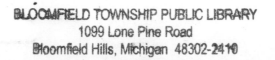

# EARTHLY DELIGHTS

Over 750 simple and delicious recipes for everyday meals
and special occasions

# EARTHLY DELIGHTS

Everyday Vegetarian Cooking

Over 750 simple and delicious recipes for everyday meals
and special occasions

## VIKKI LENG

## Thorsons
*A Division of* HarperSanFrancisco
HarperCollins*Publishers*

*Overleaf: Watermelon Wonder is as refreshing as a*
*dip in the ocean or a splash of cool water.*

First published in the United States in 1994

Library of Congress Cataloging-in-Publication Data
ISBN 0-207-18443-7

94 95 96 97 98 XXX 10 9 8 7 6 5 4 3 2 1

A BARBARA BECKETT BOOK

Produced in association with
Barbara Beckett Publishing
14 Hargrave Street, Paddington, Sydney, Australia 2021
Photography by Andrew Elton
Food styling by Donna Hay
Food stylist assistants Jody Vassallo and Vikki Leng
Copy editing by Alison Magney
Printed in Australia by The Griffin Press

The author and the publisher would like to thank the
following who supplied props for the photography.
Country Road Homewares Stores, nationally.
Accoutrement Cooks Shops, Gordon, Mosman, Bondi
Junction.
Orrefors, Kosta Boda, Miranda, Liverpool, Mosman.
David Jones stores, nationally.
Villeroy & Boch, David Jones and selected stores.

*This book is dedicated to all those*

*with a passion for living*

# Acknowledgments

To my best friend and husband, Tod, thank you for understanding me and letting me be myself, for allowing me to fulfil my dreams and for patiently and quietly tolerating a household that is often akin to a bustling restaurant. And to my children, who are blossoming into wonderful people, thank you for eating up your vegies!

The production of this book has been a mammoth project and, like all such projects, has involved a host of people. My venture (adventure) into writing books began over twelve years ago when my first publisher, Susan McCulloch, believed in my work at a time when the only book I had written was a diary! I would like to thank Sue for getting me started with my writing, a pastime that I have come to love. Thanks too to Barbara Beckett whose vision of an exciting new vegetarian cookbook inspired me and gave me the confidence to tackle such a challenging project. A fine cook and author herself, Barbara has smoothly directed this project with her artistic flair, since the very first moment of its conception. My thanks also go to Alison Magney for her valuable contribution as editor. My appreciation also goes to Lisa Highton and Alison Pressley of HarperCollins*Publishers* for their faith in and commitment to the entire project. To the food stylist, Donna Hay and sensitive photographer, Andrew Elton, congratulations and thank you for producing the wonderful illustrations in this book. I had great pleasure working with Donna and Andrew as Donna's assistant for part of this assignment; it

gave me the opportunity to witness their creativity, conscientiousness and dedication to their work, all in a relaxed manner. Thanks too, to Jody Vassallo, Donna's assistant for the remainder of the assignment. I am also grateful to my former work place, the Food and Nutrition Program, Deakin University, for all I learned whilst working with a fantastic team of professionals for a period of 5 years. It was here that I was to be launched into the age of technology—by this I mean I became familiar with the merits of computers. It wasn't long before I became positively addicted to using them. Thanks to Peter Gilbert from Deakin University for his expert advice, patience and humour whilst teaching me how to make the best use of my computer for all my projects.

To the proprietors of my favourite fruit shops and market outlets, I offer a big thank you for providing me with produce and service of outstanding quality. Thanks go particularly to the Mirabella Brothers of Doncaster, Narduzzo's and The Healthy Gourmet of the Prahran Market and Blackburn Orchards Fruit Supply.

I'd also like to express my gratitude to Rosemary and Michael Tabak of Berry King for supplying me with oodles of magnificent berries which I have enjoyed transforming into the myriad berry recipes contained in this book. The final tribute must go to none other than my taste testers who also ate up all their vegies, and thanked me for them too!

VIKKI LENG

# Contents

## Part One: Recipes for all Occasions  14

# Part Two: How to Make Your Own  238

# Part Three: The Vegetarian Diet  334

# Cook's Notes

Fresh herbs are used unless otherwise stated. If fresh herbs are unavailable, however, use half the amount of dried herbs. Use freshly grated root ginger unless preserved or ground ginger is stipulated. Use freshly ground black pepper unless white pepper or cracked black pepper is specified. Mixed spice is made up of 4 parts cinnamon, 2 parts ground ginger, 1 part ground nutmeg and 1 part ground cloves. Use low-flavoured oils, such as sunflower seed, grapeseed or safflower oils unless olive or sesame oils are called for. Use low-fat or reduced fat dairy products unless otherwise specified. Use nonfat plain yoghurt unless other varieties are called for. Yoghurt cheese (page 271) is interchangeable with cream cheese. Use light (single) cream or whipping (double) cream which has been thickened with vegetable gum rather than cream thickened with gelatine. Soy milk is interchangeable with cow's milk in most recipes. Use salt-reduced soy sauce. Use plain (all-purpose) flour when flour is indicated.

Some recipes call for prepared baking sheets, cake pans, loaf pans and dariole moulds. Simply use a pastry brush to brush them with a little melted butter or oil.

Food processors and blenders are interchangeable unless one or the other is specified. Blenders, for example, are more suitable for grinding nuts and seeds and for making light and fluffy drinks.

The microwave cooking times have been calculated according to the use of a 650 watt microwave oven. If your microwave oven is a lower wattage you will need to add 5 seconds per minute per 50 watts onto the specified cooking times. If you have a higher wattage oven, subtract 5 seconds per minute per 50 watts from the specified cooking times. Remember to use only microwave ovenproof cookware and microwave-safe plastic wrap (cling film).

Apart from these notes, remember the most important point—to enjoy the art of cooking and let your own creativity flourish!

# Weights and Measures

For accurate measurements, you will need:
• A nest of four graduated measuring cups for measuring dry ingredients. These come in ¼, ½, ⅓ and 1 cup size.
• A standard measuring cup for measuring liquids.
• A 1-litre or 4-cup measuring jug for measuring large quantities of liquid. These jugs usually show both cup and metric measures and are marked in cups and millilitres, others in imperial fluid ounces.
•A set of graduated measuring spoons. The set includes a tablespoon, teaspoon, half-teaspoon and quarter-teaspoon. Level spoon measures are used.
• Scales. Usually marked nowadays in both metric and imperial measurements. Scales are needed for weighing vegetables and other bulky items.

Weights and measures translations in this book are not exact equivalents but are brought to the nearest round figure; however, they still preserve the correct balance of ingredients. To retain that balance, follow either metric or imperial, never a mixture.

### Spoon and Cup Measurements

|              | Australia | New Zealand | United Kingdom    | United States     |
|--------------|-----------|-------------|-------------------|-------------------|
| 1 tablespoon | 20 mL     | 15 mL       | ½ fl oz (14 mL)   | ½ fl oz (14 mL)   |
| 1 cup        | 250 mL    | 250 mL      | 8 fl oz (237 mL)  | 8 fl oz (237 mL)  |

All countries use the same teaspoon measurements.

### Preheat the Oven

Always preheat an oven, unless you are reheating food. The time this takes varies with the oven. The usual time to reach a required oven temperature varies from 15 to 20 minutes. Check with the instruction book of your oven.

The correct oven temperature is essential to the success of a dish. It makes pastry crisp, a soufflé or cake rise. Sometimes oven temperatures are changed during cooking, e.g. high heat for a crispy topping, then low to cook the filling.

### Oven Temperatures and Gas Marks

| CELSIUS | FAHRENHEIT | GAS MARKS | HEAT      | CELSIUS | FAHRENHEIT | GAS MARKS | HEAT      |
|---------|------------|-----------|-----------|---------|------------|-----------|-----------|
| 110°C   | 225°F      | ¼ (S)     | very cool | 190°C   | 375°F      | 5         | fairly hot |
| 120°C   | 250°F      | ½ (S)     | very cool | 200°C   | 400°F      | 6         | fairly hot |
| 140°C   | 275°F      | 1         | cool      | 220°C   | 425°F      | 7         | hot       |
| 150°C   | 300°F      | 2         | cool      | 230°C   | 450°F      | 8         | very hot  |
| 160°C   | 325°F      | 3         | moderate  | 240°C   | 475°F      | 9         | very hot  |
| 180°C   | 350°F      | 4         | moderate  | 260°C   | 500°F      | 10        | very hot  |

Note: The gas mark S is a special setting available on some ovens used for cooking slowly, e.g. meringues.

# PREFACE

In 'Earthly Delights' Vikki Leng has used her expertise to highlight the inherent strengths of vegetarian meals to meet the modern demands for quickly prepared meals that are simple, economic, light, nutritious and tasty. The result is a book crammed with an eclectic blend of ethnic and vegetarian recipes, handy hints and useful ideas all prepared in Vikki's inimitable style.

For countless thousands of years the human body has evolved in harmony with the environment by consuming a predominantly vegetarian diet comprising an assortment of basic foods. These foods became the staples of a rich diversity of cultural cuisines that developed over time. Many of the dietary imbalances and associated nutritional health problems that have emerged in relatively recent times are attributed to the excessive consumption of highly processed foods in contemporary society. In this book, Vikki uses her flair and culinary skills to encourage people to be creative with their meals. She urges us to take full advantage of the wonderful variety and attractiveness of basic foods and cultural cuisines. Her recipes will not only help those interested in promoting their health, but also assist those concerned with protecting the environment to select foods from further down the food chain, which are less resource intensive in their production.

Scientific knowledge regarding the importance of the relationship between diet and health has increased substantially in recent years. Indeed, it has been stated that no other component of our way of life has a greater potential to influence health than the food we eat. Unfortunately, this increase in scientific knowledge has not always translated easily into clear and helpful advice for the public. Many people find the seemingly endless focus on the relationship between specific nutrients and certain diseases quite confusing. This is particularly the case because we select, prepare and eat foods, not nutrients, and most of us would prefer to eat for pleasure and health, not simply as a mechanism to avoid disease.

This book advocates simple, positive messages about food and health. It operates from the sound basis that eating a variety of basic foods is the best foundation for a healthy, balanced diet. It affirms that eating is a pleasurable experience. We enjoy the social and cultural occasions of sharing food. 'Earthly Delights' is fun and enticing, offering practical advice that converts the complex science of nutrition into enjoyable and understandable food messages with which people are familiar.

I'm sure you'll enjoy reading 'Earthly Delights' and preparing its wonderful recipes, complemented throughout by Vikki's vibrant and warm personality. Whether you are a vegetarian, non vegetarian (who wishes to expand your repertoire), interested in your health or simply someone who enjoys delicious meals, this book is for you.

Mark Lawrence, B. Sc. (Hons), Dip. Nut. Diet., M. Sc., Senior Nutritionist, Australian National Food Authority.

# Introduction

*The new style of vegetarian cooking is like a breath of fresh air.
Whether you are preparing a simple breakfast or snack or dreaming
up a feast to share with family and friends, relax and enjoy creating
light, tasty and colourful dishes from fresh seasonal produce.*

# Introduction

This book is a celebration of recipes, handy hints and ideas for both vegetarians and non vegetarians alike. Enjoy the simplicity and ease of preparation, for I believe that food preparation should be enjoyed as much as the food itself—in fact, to my mind, the enjoyment of the cooking is an integral ingredient which has a taste of its own.

I have always enjoyed meeting and getting to know people. In fact that's one of the reasons why I chose to study Home Economics for a rewarding career path—people have to eat, so what better way to enjoy their company than to offer the refreshment of one of my latest culinary creations! I happen to also love spending time shopping for seasonal produce at the markets or local fruit shop, not to mention visiting local growers to obtain 'the pick of the crop' berries and apples, and I regard scouting the ethnic food stores and delicatessens as an exciting outing, and one jam-packed with learning experiences as well. Then homeward bound to unpack, stack, store and embark upon another of my favourite pastimes—cooking. To me, the experience of preparing and sharing food with people is immensely satisfying; the rewards are well worth

*Overleaf: Celebrate the wonderful harvests of each season by enjoying quality produce, all the more satisfying when freshly picked from your own garden.*

the effort. I do appreciate, however, that many people do not share the same passion nor do they have the time for extensive shopping and cooking so I have endeavoured to keep the recipes and procedures as simple as possible for the busy modern cook.

It is a joy to shop for, prepare and share vegetarian food. There is such a wealth of ingredients to choose from—vegetables and fruits of all colours, shapes and sizes, a huge variety of dried beans, peas and lentils, nuts and seeds and soy products such as soy bean curd (tofu) and soy bean milks. All these and more, for vegetarians who also include eggs and dairy products such as milk, cheeses, buttermilk and yoghurt in their diets.

Times sure have changed. Once upon a time I was constantly asked 'Just what do vegetarians eat?' But nowadays, the people who once asked that question are themselves including delicious vegetarian dishes in their repertoire of favourite recipes. Recent research tells us that the modern consumer is seeking out ways to prepare and enjoy tasty, lighter, more nutritious, informal, economical and quickly prepared foods, and as far as I'm concerned, including more vegetarian foods in our diets is a perfect way to do just this. Most of the recipes in this book have been developed in response to this trend. In fact, it is my belief that some of the most delicious and nutritious dishes are those that can be prepared quickly and simply. Some dishes based on dried beans, peas and lentils do take a bit longer to prepare overall, but by part-preparing and storing these foods for later use, you will be ready when the hunger pangs actually strike. You'll find plenty of handy hints and ideas for how to be prepared scattered throughout this book. And for those of you who, like me, actually find it relaxing, rewarding and enjoyable to potter in the kitchen, I have provided plenty of recipes for homemade concoctions that will keep you singing over a hot stove for as long as you wish to stay there!

Economically speaking, vegetarian food generally comes up trumps! Rice and other grains, breads, pasta, soy beans and their products and most vegetables and fruits are more economical than meat and dairy products, not to mention many of the fast and take-away foods that have become so popular. For the price of a packet of soy beans, you can provide a family of four with all the protein they will need for two meals!

These days, we are encouraged by nutritionists to consume more vegetables and fruits, beans, peas and lentils, wholegrains and their products and low-fat dairy products and reduce our intake of fat (particularly saturated fats), salt and sugar. This book is based on these sound nutritional philosophies but with plenty of room to breathe. For variety, interest and excitement, I have also included a collection of recipes which I recommend only as occasional 'extras' for special occasions—luscious fruit liqueurs, creamy ice creams, spicy chutneys, sweet preserves and confections. Although these recipes characteristically contain more salt and/or sugar than dishes I prepare for everyday use, they store well and can therefore be prepared well ahead of time and placed in the pantry or freezer, ready for unsuspecting (or unexpected!) dinner guests.

It is my experience that vegetarian dishes are not only tasty, quickly and simply prepared, economical and nutritious, but they can add a carnival of colour and excitement to anyone's life—especially mine. It's been a lot of fun creating and testing all the recipes in this book. I hope it brings you much happiness as you cook up a storm in your own kitchen.

# Part One: Recipes for All Occasions

*You will find plenty of tempting recipe ideas for every day eating, including a collection of basic recipes. Use these to get started then have fun mixing and matching recipes, and adding your favourite dressings, sauces, herbs and spices.*

# Shopping, Storage and Preparation

Planning, shopping and pre-preparation are as important as the actual enjoyment I get from creating a colourful and tasty dish—and you can't have one without the other. As time for shopping and meal preparation diminishes, as it seems to be doing these days, the need for planning and pre-preparation increases.

Plan your shopping trips ahead of time and have a 'running list' at hand so you can jot down all the items you need when they first come to mind. Non-perishable items such as dried beans, peas and lentils can be bought in bulk, but don't be tempted to buy more than you will comfortably use within 3–6 months. Purchase amounts of semi-perishable items such as dried fruits, grains and flour that you will use within a month or so. It's not a bad idea to buy in bulk and divide food up amongst friends and family. A good quality olive oil, for instance, is cheaper to buy by the tin, but none of us is likely to use this amount of oil by ourselves before it loses its freshness.

When it comes to shopping for fresh fruit and vegetables it's best to make several shopping trips per week rather than one big one, if possible. Be aware of the seasonal availability of fruits and vegetables so you can plan to include new season's produce in your menus as soon as it is available. This way you will be able to enjoy the freshest of ingredients which not only look and taste far better, but are more nutritious and more economical than produce which is not in season. Choose firm fresh-looking fruits and vegetables which seem to be heavy for their size and

*Overleaf: Yoghurt Cheese, a wonderful fresh cheese you'll see mentioned throughout this book, is great for whipping up impromptu meals and snacks.*

consider when a bargain is not a bargain! Wilted or 'tired-looking' produce is sure to have a disappointing flavour and texture, not to mention diminished vitamin content, so think carefully about whether the cheaper price warrants the drop in quality. Another tip which sounds humorous is to avoid going shopping when really hungry, such as on your way home after work—research indicates that we spend much more on food at these times, and include items that we would normally be able to resist! The almighty shopping list also helps us to focus on what we came into the shop to buy in the first place.

## Storage

Store beans, peas and lentils in airtight jars in a cool dark place such as a pantry. Take particular care to store dried fruits and grains in jars that the 'pest of the pantry', the weevil, cannot penetrate. I use fruit glass preserving jars with a rubber seal. These jars are also handy if you have a problem with ants, as they cannot penetrate the rubber seal—what better place to store honey. A note about nuts—because they are high in fat, they can spoil quite quickly, so buy them in small amounts at a time and store them in an airtight jar in the pantry or in the refrigerator in hot weather. Perishable foods such as fresh milk, yoghurt, buttermilk, cheese, fresh tofu, tempeh, eggs and frozen goods should be placed in the refrigerator or freezer as soon as possible after purchasing. Try to have a few packs of ultra heat treated milk in the pantry for those times when you run out of fresh milk unexpectedly—and isn't it always when milk is in demand for those quick breakfasts.

## Pre-preparation

Many foods can be part-prepared before the actual meal time. This is a real sanity saver for busy people. People have often commented to me that vegetarian food takes a long time to prepare. But all that is needed is planning and pre-preparation of certain foods and meals can be whipped up in minutes.

## Beans, Peas, Lentils and Grains

It's true that these foods can hold up meal time if they are cooked just before they are required. I make sure I always have a supply of frozen cooked beans, peas and lentils (pages 121–5) on hand, or better still, in the freezer. They can, for example, be added to bubbling hot pots of soup during the last stage of cooking. This way they are thawed and reheated at the same time as the soup cooks. Canned beans can be kept on hand in the pantry for quick meals, too.

It is a good idea to cook grains such as rice, wheat and buckwheat (pages 109–120) in the amount that you will use for the week and store them in airtight containers in the refrigerator. Cold cooked grains are also better to use for stir-fries because the grains retain their shape far better than fresh-cooked warm grains. You can have containers of cooked grains lying in wait in the freezer, too. Frozen grains can be thawed and reheated in a steamer insert over a pot of boiling water, or in a microwave oven.

### Sauces

Sauces such as Quick Pasta Sauce (page 50) are so versatile that I always keep a space in my freezer for a container or two. As you cook your favourite pasta, thaw and reheat the sauce in a microwave oven, or in a covered saucepan over a gentle heat. Frozen sauce usually takes as long to thaw and reheat as it takes pasta to cook—very convenient. Quick Pasta Sauce also makes a great topping for pizzas, and upon adding a few drops of Tabasco Sauce, can be combined with cooked beans for a quick meal of nachos or tacos.

### Bread, Rolls, Muffins, Crêpes, Pancakes, and Waffles

Always keep a small loaf of sliced bread in the freezer for sandwiches or toast. Freezing bread is great for those who don't eat much bread or for making packed lunches. The butter or margarine can be spread more thinly on frozen bread without breaking it up and, by lunchtime, the bread will have thawed nicely. When making bread at home (pages 243-253), always make a loaf or two extra to tuck away in the freezer for later use. Frozen bread can be thawed in a microwave oven or, if you are using your conventional oven at meal times, bread can be crisped up beautifully just before you wish to serve it. As for rolls, muffins, crêpes and pancakes, they can be very successfully frozen

and thawed just before use. And waffles are given new life when toasted until crispy just before serving.

If you like making your own bread but can't seem to find enough time to wait for it to prove (rise), why not make it in two stages as I often do? This tip also provides you with a way to have oven fresh bread first thing in the morning without your having to wake up before the birds do. Simply prepare the bread dough up until the first proving (rising) the night before, then pop it in a large plastic (polythene) bag and seal, allowing room for the dough to double in size. Pop the dough in the vegetable drawer of your refrigerator where it will prove very slowly overnight (cold temperatures do not inactivate yeast, just slow down its growth). In the morning, proceed with the recipe and you should have bread on the breakfast or brunch table in an hour or so.

### Dry Roasting Nuts and Seeds

Dry roasting brings out the flavour of nuts and seeds and it's a good idea to have some stored in an airtight jar for scattering over salads, vegetables and grains. It is also easier to roast a cupful or so of nuts or seeds at a time rather than a tablespoonful or so when each recipe calls for a small amount. For the 'on top of the stove' method, sprinkle the nuts or seeds into a heavy-based saucepan (this assists with even heat distribution) and cook them over a medium-high heat, shaking the pan constantly so that the nuts brown evenly. Roast only until the nuts or seed become a pale golden brown; take care, because once they start to brown it only takes seconds to overcook them. For the oven method, spread an even layer of nuts or seeds on a baking sheet and cook them in a moderate oven (180°C/350°F) for 15–20 minutes. Check them regularly.

Once you have a supply of pre-prepared foods such as beans, peas, lentils, grains, bakery items and a tasty sauce or two, preparing meals is not a chore any more. Other foods such as fresh fruit and vegetables can be served raw for a burst of vitality, or cooked until just tender and served immediately.

# Soups and Starters

*Soups and starters can be as varied as your imagination allows. Soups alone can be light and fragrant or spicy, with an unmistakable oriental influence, or they can be robust with the flavours and textures of Mediterranean cooking. Starters can be whipped up from ripe new season's fruits just as easily as from fresh vegetables, pasta, grains and aromatic herbs.*

# Chilled Melon and Mint Soup

1.25 kg (2½ lb) honeydew melon
2 teaspoons light flavoured honey
1 cup (250 mL/8 fl oz) plain yoghurt
2 tablespoons chopped mint leaves
additional 1 cup (250 mL/8 fl oz) plain yoghurt
4 strawberries, hulls removed, cut into slivers
mint leaves

Cut the honeydew melon in half and scoop out the pips with a spoon. Cut the melon into slices and remove the skin with a vegetable peeler. Cut the melon into chunks. Using a food processor, blend the honeydew and honey until smooth, then add the yoghurt and chopped mint and continue blending for 1 minute. Chill thoroughly and serve topped with a generous spoonful of yoghurt and the strawberries and mint leaves.
*Serves 4*

# Citrus Mango Soup

*A delightful way to celebrate the mango season, this quickly prepared soup is wonderful served as it is or with a swirl of plain yoghurt.*

2 mangoes, peeled, pip removed, sliced
1 tablespoon lime *or* lemon juice
2 teaspoons finely grated lime *or* lemon rind
3 cups (750 mL/24 fl oz) freshly squeezed orange juice
¼ teaspoon ground cinnamon
fine slivers of lime *or* lemon zest (page 136)
frangipani for garnishing (optional)

Using a food processor or blender, blend the mangoes, lime (or lemon) juice, lime (or lemon) rind, orange juice and cinnamon until smooth and creamy. Chill thoroughly and serve topped with lime or lemon zest and frangipani (optional).
*Serves 4*

*Overleaf: The cool green hue and the refreshing flavour of Chilled Melon and Mint Soup does wonders for jaded appetites on hot summer days.*

# Rich Plum Soup

*Serve piping hot on cool days or icy cold to ward off the summer heat.*

400 g (14 oz) blood plums
2 cups (500 mL/16 fl oz) dark grape juice
1 cinnamon stick
2 pieces of lemon zest (page 136)
½ cup (125 mL/4 fl oz) red wine *or* blackcurrant juice
2 cups (500 mL/16 fl oz) plain yoghurt
redcurrants *or* raspberries for garnishing

Cook the plums in the grape juice with the cinnamon stick and the lemon zest until tender (about 10–15 minutes). Add the red wine (or blackcurrant juice) and cook with the lid off the pan for 5 minutes. Remove the cinnamon stick and lemon zest and push the mixture through a sieve. Reheat, or chill the soup thoroughly, before serving topped with the yoghurt and the redcurrants (or raspberries).
*Serves 4*

# Fruits of the Forest Soup

*Terrific to serve as a summer celebration.*

250 g (8 oz) raspberries
250 g (8 oz) blackberries
2 cups (500 mL/16 fl oz) apple and blackcurrant juice
½ teaspoon vanilla essence (extract)
1 tablespoon honey
½–1 cup crushed ice
1 cup (250 mL/8 fl oz) plain yoghurt
clumps of redcurrants *or* fresh berries, with leaves if possible

Blend half of the berries with the apple and blackcurrant juice, vanilla, honey and ice until smooth, using a food processor or blender. Arrange the remaining berries in soup bowls and ladle the soup over. Serve at once topped with a generous dollop of yoghurt and a clump of redcurrants (or scattered with berries).
*Serves 4*

# Pina Colada Soup

*This soup is best partly prepared ahead of time, so be sure to allow time for the soup to chill. The final stage of preparation is completed in a few seconds.*

1 large ripe pineapple, peeled and chopped
1 cup (250 mL/8 fl oz) unsweetened pineapple juice
1/2 cup (125 mL/4 fl oz) coconut cream (page 341)
1–2 tablespoons white rum or 1–2 teaspoons vanilla essence (extract)
8 pineapple sage leaves

Using a blender, purée the pineapple, adding a little of the pineapple juice. Add the remaining juice and blend until the mixture is well combined, about 10 seconds. Cover and chill the mixture for 1 hour if possible. Just before serving, add the coconut cream and the rum (or vanilla), and blend for a further 5–10 seconds. Serve at once decorated with the sage leaves.
*Serves 4*

# Summer Wine Soup

500 g (1 lb) peaches
2 cups (500 mL/16 fl oz) apple juice
1 tablespoon light flavoured honey
½ cup (125 mL/4 fl oz) sweet white wine
½ punnet (carton) strawberries, hulls removed, sliced
additional sliced strawberries

Place the peaches in a medium-sized saucepan. Combine the apple juice and the honey and pour over the peaches. Bring to the boil, then reduce the heat and cook the peaches gently until almost tender. Add the wine and simmer, with the lid off the pan, for 5 minutes then set the mixture aside to cool. Remove the skins from the peaches then slice the flesh from the pips. Using a food processor or blender, purée the peach slices then add the strawberries and blend the mixture until smooth. Chill the soup thoroughly and serve topped with the additional sliced strawberries.
*Serves 4*

# Avocado and Cucumber Soup

½ medium-sized cucumber, peeled, pips removed
1 avocado, peeled, pip removed, sliced
2 spring onions (scallions), sliced
2 garlic cloves, crushed (pressed)
juice of 1 lemon
a few drops of Tabasco Sauce
2 cups (500 mL/16 fl oz) buttermilk (page 275)
½ cup crushed ice
1 cup (250 mL/8 fl oz) Greek Yoghurt (page 273)
1–2 teaspoons finely sliced chili peppers, seeds removed

Slice the cucumber then, using a food processor, blend until smooth with the avocado, spring onions, garlic, lemon juice, Tabasco Sauce and buttermilk. Add the ice and blend for 5 seconds. Serve immediately, topping each serve with a dollop of yoghurt and the chilies.
*Serves 4–6*

# Avocado with Raspberry Vinaigrette

*The vinaigrette can be whipped up well before this dish is needed. The remainder of the preparation can be done in the wink of an eye!*

1 quantity Raspberry Vinaigrette (page 149)
2 avocados
cracked black pepper
fresh salad greens such as arugula (rocket) *or* young spinach leaves
lemon *or* lime wedges

Cut the avocados in half lengthways and remove the pip carefully. Drizzle the Raspberry Vinaigrette over and sprinkle with the pepper. Serve on a bed of salad greens with the lemon (or lime) wedges.
*Serves 4*

# Tofu Houmus

*An old-time favourite of mine, not only because it is a quick and easy recipe, but also because it's delicious and nutritious as well. Serve with corn chips, warm pita bread and a colourful selection of crispy vegetable crudités.*

250 g (8 oz) tofu, drained
2–3 garlic cloves, crushed (pressed)
2 tablespoons lemon juice
2 tablespoons tahini (page 346)
1 tablespoon soy sauce
2–3 tablespoons nonfat plain yoghurt
a few drops of Tabasco Sauce
freshly ground black pepper

Place the tofu, garlic, lemon juice, tahini, soy sauce and yoghurt into a food processor and blend until smooth. Season to taste with the Tabasco Sauce and pepper.
*Makes about 1½ cups (375 mL/12 fl oz)*

# Scrumptious Peanut Dip

3 tablespoons peanut butter
250 g (8 oz) tofu *or* light cream cheese
2 garlic cloves, crushed (pressed)
2 spring onions (scallions), sliced finely
1 tablespoon soy sauce
2–3 tablespoons nonfat plain yoghurt
a few drops of Tabasco Sauce
freshly ground black pepper
1 tablespoon dry roasted peanuts
sweet paprika

Using a wooden spoon, beat the peanut butter, tofu (or cream cheese), garlic, spring onions, soy sauce and yoghurt together until well combined. Season to taste with Tabasco Sauce and pepper and serve scattered with the peanuts and dusted with the sweet paprika.
*Makes about 1 cup (250 mL/8 fl oz)*

# Rich Tomato Dip

*This dip will seduce your taste buds with its rich tangy flavour. Especially delicious with crisp fresh celery and warm crusty bread.*

60 g (2 oz) sun-dried tomatoes
2 teaspoons tomato paste (purée)
250 g (8 oz) light cream cheese *or* tofu
2 garlic cloves, crushed (pressed)
1 tablespoon lemon juice
2 tablespoons nonfat plain yoghurt
freshly ground black pepper
a few drops of Tabasco Sauce
sweet paprika

Blend the tomatoes, tomato paste, cream cheese (or tofu), garlic, lemon juice and yoghurt until smooth using a food processor. Season to taste with the pepper and Tabasco Sauce. Serve dusted with sweet paprika.
*Makes about 1 cup (250 mL/8 fl oz)*

# Creamy Pesto Dip

*This dip captures the romance of the Mediterranean with the fragrance of basil, the texture of pine nuts, the full-bodied flavour of garlic and the characteristic tang of balsamic vinegar.*

250 g (8 oz) Yoghurt Cheese (page 271) *or* cream
   cheese
1 cup chopped basil
60 g (2 oz) pine nuts, roasted (page 17)
3 garlic cloves, crushed (pressed)
1 tablespoon balsamic vinegar
1 tablespoon finely sliced basil
additional 1 tablespoon roasted pine nuts

Using a food processor or blender, combine the cheese, basil, pine nuts, garlic and vinegar. Serve sprinkled with the basil and pine nuts.
*Makes about 1½ cups (375 mL/12 fl oz)*

*Right: Rich Tomato Dip. Enjoy the taste of summer all year round with this thick and creamy dip laced with the distinctive flavour of sun-dried tomatoes.*

# French Onion Dip

*A popular dip all round! Serve with wholemeal (whole-wheat) crackers, or add more yoghurt and dollop onto salads or stuffed vegetables.*

2 teaspoons oil
2 onions, diced finely
250 g (8 oz) light cream cheese
2 tablespoons plain yoghurt
1 tablespoon finely sliced chives
1 tablespoon soy sauce
freshly ground black pepper
additional finely sliced chives

Heat the oil in a frying pan or skillet and cook the onion over a medium-high heat, covered, for 5 minutes, stirring occasionally. Continue to cook, stirring, for about 5 minutes or until the onions become a light golden brown. Using a food processor or blender, blend the onions with the cheese, yoghurt, chives, soy sauce and pepper until smooth. Serve topped with finely sliced chives.
*Makes about 1½ cups (375 mL/12 fl oz)*

**Quick Savouries**
Swirls of thick creamy dips can be piped onto bruschetta, pumpernickel or crackers for impressive yet easy savouries. Try using Rich Tomato Dip, Creamy Avocado Dip and Pumpkin and Cream Cheese Dip. Top the swirls with chopped herbs or a dusting of spices.

# Creamy Avocado Dip

*This is especially good for piping onto toasted bread shapes or crackers or into tiny tomato shells but also doubles as a light Guacamole-type dip, great for serving with nachos and tacos (page 45).*

1 avocado, peeled, pip removed
2 garlic cloves, crushed (pressed)
a few drops of Tabasco Sauce
freshly ground black pepper
juice of ½ lemon
2 teaspoons white wine vinegar *or* apple cider vinegar
125 g (4 oz) firm tofu *or* ricotta cheese, drained well
chopped parsley *or* snipped chives, to garnish

Using a food processor, blend all the ingredients together until smooth. Serve sprinkled with the parsley (or chives).
*Makes about 1 cup (250 mL/8 fl oz)*

# Pumpkin and Cream Cheese Dip

*This delightful dip has a sweet nutty flavour and provides an interesting colour contrast when served with a selection of other dips such as Rich Tomato Dip (page 22) and Creamy Avocado Dip.*

1 cup mashed cooked pumpkin (page 93)
1 tablespoon white miso (page 343)
a few drops of Tabasco Sauce
freshly ground black pepper
125 g (4 oz) cream cheese *or* tofu, drained
1 tablespoon finely sliced chives

Using a food processor, blend the pumpkin, miso, Tabasco Sauce, pepper and cream cheese (or tofu) until smooth. Stir in the sliced chives.
*Makes 1½ cups (375 mL/12 fl oz)*

# Basic Sushi Rice

*Watching sushi rice prepared in a traditional manner is fascinating. The trick is to cool the rice as quickly as possible as the sweet vinegar is tossed through and special wooden paddles or fans are used to do this. I enjoy preparing sushi rice when I have another pair of hands which can fan as I toss.*

4 cups (1 litre/1¾ imp. pints) boiling water
2 cups short grain rice
1 tablespoon rice vinegar
3 tablespoons white wine vinegar
1 tablespoon mirin *or* dry sherry
2 teaspoons honey
2 teaspoons sugar
a pinch of salt

While the water is boiling, add the rice. Reduce the heat to a slow simmer and cook, with the lid on the pan, for 12 minutes. Remove from the heat and allow to stand for 5 minutes with the lid on the pan. Meanwhile combine the vinegars, mirin (or sherry), honey, sugar and salt thoroughly. While the rice is still hot, place it in a shallow dish and pour the flavouring mixture over. Toss the rice to combine all the ingredients well, and if you can manage it, fan the rice as you go, to cool it quickly.
*Makes about 4 cups (1 litre/1¾ imp. pints)*

### A Wholegrain Alternative

Although sushi rice is traditionally made from white rice, I often use brown rice for variety as well as nutrition. To cook brown rice, see page 109.

# Basic Nori Rolls

Filling ingredients, as suggested below
1 quantity Sushi Rice
2 sheets toasted nori (page 344)
60 g (2 oz) Japanese pickled vegetables

Spread the rice and then the filling over the nori sheets, leaving a 1 cm (⅜ in.) strip uncovered along the edge furthest from you. Place the Japanese pickled vegetables in a neat strip in the middle of the rice.

Proceed to roll the nori in a cylindrical fashion, beginning with the edge closest to you. Try to exert even pressure along the length of the nori so that you end up with neat even-sized rolls. Using a sharp cook's knife, slice each of the rolls into about 8 pieces. Arrange on a serving plate or platter accompanied by a small bowl of dipping sauce (page 97).
*Makes about 16 rolls*

# Nori Maki

*Nori Maki translates to 'salad rolls'. In Japan, nori rolls are much like the ever popular western sandwich. Why not try these delicious simply prepared rolls, which are a combination of tasty salad vegetables enveloped in toasted nori sheets.*

2 teaspoons wasabi paste (page 346)
2 sheets toasted nori (page 344)
1 quantity Basic Sushi Rice
1 small avocado, skin and pip removed, sliced thinly
1/4 small lettuce, washed and dried, trimmed and chopped

Spread 1 teaspoon wasabi paste evenly over each of the sheets of nori then prepare the rolls as for Basic Nori Rolls, topping the rice with the avocado and lettuce in place of the pickled vegetables.
*Makes about 16 rolls*

# Nori Wrapped Sweet Potato

1 kg (2 lb) sweet potato, peeled, cut into chunks
2–3 spring onions (scallions), trimmed
2 teaspoons sesame oil
2 teaspoons honey
1½ tablespoons rice vinegar *or* white wine vinegar
2 sheets toasted nori (page 344)

Cook the sweet potato until tender. If using a microwave oven, place the sweet potato in a covered container and cook on high for 10 minutes. Alternatively, steam the sweet potato for 15 minutes. Cook the spring onions until just tender by adding them to the sweet potatoes for the last 1 minute of cooking time (for microwave method) or for the last 2 minutes of cooking time (for the steaming method). Remove the spring onions and set aside, then mash the sweet potatoes while still hot. Add the sesame oil, honey and rice vinegar (or white wine vinegar) and mix well.

Spread one half of the mixture on each of the sheets of nori, leaving a 1 cm (⅜ in.) strip along the edge furthest from you. Lay the spring onions top to tail along the middle of the sweet potato mixture. Proceed to roll the nori as for Basic Nori Rolls (page 25). Arrange on a serving plate or platter accompanied by a small bowl of dipping sauce (page 96).
*Makes about 16 rolls*

# Crisp Vegetable Sushi with Nori

*These delicious rolls are often the first introduction to Japanese cuisine for many westerners, and no wonder they are keen to try more. Serve with a tasty dipping sauce such as Sweet Chili Dipping Sauce (page 97).*

2 garlic cloves, crushed (pressed)
2 tablespoons rice vinegar *or* white wine vinegar
1 tablespoon mirin *or* dry sherry
¼ teaspoon salt
1 quantity Basic Sushi Rice (page 25)
2 sheets toasted nori (page 344)
30 g (1 oz) Japanese pickled vegetables
30 g (1 oz) Japanese pickled ginger
90 g (3 oz) freshly grated vegetables such as
    carrot, turnip *or* beetroot (beets)

Mix the garlic, rice vinegar (or white wine vinegar), mirin (or dry sherry) and salt. Combine with the rice, then spread the rice mixture over the nori sheets, leaving a 1 cm (⅜ in.) strip uncovered along the edge furthest from you. Place the Japanese pickled vegetables, pickled ginger and fresh vegetables in a neat strip in the middle of the rice. Proceed to roll as for Basic Nori Rolls (page 25).
*Makes about 16 rolls*

**Storing Nori Rolls**
Nori rolls can be stored in the refrigerator for a day or two. Before cutting into rolls, wrap the mixture in plastic wrap (cling film).

*Right: Nori Wrapped Sweet Potato and Crisp Vegetable Sushi with Nori. Enjoy the Japanese-inspired flavour of these delicious nori rolls.*

# Basic Vegetable Stock

*Vegetable stock can be simply prepared from vegetable trimmings during the normal course of daily meal preparation. For instance, celery hearts and leaves, mushroom stalks, the outside leaves from lettuce and parsley and basil stalks are very flavoursome yet are often discarded rather than used again as they can be for delicious stock.*

2 carrots, scrubbed and chopped
1 large onion, skin left on, washed and sliced
1 celery heart and leaves, *or* 3 celery stalks, washed and sliced
½ cup chopped fresh herbs *or* 2 teaspoons dried herbs such as basil, parsley *or* coriander
6 cups water (1.5 litres/2½ imp. pints) water

Place all the ingredients in a large pot, cover and bring the mixture to the boil. Reduce the heat and simmer for 1 hour. Remove the stock from the heat and set aside to cool slightly. Strain the stock into a clean saucepan or container and discard the vegetables and herbs. If you are not using the stock at once, store it in the refrigerator for up to 1 week, or in the freezer for several weeks.
*Makes 4 cups (1 litre/1¾ imp. pints)*

# Miso Vegetable Stock

*Quick and tasty stocks can be prepared from the several varieties of miso available at Asian grocery stores and health food stores today. For a light flavoured stock, use white miso, otherwise known as 'shiro miso' or 'young rice miso'. For a full bodied flavour, use the mature darker misos such as hatcho or mugi miso.*

4 teaspoons hatcho *or* mugi miso (page 343), *or* 2 tablespoons shiro (white) miso (page 343)
4 cups (1 litre/1¾ imp. pints) boiling water

Blend the miso to a smooth paste with a little of the water and whisk into the remaining water.
*Makes 4 cups (1 litre/1¾ imp. pints)*

# Dashi

*Dashi sounds like just the kind of stock that would suit all of us today, with our busy lifestyles. It is, however, really a Japanese stock prepared from kombu, a delicious sea vegetable, and shiitake mushrooms which are renowned for their full bodied flavour. Both kombu and shiitake mushrooms are available at Asian grocery stores. Dashi is especially good used in clear soups, noodle and rice dishes and stir-fried vegetables dishes.*

10 cm (4 in.) piece kombu sea vegetable (page 343)
6 dried shiitake mushrooms (page 345)
4 cups (1 litre/1¾ imp. pints) water

Place the kombu, mushrooms and water in a stainless steel saucepan and set aside to soak for at least 30 minutes. Bring the mixture slowly to the boil, then remove from the heat. Strain the stock and use as required. Retain the kombu and mushrooms for use in soups, stews and stir-fries.
*Makes 4 cups (1 litre/1¾ imp. pints)*

### Adding Flavour to Dashi

A few teaspoons of soy sauce and a teaspoon of grated ginger add flavour to dashi. If you have dashi on hand, tasty oriental-style soups with their characteristic tender crisp vegetables can be prepared in minutes.

# Clear Vegetable Soup

*This is a perfect example of how quick and tasty soups can be prepared from dashi. If you enjoy tender crisp vegetables as I do, then you will find this soup a delight.*

½ teaspoon sesame oil
1 carrot, scrubbed, halved lengthways and sliced thinly
1 teaspoon grated ginger
125 g (4 oz) broccoli florets, sliced
3–4 spring onions (scallions), sliced finely
6 button mushrooms, sliced
3 cups (750 mL/24 fl oz) dashi (page 28)
1 tablespoon mirin (page 343)
freshly ground black pepper

Brush the base of a saucepan with the sesame oil and stir-fry the carrot, ginger, broccoli and spring onions for 1–2 minutes. Add the mushrooms and the dashi and bring the soup to the boil, stirring occasionally. Reduce the heat and simmer gently, covered, for 5 minutes. Season to taste with the mirin and pepper and serve at once.
*Serves 4*

# Carrot and Leek Soup

1 teaspoon sesame oil
1 onion, diced
1 teaspoon grated ginger
225 g (7 oz) carrots, scrubbed, sliced
2 leeks, trimmed, sliced, washed well
3 cups (750 mL/24 fl oz) vegetable stock
freshly ground black pepper
2 tablespoons finely sliced chives

Place the oil in a saucepan and cook the onion, ginger, carrots and leeks gently for 5 minutes, stirring occasionally. Add the stock and bring the mixture to the boil. Reduce the heat and simmer for about 10–12 minutes or until the vegetables are tender. Season to taste with the pepper and serve sprinkled with the chives.
*Serves 4–6*

# Vegetable Soup with Noodles

*A simply delicious soup, great as an afternoon pick-me-up or as a start to a main meal.*

6 dried shiitake mushrooms (page 345)
3 cups (750 mL/24 fl oz) dashi (page 28)
1 teaspoon sesame oil
1 teaspoon grated ginger
2 leeks, trimmed, sliced thinly
2 teaspoons white miso (page 343)
2 cups (225 g/7 oz) cooked noodles such as soba (page 106)
2–3 spring onions (scallions), sliced finely
freshly ground black pepper

Place the mushrooms in a small bowl and cover with the dashi. Cover and set aside to soak for at least 30 minutes. Remove the mushrooms with a slotted spoon retaining the liquid (dashi) to use later. Remove the stalks from the mushrooms and add to your stockpot. (Do not discard them—they still contain plenty of flavour.) Brush the bottom of a saucepan with the oil and stir-fry the ginger, leeks and mushrooms over a medium heat for 2 minutes. Cover and cook gently for 10 minutes, stirring occasionally, then add the dashi. Bring the soup to the boil, then reduce the heat and simmer gently for 5 minutes. Blend the miso to a smooth paste with a little soup stock and stir it into the soup. Add the noodles, spring onions and pepper and reheat the soup gently.
*Serves 4*

# A Meal of Minestrone

*A feast of flavours from the Mediterranean abound in this ever popular soup, quite often served as a light meal with crusty bread.*

2 teaspoons olive oil
1 onion, diced
2 garlic cloves, crushed (pressed)
1 carrot, scrubbed, diced
1 celery stalk, diced
125 g (4 oz) green peas, *or* green beans, sliced
1 cup (280 g/9 oz) cooked beans, or canned baked beans
250 g (8 oz) cabbage, shredded *or* chopped
2 tomatoes, peeled and diced
1 tablespoon tomato paste (purée)
2 cups (500 mL/16 fl oz) vegetable stock
½ cup (125 mL/4 fl oz) white wine
2 cups (225 g/7 oz) cooked pasta such as shells (page 104)
2 tablespoons grated Parmesan cheese
½ cup chopped parsley

Heat the oil in a saucepan and cook the onion, garlic, carrot, celery and peas (or green beans) over a medium heat with the lid on the pan for 10 minutes, stirring occasionally. Add the beans, cabbage, tomatoes, tomato paste and stock and bring the soup to the boil. Reduce the heat and simmer gently for 15 minutes. Add the wine and pasta and cook with the lid off the pan for 5 minutes. Serve sprinkled with the Parmesan cheese and chopped parsley.
*Serves 4–6*

### Sweating Vegetables

I almost always commence my soup-making with 'sweating' the vegetables, that is, cooking them in a little oil over a medium heat at the beginning of the cooking time. This develops a soup with a sweet and nutty flavour, thereby reducing the need for salt or commercial stock mixes.

*Left: Hot Peanut Soup. This flavour-packed Asian style soup is brimming with tender-crisp vegetables and spiced with fresh chili peppers.*

# Hot Peanut Soup

*Peanuts add an exotic touch and distinctive character to soups and vegetable dishes. Try this colourful spicy soup on its own or served with a dollop of thick yoghurt and warm chapatis for a light yet satisfying meal.*

2 teaspoons oil
1 onion, diced finely
1 red sweet pepper (capsicum), diced
2 garlic cloves, crushed (pressed)
1–2 teaspoons finely chopped chili peppers
1 cup (155g/5 oz) dry roasted peanuts (page 17)
4 cups (1 litre/1¾ imp. pints) vegetable stock
4 spring onions (scallions), sliced
1 tablespoon soy sauce
90 g (3 oz) beanshoots
additional 2 tablespoons dry roasted peanuts

Heat the oil and cook the onion, sweet pepper, garlic, chilies and peanuts over a medium heat for 5 minutes, stirring occasionally. Add the stock and bring the soup to the boil. Reduce the heat and simmer gently for 15 minutes. Add the spring onions and season to taste with the soy sauce. Serve topped with a small mound of beanshoots and sprinkled with the additional peanuts.
*Serves 4*

# Creamy Celery Soup

*Most of us treat celery as one of a collection of ingredients to be added to soups, salads and stews, but try using crisp fresh celery as a vegetable in its own right and you will be pleasantly surprised. The soy milk also adds a richness without the cream or butter that most creamy soups contain.*

2 teaspoons oil
2 onions, chopped
7–8 celery stalks, chopped
1 cup (250 mL/8 fl oz) vegetable stock
2 cups (500 mL/16 fl oz) soy milk
freshly ground black pepper
chopped celery leaves

Heat the oil in a saucepan and cook the onions and celery over a medium heat with the lid on the pan for 10 minutes, stirring occasionally. Add the stock and bring the mixture to the boil. Reduce the heat and simmer for 10 minutes. Blend the mixture with the soy milk until smooth using a food processor or blender. Return the soup to the saucepan and reheat without boiling. Season to taste with the pepper. Serve topped with chopped celery leaves.
*Serves 4*

# Creamy Asparagus Soup

2 teaspoons oil
1 large onion, chopped
2 garlic cloves, crushed (pressed)
1 kg (2 lb) asparagus, trimmed, sliced
1 cup (250 mL/8 fl oz) vegetable stock
2 cups (500 mL/16 fl oz) milk
cracked black pepper

Heat the oil in a saucepan and stir the onion, garlic and asparagus over a medium-high heat for 2–3 minutes. Add the stock and bring the mixture to the boil, stirring occasionally. Reduce the heat and cook over a medium heat for 15 minutes or until the asparagus is tender. Blend the mixture with the milk until smooth using a food processor or blender and reheat gently.
*Serves 4–6*

# Tomato Soup with Pesto

*Everyone's favourite, tomato soup can be laced with a diversity of flavours from ginger to bay leaves, but try this tasty soup for a summer treat when tomatoes are sun-ripened and sweet and basil is thriving—a wonderful recipe for those who grow their own vegetables.*

1 tablespoon olive oil
2 onions, diced finely
4 garlic cloves, crushed (pressed)
½ cup chopped sweet basil leaves
½ cup (60 g/2 oz) pine nuts, roasted (page 17)
1 kg (2 lb) tomatoes, peeled and diced
1 cup (250 mL/8 fl oz) vegetable stock
2 tablespoons tomato paste (purée)
½ cup (125 mL/4 fl oz) sweet white wine
2 tablespoons grated Parmesan cheese
cracked black pepper
additional 2 tablespoons roasted pine nuts

Place the oil in a saucepan and stir the onion, garlic, basil and pine nuts over a medium heat for 2–3 minutes. Add the tomatoes and cook, covered, for 5 minutes. Add the stock and tomato paste and bring the mixture to the boil, then reduce the heat and simmer for 15–20 minutes. Add the wine and cook with the lid off the pan for 5 minutes. Remove from the heat and whisk the cheese through. Season to taste with the pepper and serve sprinkled with pine nuts.
*Serves 4–6*

# Pumpkin Soup

*There is something very comforting about pumpkin soup. Whether you prefer a tasty yet light version or the thick and hearty variety as I do, pumpkin soup seems here to stay. I have therefore provided you with a recipe to serve 6 for those inevitable second helpings.*

1¾ kg (3½ lb) pumpkin, peeled and chopped
2 large onions, sliced
2 bay leaves
1 cinnamon stick
2 garlic cloves, crushed (pressed)
2½ cups (625 mL/1 imp. pint) vegetable stock
1½ cups (375 mL/12 fl oz) milk
1 tablespoon white miso (page 343),
  *or* 2 tablespoons soy sauce
freshly ground black pepper
a few drops Tabasco Sauce

Place the pumpkin, onions, bay leaves, cinnamon stick, garlic and vegetable stock in a saucepan with a lid. Bring the mixture to the boil, stirring occasionally. Reduce the heat and cook over a medium heat for 20 minutes or until the pumpkin is tender. Remove the bay leaves and blend the mixture until smooth using a food processor or blender. Stir in the milk and return the mixture to the saucepan. Bring the soup to the boil, stirring occasionally. Place the miso in a cup and blend to a smooth paste with a little of the hot soup. Remove the soup from the heat and season to taste with the miso (or soy sauce), pepper and a few drops of the Tabasco Sauce.
*Serves 6*

**Peeling Pumpkin**
I often leave the skin on when cooking pumpkin to be served as a side vegetable, but to prepare smooth creamy pumpkin soups, it is best to peel the pumpkin. The easiest and safest way to peel pumpkin is with a vegetable peeler.

# Lemony Lentil Soup

*Laced with popular ingredients of the Middle East and Mediterranean, this soup is suitable to serve in both hot or cold weather. Serve simply with warm pita bread.*

2 teaspoons olive oil
1 red onion, diced
2–3 garlic cloves, crushed (pressed)
2 teaspoons ground cumin
2 tomatoes, diced
2 tablespoons chopped preserved lemon,
  (page 302) *or* 1 tablespoon finely shredded
  lemon peel
2 cups (435 g/14 oz) cooked brown lentils
  (page 121)
2 cups (500mL/16 fl oz) vegetable stock
½ cup roughly chopped coriander
freshly ground black pepper
additional 2 tablespoons chopped preserved
  lemon *or* 1 teaspoon finely shredded lemon peel
1 tomato, diced
2 tablespoons chopped coriander *or* sliced chives
4 tablespoons plain yoghurt

Heat the oil and stir the onion, garlic and cumin over a medium heat for 2–3 minutes. Add the tomatoes and preserved lemon (or lemon peel) and continue to stir over the heat for 2–3 minutes. Add the lentils and stock and simmer the soup for 15 minutes. Stir in the coriander and pepper to taste. Combine the additional preserved lemon (or lemon peel), tomato and coriander (or chives). Serve the soup topped with the yoghurt and a spoonful of the lemon and tomato mixture.
*Serves 4*

# Baked Ricotta Cheese

*This dish is not only versatile but nutritious as well. Serve it with crusty bread and a selection of your favourite fresh and pickled vegetables.*

500 g (1lb) ricotta cheese, drained
2 teaspoons olive oil
¼ teaspoon cracked black pepper

Place the ricotta cheese on a prepared baking sheet. Brush the oil over the ricotta cheese and sprinkle with the pepper. Bake in a moderate oven (180°C/350°F) for 25 minutes.
*Serves 6*

# Baked Lattice Ricotta Cheese

*Laced with the distinctive flavours of roasted sweet pepper (capsicum) and capers, this baked ricotta cheese is transformed into a simply delicious and eye-catching first course.*

500 g (1 lb) ricotta cheese, drained
1–2 teaspoons olive oil
1 red sweet pepper (capsicum), cut into thin
  matchsticks
2 teaspoons pickled capers
freshly ground black pepper

Cut the ricotta cheese into 1 cm (½ in.) slices and arrange on a prepared baking sheet. Place the sweet pepper sticks in a small bowl and drizzle with the oil. Arrange the sticks in a lattice pattern on top of the ricotta cheese, dot with the capers and sprinkle with the pepper. Bake in a moderate oven (180°C/350°F) for 25 minutes.
*Serves 4–6*

# Bocconcini and Tomato Pesto

*This tasty dish is very simply prepared, yet makes a stunning first course. Serve warm with crusty bread to mop up every drop of the sauce.*

6 small to medium tomatoes, peeled and halved
6 pieces bocconcini cheese, halved
2 tablespoons Pesto Sauce (page 97)
2 tablespoons grated Parmesan cheese

Carefully scoop one heaped teaspoon of flesh from each of the tomato halves, retaining the flesh for use in soups and sauces. Arrange the tomatoes, cut side facing upwards, in a heatproof dish and place a piece of bocconcini in each cavity. Spoon the Pesto Sauce over and sprinkle with the cheese. Cover and bake in a moderate oven (180°C/350°F) for 10 minutes or microwave on high for 2 minutes.
*Serves 4–6*

# Roasted Garlic

*Roasted garlic is wonderful to have on hand, especially for adding to dishes that are cooked quickly as the garlic is virtually cooked already. The flavour is potent, but much milder than fresh or short cooked garlic and the texture is smooth and creamy— even spreadable.*

3–4 knobs garlic

Simply place the garlic on a baking sheet and bake in a moderate oven (180°C/350°F) for 25–30 minutes. Use as required.

**Preserving Roasted Garlic**
If you are not using the roasted garlic at once you can preserve it for several months. First allow the garlic to cool completely, then place it in a clean dry jar and cover it completely with virgin olive oil. Seal and store in a cool dark cupboard.

*Right: Baked Lattice Ricotta Cheese. Serve as the key attraction of an antipasto spread.*

# Crispy Bread Rounds

*These are delicious served with a tasty vegetable concasse or purée or as an accompaniment to a main meal soup.*

12 thick slices French bread stick
2 tablespoons tomato paste (purée)
4 pieces bocconcini cheese, sliced
3 spring onions (scallions), sliced finely
8 cloves Roasted Garlic (page 34), sliced
cracked black pepper
1 teaspoon dried oregano

Place the bread slices on a prepared baking sheet. Brush the tops of the bread slices with the tomato paste and arrange the cheese, spring onions and garlic cloves on top. Sprinkle with the pepper and oregano and bake in a moderately hot oven (190°C/375°F) for 15 minutes.
*Serves 4*

# Grilled Brie Canapes

*Quick, simple and yet stunning, this dish can be almost completely prepared ahead of time. This way you can enjoy the fluffy melt-in-the-mouth texture of the freshly cooked Brie.*

3 slices square loaf bread
1½ tablespoons Cranberry Sauce (page 305)
90 g (3 oz) Brie, sliced
chopped chives
12 small clumps of redcurrants

Toast the bread on one side until it becomes golden brown. Trim the crusts from the bread if desired and spread the cranberry sauce on the untoasted side. Cut each slice of toast into 4 fingers and top each with a slice of Brie. Just before serving, grill (broil) the fingers until the cheese begins to melt. Top each finger with two or three chopped chives and a clump of redcurrants.
*Serves 4*

# Bruschetta Shapes

*Quick and easy to prepare, these scrumptious starters can be prepared with a variety of toppings to suit the individual tastes of your family or friends. All types of bread may be used. In fact this is a good way to make use of bread that is a day or two old.*

12 slices bread
3 teaspoons olive oil
2 garlic cloves, crushed (pressed)
¼ teaspoon cracked black pepper
2 cups (185 g/6oz) shredded spinach
185 g (6 oz) feta cheese *or* bocconcini cheese, sliced
125 g (4 oz) cherry tomatoes, sliced
12 basil leaves

Cut the bread into the desired shapes using a sharp knife or a decorative biscuit (cookie) or scone (biscuit) cutter. Place the shapes on a prepared baking sheet. Place the oil in a cup and add the garlic, stirring briskly to combine well. Using a pastry brush, brush the garlic oil over the bruschetta shapes and sprinkle them with the pepper. Bake them in a hot oven (200°C/400°F) for 10 minutes. Remove from the oven and arrange the spinach, feta (or bocconcini), tomatoes and basil leaves on top.
*Serves 6*

# Ginger Roasted Tofu

*Serve with a selection of antipasto tidbits such as roasted vegetables, dips or dipping sauces and a fresh crispy salad.*

500 g (1 lb) tofu, drained
3 tablespoons pineapple juice
2 teaspoons grated ginger
2–3 garlic cloves, crushed (pressed)
1 tablespoon soy sauce
2 teaspoons sesame oil
2 teaspoons honey
¼ teaspoon cracked black pepper
2 spring onions (scallions), finely sliced
a little oil

Cut the tofu into 6 mm (¼ in.) slices. Combine the remaining ingredients and pour over the tofu. Cover and allow to stand for as long as possible (from 1 hour to all day) in the refrigerator. Drain the excess marinade from the tofu, retaining the leftover marinade for adding to soups and sauces. Place the tofu on a prepared baking sheet and bake in a hot oven (200°C/400°F) for 20 minutes.
*Serves 4–6*

# Roasted Tempeh

*Tempeh is often deep fried but I prefer to have a say in the amount of oil absorbed by food during cooking. It's easy to roast vegetable slices and even tempeh and tofu and the result is very similar to the fried version, but of course not as oily. Try this tempeh with all manner of tasty dips or dipping sauces.*

2 teaspoons oil such as peanut *or* safflower
500 g (1 lb) tempeh, cut into strips
cracked black pepper

Place the oil in a bowl and add the tempeh strips. Roll them in the oil to coat them evenly. Place the tempeh on a baking sheet and bake in a hot oven (200°C/ 400°F) until it becomes golden brown, about 25 minutes.
*Serves 4*

# Cranberry Dressed Tempeh

1 butter lettuce, trimmed, washed and patted dry
2 tablespoons Raspberry Vinegar (page 295)
1 quantity Roasted Tempeh
3 tablespoons Cranberry Sauce (page 305)
1 cup (250 mL/8 fl oz) Greek Yoghurt (page 273)
freshly ground black pepper
2 tablespoons finely sliced chives
6 lemon twists

Tear the lettuce into large bite-size pieces and place them in a bowl. Toss the lettuce with the Raspberry Vinegar, then arrange it neatly on 4 individual serving plates. Arrange the tempeh on top of the lettuce, leaving an indentation in the middle. Combine the Cranberry Sauce and Greek Yoghurt well and season to taste with the pepper. Spoon the cranberry dressing into the middle of the tempeh, sprinkle with the chives and decorate with the lemon twists.
*Serves 4*

# Tempeh with Creamy Tahini Dressing

2 cups (185 g/6 oz) young spinach leaves, trimmed, washed and spun dry
1 cup (90 g/3 oz) alfalfa sprouts (page 255)
1 quantity Roasted Tempeh
1 quantity Creamy Tahini Dressing (page 144)
125 g (4 oz) cherry tomatoes, halved

Arrange the spinach on a serving tray and place a 'nest' of alfalfa sprouts in the centre. Arrange the tempeh on top of the spinach. Spoon the dressing into the middle of the alfalfa and scatter with the cherry tomatoes.
*Serves 4*

# Main Meals and Snacks

*Often the main course is the only course we have time to prepare on a regular basis. Here is a selection of dishes which reflect the modern trend for lighter, informal eating, yet some of them can be proudly featured on formal dinner party menus. You will find a tempting variety of dishes from tasty timbales to luscious lasagnes.*

# Basic Pizza Dough

*This dough, leavened by yeast, is crusty and light—great for pizzas. Pizza yeast doughs do not have to be proved twice as for bread. Once the dough is prepared, it can be rolled out and placed directly onto the pizza or baking sheets. The dough will prove while you prepare the topping.*

½ cup (125 mL/4 fl oz) boiling water
1 teaspoon sugar
1 cup (250 mL/8 fl oz) cold water
7 g (¼ oz) active dry yeast
2 cups (250 g/8 oz) wholemeal (whole-wheat) flour
1 cup (125 g/4 oz) white flour
pinch salt (optional)
additional flour

Place the boiling water in a bowl, add the sugar and stir until it is dissolved. Add the cold water, then sprinkle the yeast on top of the water. Whisk the yeast through the water and set the mixture aside until a 'sponge' forms on top (about 5 minutes). Meanwhile, sift the flours and salt into a large bowl. Make a 'well' in the centre of the flour and pour in the yeast mixture. Mix the flour in gradually until a soft dough is formed, then turn it out onto a lightly floured surface. Knead the dough for about 5 minutes then roll it out to a 6 mm (¼ in.) thickness.
*Makes 1 large or 8 individual pizzas*

# Quick Pizza Dough

1 cup (125 g/4 oz) wholemeal (whole-wheat) self-raising flour
1 cup (125 g/4 oz) white self-raising flour
30 g (1 oz) butter, melted
1 tablespoon oil
¾ cup (185 mL/6 fl oz) milk or water

Sift the flours into a bowl and make a 'well' in the centre. Add the butter and oil and enough of the milk to bring the mixture to a soft dough consistency. Turn out onto a lightly floured surface and knead lightly for 1 minute. Roll out to a 6 mm (¼ in.) thickness.
*Makes 1 large or 8 individual pizzas*

# Polenta Pizza Dough

*Have fun testing out your creative flair, making large or individual pizzas, using a variety of doughs for the crust and varying the vegetable toppings according to the seasons. And why stop here—there is a fabulous array of cheeses suitable for topping pizzas, like bocconcini, bacio, ricotta cheese and feta cheese—all these need only 10 minutes in a hot oven to melt in tasty pools on top of your pizzas.*

½ cup (125 mL/4 fl oz) boiling water
1 teaspoon sugar
1 cup (250 mL/8 fl oz) cold water
2½ teaspoons active dry yeast
2 teaspoons oil
½ cup (90 g/3 oz) polenta
1 cup (125 g/4 oz) wholemeal (whole-wheat) flour
2 cups (250 g/8 oz) white flour
additional flour
pinch of salt

Place the boiling water in a small bowl and stir in the sugar until it's dissolved. Add the cold water and sprinkle the yeast on top. Whisk the yeast into the water and set the mixture aside until a 'sponge' forms on top (about 5 minutes). Meanwhile, sift the polenta, flours and salt into a bowl and make a 'well' in the centre. Add the yeast mixture and mix to a soft dough. Turn the dough out onto a lightly floured surface and knead for 200 'turns' (about 2 minutes). Roll out to a 6 mm (¼ in.) thickness.
*Makes 2 large pizzas or 10 individual pizzas*

### Preparing Extra Dough

It's worthwhile preparing the whole quantity, or even double quantity, even if you don't need all of it at once—it can be refrigerated or frozen for later use. Pizza dough is a great basic recipe.

*Overleaf: Polenta Pizzas with Pesto. The golden hue of the polenta provides a perfect backdrop for the summer vegetables.*

# Quick Pizzas

*These make a great snack—and kids love adding their own favourite vegetables to the topping, like grated carrot, mushrooms or even beanshoots.*

1 quantity Quick Pizza Dough (page 40)
2 tablespoons tomato paste (purée)
1½ tomatoes, diced
¾ cup (90 g/3 oz) grated tasty (mature cheddar) cheese
4 spring onions (scallions), sliced
½ sweet pepper (capsicum), diced
freshly ground black pepper

Roll the dough out into 8 individual pizzas, 2 medium pizzas or 1 large pizza and place on a prepared pizza baking sheet. Brush the dough with the tomato paste, scatter the tomatoes over and sprinkle with the cheese. Scatter the sweet pepper and spring onions over and season to taste with pepper. Bake in a hot oven (200°C/400°F) for 12–15 minutes for individual pizzas, 20 minutes for medium pizzas and 25 minutes for a large pizza.
*Makes 8 individual, 2 medium or 1 large pizza*

# Lentil Pizzarets

1 quantity Basic Pizza Dough (page 40)
½ quantity Lentil Pasta Sauce (page 52)
1 cup (125 g/4 oz) grated mozzarella cheese
½ cup sliced pitted black olives
1 red sweet pepper (capsicum), seeds removed, diced

Roll the dough out to a 6 mm (¼ in.) thickness and cut into 8–10 rounds using a large biscuit (cookie) cutter or tracing around a saucer with a knife. Place the rounds on prepared baking sheets. Spread the lentil sauce onto the pizza bases, sprinkle with the mozzarella and arrange the olives and the sweet peppers on top. Bake in a hot oven (200°C/400°F) for 20 minutes.
*Makes 8–10 individual pizzas*

# Polenta Pizzas With Pesto

*The tantalising aroma of the pesto sauce transforms these single serve pizzas into a mouthwatering delight. Serve with a light leafy salad such as Summer Greens with Mango Vinaigrette (page 130) for a main meal or serve singly for a substantial snack.*

1 quantity Polenta Pizza Dough (page 40)
3 tablespoons tomato paste (purée)
2 onions, diced finely
500 g (1lb) tomatoes, sliced
1 quantity Pesto Sauce (page 97)
300 g (10 oz) bocconcini cheese, sliced
1 red sweet pepper (capsicum), cut into thin strips
12 small sprigs basil for garnishing

Roll the dough out to a 6 mm (¼ in.) thickness and cut into about 10 rounds. Place the rounds of dough on baking sheets. Brush the rounds of dough with the tomato paste, scatter the onion over and arrange the tomato slices neatly on top. Using a pastry brush, brush about 2 teaspoons of the Pesto Sauce over each pizza and arrange the bocconcini and sweet pepper on top. Brush the remaining Pesto Sauce over the cheese and bake in a hot oven (200°C/400°F) for 20–25 minutes. Serve garnished with basil sprigs.
*Makes about 10 individual pizzas*

### Cutting Individual Pizzas

Individual pizzas can be cut into shape with a large cutter or by placing a small bowl or saucer upside down on the dough and running a sharp knife around the outside.

# Eggplant with Couscous

2 medium eggplants (aubergines), cut in half
    lengthways
1 tablespoon olive oil
1 onion, finely diced
2 garlic cloves, crushed (pressed)
1 celery stalk, diced finely
½ red sweet pepper (capsicum), diced
½ cup (90 g/3 oz) couscous
1 cup (250 mL/8 fl 0z) tomato juice *or* vegetable
    stock
juice of ½ lemon
freshly ground black pepper
3 tablespoons chopped parsley
additional chopped parsley
4 lemon wedges

Place the eggplants, cut side facing down, on a
prepared baking sheet. Brush the skins with a
little of the oil and bake in a moderate oven
(180°C/350°F) for 20 minutes. Carefully scoop
out the flesh leaving a 'shell' about 6 mm (¼ in.)
thick. Brush the insides of the eggplant shells
with half the remaining olive oil and return to
the oven for 10 minutes. Cut the eggplant flesh
into 6 mm (¼ in.) dice. Heat the remaining oil in
a frying pan or skillet and cook the onion, garlic,
celery and sweet pepper over a medium heat,
stirring occasionally, for 5 minutes. Add the
eggplant flesh and couscous and stir over a
medium heat for 2 minutes. Add the tomato juice
(or stock), cover and cook gently for 10 minutes.
Season to taste with the lemon juice and pepper
and add the parsley. Pile the couscous mixture
into the eggplant shells and serve sprinkled with
the additional chopped parsley and the lemon
wedges.
*Serves 4*

# Thai Style Vegetables

*The fragrance of the lemon zest and the richness of
the coconut cream soften the spicy flavour of this
dish. Serve with a bowl of steaming hot rice or
noodles for a tasty nutritious meal.*

2 teaspoons oil
1 onion, finely diced
4 garlic cloves, crushed (pressed)
1 tablespoon diced chili peppers *or* 2 teaspoons
    sliced dried chilies
1 teaspoon ground cumin
2 teaspoons ground coriander
1 tablespoon grated ginger
½ teaspoon ground turmeric
1 cup (225 g/7 oz) cooked chick peas (garbanzo
    beans), (page 124)
½ cup (125mL/4 fl oz) vegetable stock
500 g (1 lb) sweet potato, peeled, sliced
435 g (14 oz) tomatoes, peeled and cut into
    wedges
125 g (4 oz) green beans, trimmed and sliced
1 red sweet pepper (capsicum), seeded and sliced
finely grated rind of ½ lemon
1 cup (250 mL/8 fl oz) coconut cream (page 341)
1–2 tablespoons soy sauce
¼ teaspoon cracked black pepper

Heat the oil in a frying pan, skillet or wok, add
the onion and stir-fry for 1–2 minutes. Add the
garlic, chilies, cumin, coriander, ginger and
turmeric. Cook gently for 2 minutes, stirring all
the time. Add the chick peas and vegetable stock
and stir the mixture until it comes to the boil.
Add the sweet potato and tomato, cover and
cook over a medium heat for 10 minutes. Add
the green beans, sweet pepper, lemon rind and
coconut cream and stir well. Cook over a low
heat for a further 10 minutes. Season to taste
with the soy sauce and the pepper.
*Serves 6*

**Time Saver**
Replace the spices in this recipe with 2½
tablespoons commercial Thai Curry Paste if you
wish to save time.

*Right: Thai Style Vegetables. A harmonious blend of
aromatic spices and colourful vegetables.*

# Spicy Beans

2–3 teaspoons oil
2 onions, diced finely
2–3 garlic cloves, crushed (pressed)
2 teaspoon grated ginger
1 tablespoon ground coriander
2 teaspoons ground cumin
½–1 teaspoon ground turmeric
2 teaspoons garam masala
½ red sweet pepper (capsicum), cut into strips
3 tomatoes, peeled and chopped
3 cups (675 g/1¼ lb) cooked beans such as chick peas (garbanzo beans)
1 cup (250 mL/8 fl oz) tomato juice
3 tablespoons chopped coriander

Heat the oil in a frying pan, skillet or wok and stir-fry the onion, garlic and ginger over a medium heat for 2 minutes. Add all the spices, the sweet pepper and the tomatoes and cook, stirring, for 5 minutes. Add the chick peas and tomato juice and bring the mixture to the boil. Reduce the heat and simmer for 20 minutes. Stir in the chopped coriander and serve.
*Serves 6*

# Adzuki Bean Curry

2 teaspoons oil
1 onion, diced
2–3 garlic cloves, crushed
2 tablespoons curry paste
2 sticks celery, diced
2 cups (500 g/1 lb) cooked adzuki beans (page 123)
1 cup (250 mL/8 fl oz) vegetable stock
½ cup chopped coriander
additional coriander for garnishing

Heat the oil in a saucepan and stir-fry the onion and garlic for 2 minutes Add the curry paste, celery, adzuki beans and vegetable stock and bring the mixture to the boil, stirring occasionally. Reduce the heat, add the coriander and cover. Simmer gently for 15 minutes. Garnish with additional coriander and serve.
*Serves 4–6*

# Lentil Dahl

*This is a delightfully quick and easy recipe which is simply delicious. Enjoy with a side dish of rice or couscous.*

2 teaspoons oil
1 onion, diced finely
4 garlic cloves, crushed (pressed)
2 tablespoons curry powder
1 cup (185 g/6 oz) red split lentils, rinsed and drained
750 g (1½ lb) sweet potato, peeled, sliced
1 cup (155 g/5 oz) green peas
2 celery stalks, diced
2 cups (500 mL/16 fl oz) vegetable stock
freshly ground black pepper
1 cup (250 mL/8 fl oz) Greek Yoghurt (page 273)
4 tablespoons chopped coriander

Heat the oil in a saucepan and cook the onion for 2 minutes, stirring occasionally. Add the garlic and curry powder and stir over a medium heat for 2 minutes. Add the lentils, sweet potato, peas and celery and continue to stir over the heat for a few minutes. Add the stock and bring the mixture to the boil, stirring occasionally. Reduce the heat and cook gently for 25 minutes. Top each serve with a generous dollop of yoghurt and some chopped coriander.
*Serves 4–6*

# Chili Beans

2 teaspoons oil

2 onions, diced finely

2–3 garlic cloves, crushed (pressed)

1 red *or* green sweet pepper (capsicum), diced

½ teaspoon chili powder

4 tomatoes, chopped

2 tablespoons tomato paste (purée)

2 cups (500 mL/16 fl oz) cooked Red Kidney
   Beans (page 123)

Heat the oil and stir-fry the onion, garlic, sweet
pepper and chili powder for 2–3 minutes. Add
the tomatoes and tomato paste and cook,
stirring, for 5 minutes. Cover and simmer the
mixture for 5 minutes then add the kidney beans
and simmer gently for 12–15 minutes.
*Serves 4*

# Refried Beans

*These beans are delicious topped with Chili and
Tomato Sauce (page 48) and a generous dollop of
Yoghurt Cheese (page 271) and served with a leafy
salad.*

2 teaspoons oil

1 onion, diced

2–3 garlic cloves, crushed (pressed)

2 teaspoons minced chili peppers

½ red sweet pepper (capsicum), diced

3 cups (675 g/1¼ lb) cooked Red Kidney Beans
   (page 123)

½ cup chopped coriander

Place the oil in a saucepan, frying pan or skillet
and stir-fry the onion, garlic, chilies and sweet
pepper over a medium-high heat for 3–5
minutes. Add the beans and cook, covered, for
10 minutes. Using a potato masher or fork, mash
the beans then stir the coriander through.
*Serves 4*

# Vegetable Nachos

2 teaspoons oil

1 onion, diced

2 garlic cloves, crushed (pressed)

1 celery stalk, diced

2 carrots, scrubbed and grated

1 cup (155 g/5 oz) green peas

1 cup (250 mL/8 fl oz) vegetable stock

250 g (8 oz) packet corn chips

1 cup (125 g/4 oz) grated tasty (mature cheddar)
   cheese

Heat the oil and stir-fry the onion, garlic, celery
and carrot for 3–5 minutes. Add the peas and
stock and cook until the vegetables are tender,
about 10–15 minutes. Place half the corn chips
in 4 ovenproof dishes and sprinkle half the
cheese over. Bake in a moderately hot oven
(190°C/375°F) for 10 minutes. Top with the
vegetable mixture and the remaining chips and
cheese. Bake for a further 10 minutes.
*Serves 4*

# Basic Tacos

1 quantity Chili Beans

8 large taco shells

½ cucumber, seeds removed, diced

1 tomato, diced

3 spring onions (scallions), sliced finely

chopped parsley *or* coriander

1 cup (125 g/4 oz) grated tasty (mature cheddar)
   cheese

1 cup (250 mL/8 fl oz) Greek Yoghurt (page 273)
   *or* Yoghurt Cheese (page 271)

Place the Chili Beans in a saucepan, cover and
heat gently. Meanwhile crisp the taco shells by
heating in a moderate oven (180°C/350°F) for
3–5 minutes, or by cooking on medium heat in a
microwave for 1 minute. Combine the cucumber,
tomato, spring onions and parsley (or coriander).
Just before serving, spoon the Chili Beans into
the taco shells and sprinkle with the grated
cheese. Top each with a generous spoonful of
yoghurt and the vegetable mixture.
*Serves 4*

# Pumpkin and Spinach Terrine

*A sweet and nutty dish which doubles as an appetiser or a satisfying main meal when served with a vibrant green vegetable such as Succulent Broccoli (page 72). For a splash of colour, serve on a bed of Tomato and Ginger Concasse.*

1 kg (2 lb) pumpkin, cooked and mashed
1 tablespoon white miso (page 343)
225 g (7 oz) cashew pieces
1 teaspoon oil
225 g (7 oz) spinach, stalks removed, washed well
500 g (1 lb) Baked Ricotta Cheese (page 34), sliced

Combine the pumpkin with the miso and the cashew pieces. Brush the inside of a terrine dish or loaf pan with the oil. Pat the spinach dry with a clean tea towel and put aside 12–16 leaves (depending on size). Blanch, steam or microwave the remaining spinach until it is wilted down (page 94). Squeeze out excess moisture and chop. Line the base and the sides of the prepared dish with the whole spinach leaves. Place half of the pumpkin mixture in the dish, spreading it out evenly. Press the mixture down firmly to ensure the mixture fits into the dish neatly. Place half of the ricotta cheese slices on top of the pumpkin. Top with the remaining chopped spinach, then the remaining pumpkin mixture and ricotta cheese slices. Place the remaining whole spinach leaves on top of the ricotta cheese and cover the dish with aluminium foil. Bake in a moderate oven (180°C/350°F) for 30 minutes. Allow to cool in the dish before turning out and slicing.
*Serves 6–8*

*Left: Pumpkin and Spinach Terrine. Studded with cashews, this colourful terrine makes a light yet satisfying dish.*

# Tomato and Ginger Concasse

*Served hot or cold, this sauce adds both a burst of flavour and a splash of colour to a variety of dishes.*

2 teaspoons oil
1 onion, finely chopped
3 teaspoons grated ginger
¼ teaspoon chili powder
500 g (1 lb) ripe tomatoes, peeled and chopped
1 cup (250 mL/8 fl oz) apple juice
1 teaspoon honey
2 teaspoons apple cider vinegar

Heat the oil and stir-fry the onion, ginger and chili powder over a medium heat for 2 minutes. Add the tomatoes and the apple juice and bring the mixture to the boil. Reduce the heat, cover and simmer gently for 10 minutes. Remove from the heat and stir in the honey and the cider vinegar. Push the mixture through a sieve.
*Makes about 2 cups (500 mL/16 fl oz)*

# Tofu Chili Burgers

*Tofu is quite bland on its own and needs spicing up to win the hearts of burger lovers—it's the chili in these burgers that makes all the difference. Serve with Quick Satay Sauce (page 99) and tender crisp vegetables or a crispy salad.*

375 g (12 oz) firm tofu, drained and mashed
¼ teaspoon chili powder
1 tablespoon tomato paste (purée)
8 spring onions (scallions), sliced
2–3 garlic cloves, crushed (pressed)
2 tablespoons chick pea flour (besan flour)
1 tablespoon oil

Combine all the ingredients except the oil thoroughly and form the mixture into 12 burgers. Heat the oil in a frying pan or skillet and cook the patties for 2–3 minutes each side. Drain well on paper towels (absorbent kitchen paper) to remove excess oil.
*Makes about 12*

# Tofu Burgers

*These burgers are always popular served as a snack in a sandwich or a bun, but for a special touch, serve on toasted focaccia with Fresh Mango Relish (page 304), crisp fresh alfalfa sprouts and wild salad greens.*

375 g (12 oz) firm tofu, drained and mashed
2 tablespoons soy sauce
2 tablespoons peanut butter
8 spring onions (scallions), sliced
½ cup (60 g/2 oz) quick-cooking oats
2 tablespoons oil

Combine all the ingredients except the oil thoroughly, adding enough oats to bring the mixture to a 'soft dough consistency'. Form the mixture into burgers. Heat the oil in a frying pan or skillet and cook the patties for 2–3 minutes each side. Drain well on paper towels (absorbent kitchen paper) to remove excess oil.
*Makes about 12*

# Lentil Burgers

1 cup (225 g/7 oz) cooked brown lentils
  (page 121), well-drained
1 onion, diced finely
1–2 garlic cloves, crushed (pressed)
1 carrot, scrubbed and grated
1 celery stalk, diced finely
1 egg, beaten
1–2 tablespoons crunchy peanut butter
1 tablespoon soy sauce
½ cup chopped parsley
freshly ground black pepper
½ cup (60 g/2 oz) wholemeal (whole-wheat) flour
1 cup (155 g/5 oz) quick-cooking oats
1 tablespoon oil

Combine all the ingredients except the oil thoroughly, adding enough oats to bring the mixture to a 'soft dough consistency'. Form the mixture into burgers. Heat the oil in a frying pan or skillet and cook the patties for 2–3 minutes each side. Drain well on paper towels (absorbent kitchen paper) to remove excess oil.
*Makes about 12*

# Mushroom and Hazelnut Burgers

*Serve these tasty burgers in a fresh wholemeal (whole-wheat) roll with crispy salad greens and a dollop of Tofu Houmus (page 22) or with a colourful sauce such as Spiced Carrot Purée (page 99) or Tomato and Ginger Concasse (page 47), baked jacket potatoes and a leafy salad.*

250 g (8 oz) mushrooms, chopped
125 g (4 oz) coarsely ground hazelnuts
1 onion, diced finely
1 celery stalk, diced finely
2 garlic cloves, crushed (pressed)
1 tablespoon soy sauce
3 tablespoons chick pea flour (besan flour)
1 egg *or* 60 g (2 oz) tofu, drained and mashed
2 tablespoons finely sliced chives
freshly ground black pepper
1 tablespoon oil

Combine all the ingredients except the oil well and form the mixture into 8 burgers. Heat the oil in a frying pan or skillet and cook over a medium-high heat for 3–4 minutes on each side.
*Makes 8*

# Chili and Tomato Sauce

2 teaspoons oil
1 onion, diced finely
2 garlic cloves, crushed (pressed)
½ red sweet pepper (capsicum), diced
2 teaspoons minced chili peppers
500 g (1 lb) tomatoes, peeled and chopped
freshly ground black pepper

Heat the oil in a saucepan and stir the onion, garlic, sweet pepper and chilies over a medium-high heat for 2–3 minutes. Add the tomatoes and bring the mixture to the boil. Reduce the heat and simmer the mixture for 10 minutes. Season to taste with the pepper. Serve as it is or blend until smooth using a food processor or blender.
*Makes about 2 cups (500 mL/16 fl oz)*

# Roasted Soy and Cashew Burgers

*The sweet nutty flavour of the cashews shines through in these burgers which are delicious served with a spoonful of your favourite relish or chutney.*

2 cups cooked soy beans (page 124) chopped
125 g (4 oz) cashew pieces
1½ cups (375 g/12 oz) cooked mashed pumpkin
8 spring onions (scallions), sliced finely
2 garlic cloves, crushed (pressed)
1 tablespoon soy sauce
2 tablespoons wholemeal (whole-wheat) flour *or* chick pea flour (besan flour)
freshly ground black pepper
1 teaspoon oil

Combine all the ingredients except the oil. Form the mixture into patties, place on a prepared baking sheet and brush the tops with the oil. Bake in a moderately hot oven (190°C/375°F) for 25 minutes.
*Makes about 12*

# Avocado Foccacia

4 slabs foccacia, or other Italian bread
1 avocado, peeled, pip removed, sliced
juice of ½ lemon
cracked black pepper
8 spinach leaves, washed and dried
4 slices feta cheese
8 slices tomato
1 cup (125 g/4 oz) grated tasty (mature cheddar) cheese

Toast the foccacia on one side. Mash the avocado with the lemon juice and pepper and spread on the foccacia. Top with the spinach leaves, feta, tomato and grated cheese. Grill (broil) until the cheese melts.
*Serves 4*

# Avocado Timbales

*The richness of guacamole is captured in this delectable dish which is transformed into an eye catching meal when served with Tomato and Ginger Concasse (page 47) and tender-crisp vegetables such as broccoli and carrots.*

3 ripe avocados, skin and pip removed
6 spring onions (scallions), sliced
1 tablespoon finely sliced chives
2–3 garlic cloves, crushed (pressed)
juice of 1 lemon
a few drops of Tabasco Sauce
½ cup (60 g/2 oz) finely chopped spinach leaves
250 g (8 oz) Yoghurt Cheese (page 271) *or* light cream cheese
1 cup (250 mL/8 fl oz) milk
1½ teaspoons pure agar agar powder
1 finely sliced chili pepper, seeds removed

Using a food processor, blend the avocado, spring onions, chives, garlic, lemon juice, Tabasco Sauce and spinach until smooth. Add the Yoghurt Cheese (or light cream cheese) and blend for 30 seconds. Place the milk in a small saucepan and sprinkle the agar agar powder on top. Bring the mixture to the boil, stirring constantly, then reduce the heat and simmer for 1 minute. Remove from the heat and add to the avocado mixture while the processor is running.

Once the ingredients are thoroughly combined, it is important to pour the mixture immediately into wetted individual moulds before the mixture sets. If the mixture becomes too thick to pour, simply spoon the mixture into the moulds, tapping them on the bench firmLy to ensure there are no large pockets of air between the mixture and the moulds. Chill for at least 30 minutes, then serve topped with the finely sliced chilies.
*Makes 6*

# Tomato and Ginger Timbales

*Serve these timbales with a crispy salad, a generous dollop of Tofu Mayonnaise (page 145) and fresh crusty bread for a delicious light meal.*

3 medium tomatoes, peeled and sliced
½ white onion, chopped
2 garlic cloves, crushed (pressed)
juice of ½ lemon
2 teaspoons honey
1½ teaspoons grated ginger
cracked black pepper
1 cup (250 mL/8 fl oz) tomato juice
1½ teaspoons pure agar agar powder

Blend the tomatoes, onion, garlic, lemon juice, honey, ginger and pepper until smooth using a food processor. Place the tomato juice and agar agar powder in a small saucepan and bring to the boil, stirring constantly. Reduce the heat and cook for 1 minute, stirring. While the food processor is operating, add the agar agar mixture to the tomato mixture and blend for about 20 seconds. Immediately pour the mixture into 6 wetted moulds and chill before serving.
*Makes 6*

*Right: Tomato and Ginger Timbales and Sweet Potato and Leek Timbales are as quick and easy to prepare as they are delicious.*

# Sweet Potato and Leek Timbales

500 g (1 lb) sweet potato, peeled and sliced
2 teaspoons grated ginger
2 teaspoons honey
1 cup (250 mL/8 fl oz) coconut milk (page 341)
young leeks, trimmed, sliced thinly lengthways
2 eggs
freshly ground black pepper

Cook the sweet potato with the ginger, honey and coconut milk in a saucepan, covered, over a medium heat for 15 minutes, or in a microwave oven on high for 8 minutes, until tender. Meanwhile, place the leek slices in a heatproof bowl and cover with boiling water. Allow to stand for 10 seconds only then scoop the leeks out with a slotted spoon. Arrange the leek slices around the sides of 6 moulds. Using a food processor or blender, blend the sweet potato mixture until smooth with the eggs and pepper. Pour the mixture into the moulds and cover with aluminium foil. Steam for 10–15 minutes and allow to stand for 2 minutes. Cool slightly before turning out of the moulds.
*Makes 6*

# Quick Pasta Sauce

2 teaspoons oil
1 onion, diced finely
4 garlic cloves, crushed (pressed)
500 g (1 lb) tomatoes, peeled and chopped
½ cup (125 mL/4 fl oz) tomato juice
2 tablespoons tomato paste (purée)
freshly ground black pepper

Heat the oil in a medium sized saucepan and cook the onion over a medium heat, with the lid on the pan, for 2–3 minutes. Add the garlic, tomatoes, tomato juice and tomato paste and bring the mixture to the boil, stirring occasionally. Reduce the heat, cover and cook the sauce over a medium heat for 15 minutes, stirring occasionally. Season with the pepper.
*Makes about 3 cups (750mL/24 fl oz)*

# Lentil Pasta Sauce

*Serve on a bed of your favourite pasta or use to make a delicious lasagne or pizza (page 41).*

2 teaspoons oil
1 onion, diced
4 garlic cloves, crushed (pressed)
2 celery stalks, diced finely
375 g (12 oz) tomatoes, diced
2 cups (500 mL/16 fl oz) vegetable stock
3 tablespoons tomato paste (purée)
2 cups (435 g/14 oz) cooked brown lentils
  (page 121)
½ cup chopped parsley
freshly ground black pepper

Heat the oil in a saucepan and cook the onion, garlic and celery, covered, over a medium heat for 5 minutes. Add the tomatoes, stock and tomato paste and bring the mixture to the boil, stirring occasionally. Reduce the heat and simmer the sauce, covered, for 15 minutes. Add the lentils, cover, and cook gently for 10 minutes. Stir in the parsley and season to taste with the pepper.
*Serves 4*

# Lentil Lasagne

*This hearty and filling lasagne is an old time favourite of my family and friends.*

double quantity Lentil Pasta Sauce
250 g (8 oz) instant lasagne sheets
1 quantity Cheesy Sauce (page 101)
chopped parsley

Prepare or reheat the lentil sauce so that it is bubbling hot. When using instant pasta sheets it's very important to use hot pasta sauce to ensure that the lasagne starts cooking as soon as it is assembled. Assemble layers of lasagne sheets and lentil sauce in an ovenproof dish. Top with a layer of the cheese sauce. Bake the lasagne in a moderate oven (180°C/350°F) for 45 minutes. Serve sprinkled with the chopped parsley.
*Serves 8*

# Sweet Potato Lasagne

*This is one of my sister's culinary creations and is sweet, nutty and irresistible—just like her! Served with a tangy, green salad and crusty bread, this lasagne is a real treat.*

1 quantity Quick Pasta Sauce (page 50)
250 g (8 oz) instant lasagne sheets
2 cups (435 g/14 oz) cooked (page 123) *or* canned
  red kidney beans, drained
500 g (1 lb) sweet potato, cooked and puréed
double quantity Light White Sauce (page 101)
90 g (3 oz) mushrooms, sliced
½ cup (60 g/2 oz) grated mozzarella cheese

Place half the pasta sauce on the base of a lasagne dish and top with a layer of lasagne. Spread the beans on top of the lasagne, top with another layer of lasagne, then the remaining pasta sauce and another layer of lasagne. Spread the sweet potato over the lasagne, top with another layer of lasagne, half the white sauce, mushrooms and more lasagne. Finally top with the remaining white sauce and the mozzarella. Bake in a moderate oven (180°C/350°F) for 45 minutes.
*Serves 8*

# Vegetable Layer Lasagne

double quantity Quick Pasta Sauce (page 50)
375 g (12 oz) carrots, scrubbed and grated
½ cup chopped parsley
500 g (1 lb) ricotta cheese, mashed
185 g (6 oz) mushrooms, sliced
2 tablespoons soy sauce
250 g (8 oz) packet instant lasagne sheets
¾ cup (90 g/3 oz) grated tasty (mature cheddar)
   cheese

Heat the pasta sauce through until boiling, then stir in the carrots and parsley and cook, covered, for 10 minutes. Combine the ricotta cheese, mushrooms and soy sauce. Arrange consecutive layers of lasagne sheets and pasta sauce in an ovenproof dish, with a layer of the ricotta cheese and mushroom mixture in the middle and finishing with a layer of pasta sauce sprinkle with the cheese. Bake in a moderate oven (180°C/350°F) for 45 minutes.
*Serves 8*

# Baked Tofu Satay Slices

*Great as a sandwich filling, or sliced and added to stir-fried vegetables, noodles or rice.*

500 g (1 lb) tofu, well drained
1 cup (250 mL/8 fl oz) hot vegetable stock
3 tablespoons peanut butter
1 tablespoon soy sauce
2–3 garlic cloves, crushed (pressed)
freshly ground black pepper
1 teaspoon finely chopped red chili peppers
   (optional)

Cut the tofu into slices approximately 1 cm (½ in.) thick and place on a prepared baking sheet. Combine the stock, peanut butter, soy sauce, garlic, pepper and chili pepper, if using. Brush this mixture over the tofu slices and bake in a moderately hot oven (190°C/375°F) for 20–25 minutes.
*Serves 4–6*

# Baked Sesame Tofu

*Serve drizzled with a delicious dipping sauce (page 97).*

500 g (1 lb) tofu, drained
1 tablespoon soy sauce
1 teaspoon grated ginger
1 teaspoon honey
1 tablespoon finely sliced chili peppers
2 garlic cloves, crushed (pressed)
1 teaspoon sesame oil
a little additional sesame oil
1 tablespoon sesame seeds
2 tablespoons chopped coriander

Cut the tofu into 1 cm (½ in.) cubes and place in a bowl. Combine the soy sauce, ginger, honey, chili pepper, garlic and sesame oil and pour the mixture over the tofu, tossing carefully to ensure the tofu is covered with the flavouring ingredients. Spread the tofu evenly over a prepared baking sheet. Sprinkle with the sesame seeds and bake in a hot oven (200°C/400°F) for 20–25 minutes. Sprinkle with the coriander.
*Serves 4*

# Braised Tofu

*Once you have the marinated tofu on hand, this is a quick dish to prepare. Serve over steaming hot noodles or rice for a tasty nutritious meal.*

375 g (12 oz) firm tofu, drained, cut into cubes
1 quantity Ginger and Soy Dipping Sauce
  (page 96)
2 teaspoons sesame oil
6 spring onions (scallions), sliced
1 carrot, scrubbed and sliced
125 g (4 oz) green beans, sliced
125 g (4 oz) button mushrooms, sliced
1 tablespoon arrowroot
1½ cups (375 mL/12 fl oz) vegetable stock
125 g (4 oz) beanshoots

Marinate the tofu in the dipping sauce for a minimum of 1 hour (or all day, or overnight if this is convenient). Heat the oil in a frying pan, skillet or wok and stir-fry the spring onions, carrots and green beans for 5 minutes. Add the mushrooms and continue stir-frying for 5 minutes. Blend the arrowroot to a smooth paste with a little of the stock, then combine with the remaining stock. Add the stock to the vegetables and stir until boiling. Reduce the heat and carefully stir in the tofu, including the marinade. Simmer the mixture gently for 5 minutes. Stir in the beanshoots and serve at once.
*Serves 4–6*

# Tofu Cacciatore

*A popular dish all round as the tofu readily absorbs the flavours of the mushrooms and wine. Serve with tender-crisp vegetables and fresh bread.*

500 g (1 lb) firm tofu, drained and sliced
2 teaspoons olive oil
freshly ground black pepper
4 spring onions (scallions), sliced
125 g (4 oz) mushrooms, sliced
½ cup (125 mL/4 fl oz) white wine
1 quantity Quick Pasta Sauce (page 50)

Arrange the tofu slices in a single layer on a prepared baking sheet. Brush the tofu with ½ teaspoon of the oil and sprinkle with the pepper. Bake in a hot oven (200°F/400°F) for 20 minutes. Meanwhile, place the remaining oil in a frying pan, skillet or wok and stir-fry the spring onions and mushrooms for 2 minutes. Add the wine and cook for 5 minutes. Stir in the Quick Pasta Sauce and heat gently. Combine with the tofu and serve.
*Serves 4–6*

# Tofu Pastry

*This pastry is very pliable, fun to work with and gives a surprisingly good result. The bonus is that it is much lower in fat than conventional pastry.*

2 cups (250 g/8 oz) wholemeal (whole-wheat)
  flour
1 teaspoon baking powder
90 g (3 oz) tofu, drained and mashed
1 tablespoon oil
½ cup (125 mL/4 fl oz) water
additional flour

Sift the flour and baking powder and make a 'well' in the centre. Combine the tofu and the oil and add to the 'well' with the water. Work the mixture until it forms a soft dough, then turn it out onto a lightly floured surface and knead for 30 seconds only. Use as required.
*Makes 2 pastry shells (page 57) or the top and bottom of a family sized pie.*

*Right: Tofu Cacciatore. The robust flavours in this Italian-inspired dish are perfect for dressing up tofu.*

# Basic Wholemeal Pastry

*This pastry has less fat, is easier to work with and rolls out well. It also crisps up nicely in the oven.*

2 cups (250 g/8 oz) wholemeal (whole-wheat) flour
½ teaspoon baking powder
30 g (1 oz) butter, melted
1 tablespoon oil
½ cup (125 mL/4 fl oz) water
additional flour

Sift the flour and baking powder and make a 'well' in the centre. Add the butter, oil and water to the 'well' and gradually work the mixture into a soft dough using your hand if you can bear it, or a wooden spoon if you prefer not to submerge yourself in food as I do. Turn the dough out onto a lightly floured surface and knead lightly for 30–60 seconds only. Roll out and use as required.
*Makes 2 pastry shells (page 57) or the top and bottom of a family-sized pie*

# Cheesy Leek Flan

2–3 teaspoons oil
1 bunch leeks, washed, trimmed and sliced
4 eggs, beaten
1 cup (250 mL/8 fl oz) plain yoghurt
freshly ground black pepper
1 prepared pastry shell (page 57)
1 cup (125 g/4 oz) grated tasty (mature cheddar) cheese

Heat the oil and cook the leeks over a medium heat, covered, for 5–10 minutes, then set aside to cool to lukewarm. Combine the eggs, yoghurt and pepper. Place the leeks on the base of the prepared pastry shell and pour the egg mixture over. Sprinkle with the cheese and bake in a moderately hot oven (190°C/375°F) for 30 minutes.
*Serves 8–10*

# Vegetable Cheese Pies

*My favourite topless pies with a golden brown cheesy topping.*

1 quantity Basic Wholemeal Pastry
1 kg (2 lb) pumpkin, peeled and diced
1 carrot, scrubbed and diced
1 onion, diced
2 garlic cloves, crushed (pressed)
250 g (8 oz) cauliflower, chopped
1 cup (155 g/5 oz) green peas
1 cup (250 mL/8 fl oz) vegetable stock *or* water
½ cup chopped parsley
freshly ground black pepper
2 cups (250 g/8 oz) grated tasty (mature cheddar) cheese
2 tomatoes, sliced thickly
chopped parsley

Place the pumpkin, carrot, onion, garlic, cauliflower, peas and stock (or water) in a large saucepan. Cover and bring the mixture to the boil. Reduce the heat and simmer the mixture for 25–30 minutes, or until the pumpkin is very tender. Alternatively halve the amount of stock and place all the above ingredients in a microwave-proof dish, cover and cook on high for 15 minutes. Add the parsley and pepper to taste and set aside to cool completely. Drain any excess liquid and retain to use in soups or sauces.

Cut the pastry to fit 8 individual or 2 family-size flan tins (pie pans). Bake in a moderately hot oven (190°C/375°F) for 10 minutes. Place the filling in the pastry shells and sprinkle the cheese evenly over the tops. Bake in a moderately hot oven (190°C/375°F), 20 minutes for individual pies and 30 minutes for family-size pies. Top with the tomato slices and parsley
*Makes 8 individual or 2 family-size pies*

# Golden Onion Flan

*The sweetness of this delicious flan comes from the slow cooking of the onions which causes them to caramelise. Serve with a crispy green salad.*

3 teaspoons oil
5 onions, diced
6 eggs, beaten
1 cup (250 mL/8 fl oz) plain yoghurt
2 teaspoons rosemary leaves
freshly ground black pepper
1 tablespoon soy sauce
1 prepared pastry shell using BasicWholemeal
   Pastry (page 56)

Heat the oil in a frying pan, skillet or wok and cook the onion over a medium heat, covered, for 5 minutes. Remove the cover and continue to cook over a medium heat, stirring occasionally, until they become a light golden brown, about 5 minutes. Set the onions aside to cool. Blend the eggs and yoghurt until smooth and add the rosemary, pepper and soy. Place the onion on the base of the prepared pastry shell and pour the egg mixture on top. Bake in a hot oven (200°C/400°F) for 10 minutes, then reduce the heat and bake in a moderate oven (180°C/350°F) for 20 minutes.
*Serves 6*

### Egg Substitute

If you wish to omit the eggs, you can still have your flan and eat it too—substitute the eggs and yoghurt with 500 g (1 lb) tofu and 1 cup (250 mL/8 fl oz) soy milk. All you need to do is blend the tofu and the soy milk in a food processor or blender until it is smooth.

# Spicy Sweet Potato Flan

*Serve with a leafy green salad and a small scoop of light cream cheese.*

2 teaspoons oil, sesame if possible
1 onion, diced finely
2 garlic cloves, crushed (pressed)
1 teaspoon ground cardamom
1 teaspoon grated ginger
1 teaspoon minced chili peppers
1 kg (2 lb) sweet potato, peeled and diced
3 tablespoons Coconut Cream (page 341)
225 g (7 oz) tofu, drained and mashed
freshly ground black pepper
3 tablespoons chopped coriander
1 prepared pastry shell
**additional chopped coriander for topping**

Heat the oil in a saucepan and stir-fry the onion, garlic, cardamom, ginger and chili peppers over a medium heat for 2 minutes. Add the sweet potato and coconut cream and cook over a medium heat, covered, until the sweet potato is very tender, about 20 minutes. Using a food processor or blender, blend the sweet potato with the tofu until smooth, then stir through the coriander and pepper to taste. Set the mixture aside to cool. Spread the mixture out in the prepared pastry shell and bake in a moderately hot oven (190°C/375°F) for 30 minutes.
*Serves 8–10*

### Preparing Pastry Shells

To prepare a pastry shell, divide the pastry in half and roll each piece out to a 12 mm (½ in.) thickness. Roll up on a rolling pin, unroll the pastry into the pan and press onto the bottom and sides. Run the rolling pin over the pan's rim to trim the edges neatly. Bake in a moderately hot oven (190°C/375°F) for 10 minutes before filling. If you only need one pastry shell immediately, it is a good idea to freeze the other for later use.

# Farmhouse Omelette

*This is a dish to whip up for a simple meal at the end of the week, and a perfect way to use up leftover vegetables from the night before. Even stir-fried vegetables or spicy vegetable dishes such as Spicy Potato Sauté (page 80) can be used instead of the potato and green peas, so have fun creating your own delicious versions.*

2 teaspoons oil
1 onion, diced
4 eggs
2 teaspoons soy sauce
freshly ground black pepper
2 potatoes, scrubbed, cooked (page 93) and diced
½ cup (90 g/3 oz) green peas *or* beans, cooked, (page 96)
½ cup (60 g/2 oz) grated tasty (mature cheddar) cheese
2 tomatoes, sliced
½ cup chopped parsley

Heat the oil in a frying pan or skillet and stir-fry the onion over a medium heat for 1 minute. Cover and cook for 2–3 minutes or until the onion becomes translucent. Whisk the eggs with the soy sauce and pepper and add the onions. Return the mixture to the pan and when the eggs begin to set, scatter the potatoes and peas over the top. Cook, covered, until the eggs have set, then sprinkle the cheese over. Cook the omelette under a hot grill (broiler) until the cheese melts, then top with the tomato slices and parsley.
*Serves 6*

# Feta Frittata

*A quick and easy recipe, delicious served with crusty bread and a fresh tomato salad.*

2 teaspoons oil
6 eggs, beaten
freshly ground black pepper
4 spring onions (scallions), sliced finely
125 g (4 oz) feta cheese
½ cup halved black olives

Heat the oil, pour in the egg, cover and cook over a medium heat for 5–8 minutes. Sprinkle with the pepper and spring onions and arrange the feta and olives on top. Cook under a hot grill (broiler) until bubbling hot and serve at once.
*Serves 4*

# Baked Tofu Frittata

*Serve hot or warm with baked seasonal vegetables and a tasty sauce or purée.*

1 medium carrot, scrubbed and diced
1 cup (155 g/5 oz) green peas
500 g (1 lb) firm tofu, mashed
2 eggs, beaten
1 tablespoon white miso (page 343)
freshly ground black pepper
½ red sweet pepper (capsicum), diced
4 spring onions (scallions), sliced
½ cup chopped parsley

Cook the carrot and peas until tender. Blend the tofu, eggs, miso and pepper until smooth. Combine the peas, carrots, sweet pepper and spring onions with the tofu mixture and place in a prepared terrine dish. Bake in a moderately hot oven (190°C/375°F) for 30 minutes. Sprinkle with the parsley before serving.
*Serves 4*

*Left: Feta Frittata. A flavour-packed dish that can be whipped up in minutes.*

# Basic Waffles

¾ cup (90 g/3 oz) wholemeal (whole-wheat)
  self-raising flour
¾ cup (90 g/3 oz) white self-raising flour
2 eggs, separated
1½ cups (375 mL/12 fl oz) milk

Place the flours in a bowl and make a 'well' in
the centre. Whisk the egg yolks and milk
together and pour into the 'well'. Beat the
mixture for 1–2 minutes then set aside for 5–10
minutes if possible. Whisk the egg whites until
soft peaks form and carefully fold into the
mixture. Preheat the waffle iron and cook ½
cupfuls of the mixture at a time until the waffles
are golden brown (about 2 minutes).
*Makes 6*

# Cheesy Waffles

*These crispy and tasty waffles make a great snack
on their own, a special accompaniment for soups or
hotpots and can also form the base for a light meal.*

1½ cups (185 g/6 oz) wholemeal (whole-wheat)
  self-raising flour
½ cup (60 g/2 oz) grated tasty (mature cheddar)
  cheese
2 eggs, separated
½ cup (125 g/4 fl oz) plain yoghurt
1¼ cups (310 mL/10 fl oz) milk
1 tablespoon grainy mustard
freshly ground black pepper

Follow the method for Basic Waffles, adding the
cheese to the flour and combining the yoghurt
and mustard with the egg yolks and milk. Season
to taste with the pepper before cooking.
*Makes 6*

# Polenta Waffles with Chili Beans

1 cup (125 g/4 oz) wholemeal (whole-wheat)
  self-raising flour
½ cup (90 g/3 oz) polenta
225 g (7 oz) tofu
2 tablespoons oil
1¼ cups (310 mL/10 fl oz) milk
½ teaspoon bicarbonate of soda (baking soda)
  dissolved in 1 tablespoon boiling water
1 avocado, peeled, pip removed, diced
1 tomato, diced
2 spring onions (scallions), sliced finely
1 tablespoon lemon juice
1 quantity Chili Beans (page45)
1½ cups (375 mL/12 fl oz) Greek Yoghurt
  (page 273)

Using a food processor, blend the flour, polenta,
tofu, oil, milk and bicarbonate of soda until
smooth. Set aside for 15 minutes if possible, to
soften the polenta. Cook in ½ cupfuls as for Basic
Waffles. Serve at once or reheat in a moderate
oven (180°C/350°F) for 10 minutes or in a
microwave oven for 2 minutes. Combine the
avocado, tomato, spring onions and lemon juice.
Serve each waffle topped with the chili beans, a
generous dollop of yoghurt and the avocado and
tomato mixture.
*Serves 6*

### Pancake Substitutes

If you do not have a waffle maker, do not
despair! Although waffles look great, you can
make pancakes faster, almost as fast as a hungry
herd can devour them. Simply cook large
spoonfuls of the mixture in a moderately hot
frying pan or skillet which has been brushed
with a little oil.

# Super Soy Pancakes

*These egg and dairy free pancakes are light and tasty and versatile too. This mixture can be used as a base for any of the following vegetable pancakes. Simply fold the vegetables through once you have prepared the mixture.*

125 g (4 oz) tofu, drained and mashed
1 tablespoon oil
1 cup (250 mL/8 fl oz) soy milk
1½ cups (185 g/6 oz) wholemeal (whole-wheat)
    self-raising flour
freshly ground black pepper
1—2 additional teaspoons oil

Using a food processor, blend the tofu, oil and soy milk until smooth. Add the flour and pepper and blend for a further 10 seconds. Heat the oil in a frying pan or skillet and cook large spoonfuls of the mixture until bubbles rise and begin to burst on the uncooked side. Turn the pancakes over carefully and cook for 2 minutes on the other side.
*Makes 12*

# Vegetable Pancakes

1½ cups (185 g/6 oz) wholemeal (whole-wheat)
    self-raising flour
2 eggs
1¼ cups (310 mL/10 fl oz) milk
1 tablespoon soy sauce
1 carrot, scrubbed, grated
6 spring onions (scallions), sliced finely
90 g (3 oz) beanshoots *or* chopped cabbage
freshly ground black pepper

Using a food processor, blend the flour, eggs, milk and soy sauce until smooth. Transfer the mixture to a bowl and fold in the remaining ingredients. Heat a teaspoon of oil in a frying pan or skillet and cook large spoonfuls of the mixture until bubbles rise and begin to burst on the uncooked side. Turn the pancakes over carefully and cook for 2 minutes on the other side.
*Makes 12*

# Cheese and Leek Pancakes

*Delicious served on their own as a snack or served with tender crisp green vegetables and a tasty sauce.*

1½ cups (185 g/6 oz) wholemeal (whole-wheat)
    self-raising flour
2 eggs
1 cup (250 mL/8 fl oz) milk
90 g (3 oz) leeks, sliced
3 tablespoons sliced chives
½ cup (60 g/2 oz) grated cheese
freshly ground black pepper

Blend the flour, eggs and milk until smooth. Add the remaining ingredients and combine well. Heat a teaspoon of oil in a frying pan or skillet and cook large spoonfuls of the mixture until bubbles rise and begin to burst on the uncooked side. Turn the pancakes over carefully and cook for 2 minutes on the other side.
*Makes 12*

# Spinach Pancakes

1½ cups (185 g/6 oz) wholemeal (whole-wheat)
    self-raising flour
2 eggs
1¼ cups (310 mL/10 fl oz) milk
½ bunch spinach, trimmed, washed and chopped
6 spring onions (scallions), sliced
freshly ground black pepper
1 teaspoon oil

Blend the flour, eggs and milk until smooth. Add the remaining ingredients and combine well. Heat the oil in a frying pan or skillet and cook large spoonfuls of the mixture until bubbles rise and begin to burst on the uncooked side. Turn the pancakes over carefully and cook for 2 minutes on the other side.
*Makes 12*

# Spinach and Cheese Pancake Stack

*These pancakes are delicious served surrounded with a colourful sauce such as Tomato and Ginger Concasse (page 47).*

12 Spinach Pancakes (page 61)
125 g (4 oz) tasty (mature cheddar) cheese, sliced
8 large slices tomato
2 tablespoons finely sliced chives

Arrange 4 pancakes in an ovenproof dish. Top each with a slice of cheese and a slice of tomato then top with the remaining pancakes. Arrange the remaining cheese on top, and bake in a moderate oven (180°C/350°F) for 12–15 minutes or cover with microwave proof plastic wrap (cling film) and cook in a microwave oven on high for 3 minutes. Top with the remaining tomato slices and serve sprinkled with the chives.
*Makes 4*

# Cheesy Leek Pancakes with Asparagus

8 Cheese and Leek Pancakes (page 61)
1 quantity Cheese Sauce (page 101)
1 tablespoon prepared grainy mustard
1 kg (2 lb) asparagus, trimmed and cooked (page 72)
2 tablespoons finely sliced chives
cracked black pepper

Arrange 4 pancakes in an ovenproof dish. Combine the Cheese Sauce with the mustard. Top each pancake with 3 or 4 asparagus spears and 3 tablespoons of the sauce. Top with another pancake then cover with aluminium foil. Cook in a moderate oven (180°C/350°F) for 10–12 minutes or cover with microwave proof plastic wrap (cling film) and cook on high in a microwave oven for 3 minutes. Serve topped with the additional sauce and sprinkled with the chives and the pepper.
*Serves 4*

# Vegetable Satay Pancake Stack

12 Vegetable Pancakes (page 61)
1 quantity Quick Satay Sauce (page 99)
8 large slices tomato
1 quantity Chili and Garlic Sauce (page 99)

Arrange 4 pancakes in an ovenproof dish and spread thickly with half the satay sauce. Top each with a tomato slice and then with another pancake. Top with the remaining sauce, tomato slices and pancakes. Cover with aluminium foil and bake in a moderate oven (180°C/350°F) for 10–12 minutes or cover with microwave proof plastic wrap (cling film) and cook in a microwave oven on high for 3 minutes. Serve drizzled with the Chili and Garlic Sauce.
*Makes 4*

# Antipasto Pancakes

*Serve hot with soup or on their own as a snack.*

1½ cups (185 g/6 oz) wholemeal (whole-wheat) self-raising flour
2 eggs
1¼ cups (310 mL/10 fl oz) milk
125 g (4 oz) feta cheese, drained well
8 sun-dried tomatoes, sliced
½ cup chopped basil leaves
freshly ground black pepper
1–2 teaspoons oil

Blend the flour, eggs and milk until smooth. Add the remaining ingredients and combine well. Heat a teaspoon of oil in a frying pan or skillet and cook large spoonfuls of the mixture until bubbles rise and begin to burst on the uncooked side. Turn the pancakes over carefully and cook for 2 minutes on the other side.
*Makes 12*

*Right: Bursting with the goodness of wholemeal flour and fresh vegetables, Vegetable Satay Pancake Stack makes a tasty light meal or snack.*

# Bread Crusted Vegetable Pies

*These delicious pies are as nutritious as they are delicious, and are very easy to make. Once prepared, they can be individually wrapped and frozen for later use—great thawed and reheated in the microwave for a quick light meal or snack.*

2 teaspoons oil
1 onion, diced
1 carrot, scrubbed and diced
2 celery stalks, diced
2 tomatoes, diced
6 round wholemeal (whole-wheat) rolls
1 cup (185 g/6 oz) sweet corn kernels
1 cup (225 g/7 oz) beans such as cooked or
   canned red kidney beans
freshly ground black pepper
a few drops of Tabasco Sauce
½ cup (60 g/2 oz) grated tasty (mature cheddar)
   cheese

Heat the oil in a saucepan and cook the onion, carrot, celery and tomatoes over a medium heat, covered, for 5 minutes. Cut the tops off the bread rolls and pull out the bread, leaving 6 mm (¼ in.) thick crusts. Using a food processor or blender, process the bread into coarse breadcrumbs. Combine the cooked vegetable mixture with the breadcrumbs, sweet corn and beans and season to taste with the pepper and Tabasco Sauce. Pile the mixture into the bread crusts and top with the cheese. Bake in a moderate oven (180°C/350°F) for 15 minutes.
*Makes 6*

# Double Crust Spinach Pizza

*Try using yeast dough instead of pastry to make crusty topped pies. The basic pizza dough I have used in this recipe makes a wonderfully satisfying pie yet it contains no fat. Serve with a tasty sauce on the side or a crispy dressed salad.*

1 tablespoon oil
1 onion, diced
2 garlic cloves, crushed (pressed)
2 bunches spinach, blanched (page 94) and
   chopped
225 g (7 oz) feta cheese, crumbled, *or* 225 g (7 oz)
   tofu, drained and combined with 1 tablespoon
   soy sauce
1 quantity Basic Pizza Dough (page 40)
freshly ground black pepper

Heat the oil in a saucepan and stir-fry the onion and garlic for 2 minutes, then add the spinach. Combine with the feta (or tofu) and season to taste with the pepper. Prepare the pizza dough and divide the dough in half. Set one half aside and cover with a tea towel. Roll out the other half to a 6 mm (¼ in.) thickness and arrange on a prepared pizza tray or baking sheet. Spread the filling evenly over the pizza base. Knead the remaining dough and roll out to a 6 mm (¼ in.) thickness. Arrange on top of the vegetable mixture and tuck the edges under. Brush with a little warm water and prick the top with a skewer. Set the pizza aside for 10 minutes, then bake in a hot oven (200°C/400°F) for 20–25 minutes.
*Makes 1 large pizza*

# Savoury Cheese Balls

*It is well worthwhile preparing a double quantity of this recipe as the balls can be stored in the refrigerator for up to one week, or in the freezer for several weeks, and can be reheated at a moment's notice. Delicious served with Quick Tomato Braise (page 77).*

1 cup (155 g/5 oz) quick cooking oats
155 g (5 oz) ricotta cheese *or* tofu (page 346)
1 onion, finely diced
2 garlic cloves, crushed
½ cup (60 g/2 oz) grated tasty (mature cheddar) cheese
½ cup chopped parsley
1 egg, beaten
freshly ground black pepper
1 cup (90 g/3oz) fresh breadcrumbs

Mix all the ingredients thoroughly and form into balls about the size of a walnut. Place on a prepared baking sheet and bake in a moderately hot oven (190°C/375°F) for 20–25 minutes.
*Makes 18*

# Crispy Phyllo Tartlets

4 sheets phyllo pastry
1 tablespoon oil
½ bunch spinach, blanched and chopped (page 94)
125 g (4 oz) ricotta cheese
½ cup (60 g/2 oz) grated tasty (mature cheddar) cheese
freshly ground black pepper

Lay 2 double sheets of phyllo out and brush the top sheets with a little of the oil. Fold the sheets over to enclose the oiled sheets and cut each of the phyllo sheets into 8 squares. Brush the insides of 8 muffin tins (pans) with a little of the oil and place a square of phyllo into each tin, oiled surface facing upwards. Top with the remaining squares. Add the combined filling ingredients and bake in a moderate oven (180°C/350°F) for 20 minutes.
*Makes 8*

# Golden Haloumi Cheese

*Haloumi cheese is a wonderful Greek cheese, which is traditionally cooked until golden brown in olive oil. Serve simply on a bed of fresh salad greens.*

250 g (8 oz) haloumi cheese (page 343)
2 teaspoons olive oil
¼ cup chopped parsley
lemon wedges

Place the haloumi cheese in a bowl and cover with water. Allow to stand for 1 hour. Drain well and pat dry with a clean tea towel. Cut the cheese into 6 mm (¼ in.) slices. Heat a frying pan or skillet with the olive oil and fry the cheese for 1 minute each side until it becomes golden brown. Make sure the oil is quite hot before you start frying. This will help the cheese absorb as little oil as possible and you will have crisp golden brown haloumi. Serve topped with the parsley and the lemon wedges on the side.
*Serves 4*

**Soaking Haloumi**
Haloumi cheese must first be soaked to remove excess salt. It's a good idea to soak haloumi cheese as soon as you bring it home. It can then be drained and wrapped in a clean tea towel and stored in the refrigerator for 2-3 days.

# Tiny Cheese Money Bags

*Serve these crispy parcels with tender crisp steamed or stir-fried vegetables with a delicious sauce on the side.*

250 g (8 oz) feta cheese, crumbled
250 g (8 oz) ricotta cheese, mashed
3 tablespoons chopped herbs
3 tablespoons chopped pitted olives
2 garlic cloves, crushed (pressed)
cracked black pepper
4 sheets phyllo pastry
2 teaspoons oil such as olive
8 chives

Combine the feta, ricotta cheese, herbs, olives, garlic and pepper. Cut the phyllo pastry sheets into 4. Lay out 8 squares of phyllo (double thickness) and place a spoonful of the cheese mixture in the middle of each sheet. Pull the ends of the pastry up towards the middle and twist the pastry carefully so that a 'money bag' is formed. Tie a chive around each of the money bags. Brush the money bags with a little oil and place on a prepared baking sheet. Bake in a moderately hot oven (190°C/375°F) for 15–20 minutes.
*Makes 8*

**Low-Fat Phyllo**
The traditional method for preparing phyllo pastry makes use of lashings of melted butter. This is not essential, however. Characteristically crispy phyllo pastry can be produced using only a little fat, in the form of polyunsaturated or mono-unsaturated vegetable oil. Some tricks involve the use of nonfat plain yoghurt while others use ground nuts to keep the sheets of phyllo separate and light.

# Eggplant Mozzarella

*Serve hot, warm or cold with a tangy dressing and salad greens. This dish can be prepared ahead of time to the stage of coating the eggplant (aubergine) with the polenta (cornmeal) mixture, the spin off effect being that the polenta coating will then 'stay where it's put' during cooking.*

2 medium eggplants (aubergines)
4 tablespoons plain yoghurt
1 tablespoon balsamic vinegar
4 garlic cloves, crushed (pressed)
1 tablespoon soy sauce
¼ teaspoon cracked black pepper
3 tablespoons polenta (cornmeal)
3 tablespoons grated Parmesan cheese
175 g (6 oz) mozzarella cheese, sliced
toothpicks (cocktail sticks)
1 quantity Quick Pasta Sauce (page 50)
additional 2 tablespoons grated Parmesan cheese

Cut the eggplant into crossways slices and place them in a bowl. Combine the yoghurt, vinegar, garlic, soy sauce and pepper and pour over the eggplant slices. Toss the mixture to coat the eggplant. Combine the polenta and the Parmesan cheese. Coat the eggplant slices with the polenta mixture and place on a prepared baking sheet. Bake in a moderately hot oven (190°C/375°F) for 25 minutes. Layer the eggplant slices in an ovenproof dish with the mozzerella slices in between.Pour the pasta sauce over and sprinkle with the additional Parmesan. Bake for a further 15 minutes.
*Serves 4*

*Right: Tiny Cheese Money Bags. Light and crispy, phyllo pastry is perfect for encasing tasty fillings such as feta and ricotta cheese laced with olives and fresh herbs.*

# Bocconcini Bakes

*The bocconcini develops a chewy texture when cooked, making this a light but satisfying dish. Serve with a dressed leafy salad.*

375 g (12 oz) bocconcini cheese, sliced
1 quantity Quick Pasta Sauce (page 50)
½ bunch spinach, blanched (page 94) and chopped finely
cracked black pepper
grated mozzarella cheese

Arrange 2 layers each of bocconcini, pasta sauce and spinach in 4 prepared moulds. Sprinkle with pepper to taste and the grated mozzarella. Bake in a moderately hot oven (190°C/375°F) for 25 minutes.
*Serves 4*

# Panir with Eggplant

1 medium-sized eggplant (aubergine), trimmed
1 tablespoon oil
1 onion, diced finely
2 garlic cloves, crushed
2 teaspoons ground coriander
1 teaspoon ground cumin
1 teaspoon grated ginger
2 ripe tomatoes, peeled and diced
½ cup (125 mL/4 fl oz) vegetable stock
225 g (7 oz) panir (page 271), sliced
freshly ground black pepper

Cut the eggplant in half lengthways, then cut into 6 mm (¼ in.) crossways slices. Place the eggplant slices on a prepared baking sheet. Brush the slices lightly with some of the oil and bake in a moderate oven (180°C/350°F) for 20 minutes. Meanwhile, heat the remaining oil in a frying pan or skillet and stir the onion, garlic, coriander, cumin and ginger over a medium heat for 2–3 minutes. Add the tomatoes and cook, with the lid on, for 10 minutes, stirring occasionally. Add the stock and the eggplant slices and simmer for 5 minutes. Stir in the panir carefully, reheat gently and serve.
*Serves 4–6*

# Spicy Panir

*Simple to prepare yet tasty and nutritious to eat, especially when served with hot chapatis or steaming hot noodles or rice.*

1 tablespoon peanut oil
1 onion, diced finely
2 garlic cloves, crushed (pressed)
2 teaspoons garam masala
2 teaspoons finely sliced chili peppers, seeds removed
1 teaspoon grated ginger
375 g (12 oz) tomatoes, peeled, and diced
1 teaspoon honey
½ cup (125 mL/4 fl oz) tomato juice *or* vegetable stock
225 g (7 oz) panir (page 271), cut into cubes
6 spring onions (scallions), sliced
freshly ground black pepper

Heat the oil in a frying pan or skillet and stir-fry the onion, garlic, garam masala, chilies and ginger over a medium heat for 2–3 minutes. Add the tomatoes, honey and tomato juice (or stock) and cook with the lid on for 15 minutes, stirring occasionally. Add the panir and spring onions and stir carefully through the sauce to ensure all the cubes are evenly coated. Reheat gently, stirring as little as possible to prevent breaking up the panir.
*Serves 4*

### Panir Variations
For an interesting texture contrast, add toasted sesame seeds or dry roasted peanuts when stirring in the panir. And for a quick transformation into a dairy free dish, simply substitute Roasted Tempeh or Ginger Roasted Tofu (page 37) for the panir.

# Basic Rice Paper Rolls

*Available at Asian grocery stores and some supermarkets, rice paper is a wonderful ingredient to have tucked away in the pantry. It is easy and fun to use, can be wrapped around all sorts of tasty fillings and can be prepared well ahead of time. Serve cold or steam for 1–2 minutes to warm.*

12 sheets rice paper
2 cups (500 mL/16 fl oz) warm water
3 cups filling of your choice

Immerse the rice paper in the warm water for 5–10 seconds or until it becomes pliable. Remove immediately from the water and lay the rice paper on a clean dry tea towel. Place about ¼ cup of the filling at the end of the rice paper closest to you and begin rolling, folding the side edges of the rice paper as you roll. Place the rolls on a serving plate, with the ends of the rice paper tucked underneath.
*Makes 12 rolls*

# Tofu Satay Rolls

1 teaspoon sesame oil
8 spring onions (scallions), sliced finely
2 garlic cloves, crushed (pressed)
¼ teaspoon chili powder
1 tablespoon desiccated coconut
3 tablespoons crunchy peanut butter
1 tomato, diced
1 tablespoon tomato paste (purée)
freshly ground black pepper
1 quantity Baked Tofu Satay Slices (page 53)
12 sheets rice paper
2 cups (500 mL/16 fl oz) warm water

Heat the oil in a frying pan, skillet or wok and stir-fry the spring onions, garlic, chili powder and coconut over a medium heat for 2 minutes. Add the peanut butter, tomato, tomato paste and pepper and cook, covered, for 5 minutes. Remove from the heat and stir in the tofu. Assemble the rolls as for Basic Rice Paper Rolls.
*Makes 12 rolls*

# Vegetable Rolls

*Laced with the distinctive flavours of ginger, garlic and miso, these tasty rolls are wonderful served with a salad of summer greens for a light meal on a hot day. Serve with a little soy sauce or your favourite dipping sauce (page 97) on the side.*

1 teaspoon sesame oil
1 onion, diced *or* 8 spring onions (scallions), finely sliced
1 teaspoon grated ginger
2 garlic cloves, crushed
1 carrot, scrubbed and grated
⅛ cabbage, trimmed, washed and chopped
125 g (4 oz) beanshoots
2 teaspoons white miso (page 343)
1 tablespoon water
12 sheets rice paper
2 cups (500 mL/16 fl oz) warm water

Heat the oil in a frying pan, skillet or wok and stir-fry the onion (or spring onions), ginger and garlic for 1–2 minutes, then cover and cook for 2 minutes. Add the carrot and cabbage and continue to cook, covered, for 3 minutes, then add the beanshoots and cook for a further 2 minutes. Place the miso in a cup and blend to a smooth paste with the water. Stir the miso through the vegetables and set aside to cool. Assemble the rolls as for Basic Rice Paper Rolls.
*Makes 12 rolls*

# Vegetables and Sauces

*These days, vegetables can take pride of place as main course dishes,
yet can still be served simply so that their true character shines
through. I'm sure the less fuss vegetables receive, the happier they
are—so dress them up simply with fresh herbs or try some of the
lighter tasty sauces and purées in this chapter.*

# Lemon Dressed Asparagus

*Fresh new season's asparagus has a wonderful flavour of its own, yet is further enhanced by the tang of lemon juice and the heat of cracked black pepper.*

1 kg (2 lb) asparagus, trimmed
1 quantity Lemony Pepper Dressing (page 149)

To trim the asparagus, simply hold each spear firmly and snap the coarse ends off. Some people peel asparagus with a special peeler or small sharp knife but I personally feel this is unnecessary if you have fresh young asparagus. To steam the asparagus, place in a steamer insert and steam for 10 minutes; to cook it in a microwave, place it in a microwave-proof dish, cover and cook on high for 4–5 minutes. While still warm, arrange the asparagus neatly on a serving platter and drizzle with the dressing.
*Serves 4–6*

### Storing Asparagus

When shopping, choose bright crisp asparagus and prepare it as soon as possible. To store it for a day or two, first wrap in a paper towel (absorbent kitchen paper), place in a plastic (polythene) bag and store it in the vegetable compartment of your refrigerator.

# Peas with Ginger

1½ kg (3 lb) green peas, shelled
2 tablespoons preserved ginger syrup *or*
  ¼ teaspoon ground ginger mixed with
  1 tablespoon honey
freshly ground black pepper

Steam the peas for 10–12 minutes, or place in a microwave-proof dish with 2 tablespoons water, cover and cook on high for 8 minutes, stirring the peas after 4 minutes. As soon as the peas are cooked, toss in the ginger syrup (or the ginger and honey mixture) and season to taste with the pepper.
*Serves 4*

# Succulent Broccoli

*This recipe is so quick and easy you can leave it to the last moment to prepare. Green vegetables seem to come alive when cooked until just tender and, with the combined flavours in the dressing, this broccoli will never be left on the plate! This dish also doubles as a great appetiser.*

500 g (1lb) broccoli, trimmed
4 tablespoons mirin (page 343)
1 garlic clove, crushed (pressed)
1 teaspoon sesame oil
cracked black pepper

Cut the broccoli into florets and peel and slice the stalks. Cook the broccoli until tender crisp (page 85). Meanwhile, place the remaining ingredients in a screw-top jar and shake to combine. As soon as the broccoli is cooked, toss carefully with the dressing and serve at once.
*Serves 4*

### Retaining Flavour

Cook vegetables quickly with as little moisture as possible by stir-frying in a minimum of oil, dry baking, steaming or cooking in a microwave oven. Maximum retention of flavour, texture and nutrients can be achieved if water is not permitted to dilute the flavour. You'll find there is no need to add salt, butter or rich sauces.

*Overleaf: Lemon Dressed Asparagus. Cook until tender-crisp and dress simply to bring out the stunning colour and flavour of this special vegetable.*

# Real Vegetable Spaghetti

*Spaghetti squash is a fascinating vegetable. When cooked, the flesh can be fluffed up with a fork so that it resembles spaghetti, hence its name. You'll love this dish for its flavour, and there is a bonus— the 'spaghetti' can be served straight from the vegetable so there are fewer dishes to wash!*

1 medium spaghetti squash
1 quantity Quick Pasta Sauce (page 50), heated
2 tablespoons grated Parmesan cheese

Place the squash in a large saucepan and half cover with water. Bring the water to the boil and boil the squash for 25–30 minutes. When the squash is cooked, cut it in half and remove the seeds. To cook the squash in a microwave, first cut it in half and remove seeds. Peel and slice and place in a microwave-proof dish. Sprinkle with 1 tablespoon water, cover and cook on high for 5 minutes. Allow to stand for 2 minutes. Using a fork, fluff up the flesh and toss the hot pasta sauce through. Sprinkle with the cheese and bake in a moderately hot oven (190°C/375°F) for 10 minutes.
*Serves 4*

# Mirin Carrots

*Some of the popular flavours of Japanese cooking mingle in this simple dish which makes a wonderful light vegetable accompaniment.*

2 teaspoons sesame oil
1 teaspoon grated ginger
500 g (1lb) carrots, trimmed and sliced diagonally
4 spring onions (scallions), sliced finely
2 tablespoons mirin (page 343) *or* dry sherry
cracked black pepper

Heat the oil in a saucepan and stir-fry the ginger, carrots and spring onions for 2–3 minutes. Add the mirin (or dry sherry) and cook gently for 10 minutes. Season to taste with the pepper.
*Serves 4*

# Spiked Baby Carrots

*Start off with crisp young carrots and you cannot go wrong with this recipe—the citrus tang complements the carrots beautifully while the fresh parsley provides a wonderful colour contrast.*

2 bunches baby carrots, trimmed and washed
3 tablespoons orange juice
2 teaspoons honey
½ cinnamon stick, broken in half
1 tablespoon Orange Liqueur (page 329)
3 tablespoons chopped parsley

Cook the carrots until tender (page 93). Place the orange juice, honey, cinnamon stick and liqueur in a small saucepan and simmer for 1 minute. Remove the cinnamon stick and drizzle the sauce over the carrots. Serve sprinkled with the parsley.
*Serves 6*

# Zucchini with Almonds

2 teaspoons oil
1–2 garlic cloves, crushed (pressed)
3 tablespoons slivered almonds
500 g (1 lb) zucchini (courgettes), trimmed and cut into strips
freshly ground black pepper

Heat the oil and stir-fry the garlic and almonds over a medium heat for 1–2 minutes. Add the zucchini and cook, covered, for 5 minutes, or until the zucchini become tender-crisp. Season to taste with the pepper.
*Serves 4*

### Choosing Zucchini

When shopping, choose young firm zucchini (courgettes) with a glossy skin. Young zucchini are more flavoursome than their larger more mature counterparts.

# Hijike Carrots

15 g (½ oz) hijike (page 343)
½ cup (125 mL/4 fl oz) water
1 teaspoon sesame oil
1 teaspoon grated ginger
3 spring onions (scallions), sliced diagonally
500 g (1 lb) carrots, cut into sticks
2 tablespoons mirin (page 343) *or* dry sherry
freshly ground black pepper

Break the hijike into short lengths, then place it in a small bowl and pour the water over. Cover and set aside for 20 minutes. Heat the oil in a frying pan, skillet or wok and stir-fry the ginger, spring onions and carrots over a medium–high heat for 3–5 minutes. Add the mirin (or dry sherry), cover and cook, for 2–3 minutes. Drain the liquid from the hijike and add the hijike to the carrots. Season to taste with the pepper and reheat gently.
*Serves 4*

**A Flavour Boost**
Retain the hijike soaking water. It is very flavoursome and can be added to soups or sauces.

# Carrots with Dill

1 teaspoon oil
1–2 teaspoons dill seeds
500 g (1lb) carrots, scrubbed and sliced
 diagonally
3 tablespoons vegetable stock
freshly ground black pepper
2 tablespoons chopped dill

Heat the oil in a saucepan and add the dill seeds and the carrots. Cover and cook over a medium heat for 5 minutes. Add the stock and pepper and continue to cook for another 5 minutes. Stir in the chopped dill and serve.
*Serves 4*

# Sesame Beans

*Green beans are delicious cooked until they are tender-crisp, as they are in this side dish which doubles as a salad dressed simply with a squeeze of lemon juice and sprinkled with chopped coriander.*

2 teaspoons sesame oil
¼ teaspoon ground ginger
1 tablespoon sesame seeds
500 g (1 lb) green beans, trimmed and sliced
 diagonally
1 tablespoon mirin (page 343) *or* apple juice

Heat the oil in a frying pan, skillet or wok and stir-fry the ginger and sesame seeds over a medium heat for 1–2 minutes. Add the beans and the mirin (or apple juice) and cook, covered, for 5 minutes. Cook, uncovered, for 5 more minutes, stirring occasionally.
*Serves 4*

# Cabbage with Poppy Seeds

*Cabbage seems like a completely different vegetable when it is cooked this way. The crisp texture is offset by the poppy seeds which also provide an interesting colour contrast.*

2 teaspoons oil
1 tablespoon poppy seeds
¼ cabbage, trimmed, washed and shredded finely
3 tablespoons fruit juice *or* water
freshly ground black pepper

Brush the bottom of a large frying pan, skillet or wok with the oil and add the poppy seeds. Cook over a medium heat, shaking the pan, for 1 minute. Add the cabbage and cook over a medium heat, stirring, for 2–3 minutes. Reduce the heat, add the juice (or water) and place a lid on the pan. Cook the cabbage for 2 minutes or until it is just tender but still a vibrant green. Season with the pepper.
*Serves 4*

*Left: Cooked lightly with a minimum of moisture, Cabbage with Poppy Seeds retains its colour well.*

# Broad Beans with Cabbage

*Simply delicious, this dish makes a great accompaniment for burgers and savoury tarts.*

1–2 teaspoons oil
1 onion, diced, *or* 8 spring onions (scallions), sliced
375 g (12 oz) broad (fava) beans, cooked (page 96)
2 tomatoes, diced
¼ small cabbage, trimmed, washed and shredded finely
3 tablespoons chopped parsley
freshly ground black pepper

Heat the oil and stir-fry the onion (or spring onions) over a medium heat for 2–3 minutes. Add the broad beans and tomatoes and cook, covered, for 5 minutes. Stir in the cabbage and the parsley and cook, covered, for 5 minutes. Season to taste with the pepper.
*Serves 4–6*

**Blanching Broccoli or Cauliflower**
Place the trimmed broccoli (or cauliflower) florets in a heatproof bowl and completely cover with boiling water. Allow to stand for 1 minute, then quickly and carefully drain the water off. Plunge the florets into icy water for 1 minute to refresh them and prevent further cooking. Spread the broccoli (or cauliflower) out on a clean dry tea towel to drain. Use as soon as possible, or place the florets in an airtight container and store in the refrigerator for 1 day.
Serves 4

# Garlic Mushrooms

1 tablespoon oil
1 large onion, diced
4 garlic cloves, crushed (pressed)
250 g (8 oz) mushrooms, wiped over, stalks removed
½ cup (125 mL/4 fl oz) vegetable stock
½ cup (125 mL/4 fl oz) white wine
2 teaspoons white miso *or* soy sauce
½ cup chopped parsley
cracked black pepper

Heat the oil in a frying pan, skillet or wok over a medium heat. Add the onion and garlic and cook, stirring, for 2 minutes. Add the mushrooms and the vegetable stock and stir over the heat for 1 minute. Place a lid on the pan and cook for 5 minutes. Add the white wine and cook for 5 minutes with the lid off the pan. If using miso, place it in a cup and blend to a smooth paste using a little of the liquid in the pan. Add the miso (or soy sauce) and stir through the mushrooms. Add the parsley, season to taste with the pepper and serve at once.
*Serves 4*

**Buying Mushrooms**
When shopping, choose firm sweet smelling mushrooms and buy only the amount you will use within a day or two. To retain maximum freshness and to prevent them from sweating and spoiling, store mushrooms in a brown paper bag in the vegetable compartment of your refrigerator.

# Mushrooms and Tomatoes

2 teaspoons olive oil
4 spring onions (scallions), sliced
225 g (7 oz) mushrooms
375 g (12 oz) tomatoes, peeled and sliced
1 teaspoon honey
2–3 tablespoons dry white wine

Heat the oil in a frying pan, skillet or wok and stir-fry the spring onions and mushrooms over a medium–high heat for 2–3 minutes. Add the tomatoes and honey and continue to cook, covered, for 5 minutes. Stir in the wine. Cook, uncovered, for 5 minutes, stirring occasionally. Season to taste with the pepper.
*Serves 4–6*

# Quick Tomato Braise

1 teaspoon oil
1 onion, diced
½ sweet pepper (capsicum), seeds removed, diced
500 g (1 lb) tomatoes, peeled and sliced
1 teaspoon honey
freshly ground black pepper

Heat the oil in a saucepan and stir-fry the onion and sweet pepper over a medium heat for 2–3 minutes. Add the tomatoes and honey and bring the mixture to the boil. Reduce the heat and simmer, covered, for 10 minutes. Season to taste with the pepper.
*Serves 4–6*

**Peeling Tomatoes**
To peel tomatoes, place them in a heatproof bowl and cover them completely with boiling water. Allow them to stand for 1 minute, drain off the water and cover the tomatoes with cold water. The skin should now be easily peeled off. The skins of tomatoes can also be easily removed by first roasting or grilling (broiling) the tomatoes under a high heat.

# Mushrooms with Ginger

*This Japanese inspired dish is laced with the flavour of ginger, spring onions and coriander with a hint of sesame.*

1 teaspoon sesame oil
1 teaspoon grated ginger
3 garlic cloves, crushed (pressed)
3 spring onions (scallions), sliced on the diagonal
250 g (8 oz) button mushrooms, trimmed
2–3 tablespoons mirin (page 343) *or* dry white wine *or* fruit juice
freshly ground black pepper
½ cup chopped coriander

Heat the oil in a frying pan, skillet or wok and stir-fry the ginger, garlic and spring onions over a medium heat for 2–3 minutes. Add the mushrooms and cook, covered, for 2–3 minutes. Add the wine (or fruit juice) and cook, uncovered, for 5 minutes. Stir in the pepper and coriander.
*Serves 4–6*

# Orange Glazed Sweet Potato

2 medium-sized sweet potatoes, peeled
1½ teaspoons sesame oil
2 teaspoons honey
2 tablespoons orange juice
1 tablespoon finely sliced chives
freshly ground black pepper

Cut the sweet potatoes into 6 mm (¼ in.) diagonal slices and spread out in an even layer in prepared ovenproof dish. Combine the oil, honey and orange juice and brush the mixture over the sweet potato slices. Dust with the pepper, cover with a lid or aluminium foil and bake in a moderate oven (180°C/350°F) for 15 minutes. Remove the cover (or foil) and brush the sweet potatoes with the remaining juice mixture and continue baking, uncovered, for 15 minutes. Sprinkle with the chives and pepper.
*Serves 4*

# Baked Sweet Corn

4 sweet corn cobs, husks removed, trimmed
1 quantity Sweet Chili Dipping Sauce (page 97)
chopped coriander *or* parsley
½ teaspoon oil

Remove the silk from the corn and cut the cobs in half crossways. Place the cobs in a bowl, drizzle the sauce over and sprinkle with the coriander (or parsley). Cover and set aside for 15 minutes. Arrange the corn cobs in a prepared ovenproof dish and pour any excess sauce over, then cover and bake in a moderate oven (180°C/350°F) for 30 minutes.
*Serves 4*

# Asparagus with Raspberry Vinaigrette

*Fresh cooked asparagus makes a superb appetiser as well as a vegetable accompaniment. Be sure to cook it until it is just tender to ensure it becomes a vibrant green. This recipe presents asparagus very simply—the best way to serve most vegetables!*

1kg (2 lb) asparagus, trimmed
4 tablespoons Raspberry Vinaigrette (page 149)
cracked black pepper

Cook the asparagus until just tender by placing in a covered microwave-proof container and cooking on high for 5 minutes, or by steaming for 10 minutes. Arrange the asparagus on serving plates and, just before serving, drizzle with the dressing and top with the pepper.
*Serves 4*

# Fruity Red Cabbage

*I love the colour of red cabbage, which can be retained by adding a splash of cider vinegar as it cooks. The tang of the vinegar is softened by the sweetness of the apple and raisins which make good partners for red cabbage. Serve this colourful dish hot, warm or cold as a side vegetable or a relish.*

¼ small red cabbage, trimmed, washed and chopped
2 green apples, unpeeled and diced
½ cup (90 g/3 oz) raisins
2 white onions, chopped
2 tablespoons apple juice
1 teaspoon honey
2 tablespoons apple cider vinegar
freshly ground black pepper

Place all the ingredients in a saucepan, cover and cook for 20 minutes, stirring occasionally. This is a great recipe for the microwave—cover and cook on high for 10 minutes. Stand for 5 minutes.
*Serves 6*

# Coconut Poached Carrots

*Coconut and carrots harmonise well with the distinctive flavour of cardamom in this special yet simple recipe.*

1 teaspoon oil
½ teaspoon ground cardamom
4 spring onions (scallions), sliced
1 teaspoon finely grated orange rind
500 g (1 lb) carrots, scrubbed and sliced diagonally
1 cup (250 mL/8 fl oz) coconut milk (page 341)
freshly ground black pepper

Heat the oil and stir the cardamom, spring onions, orange rind and carrots over a medium heat for 2 minutes. Stir in the coconut milk and cook, covered, for 10 minutes. Season to taste with the pepper.
*Serves 4*

*Right: Fruity Red Cabbage. A wonderful way to add a splash of colour and sweetness to winter meals.*

# Beetroot with Garlic

*A simple side dish—serve as it is or top with a dollop of plain yoghurt.*

3 beetroots (beets), trimmed and scrubbed
2–3 garlic cloves, crushed (pressed)
1 tablespoon lemon juice
½ cup chopped parsley
freshly ground black pepper

Steam or microwave the beetroot until tender (page 93), rub off the skin and cut the flesh into strips or slices. While hot, toss with the garlic, lemon juice, parsley and pepper. Serve warm.
*Serves 4*

# Garlic Potatoes

2 teaspoons oil
3 garlic cloves, crushed (pressed)
500 g (1 lb) potatoes, cooked (page 96) and sliced
3 tablespoons chopped parsley
squeeze of lemon juice
freshly ground black pepper

Heat the oil in a frying pan, skillet or wok and stir-fry the garlic for 1 minute. Add the potatoes, parsley, lemon juice and pepper and cook over a medium heat for 3–5 minutes.
*Serves 4–6*

# Rosemary Potatoes

500 g (1 lb) potatoes, cooked (page 93) and sliced
2 teaspoons oil
1 tablespoon rosemary
½ cup chopped parsley
cracked black pepper

Arrange the potatoes in a prepared ovenproof dish. Combine the oil, rosemary and parsley and sprinkle over the potatoes. Cover with a lid or aluminium foil and bake in a moderate oven (180°C/350°F) for 20 minutes, removing the lid (or foil) for the last 10 minutes of cooking time.
*Serves 4*

# Spicy Potato Sauté

*This is a side dish with a difference which doubles as a light meal when served with warm chapatis.*

750 g (1½ lb) potatoes, scrubbed and cut into wedges
2 teaspoons oil
1 teaspoon minced chili peppers
2 garlic cloves, crushed (pressed)
2 teaspoons ground coriander
1 teaspoon ground cumin
½ teaspoon turmeric powder
½ cup (125 mL/4 fl oz) vegetable stock *or* water
½ cup chopped coriander *or* parsley
cracked black pepper

Cook the potatoes until just tender (page 93). Meanwhile, heat the oil in a wok, frying pan or skillet and stir-fry the chilies, garlic and spices over a medium–high heat for 2–3 minutes. Add the stock (or water), coriander (or parsley) and stir in the potatoes. Continue to cook, covered, for 5 minutes, then season to taste with the pepper.
*Serves 4–6*

# Potatoes with Paprika

750 g (1½ lb) potatoes, scrubbed
2 teaspoons oil
1½ teaspoons sweet paprika
8 spring onions (scallions), sliced
freshly ground black pepper
1 cup (250 mL/8 fl oz) plain yoghurt
2 tablespoons finely sliced chives

Cook the potatoes until just tender (page 93), then cut into cubes or slices. Heat the oil in a frying pan, skillet or wok and stir-fry the paprika and the spring onions over a medium–high heat for 1–2 minutes. Add the potatoes and pepper and cook, stirring occasionally, for 2–3 minutes. Serve topped with the yoghurt and chives.
*Serves 4*

# Baked Jacket Potatoes

*Serve these ever-popular potatoes as a side dish dusted with cracked black pepper and freshly chopped herbs. For a light meal, sprinkle with grated tasty cheese, top with a scoop of Yoghurt Cheese (page 271) or light sour cream and drizzle with Chili and Garlic Sauce (page 99) for a splash of colour and a burst of flavour.*

**4 large potatoes, scrubbed**

Place the potatoes on a prepared baking sheet. Bake in a moderately hot oven (190°C/375°F) for 45 minutes–1 hour. To cook in a microwave oven, prick the skins with a skewer and microwave on high for 10-12 minutes. Allow to stand for 2 minutes. Split the potatoes open and serve while piping hot.
*Serves 4*

# Mashed Potatoes

*Good old fashioned mashed potatoes were laden with lashings of butter and milk and more than a good pinch of salt. In tune with lighter yet still tasty food, why not try this version which is surprisingly delicious, especially when laced with the fresh herbs.*

**500 g (1 lb) potatoes, peeled and sliced**
**½ cup (125 mL/4 fl oz) plain yoghurt or milk**
**a little salt (optional)**
**freshly ground black pepper**
**2 tablespoons chopped parsley or chives**
  **(optional)**

Cook the potatoes until very tender (page 93). Mash with a potato masher then using a wooden spoon and a strong wrist beat in the yoghurt (or milk). Season to taste with the pepper and, if liked, stir in the parsley (or chives).
*Serves 4*

# Cheesy Potatoes

*This dish is a richer version of mashed potatoes and makes a delicious side vegetable but can also be the crowning glory for vegetable pies. Simply place the potatoes in a piping bag and pipe them onto the filling rather than topping the pie with pastry.*

**500 g (1 lb) potatoes, peeled and sliced**
**125 g (4 oz) ricotta cheese**
**½ cup (60 g/2 oz) grated tasty (mature cheddar)**
  **cheese**
**freshly ground black pepper**
**2 tablespoons finely sliced chives**

Cook the potatoes until very tender (page 93). Mash with a potato masher then using a strong wrist and a wooden spoon, beat in the ricotta cheese and the tasty cheese. Season to taste with the pepper and stir the chives through.
*Serves 4*

# Ginger Glazed Parsnips

**500 g (1 lb) young parsnips, scrubbed or peeled**
**2 teaspoons sesame oil**
**3 tablespoons preserved ginger syrup or**
  **3 teaspoons honey and ½ teaspoon ground**
  **ginger**
**½ cup (125 mL/4 fl oz) freshly squeezed orange**
  **juice**
**freshly ground black pepper**
**2 tablespoons chopped parsley**

Slice the parsnips diagonally. Heat the oil in a frying pan, skillet or wok and stir-fry the parsnips for 2 minutes. Combine the ginger syrup (or honey and ginger) with the orange juice and drizzle the mixture over the parsnips. Cover and cook gently for 10–12 minutes or until tender. Season to taste with the pepper and sprinkle with the parsley.
*Serves 4*

# Roasted Fennel

*A delicious addition to an antipasto platter, fennel becomes even more flavoursome when roasted.*

2 bulbs Florence fennel (finocchio)
2 teaspoons olive oil
cracked black pepper

Trim the feathery fronds and stalks from the fennel bulbs, retaining the fronds as decoration. Cut the bulbs in half lengthways. Place the bulbs cut side down on a prepared baking sheet. Brush the fennel with the oil and sprinkle with the pepper. Bake in a moderately hot oven (190°C/375°F) for 35 minutes or until the fennel is tender when checked with a skewer.
*Serves 4–6*

# Roasted Tomatoes

6 medium-sized tomatoes, peeled
2–3 teaspoons olive oil
3 spring onions (scallions), sliced finely, *or* ¼ red onion, diced finely
2–3 garlic cloves, peeled, cut into slivers
cracked black pepper

Cut the tomatoes in half crossways and place cut side down on a prepared baking sheet. Brush with a little of the oil and scatter the spring onions (or onion) and garlic over the top. Sprinkle with the pepper and bake in a moderately hot oven (190°C/375°F) for 25–30 minutes.
*Serves 6*

# Roasted Mushrooms

*Packed full of flavour and with a satisfying chewy texture, it's no wonder that roasted mushrooms are one of the most popular tidbits to disappear from the vegetable platter when I serve antipasto meals. Try them laced with a garlic marinade too.*

12 large cap mushrooms
1 quantity Ginger and Soy Dipping Sauce (page 96)

Trim the ends off the mushroom stalks and place the mushrooms in a bowl. Drizzle the sauce over, cover and set aside for 15 minutes. Arrange the mushrooms on a prepared baking sheet. Bake in a moderately hot oven (190°C/375°F) for 25–30 minutes.
*Serves 6*

# Roasted Red Onions

*The colour of red onions provides a lift to a meal of tender-crisp steamed vegetables and adds a special touch to burgers too. But it's the sweetness developed during the roasting process that wins the hearts of many. The pièce de résistance is the fruity overtone provided by the raspberry vinaigrette.*

4 small red onions
cracked black pepper
2 teaspoons olive oil
2 tablespoons Raspberry Vinaigrette (page 149)

Trim the onions and cut them in half lengthways. Place them face down on a prepared baking sheet, then brush the tops of the onions with the oil and sprinkle with the pepper. Bake in a moderately hot oven (190°C/375°F) for 35 minutes or until the onions are tender when checked with a skewer. Serve drizzled with the Raspberry Vinaigrette.
*Serves 4–6*

*Right: The succulence of roasted vegetables like Roasted Tomatoes, Roasted Fennel and Roasted Mushrooms and the sweet nutty flavour of Baked Ricotta Cheese (page 34) make them popular as starters, side dishes and even as sandwich fillings.*

# Roasted Beetroot

*If you have not savoured the flavour of roasted beetroot, you're in for a real surprise. It is sweet and nutty with a real depth of flavour. I like to serve it with a selection of other colourful vegetables as part of an informal antipasto meal.*

**3 medium-sized beetroot (beets), scrubbed**
**cracked black pepper**
**1 tablespoon cider vinegar**

Cut the beetroot in half crossways and place cut side down on a prepared baking sheet. Bake in a moderately hot oven (190°C/375°F) for 25–30 minutes. Allow the beetroot to cool slightly and peel. Cut into slices, wedges or strips and sprinkle with the pepper and cider vinegar.
*Serves 6*

# Roasted Sweet Peppers

*Roasted sweet peppers make delicious additions to pasta and sauces.*

**2 sweet peppers (capsicums)**

Slice the sweet peppers and remove the seeds. Cook the sweet peppers under a hot grill (broiler) until the skin is blistered and charred. Alternatively, place whole peppers on a baking sheet and bake in a very hot oven (230°C/450°F) for 20 minutes, turning them over every 5 minutes. Plunge into cold water to cool quickly, then remove the skin.
*Serves 4*

# Roasted Parsnips

*Parsnip is wonderful roasted, its full-bodied flavour developing in the direct dry heat of the oven. Serve it simply, warm or cold, plain or doused in a delicious dressing.*

**500 g (1 lb) parsnips, peeled**
**1½ teaspoons sesame oil**
**cracked black pepper**

Cut the parsnip into 12 mm (½ in.) thick diagonal slices. Arrange the parsnip on a prepared baking sheet. Brush the parsnip with the oil and sprinkle with the pepper. Cover with aluminium foil and bake in a moderately hot oven (190°C/375°F) for 25–30 minutes, removing the cover for the last 10 minutes.
*Serves 4–6*

# Roast Pumpkin

*Served hot, warm or cold, roast pumpkin has come a long way! It even makes a scrumptious sandwich filling—why not try it partnered by feta cheese and fresh tomato with foccacia for a real treat.*

**500 g (1 lb) pumpkin**
**2 teaspoons pumpkin oil *or* safflower oil**
**2 tablespoons pepitas (pumpkin seeds) (optional)**
**freshly ground black pepper**

Cut the pumpkin into 12 mm (½ in.) thick slices. Arrange the pumpkin on a prepared baking sheet. Brush the pumpkin with the oil and sprinkle with the pepitas and the pepper. Cover with aluminium foil and bake in a moderately hot oven (190°C/375°F) for 25–30 minutes, removing the cover for the last 10 minutes of cooking time.
*Serves 4*

# Basic Cooked Broccoli or Cauliflower

*Like other dark green vegetables, broccoli is an excellent source of vitamins A and C so it's a pity that it has been mistreated in the past. Cauliflower has also suffered a poor reputation from over cooking. Fortunately though, we are beginning to appreciate tender-crisp cooked vegetables—so that their true colours literally shine through.*

500 g (1 lb) broccoli *or* cauliflower, trimmed and
    washed

Cut the broccoli (or cauliflower) into florets and chop the stalks. You may wish to peel the stalks using a vegetable peeler if they are coarse. Steam the broccoli (of cauliflower) for 5–6 minutes or place in a microwave-proof dish, cover and cook on high for 2–3 minutes.
*Serves 4*

# Broccoli with Peanuts

*Delicious served as a salad dressed with Orange Sesame Dressing (page 139).*

1 quantity Basic Cooked Broccoli (see above)
1 teaspoon sesame oil
2 spring onions (scallions), sliced finely
⅔ cup (90 g/3 oz) dry roasted peanuts
cracked black pepper

Heat the oil in a frying pan, skillet or wok and stir-fry the spring onions and peanuts for 2 minutes. Add the broccoli and toss lightly. Season with the pepper and serve.
*Serves 4*

# Brussels Sprouts with Tomatoes

*For a light main meal, place the mixture in a casserole dish, sprinkle with Parmesan cheese and bake in a moderately hot oven (190°C/375°F) until golden brown. Serve with fresh crusty bread.*

1 teaspoon oil
1 onion, diced finely
2 garlic cloves, crushed (pressed)
3 tablespoons pine nuts
250 g (8 oz) tomatoes, peeled and chopped
1 teaspoon honey
375 g (12 oz) Brussels sprouts, trimmed and
    halved
freshly ground black pepper

Heat the oil in a frying pan, skillet or wok and stir-fry the onion, garlic and pine nuts for 2–3 minutes. Add the tomatoes, honey and the sprouts and cook, covered, for 10 minutes, then season with the pepper.
*Serves 4*

# Sesame Spinach

*This quick and simple dish only takes a few minutes from start to finish and you will be rewarded with vibrant green spinach that still has some life in it. Serve at once because holding green vegetables for too long not only affects their appearance; it also depletes their nutritional value.*

2 teaspoons sesame oil
1 tablespoon sesame seeds
1 bunch spinach, trimmed, washed and chopped
1 tablespoon mirin (page 343) *or* orange juice
cracked black pepper

Heat the oil in a frying pan, skillet or wok and stir-fry the sesame seeds over a medium heat for 2–3 minutes. Add the spinach and cook, stirring, until the spinach 'wilts down'. Stir in the mirin (or orange juice) and season to taste with the pepper.
Serves 4

# Bok Choy Stir-Fry

*The mustard-like flavour of Bok Choy cabbage marries well with the garlic and ginger to give a full flavoured dish. Bok Choy is often enjoyed in mixed stir-fried vegetable dishes but I feel it deserves to be savoured in its own right.*

1 teaspoon oil
2 garlic cloves, crushed (pressed)
1–2 teaspoons grated ginger
1 tablespoon finely sliced lemon grass
1 Bok Choy cabbage, trimmed, shredded, rinsed
  and shaken dry
2 tablespoons plum sauce *or* mirin (page 343)

Heat the oil in a frying pan, skillet or wok and stir-fry the garlic, ginger and lemon grass over a medium heat for 2 minutes. Add the cabbage and stir-fry for 2–3 minutes. Stir the plum sauce (or mirin) through and cook, covered, for 5 minutes.
*Serves 4*

### Cooking Cabbage

Freshly washed cabbage which has been shaken dry cooks well in a wok. The direct heat converts the water clinging to the leaves to steam, thereby preventing the leaves from scorching on the surface of the hot pan.

# Green Bean Stir-Fry

*Green beans have always been a popular ingredient in stir-fried vegetable dishes. Using this method, the beans become an appetising bright green, a far cry from the overcooked boiled beans of yesteryear.*

2 teaspoons oil
375 g (12 oz) green beans, topped and tailed
1 small red sweet pepper (capsicum), seeded and
  cut into strips
90 g (3 oz) bean shoots
cracked black pepper

Heat the oil in a frying pan, skillet or wok and stir-fry the beans and the sweet pepper for 8–10 minutes, or until they become tender crisp. Stir in the bean shoots and season to taste with the pepper.
*Serves 4*

# Braised Brussels Sprouts

*I really enjoy cooking this dish for sworn 'sprout detesters' because they cannot believe that these Brussels sprouts are the same vegetable as the grey-green soggy sprouts they had to endure as children. Like all green leafy vegetables, Brussels sprouts should never be over cooked, and the closest I will ever come to cooking them in water is by steaming.*

500 g (1 lb) Brussels sprouts, trimmed
2 teaspoons oil
freshly ground black pepper

Shred the sprouts, place in a colander and rinse with cold water. Heat a frying pan, skillet or wok and add the oil. Add the sprouts and stir-fry for 5–8 minutes, or until the sprouts are tender crisp and a vibrant green. Season to taste with the pepper.
*Serves 4*

*Left: Enjoy the tender-crisp texture and the enticing colour of Green Bean Stir-Fry. Quick cooking brings out the best in green vegetables.*

# Fennel with Lemon and Ginger

*Fennel has been too often overlooked except by the wise people of the Mediterranean who have been enjoying its delightful aniseed flavour all along. The lemon and ginger adds a new dimension to this tasty vegetable.*

1 teaspoon oil
4 spring onions (scallions), sliced
1 teaspoon grated ginger
2 Florence fennel bulbs (finoccio) trimmed and sliced
juice of 1 lemon
1 teaspoon honey
2 tablespoons chopped fennel leaves

Heat the oil in a frying pan, skillet or wok, add the spring onions, ginger and fennel and stir-fry over a medium–high heat for 3–5 minutes. Stir the lemon juice and honey through, cover and cook for 5 minutes. Stir the fennel leaves through and serve at once.
*Serves 4*

# Basic Cooked Green Peas

*Podding new season's green peas is a worthwhile task—just remember to allow for those that get popped into the mouths of hungry podders along the way.*

1½ kg (3 lb) green peas, shelled

To steam the peas, place them in a steamer insert and steam for 10–12 minutes, or place in a microwave-proof dish with 2 tablespoons water, cover and cook on high for 8 minutes, stirring the peas after 4 minutes.
*Serves 4*

# Spinach and Potato Sauté

*A colourful dish, the turmeric turning the potatoes a subtle gold and the spinach becoming an intense green. The coconut milk and the lemon rind add fragrance.*

500 g (1 lb) potatoes, scrubbed and sliced
2 teaspoons oil
1 teaspoon minced chili peppers
2 garlic cloves, crushed (pressed)
¼ teaspoon turmeric powder
8 spring onions (scallions), sliced diagonally
½ bunch spinach, trimmed, washed and chopped
½ teaspoon finely grated lemon rind
½ cup (125 mL/4 fl oz) coconut milk (page 341)
cracked black pepper

Cook the potatoes until tender (page 93). Heat the oil in a frying pan, skillet or wok and stir-fry the chili peppers, garlic, turmeric powder and spring onions for 2–3 minutes. Add the potatoes, spinach, lemon rind and coconut milk and cook, covered, for 2–3 minutes. Season to taste with the pepper.
*Serves 4*

# Brussels Sprouts with Mushrooms

2 teaspoons oil
250 g (8 oz) mushrooms, trimmed and sliced
375 g (12 oz) Brussels sprouts, trimmed and shredded
freshly ground black pepper

Heat the oil in a frying pan, skillet or wok and stir-fry the mushrooms over a medium–high heat for 2 minutes. Add the Brussels sprouts and pepper and stir-fry for 2 minutes. Cover and cook for 2–3 minutes only, then remove from the heat and serve at once.
*Serves 4–6*

# Broccoli au Gratin with Almonds

*Broccoli seems to be raised to new heights when partnered by roasted almonds. This dish can be served as an appetiser or a side dish.*

500 g (1 lb) broccoli, trimmed
1 quantity Light White Sauce (page 101)
2 tablespoons slivered almonds

Cut the broccoli into florets and cut the stalks into 6 mm (¼ in.) dice. Microwave the broccoli in a covered container on high for 5 minutes, or steam for 10 minutes in a steamer insert. Place the broccoli stalks in one ovenproof dish or 4 individual dishes and top with the broccoli florets. Pour the sauce over and scatter with the slivered almonds. Bake in a moderately hot oven (190°C/375°F) for 20 minutes.
*Serves 4*

# Cheese-topped Witloof

*A simple dish which allows the flavour of the witloof to speak for itself.*

4 witloof (Belgian endive), washed and patted dry
½ cup (60 g/2 oz) grated tasty (mature cheddar) cheese
cracked black pepper
2 tablespoons finely sliced chives

Cook the witloof until almost tender by steaming for 10 minutes. Alternatively, place it in a microwave-proof dish, cover and cook on high for 5 minutes. Place the witloof in a heatproof dish, sprinkle with the cheese and pepper and cook under a hot grill (broiler) until the cheese melts. Alternatively, cook on high in the microwave for 2 minutes. Serve sprinkled with the chives.
*Serves 4*

# Baked Tomatoes with Gruyère

12 small tomatoes
freshly ground black pepper
90 g (3 oz) Gruyère cheese
2 tablespoon chopped chives
1 teaspoon dill
12 small basil leaves

Using a small sharp serrated knife, cut a 6 mm (¼ in.) slice from the bottom of each tomato. Set aside to use as 'lids'. Using a metal teaspoon carefully scoop the seeds out of each tomato. Dust the insides of the tomatoes with the pepper and place the tomatoes in an ovenproof dish. Cut the cheese into 12 cubes. Place a cube of cheese inside each tomato and sprinkle with the chives and dill. Place the 'lids' on the tomatoes and bake in a moderate oven (180°C/350°F) for 15 minutes. Decorate with the basil leaves and serve.
*Serves 6*

# Baked Potato Chips

*Baking thin slices of firm vegetables which have been brushed with a little oil results in surprisingly scrumptious 'non oily' chips, not only nicer to eat but much lower in fat than the usual deep fried chips. Try these potato chips sprinkled with a spicy dukkah (page 100) for something different.*

500 g (1 lb) potatoes, scrubbed and cut into 6 mm (¼ in.) slices
1½ teaspoons oil
freshly ground black pepper *or* paprika

Arrange the potato slices on a prepared baking sheet. Brush the tops of the potatoes with the oil and dust with pepper (or paprika). Bake in a moderately hot oven (190°C/375°F) for 30–35 minutes.
*Serves 4*

# Baked Parsnip Chips

*Parsnips are wonderful roasted so why not enjoy them as chips as well? They are delicious on their own or topped with a dollop of Greek Yoghurt (page 273) or light sour cream.*

500 g (1 lb) parsnips, scrubbed and cut into 6 mm
    (¼ in.) diagonal slices
1½ teaspoons oil
freshly ground black pepper *or* paprika

Arrange the parsnip slices on a prepared baking sheet. Brush the tops of the parsnips with the oil and dust with pepper (or paprika). Bake in a moderately hot oven (190°C/375°F) for 30–35 minutes.
*Serves 4*

# Braised Leeks with Pine Nuts

1 teaspoon sesame oil
3 tablespoons pine nuts
2 bunches young leeks, trimmed, washed and
    sliced thickly on the diagonal
2 tablespoons mirin (page 343) dry sherry *or*
    orange juice
3 tablespoons water
½ cup chopped parsley
freshly ground black pepper

Heat the oil in a frying pan, skillet or wok and stir-fry the pine nuts for 2 minutes over a medium heat. Add the leeks and continue to stir-fry for 5 minutes. Add the mirin (or sherry or orange juice), water and parsley and cook, covered, for 5 minutes. Season to taste with the pepper.
*Serves 4–6*

# Baked Sesame Pumpkin Chips

*Pumpkin has never tasted so good—baking and stir-frying are two methods which suit the character of pumpkin, which becomes sweet and nutty when cooked in direct heat. The sesame seeds make this flavour more pronounced while the sweet pepper adds its own distinctive flavour and splash of colour.*

500 g (1 lb) pumpkin, scrubbed and cut into
    6 mm (¼ in.) slices
1 teaspoon oil
freshly ground black pepper
4 spring onions (scallions), finely sliced
½ red sweet pepper (capsicum), seeded and diced
    finely
1 tablespoon sesame seeds

Arrange the pumpkin slices on a prepared baking sheet. Brush the tops of the pumpkin with the oil, dust with pepper and sprinkle with the spring onions, sweet pepper and sesame seeds. Bake in a moderately hot oven (190°C/375°F) for 30–35 minutes.
*Serves 4*

# Marinated Cherry Tomatoes

225 g (7 oz) cherry tomatoes, cut in half
1 tablespoon olive oil
1 tablespoon pickled capers
1 teaspoon finely sliced chili peppers
2–3 garlic cloves, crushed (pressed)
1 tablespoon balsamic vinegar
2 tablespoons finely sliced chives
cracked black pepper

Place the cherry tomatoes in a bowl. Combine the remaining ingredients and toss through the tomatoes. Cover and stand for 15–20 minutes if possible before serving.
*Serves 4*

*Right: Braised Leeks with Pine Nuts. Leeks, most commonly used in soups and stews, can also make a delightful vegetable accompaniment.*

# Summer Festival Platter

*Celebrate the flavours, colours and fragrances of summer's harvest with this platter which serves as a special light meal or an appetiser. Light and lively is an apt description for this simply prepared dish. My enjoyment in preparing such dishes begins at the market or local fruit shop where summer is announced with the perfume of the first of the season's stone fruits, mangoes and ripe red berries. Once home, I simply refresh the fruits and vegetables and arrange them on a platter as simply as possible just before serving.*

1 butter lettuce, trimmed and washed
125 g (4 oz) snow peas (mangetout), washed and trimmed
125 g (4 oz) cherry tomatoes, washed
1 large *or* 2 small mangoes, peeled and sliced
1 banana, peeled and sliced on the diagonal
250 g (8 oz) strawberries, washed, hulls left on
6–8 edible blossoms such as nasturtiums *or* marigolds
2 tablespoons Raspberry *or* Strawberry Vinegar (pages 295 and 296)
¼–½ teaspoon cracked black pepper

Arrange the vegetables and fruit attractively but simply on a platter or individual serving plates. Top with the blossoms or petals which have been separated from the blossoms. Just before serving, drizzle with the vinegar and sprinkle with the pepper.
*Serves 6*

# Winter Vegetable Platter

*This combination of vegetables is great for a splash of colour in the cooler months. Make up a large platter or small individual serves, but no matter what size this platter is, it is a feast for sore eyes. Serve accompanied with a delicious dip or sauce and wedges of warmed pita bread. Quick Satay Sauce (page 99) transforms this dish into a gado-gado look-a-like, while a light dipping sauce (page 96) will allow you to experience some of the much loved flavours of Japanese cooking.*

250 g (8 oz) pumpkin, skin left on, cut into wedges
250 g (8 oz) broccoli florets
250 g (8 oz) cauliflower florets
baby potatoes (steamed *or* microwaved)
3–4 radicchio leaves *or* 2 red cabbage leaves, trimmed and shredded
1 avocado, peeled, pip removed, sliced
4–5 spring onions (scallions), trimmed
whole or finely sliced chili peppers for decorating

Cook the pumpkin until just tender (page 93). Place the broccoli and cauliflower florets in a heatproof bowl, cover with boiling water and allow to stand for 1 minute. Drain well and cover with cold water (adding ice if you have it) and allow the vegetables to soak for about 1 minute until they have cooled down. Spread them out to dry on a thick clean tea towel. Arrange all the vegetables neatly on one large platter or 6 small platters and serve warm or cold.
*Serves 6*

# Basic Cooked Pumpkin or Sweet Potato

*I frequently make use of cooked pumpkin and sweet potato in a range of dishes from terrines and flans to salads and pasta. Cooked puréed pumpkin can also be whisked into sauces to add colour and flavour, especially to tomato-based pasta sauces in winter when canned or bottled tomatoes are lacking the sweetness of ripe fresh tomatoes. 1 kg (2 lb) raw pumpkin or sweet potato yields 4 cups of purée when cooked.*

**1 kg (2 lb) pumpkin *or* sweet potato**

Cut the pumpkin (or sweet potato) into slices and peel using a vegetable peeler. If using pumpkin, remove the seeds. Steam for 12–15 minutes or place in a microwave-proof dish, cover and cook on high for 6 minutes.
*Serves 4*

# Basic Cooked Beetroot

*I really enjoy a variety of dishes made from beetroot, especially salads and hot side dishes, but I do like home-pickled beetroot (page 300) too. Enjoy experimenting with this surprisingly sweet vegetable.*

**500 g (1 lb) beetroot (beets), trimmed and scrubbed**

To boil beetroots, place the whole beetroots in a saucepan and half cover with water. Bring the water to the boil and cook the beetroots for 45 minutes. When cool enough to handle, rub the skins off. To steam the beetroots, place in a steamer insert and steam for 30 minutes. To cook in a microwave oven, pierce the skins and place in a microwave-proof dish. Cook, covered, on high for 12–13 minutes.
*Serves 4*

**Trimming Beetroot**
When trimming the beetroot, be sure to leave about 2 cm (¾ in.) of the stalk attached as this will prevent the colour from bleeding out.

# Basic Cooked Potatoes

*There are now many exciting varieties of potatoes on the market and you will be amazed at the differences in flavour—some are positively buttery in texture with no added butter in sight, others have a delicious sweet nutty flavour. To really appreciate the true flavour of potatoes, choose unblemished ones with no sign of sprouting and prepare them simply.*

**750 g (1½ lb) potatoes, scrubbed or peeled**

To steam the potatoes, cut them in half or quarters, place them in a steamer insert and steam for 20 minutes. To cook them in a microwave oven, pierce the skins and place the potatoes in a microwave-proof dish, cover and cook on high for 12 minutes.
*Serves 4*

# Basic Cooked Carrots

*When shopping for carrots, choose bright crisp carrots and there will be no need to peel them. Just give them a quick buff with a vegetable brush and they are ready to be cooked simple and quickly.*

**500 g (1 lb) carrots, scrubbed, trimmed and sliced, or cut into matchsticks**

To steam the carrots, place them in a steamer insert and steam for 12–15 minutes. To cook them in a microwave, place them in a microwave-proof dish, add 2 tablespoons water, cover and cook on high for 8 minutes, stirring the carrots after 4 minutes
*Serves 4*

# Basic Cooked Spinach

*Like most other green leafy vegetables, spinach has often been abused in the past, submitted to the mercy of boiling salted water with the addition of bicarbonate of soda to keep the green colour. If only the spinach had been cooked quickly and simply to begin with there would have been no need for the bicarbonate of soda. Enjoy the flavour and texture of quick-cooked spinach as a side vegetable.*

**1 kg (2 lb) spinach**

Trim the roots and stalks from the spinach, retaining the stalks for use in stock. Wash the spinach thoroughly in several changes of water to remove the sand from between the leaves. Tear the leaves into rough pieces or shred them roughly.

To **blanch** the spinach, place the spinach in a large heatproof bowl or saucepan and cover completely with boiling water. Allow to stand for 30–60 seconds only then drain the water completely and cover quickly with cold (iced if possible) water to prevent further cooking. To **steam** the spinach, place it in a steamer insert and steam for 10 minutes. To cook spinach in a **microwave**, place the spinach in a microwave-proof dish, cover and cook on high for 4 minutes, then stand for 1 minute.
*Serves 4*

### Spinach Purée
This amount of cooked spinach makes 2 cups of spinach purée which can be used to make spinach pasta (page 291) and pasta fillings.

*Right: Cooked until tender-crisp, the golden colour of pumpkin intensifies and the flavour becomes sweet and nutty in Pumpkin Stir-Fry.*

# Pumpkin Stir-Fry

*Here's a quick and easy way to revitalise the hearts of those who had to eat mashed pumpkin as children! Serve this tasty stir-fry as a side dish or turn it into a simple light meal by serving with a side dish of noodles or Cardamom Rice (page 109).*

**2 teaspoons oil, preferably sesame**
**500 g (1 lb) pumpkin, cut into sticks**
**½ red sweet pepper (capsicum) cut into strips**
**¼ teaspoon chili powder**
**6 spring onions (scallions), sliced diagonally**
**2 tablespoons water**
**½ cup (60 g/2 oz) cashews *or* walnuts, dry roasted (page 17)**
**freshly ground black pepper**

Heat the oil in a wok, frying pan or skillet and stir-fry the pumpkin for 10 minutes. Add the sweet pepper, chili powder, spring onions and the water and cook, covered, for 5 minutes. Toss through the cashews (or walnuts) and pepper.
*Serves 4*

# Stir-Fried Vegetables

**2 teaspoons sesame oil**
**1 onion, cut into thin wedges**
**2 garlic cloves, crushed (pressed)**
**2 teaspoons grated ginger**
**2 carrots, scrubbed and cut into half-moons**
**1 celery stalk, sliced diagonally**
**8 spring onions (scallions), sliced diagonally**
**1 x 250 g (8 oz) can water chestnuts, drained**
**½ cup (125 mL/4 fl oz) pineapple juice**
**1 tablespoon soy sauce**
**2 tablespoons mirin (page 343) *or* dry sherry**

Heat the oil in a wok, large frying pan or skillet and stir-fry the onion, garlic and ginger over a medium heat for 2 minutes. Add the carrots, celery, spring onions and water chestnuts and stir-fry for 2–3 minutes. Add the pineapple juice, cover and cook for 3–5 minutes only. Stir in the soy sauce and mirin (or dry sherry) and serve at once.
*Serves 4*

# Basic Cooked Broad Beans

*Broad beans marry well with garlic and tomatoes, so once they are cooked they are delicious added to braises and salads with a simple dressing.*

**1½ kg (3 lb) broad (fava) beans, shelled**

Place the beans in a steamer insert and steam for 30–35 minutes or until tender. To cook in a microwave, place in a microwave-proof dish and add 4 tablespoons boiling water. Cover and cook on high for 15–20 minutes, stirring the beans half way through the cooking time. Allow to stand for 5 minutes. When cool enough to handle, slip the beans out of their skins.
*Serves 4*

# Basic Cooked Green Beans

**500 g (1 lb) green beans, trimmed and cut into
2.5 cm (1 in.) lengths**

To steam the beans, place them in a steamer insert and steam for 10–12 minutes. To cook them in a microwave, place them in a microwave-proof dish, cover and cook on high for 5–6 minutes, stirring the beans after 3 minutes.
*Serves 4*

# Ginger and Soy Dipping Sauce

*Whoever said 'the best sauce is hunger' was spot on as far as I am concerned! When sauces are mentioned, we often think of thick or creamy roux-based sauces. Modern trends have led creative cooks to experiment with myriad light and lively sauces such as this and other bitey dipping sauces.*

**3 garlic cloves, crushed (pressed)**
**3 teaspoons grated ginger**
**1 teaspoon sesame oil**
**2 teaspoons honey**
**3 tablespoons soy sauce**
**½ cup (125 g/4 fl oz) unsweetened pineapple juice**

Place all the ingredients in a screw top-jar and shake well.
*Makes about 1 cup (250 mL/8 fl oz)*

# Orange and Sesame Dipping Sauce

**¾ cup (185 mL/6 fl oz) orange juice**
**2 teaspoons honey**
**2 teaspoons sesame oil**
**1 garlic clove, crushed (pressed)**
**1 teaspoon grated ginger**
**1 tablespoon soy sauce**
**1 teaspoon finely sliced chili peppers (optional)**

Place all the ingredients in a screw-top jar and shake well.
*Makes about 1 cup (250 mL/8 fl oz)*

# Pesto Sauce

2 cups basil leaves
1 cup parsley
3 tablespoons olive oil
4–5 garlic cloves, crushed (pressed)
½ cup (60 g/2 oz) pine nuts, roasted (page 17)
freshly ground black pepper
1–2 tablespoons grated Parmesan cheese

Using a food processor, chop the basil leaves
and the parsley, then add the oil, garlic and pine
nuts. Place the mixture in a bowl and stir in the
pepper and the cheese. If not using at once, store
in an airtight container in the refrigerator.
*Serves 4*

# Ricotta Pesto

*This delicous pesto is much lower in fat than
traditional recipes, the ricotta taking the place of
most of the usual olive oil. By the way, this sauce is
great for spreading on top of canapés and bruschetta
as well.*

375 g (12 oz) ricotta cheese, crumbled
1 tablespoon grated Parmesan cheese
2 cups chopped basil leaves
freshly ground black pepper
3 garlic cloves, crushed (pressed)
½ cup chopped parsley
1 tablespoon olive oil

Combine all the ingredients well and toss
through the freshly cooked pasta of your choice.
*Serves 4*

# Pumpkin and Pecorino Sauce

*Great with pasta, especially gnocchi (page 108).*

500 g (1 lb) pumpkin, peeled and chopped
1 large onion, diced
2 garlic cloves, crushed (pressed)
1 cup (250 mL/8 fl oz) vegetable stock
½ cup (125 mL/4 fl oz) milk
2 teaspoons white miso (page 343)
2 tablespoons finely sliced chives
cracked black pepper
2 tablespoons grated Pecorino cheese

Place the pumpkin, onion, garlic and vegetable
stock in a saucepan with a lid. Bring the mixture
to the boil, stirring occasionally. Reduce the heat
and cook over a medium heat for 20 minutes or
until the pumpkin is tender. Blend the mixture
with the milk until smooth, using a food
processor or blender, and return the mixture to
the saucepan. Bring the sauce to the boil, stirring
occasionally. Place the miso in a cup and blend to
a smooth paste with a little of the hot sauce.
Remove the sauce from the heat, stir in the miso
mixture and the chives and season to taste with
the pepper. Stir in the Pecorino cheese.
*Serves 6*

# Sweet Chili Dipping Sauce

1 teaspoon honey
1 red chili pepper, seeds removed, sliced finely
2 teaspoons chives, finely chopped
2 teaspoons white miso (page 343)
2 garlic cloves, crushed (pressed)
3 tablespoons mirin (page 343) *or* dry sherry
½ cup (125 mL/4 fl oz) vegetable stock

Place all the ingredients in a screw-top jar and
shake well.
*Makes about 1 cup (250 ml/8 fl oz)*

# Fresh Mango Salsa

*The heat from the ginger and chilies will wake up your taste buds so they can appreciate the wonderful nectar-like flavour of the fresh mango. This salsa is particularly delicious served with baked tofu, burgers, cheese and crusty bread or crackers.*

1 large ripe mango, peeled and diced
1 small white *or* red onion, diced finely
2 spring onions (scallions), sliced finely
2 chili peppers, seeded and sliced finely
2 teaspoons grated ginger
freshly ground black pepper
2 teaspoons honey
1 tablespoon lemon *or* lime juice
1 teaspoon finely grated lime *or* lemon rind

Combine all the ingredients and allow to stand for 1 hour before serving. If not using at once, store in a covered container in the refrigerator for up to 5 days.
*Makes about 1 cup (250 mL/8 fl oz)*

# Spiced Carrot Purée

*This wonderful purée is great served alongside burgers or terrines and provide a burst of colour and flavour.*

2 teaspoons sesame oil
½ onion, diced
1 teaspoon grated ginger
750 g (1½ lb) carrots, trimmed and sliced
½ cup (125 mL/4 fl oz) orange juice
½ cinnamon stick
freshly ground black pepper

Heat the oil and stir-fry the onion, ginger and carrots for 5 minutes. Add the orange juice and cinnamon stick and simmer gently for 10–15 minutes or until the carrots are tender. Remove the cinnamon stick and purée the carrots using a food processor, or push them through a coarse sieve. Reheat gently and season to taste with the pepper.
*Serves 4*

# Quick Satay Sauce

1 teaspoon oil
1 onion, diced finely
2 garlic cloves, crushed (pressed)
½ red sweet pepper (capsicum), seeded and diced
3 tomatoes, peeled and chopped
2 tablespoons tomato paste (purée)
3 spring onions (scallions), sliced finely
1 cup (155 g/5 oz) dry roasted peanuts
1 tablespoon soy sauce
freshly ground black pepper
a few drops of Tabasco Sauce

Heat the oil and stir-fry the onion, garlic and sweet pepper for 2–3 minutes. Add the tomatoes, tomato paste, spring onions and peanuts and stir over a medium heat until the mixture comes to the boil. Simmer gently for 10 minutes, stirring occasionally. Stir in the soy sauce, pepper and Tabasco Sauce to taste. Serve as it is or blend to the desired consistency using a food processor or blender.
*Makes about 2 cups (500 mL/16 fl oz)*

# Chili and Garlic Sauce

2 teaspoons oil
2 tablespoon minced chili peppers
10 garlic cloves, crushed (pressed)
500 g (1 lb) tomatoes, peeled and chopped
2 tablespoons tomato paste (purée)
freshly ground black pepper
1 tablespoon balsamic vinegar

Heat the oil in a saucepan and stir-fry the chili peppers and garlic over a medium–high heat for 2–3 minutes. Add the tomatoes and tomato paste, bring the mixture to the boil. Reduce the heat and simmer gently, covered, for 15 minutes. Season to taste with the pepper, add the balsamic vinegar and blend until smooth using a food processor or blender.
*Makes about 1½ cups (375 mL/12 fl oz)*

*Left: In tune with today's lighter sauces, Fresh Mango Salsa adds a burst of vitality to all manner of dishes.*

# Sweet and Sour Sauce

*Tangy, spicy and fruity all at once, this simple sauce does wonders when it comes to adding vitality to freshly cooked seasonal vegetables. Use it to douse crispy roasted tofu and tempeh (page 37) or to drizzle over a piping hot bowl of noodles or rice for a snack or light meal.*

2 teaspoons sesame oil
½ onion, cut into thin wedges
6 spring onions (scallions), sliced
2 garlic cloves, crushed (pressed)
1 teaspoon grated ginger
1 red sweet pepper (capsicum), seeded and cut into thin strips
4 tablespoons chopped pitted dates
2 tablespoons plum sauce
1 cup (250 mL/8 fl oz) unsweetened canned pineapple juice
3 tablespoons rice vinegar *or* white wine vinegar
1 tablespoon soy sauce
2 teaspoons arrowroot, blended to a smooth paste with 1 tablespoon water

Place the oil in a saucepan or wok and stir-fry the onion, spring onions, garlic, ginger and sweet pepper for 2 minutes over a medium-high heat. Cover and continue to cook for 2 minutes, then add the dates (or plum sauce), vinegar and the juice and cook, stirring, until the sauce boils. Stir in the soy sauce and arrowroot mixture and cook, stirring, until the sauce thickens.
*Makes about 2 cups (500 ml/16 fl oz)*

# Sesame Dukkah

*How many of us immediately think of sauces as pouring consistency? What about these wonderful Middle Eastern dukkahs? Dukkahs are blends of condiments which portions of food can be dipped into to add flavour.*

½ cup (60 g/2 oz) sesame seeds
½ cup (60 g/2 oz) almonds
2 tablespoons coriander seeds

Heat a frying pan, skillet or wok and roast the seeds and almonds by stirring over a medium–high heat for 5 minutes. Place the mixture in a food processor and process for 1 minute.
*Makes about 1 cup (250 mL/8 fl oz)*

# Herbed Yoghurt Dukkah

*Use as a dipping sauce or drizzle over crisp cooked greens.*

1 cup (250 mL/8 fl oz) plain yoghurt
½ cup chopped herbs
freshly ground black pepper
a few drops Tabasco Sauce
additional chopped herbs for garnishing

Combine all the ingredients, place in a serving bowl and top with chopped herbs.
*Makes about 1 cup (250 mL/8 fl oz)*

# Almond and Mint Dukkah

½ cup (60 g/2 oz) almonds
2 tablespoons coriander seeds
2 tablespoons chopped mint

Heat a frying pan, skillet or wok and roast the almonds and seeds by stirring over a medium–high heat for 5 minutes. Allow the mixture to cool, then place in a food processor and process with the mint for 1 minute.
*Makes about ½ cup (125 mL/4 fl oz)*

# Tomato Concasse

*Before making this concasse, I prefer to cook the tomatoes lightly, which helps to extract the juice from the flesh as well as enabling other flavours to infuse in a gentle heat.*

500 g (1 lb) tomatoes, peeled and chopped
1 teaspoon honey
freshly ground black pepper

Place the tomatoes and honey in a saucepan and bring the mixture to the boil. Reduce the heat and simmer gently, covered, for 10 minutes. Season to taste with the pepper and blend until smooth using a food processor or blender then push the mixture through a coarse sieve.
*Makes about 1½ cups (375 mL/12 fl oz)*

# Lemon, Ginger and Honey Sauce

*Tangy, sweet and sour, this translucent sauce adds gloss to broccoli, carrots, spinach. Serve hot or cold.*

2 teaspoons sesame oil
2 garlic cloves, crushed (pressed)
3 teaspoons grated ginger
3 teaspoons honey
½ cup (125 mL/4 fl oz) lemon juice, strained
3 teaspoons arrowroot
1 tablespoon white miso (page 343) *or* soy sauce
1 cup (250 mL/8 fl oz) water

Heat the sesame oil in a small saucepan and cook the garlic and ginger over a low heat, stirring, for 2 minutes then remove from the heat and add the honey and lemon juice. Place the arrowroot in a small bowl and blend to a smooth paste with a little of the water. Stir in the miso (or soy sauce), then gradually add the remaining water. Add this mixture to the lemon and ginger mixture and cook, stirring constantly, over a medium heat until the mixture thickens.
*Makes about 2 cups (500 mL/16 fl oz)*

# Light White Sauce

*I regard this basic white sauce as an artist's clean canvas—I like to throw in whatever flavour that springs to mind according to the use I have planned for it. Try adding grated mature cheese, grainy mustard or fresh herbs—even a blob of curry paste thrown in while reheating gives this sauce a new look.*

2 teaspoons oil
½ onion, diced finely
4 tablespoons plain (all-purpose) flour
1½ cups (375 mL/12 fl oz) milk
½ cup (125 mL/4 fl oz) vegetable stock
2 teaspoons white miso (page 343) blended to a
    paste with 1 tablespoon water
white pepper

Heat the oil in a saucepan and cook the onion over a low heat with the lid on the pan for 2–3 minutes. Add the flour and stir over a low heat for 1 minute. Add the milk and vegetable stock and cook, stirring constantly, over a medium heat until the mixture comes to the boil. Reduce the heat and cook, stirring, for another minute. Remove from the heat and season to taste with the miso mixture and the pepper.
*Makes about 2 cups (500 mL/16 fl oz)*

### Low-Fat Cheesy Sauce
This sauce is modified to contain much less fat without sacrificing flavour and texture. I like to use this for lasagne, or for whipping up au gratin vegetables. To make, omit the miso in the sauce and stir in ¼ cup grated tasty (mature cheddar) cheese.

# Pasta, Pulses and Grains

*What a world of shapes, textures, flavours and colours these words conjure up, not to mention the world trip one can take when linking each grain and pasta with its cultural heritage. If variety really is the spice of life, let's spice our lives up by adding some new varieties of pasta, pulses and grains to our usual kitchen repertoire.*

# Basic Cooked Pasta

*There are a few tricks to cooking pasta. Firstly, it's important to use plenty of water, which should be brought to the boil before adding the pasta. During cooking, the water should be kept at a rolling boil, both to cook the pasta thoroughly and to keep it moving in the water rather than sinking and congealing on the bottom of the pan. Pasta usually doubles its original volume when cooked. As a guide, allow 125 g (4 oz) uncooked pasta per 4 serves for appetiser dishes or accompaniments and 250 g (8 oz) uncooked pasta per 4 serves for main dish meals.*

3 quarts (3 litres/4¾ imp. pints) boiling water
250 g (8 oz) pasta

When the water is at a rolling boil, slowly add the pasta. The trick is to keep the water boiling. If the water stops boiling, place the lid on the pan until the water returns to boiling point, then remove the lid and continue cooking until the pasta is 'al dente' or just tender. The cooking time varies according to the size and shape of the pasta and whether it is fresh or dried. As soon as the pasta is cooked, drain the water completely to prevent further cooking. Some people like to rinse the pasta by running cold water through it to prevent the pasta sticking to itself and the pan.
*Serves 4*

### Using Soy Pasta

Soy pasta can be cooked in much the same way as penne, spirals or shells. Soy pasta retains its shape well, is flavoursome, easily managed by children and is great for adding variety to the menu.

# Cooked Spaghetti or Fettucine

*Spaghetti was probably the first introduction to pasta for many of us and seems to have maintained its status throughout our lives. Serve it as a first course or main meal dish topped with a variety of tasty sauces from Quick Pasta Sauce (page 50) and flavour packed Pesto Sauce (page 97) to Pumpkin and Pecorino Sauce (page 97). You can buy solid, tubular and wholemeal (whole-wheat) varieties. The cooking time varies according to the type you use, as specified below.*

3 quarts (3 litres/4¾ imp. pints) boiling water
250 g (8 oz) spaghetti *or* fettucine

When the water is at a rolling boil, gradually add the spaghetti, keeping the water boiling. Boil the spaghetti for 10–12 minutes or until it is 'al dente'. Solid spaghetti takes 12–14 minutes to cook. Wholemeal spaghetti takes 18–20 minutes to cook. Drain the spaghetti immediately and use as required.
*Serves 4*

# Cooked Spiral Shell and Penne Pasta

*Penne, spiral and shell are wonderful pastas which can be served as appetisers or main meal dishes, added to stir-fried vegetables and used to make delicious salads—all this and they're easy to eat as well.*

3 quarts (3 litres/4¾ imp. pints) boiling water
250 g (8 oz) penne *or* spiral *or* shell pasta

When the water is at a rolling boil, gradually add the pasta, keeping the water boiling. Boil the pasta for 10–12 minutes or until it is 'al dente'. Drain the pasta immediately and use as required.
*Serves 4*

*Overleaf: Pasta of Greens. A harmonious blend of al dente pasta, quick-cooked green vegetables, creamy avocado and fresh herbs.*

# Pasta with Broccoli

2 teaspoons olive oil
2 garlic cloves, crushed (pressed)
4 spring onions (scallions), sliced finely
250 g (8 oz) broccoli, blanched (page 76) and
    sliced
½ cup (60 g/2 oz) pine nuts
½ cup chopped parsley
½ cup chopped basil leaves
cracked black pepper
1 quantity Cooked Fettucine (page 104)
Parmesan cheese for topping

Heat the oil in a wok and stir-fry the garlic over
a medium heat for 1 minute. Add the spring
onions, broccoli and pine nuts and stir-fry for
3–5 minutes. Add the parsley, basil and pepper.
Toss this mixture through the freshly cooked
pasta and serve at once topped with Parmesan
cheese.
*Serves 4*

# Vegetable Pasta Bake

1 quantity Quick Pasta Sauce (page 50)
1 red sweet pepper (capsicum), diced
4 spring onions (scallions), sliced
125 g (4 oz) mushrooms, sliced
½ cup chopped parsley
1 quantity Cooked Macaroni (page 108)
½ cup (60 g/2 oz) grated tasty (mature cheddar)
    cheese
additional chopped parsley
1 tablespoon pickled capers
1 tablespoon sliced black olives

Place the pasta sauce in a saucepan and add the
sweet pepper, spring onions, mushrooms and
parsley. Bring the mixture to the boil, then
reduce the heat and simmer, covered, for 5
minutes. Spread the pasta over the base of an
ovenproof dish and pour the vegetable mixture
over. Sprinkle with the cheese and bake in a
moderate oven (180°C/350°F) for 25 minutes.
Sprinkle with parsley, capers and olives and
serve.
*Serves 6*

# Pasta of Greens

*This dish is quite quick and simple to prepare.
While the water for the pasta is heating, and the
pasta is cooking, prepare the vegetables so that the
whole dish can be assembled as soon as the pasta is
cooked.*

500 g (1 lb) asparagus, trimmed, and sliced on the
    diagonal
2 garlic cloves, crushed (pressed)
1 tablespoon olive oil
cracked black pepper
2 avocados, peeled, pip removed, diced *or* sliced
4 spring onions (scallions), sliced finely
½ bunch spinach, blanched and chopped (page 94)
250 g (8 oz) snowpeas (mangetout) trimmed and
    blanched
1 cup chopped parsley
½ cup chopped basil leaves
1 quantity cooked fettucine (page 104)
2 oz (60 g) freshly shaved Parmesan cheese
additional 3 tablespoons chopped parsley

Cook the asparagus until just tender by
steaming for 5 minutes or place it in a
microwave-proof dish, cover and cook on high
for 2–3 minutes. Combine the garlic with the
olive oil and the black pepper. Add the avocados,
spring onions, spinach, asparagus, snowpeas,
parsley and basil. Toss the vegetables through the
freshly cooked pasta and serve at once topped
with the Parmesan cheese and additional
chopped parsley.
*Serves 4*

### A Cold Variation
This pasta is also delicious served cold as a
salad—simply squeeze the juice of 1 lemon over,
sprinkle with 1 tablespoon balsamic vinegar and
toss the pasta carefully to combine all the
ingredients.

# Basic Cooked Noodles

*Noodles are cooked a little differently to other pasta varieties in that they take less time to cook and require less cooking water. They are often cooked in a tasty stock and served in the broth and have recently become a popular snack, especially with hungry teenagers.*

4 cups (1 litre/1¾ imp. pints) boiling water *or* vegetable stock
250 g (8 oz) noodles

Cook the noodles until just tender, about 5 minutes for plain noodles and up to 15 minutes for wholemeal (whole-wheat) noodles such as Soba Noodles. Immediately drain the noodles into a colander, then plunge the colander into a sink of cold water. This will ensure that the strands of noodles remain separate instead of continuing to cook in their own heat and sticking together.
*Serves 4*

# Cooked Soba and Udon Noodles

*Soba and udon noodles are much valued in Japan. Soba noodles are made from buckwheat flour or a mixture of whole meal flour and buckwheat flour while udon noodles are made from whole meal flour. Pasta varieties like these noodles are more nutritious than pasta varieties prepared from white flour because they contain more than twice as much dietary fibre and more vitamins and minerals.*

2 quarts (2 litres/3¼ imp.pints) boiling water
250 g (8 oz) soba *or* udon noodles

When the water is at a rolling boil, gradually add the noodles, keeping the water boiling. Boil the noodles for 10–15 minutes or until they are just tender. Drain immediately and use as required.
*Serves 4*

# Noodles with Broth

*A quick dish of Chinese or Japanese noodles like this one can be whipped up in minutes and enjoyed for a snack or a light meal.*

4 cups (1 litre/1¾ imp. pints) vegetable stock *or* dashi (page 28)
8 spring onions (scallions), sliced finely
1 celery stalk, diced finely
½ carrot, scrubbed and sliced into thin half-moons
185 g (6 oz) noodles
90 g (3 oz) bean shoots
1 tablespoon soy sauce

Place the stock, spring onions, celery and carrots in a saucepan and bring the mixture to the boil. Add the noodles and return the stock to the boil. Simmer the broth for 5 minutes, then stir the bean shoots and soy sauce through and serve at once.
*Serves 4*

# Cooked Cellophane Noodles

*As their name implies, cellophane noodles become transparent when cooked. They are made from bean starch paste rather than wheat flour. If pre-soaked, they only take a few minutes to cook and are ready to add to a variety of dishes from soups and stir-fries to spicy curries.*

4 cups (1 litre/1¾ imp. pints) boiling water
250 g (8 oz) cellophane noodles

Place the noodles in a saucepan and cover completely with water. Set the noodles aside to soak for 10–15 minutes. Drain immediately and use as required. If boiling on their own, they should be cooked for 3–5 minutes, then drained thoroughly before using.
*Serves 4*

*Right: Based on Japanese and Chinese noodles, dishes like Noodles with Broth are simple, delicious and nutritious.*

# Soba Noodles with Dashi

*This can be enjoyed as a side dish or can form the basis of a delicious and nutritious light meal when served topped with tender crisp steamed seasonal vegetables.*

2 cups (500 mL/16 fl oz) dashi (page 28)
250 g (8 oz) soba noodles
3 spring onions (scallions), sliced finely
2 tablespoons mirin (page 343)
1 tablespoon soy sauce

Place the dashi in a saucepan, cover and bring to the boil. Add the noodles and spring onions and return the mixture to the boil. Simmer for 15 minutes, then remove the noodles using tongs. Place in serving bowls. Add the mirin and soy sauce to the dashi and reheat gently without boiling. Pour the dashi over the noodles and serve at once.

*Serves 4*

# Cooked Ravioli or Tortellini

*Ravioli and tortellini are very popular served as appetisers and main meal dishes, accompanied by a salad of fresh greens and crusty bread. There are many varieties now available at supermarkets and specialty food shops, the vegetarian varieties usually sporting a filling of ricotta cheese and/or spinach.*

3 quarts (3 litres/4¾ imp. pints) boiling water
435 g (14 oz) ravioli *or* tortellini

When the water is at a rolling boil, gradually add the ravioli (or tortellini), keeping the water boiling. Boil the pasta for 5–8 minutes or until it is 'al dente'. Using a slotted spoon, carefully remove the pasta and serve as soon as possible to prevent it from sticking to itself.

*Serves 4*

# Cooked Macaroni

*Thank goodness there is more to macaroni than good old macaroni cheese! I remember years ago it was the dish that was considered a good standby for vegetarians and used to be the main recipe taught in Home Economics at school when vegetarian cooking was studied. Enjoy going beyond macaroni cheese by adding cooked macaroni to vegetable-laden soups such as A Meal of Minestrone (page 31) or team it up with dry roasted nuts, crispy vegetables and luscious dressings to create interesting nutritious salads.*

3 quarts (3 litres/4¾ imp. pints) boiling water
250 g (8 oz) macaroni

When the water is at a rolling boil, gradually add the macaroni while keeping the water boiling. Boil the macaroni for 8–10 minutes or until it is 'al dente'. Strain the macaroni through a colander and rinse with cold water if not using at once.

*Serves 4*

# Cooked Gnocchi

*Served topped with any type of pasta sauce, gnocchi is an especially popular appetiser dish. To make your own fresh gnocchi, see page 293.*

3 quarts (3 litres/4¾ imp. pints) boiling water
435 g (14 oz) gnocchi

When the water is at a rolling boil, gradually add the gnocchi, keeping the water boiling. Boil the gnocchi until it is 'al dente', about 5 minutes. Remove with a slotted spoon and serve as soon as possible.

*Serves 4*

# Gnocchi with Pumpkin and Pecorino

*Serve as an appetiser with a side salad of dressed fresh greens. To make your own gnocchi, see page 293.*

435 g (14 oz) gnocchi
1 quantity Pumpkin and Pecorino Sauce (page 97)
2 tablespoons grated Pecorino cheese
2 tablespoons finely sliced chives

Cook the gnocchi until tender, drain and pour the hot sauce over. Carefully toss the gnocchi to coat each piece with the sauce. Serve immediately topped with grated Pecorino and finely sliced chives.
*Serves 4*

# Cauliflower Gnocchi

*Serve on its own as an appetiser or with a crispy salad and fresh crusty bread for a light meal.*

435 g (14 oz) cauliflower, chopped
1 quantity Quick Pasta Sauce (page 50)
3 tablespoons chopped parsley
435 g (14 oz) gnocchi, cooked (page 108)
½ cup grated tasty (mature cheddar) cheese
additional chopped parsley

Steam or microwave the cauliflower until tender and combine with the pasta sauce and the parsley. Stir the gnocchi through the sauce and place in an ovenproof dish. Sprinkle with the cheese and bake in a moderate oven (180°C/350°F) for 20 minutes. Sprinkle with the additional parsley and serve.
*Serves 4*

# Cooked Brown Rice

*Brown rice contains more dietary fibre, vitamins and minerals than white rice and has a satisfying chewy texture. It's perfect for making stir-fried dishes because the grains are far less likely to stick together.*

2 cups (375 g/12 oz) brown rice
3 cups (750 mL/24 fl oz) water

Place the rice and water into a saucepan, cover and bring the mixture to the boil. Reduce the heat and simmer gently for 15 minutes. Turn off the heat and allow the rice to stand, covered, for 5–10 minutes. Fluff up the rice with a fork and serve.
*Makes about 4 cups*

**Quick Brown Rice**
For speed, try using the quick-cook variety of brown rice. For those who prefer the softer texture of white rice, quick-cook brown rice has a similar texture but is more nutritious.

# Cardamom Rice

*Simply delicious served with spicy vegetable dishes.*

3 cardamom pods
2 cups (375 g/12 oz) Basmati rice
2 cups (500 mL/16 fl oz) coconut milk
1 teaspoon grated ginger

Place the cardamom pods in a saucepan and dry roast by shaking the pan over a medium–high heat for 2–3 minutes. Add the rice, coconut milk and ginger, then cover and bring the mixture to the boil. Reduce the heat and simmer gently for 10 minutes. Turn off the heat and allow the rice to stand, covered, for 5 minutes. Fluff up the rice with a fork, remove the cardamom pods and serve.
*Serves 4*

# Coconut Rice with Vegetables

*This dish makes a colourful addition to spicy main meal dishes or, accompanied by a special salad such as Summer Greens with Mango Vinaigrette (page 130), makes a stunning appetiser.*

¼ teaspoon *or* a good pinch of saffron strands
¾ cup (185 mL/6 fl oz) water or vegetable stock
1 cup (185 g/6 oz) Basmati rice
1 cup (250 mL/8 fl oz) coconut milk (page 341)
1 piece of lemon grass *or* 1 teaspoon finely grated lemon rind
freshly ground black pepper
1–2 teaspoons sesame *or* peanut oil
1 red onion, diced
2 garlic cloves, crushed (pressed)
1 red sweet pepper (capsicum), seeds removed and cut into strips
fine slivers of lemon zest

Place the saffron in a heavy based saucepan and dry roast by shaking the pan over a medium–high heat for 10–20 seconds. Crush the saffron using a mortar and pestle then, using a pastry brush, brush as much saffron from the mortar as possible. Return the saffron to the saucepan, add the water (or stock), rice, coconut milk, lemon grass (or lemon rind) and the pepper to the saucepan and bring the mixture to the boil. Reduce the heat, cover and cook the rice gently for 10 minutes. Remove the rice from the heat and set aside. Heat the oil in a frying pan, skillet or wok and add the onion, garlic and sweet pepper and stir-fry over a medium–high heat for 5 minutes. Carefully combine the rice with the vegetables and serve at once sprinkled with fine slivers of lemon zest.
*Serves 4–6*

# Rice Timbales

*Serve as a side dish or accompany with a tangy green salad and a dollop of creamy dressing on the side such Creamy Tahini Dressing (page 144) for a light appetiser.*

1 quantity cooked rice such as Coconut Rice with Vegetables
¼ teaspoon sesame oil

Brush 6 timbale moulds or decorative moulds such as heart shaped moulds very lightly with the oil to prevent the rice from sticking. While the rice mixture is hot, press it into the moulds. Allow the rice to cool, then carefully turn the timbales out.
*Serves 6*

# Saffron Rice

*Saffron, one of the most expensive spices in the world, transforms rice into a special dish by giving it a wonderful golden glow.*

pinch of saffron threads
3 cups (750 mL/24 fl oz) water
2 cups (310 g/10 oz) brown rice

Dry roast the saffron by placing it in a heavy based saucepan and shaking it over a medium–high heat for 10–20 seconds. Take care not to burn the saffron threads or this could become quite an expensive dish. Tip the saffron into a mortar and grind it to a powder using a pestle. Return the saffron to the saucepan and add the water and the rice. Continue to cook as for Cooked Brown Rice (page 109).
*Serves 4*

*Right: Tinted with the golden glow of saffron and scented with lemon, Coconut Rice with Vegetables is a delightful side dish.*

# Sesame Rice

*The sesame seeds add a roasted nutty flavour and an interesting texture contrast to this rice. The bonus is that sesame seeds act as complementary protein for the rice, considerably improving its food value.*

2 teaspoons sesame oil
3 tablespoons sesame seeds
5 spring onions (scallions), sliced finely
1 quantity cold Cooked Brown Rice (page 109)
freshly ground black pepper

Heat the oil in a frying pan, skillet or wok and stir-fry the sesame seeds and spring onions over a medium–high heat until the seeds become golden brown. Add the rice and pepper and toss the mixture over a medium heat for 5–10 minutes.
*Serves 4*

# Herbed Rice

2 teaspoons sesame oil
2 teaspoons cumin seeds
5 spring onions (scallions), sliced finely
1 cup chopped coriander *or* parsley
1 quantity cold Cooked Brown Rice (page 109)
freshly ground black pepper

Heat the oil in a frying pan, skillet or wok and stir-fry the cumin seeds and spring onions over a medium–high heat until the seeds become golden brown. Add the coriander (or parsley), rice and pepper and toss the mixture over a medium heat for 5 minutes.
*Serves 4*

# Rice and Pistachio Pilaf

90 g (3 oz) shelled pistachio nuts
2–3 teaspoons olive oil
1 onion, diced finely, *or* 5 spring onions (scallions), sliced
2–3 garlic cloves, crushed (pressed) (optional)
125 g (4 oz) green beans, sliced
1 quantity cold Cooked Brown Rice (page 109)
2 ripe tomatoes, diced
freshly ground black pepper

Place the pistachio nuts in a small heatproof bowl and cover with boiling water. Allow to stand for 2–3 minutes. Drain the water and slide the skins off the nuts, then spread them out to dry on a clean tea towel. Heat the oil in a frying pan, skillet or wok and stir-fry the onion (or spring onions), garlic, pistachio nuts and green beans over a medium-high heat for 2–3 minutes. Add the rice and tomatoes, cover and cook over a medium heat for 5 minutes. Season to taste with the pepper.
*Serves 4*

# Tasty Fried Rice

2 teaspoons oil
1 onion, diced finely
1 cup (90 g/3 oz) shredded cabbage
1 quantity cold Cooked Brown Rice (page 109)
2 eggs, beaten
freshly ground black pepper
soy sauce

Heat the oil in a frying pan, skillet or wok and stir-fry the onion and cabbage over a medium heat for 2–3 minutes. Add the rice and cook, stirring occasionally, for 5 minutes. Meanwhile heat a small frying pan or skillet and cook the beaten eggs, covered, over a medium heat for 2–3 minutes. Turn the egg out onto a wooden board and cut it into strips. Carefully stir the egg through the rice and season to taste with the soy sauce.
*Serves 4*

# Mexican Rice

*This dish is as versatile as it is tasty—serve as a colourful side dish or as a tasty light meal topped with diced avocados and tomatoes which have been doused in lemon or lime juice.*

1–2 teaspoons oil
1 onion, diced
2 cloves garlic, crushed (pressed)
6 spring onions (scallions), sliced finely
¼–½ teaspoon chili powder
½ red sweet pepper (capsicum), diced
1 cup (155 g/5 oz) long grain rice
2 cups (500 mL/16 fl oz) water *or* vegetable stock
1 tablespoon tomato paste (purée)
freshly ground black pepper
3 tablespoons chopped coriander *or* parsley

Heat the oil in a frying pan, skillet or wok and stir-fry the onion, garlic, spring onions, chili powder and sweet pepper over a medium heat for 2–3 minutes. Add the rice and stir-fry over a medium–high heat for 3 minutes. Add the water (or stock) and the tomato paste and bring the mixture to the boil, stirring occasionally. Cover and cook for 12–15 minutes, stirring occasionally. Season to taste with the pepper and stir the coriander (or parsley) through.
*Serves 4*

# Quick Vegetable Risotto

1 tablespoon oil
1 onion, diced
1 sweet pepper (capsicum), diced
2 garlic cloves, crushed (pressed)
1 cup green peas
2 tomatoes, diced
a few drops Tabasco Sauce
freshly ground black pepper
1 quantity Cooked Brown Rice (page 109)
1 cup (125 g/4 oz) grated tasty (mature cheddar) cheese
1 avocado, peeled, pip removed, diced
2 tomatoes, diced

Heat the oil and stir-fry the onion, sweet pepper, garlic and peas for 2–3 minutes. Add the tomatoes and Tabasco Sauce to the onion mixture and cook over a medium heat for 5 minutes. Stir the rice through and continue to cook, covered, for 5 minutes. Remove from the heat and stir the cheese through. Serve topped with the avocado and tomatoes.
*Serves 4*

# Cooked Couscous

*A wonderful Northern African food, couscous is perfect for serving with spicy stews both to calm down the heat of the spices and to absorb the delicious juices. Prepared from semolina with the addition of wheat flour, couscous could really be labelled as pasta, but it is more often treated and served as a grain. But no matter what the label, it is a great food to have in the pantry.*

2 cups (375 g/12 oz) couscous
2 cups (500 mL/16 fl oz) water *or* vegetable stock
freshly ground black pepper

Place the couscous into a saucepan and dry roast over a medium–high heat for 2–3 minutes. Add the water (or stock), cover and cook gently for 5 minutes. Remove from the stove and allow to stand for 2–3 minutes before fluffing up the couscous with a fork. Season to taste with the pepper.
*Makes about 4 cups*

# Couscous with Mint

2 cups (375 g/12 oz) couscous
2 cups (500 mL/16 fl oz) water *or* vegetable stock
3 tablespoons chopped mint leaves
½ cup chopped parsley
juice of 1 lemon
freshly ground black pepper

Place the couscous into a saucepan and dry roast over a medium heat for 2–3 minutes. Add the water (or stock) and cover and cook gently for 5 minutes. Stir in the mint, parsley and lemon juice and season to taste with the pepper. Cover the saucepan and allow to stand for 5 minutes so that the flavours infuse.
*Serves 4*

# Vegetable Couscous with Pine Nuts

2 teaspoons oil
1 onion, diced
½ cup (60 g/2 oz) pine nuts
3–4 garlic cloves, crushed (pressed)
1 celery stalk, diced
4–6 baby carrots, washed, trimmed and sliced
    diagonally
125 g (4 oz) green beans, sliced
2 cups (375 g/12 oz) couscous
1½ cups (375 mL/12 fl oz) water *or* vegetable
    stock
2 tablespoons soy sauce
freshly ground black pepper

Heat the oil in a saucepan and stir-fry the onion, pine nuts, garlic, celery, carrots and beans for 2 minutes. Add the couscous and stir over a medium heat for 2–3 minutes. Add the water (or stock), cover and cook gently for 10 minutes. Season to taste with the soy sauce and pepper.
*Serves 4*

# Fruity Couscous

*Delicious served topped with a dollop of Creamy Tahini Dressing (page 144) and sprinkled with chopped coriander. In the Middle Eastern countries, dried fruits and nuts are standard fare in grain dishes. Try adding fresh dates for an authentic dish.*

2 teaspoons olive oil
1 onion, diced
1 apple, diced
1 tablespoons ground cumin
2 tablespoons ground coriander
1 celery stalk, diced
½ red sweet pepper (capsicum), diced
½ cup (60 g/2 oz) peanuts
½ cup (60 g/2 oz) sultanas *or* raisins
1 cup (185 g/6 oz) couscous
1½ cups (375 mL/12 fl oz) vegetable stock *or*
    water
3 spring onions (scallions), sliced finely

Heat the oil and stir-fry the onion, apple, cumin, coriander, celery and sweet pepper for 2–3 minutes. Add the peanuts, sultanas (or raisins) and couscous and stir over the heat for 2 minutes. Add the stock (or water) and the spring onions, cover and cook over a medium heat for 10 minutes.
*Serves 4*

*Left: Fruity Couscous is perfect for serving hot with spicy soups or stews. For a salad with a difference, serve it cold.*

# Cooked Millet

*Enjoy millet as a light and fluffy alternative to rice, incorporating it into stir-fries and pilafs or simply serve it as a side dish with spicy vegetable stews and casseroles.*

1⅓ cups (250 g/8 oz) hulled millet
4 cups (1 litre/1¾ imp. pints) water *or* stock

Place the millet into a medium-sized saucepan and roast by shaking the pan over a medium–high heat for 2–3 minutes. Add the water (or stock) and bring the mixture to the boil, stirring occasionally. Reduce the heat, cover and simmer the millet gently for 30–35 minutes. Remove the saucepan from the stove and allow the millet to stand for 5 minutes before fluffing it up with a fork. Serve at once or allow the millet to cool before storing it in the refrigerator for up to 1 week.
*Makes about 4 cups*

# Orange Millet

1 cup (185 g/6 oz) millet
2 carrots, grated
1 teaspoon finely grated orange rind
3 cups (750 mL/24 fl oz) water
½ cup (125 mL/4 fl oz) orange juice
grated nutmeg
freshly ground black pepper

Place the millet into a saucepan and dry roast by shaking the pan over a medium–high heat for 2–3 minutes. Add the carrot, rind and water, cover and cook as for Basic Millet, pouring the orange juice over before standing for 5 minutes. Add the nutmeg and pepper and fluff the millet up with a fork.
*Serves 4*

# Millet and Cashew Pilaf

*Adding the cashews to this dish drastically improves its nutritive value by increasing the fibre content and improving the quality of the protein. Apart from all this, it is important to remember that it is simply delicious to eat!*

2 teaspoons sesame oil
6 spring onions (scallions), sliced finely
½ cup (60 g/2 oz) cashews
1 quantity cold Cooked Millet
freshly ground black pepper

Heat the oil in a frying pan, skillet or wok and stir-fry the spring onions and cashews over a medium heat for 2–3 minutes. Stir in the millet and season to taste with the pepper.
*Serves 4*

**Enhancing Flavour**
For a quick flavour burst, cook grains in vegetable stock, add fresh herbs to the cooking water or cook them in a steamer insert over stews or soups—this not only helps infuse the grains with flavour, it also conserves energy.

# Cooked Wheat

*Cooked wheat makes delicious pilafs with a sweet nutty flavour and a satisfying chewy texture.*

2 cups (375 g/12 oz) wheat
4 cups (1 litre/1¾ imp. pints) water

Place the wheat in a container or bowl and pour in the water. Cover and allow to stand all day or overnight to soften the wheat. Place the wheat and water into a medium-sized saucepan and bring the mixture to the boil. Simmer, covered, until the wheat is tender, about 1 hour.
*Makes about 4 cups*

# Cooked Barley

*Like other whole grains, barley is rich in dietary fibre, vitamins and minerals and is a delicious addition to soups and stews.*

2 cups (375 g/12 oz) pot barley
4 cups (1 litre/1¾ imp. pints) water

Place the barley into a container or bowl and pour in the water. Cover and allow to stand all day or overnight. If soaking in warm weather, place the container in the refrigerator to prevent the water from becoming warm which causes the barley to start fermenting. Place the barley and water into a medium-sized saucepan and bring the mixture to the boil. Simmer, covered until the barley is tender, about 1 hour.
*Makes about 4 cups*

# Lemon Scented Barley

*I use this fragrant barley as an accompaniment to a colourful selection of steamed or baked vegetables or spicy vegetable stews. It also serves as a great base for tasty salads. Try adding diced apples, raisins and walnuts for a quick and easy winter salad.*

1 cup (185 g/6 oz) pot barley
3 slices lemon, skin left on
2 cups (500 mL/16 fl oz) water
juice of 1 lemon
2 tablespoons finely sliced chives *or* chopped
    parsley
freshly ground black pepper

Cook as for Basic Barley, adding the lemon slices to the barley before cooking. Once the barley is cooked, remove the lemon slices and stir in the lemon juice and chives (or parsley). Season to taste with the pepper. Cover the saucepan and set aside to allow the flavours to infuse.
*Serves 4*

# Barley Casserole

*A tasty warming winter dish, and economical too.*

2 teaspoons oil
1 onion, diced
2–3 celery stalks, diced
250g (8 oz) mushrooms, sliced
1 tablespoon flour
1 tablespoon grainy mustard
1¼ cups (310 mL/10 fl oz) milk
2 tablespoons arrowroot
2 tablespoons water
90 g (3 oz) tasty (mature cheddar) cheese, grated
½ quantity Cooked Barley (opposite)

Heat the oil in a saucepan and stir-fry the onion and celery for 1 minute, then cover and cook for 2 minutes. Stir in the mushrooms followed by the flour and cook uncovered for 1 minute. Add the mustard and the milk. Cook, stirring constantly, over a medium–high heat until the mixture comes to the boil. Reduce the heat and cook, still stirring, for 1 minute then remove from the heat. Place the arrowroot into a medium-sized heatproof bowl and blend to a smooth paste with the water. Add the hot sauce mixture, beating with a wire whisk or wooden spoon. Return the mixture to the saucepan and heat gently until the sauce thickens. Stir in half the cheese and the barley and place the mixture into an ovenproof dish and sprinkle with the remaining cheese. Bake in a moderate oven (180°C/350°F) for 30 minutes.
*Serves 4–6*

# Basic Polenta

*A popular food in Northern Italy, polenta is traditionally prepared with the addition of plenty of butter, in much the same way as old fashioned mashed potatoes were made. Basic cooked polenta can be eaten hot as porridge or allowed to cool before slicing and grilling (broiling) until golden brown. Great served with a tasty sauce such as Tomato and Ginger Concasse (page 47).*

4 cups (1 litre/1¾ imp. pints) boiling water
1 cup (155 g/5 oz) fine polenta (cornmeal)

Bring the water to the boil and add the polenta in a slow steady stream, stirring as you go. Cook, stirring, until a thick porridge is formed. Continue to cook, stirring, for 5–10 minutes. The cooking time varies according to the type of polenta you are using—coarsely ground polenta may take up to 20 minutes to cook. Serve at once as a porridge or spread the mixture out in a shallow dish and allow it to set.
*Serves 4–6*

# Baked Sesame Polenta

*This sweet nutty polenta is delicious served piping hot straight from the oven and doused in Quick Pasta Sauce (page 50).*

4 cups (1 litre/1¾ imp. pints) boiling water
1 cup (185 g/6 oz) fine polenta (cornmeal)
6 spring onions (scallions), sliced finely
½ cup (90 g/3 oz) sesame seeds, roasted (page 17)
additional 1 tablespoon sesame seeds

Place the water in a saucepan and slowly add a 'stream' of polenta, stirring constantly. Cook, stirring, for 5–10 minutes until the mixture resembles creamy mashed potatoes. Add the spring onions and sesame seeds and cook for 2–3 minutes. Spread the mixture out in a prepared rectangular pan and quickly sprinkle with the additional sesame seeds before the mixture sets. Bake in a moderately hot oven (190°C/375°F) for 20 minutes. Serve at once or set aside for later use.
*Serves 4–6*

# Antipasto Polenta

*Serve this flavour packed polenta as it is, sliced with a selection of antipasto delights, or grill (broil) until it becomes crispy and golden brown on the outside. Enjoy it as a sandwich filling or serve it with a tasty dressing and a crispy salad. Cook in a terrine dish or a swiss roll (jelly roll) pan, depending on how you wish to serve it.*

4 cups (1 litre/1¾ imp. pints) boiling water
1 cup (185 g/6 oz) polenta (cornmeal)
6 spring onions (scallions), sliced finely
8 sun-dried tomatoes, sliced
½ red sweet pepper (capsicum), diced finely
3 tablespoons sliced pitted olives
2–3 garlic cloves, crushed (pressed)
2–3 tablespoons grated Parmesan cheese
½ cup chopped parsley *or* basil

Place the water in a saucepan and slowly add a 'stream' of polenta, stirring constantly. Cook, stirring, for 5–10 minutes until the mixture resembles creamy mashed potatoes. Add all the remaining ingredients and spread the mixture out in a prepared baking dish. Serve at once or set aside for later use.
*Serves 6–8*

*Right: Grilled until golden brown and packed with sun dried tomatoes, red sweet peppers and olives, Antipasto Polenta is tasty served on its own as a snack, or as an accompaniment for soups and stews.*

# Cooked Buckwheat

*Grains such as rice, millet, wheat, buckwheat and barley are great alternatives to porridge, potatoes, pasta and bread and add variety to the menu as well as to the diet. Buckwheat is also known as kasha, its Russian name. It is popular cooked as a hot porridge to warm the body on cold winter mornings.*

2 cups (375 g/12 oz) buckwheat
4 cups (1 litre/1¾ imp. pints) water

Place the buckwheat into a medium-sized saucepan and dry roast by shaking the pan over a medium–high heat for 2–3 minutes. Add the water and bring the mixture to the boil, stirring occasionally. Reduce the heat, cover and simmer gently for 25–30 minutes. Remove from the stove and allow to stand (covered if the buckwheat is dry, uncovered if the buckwheat is moist) for 5 minutes before fluffing the buckwheat up with a fork and serving.
*Makes about 4 cups*

**Absorption Method**
Cooking grains by the 'absorption method' outlined above helps to retain maximum flavour and nutrients and, because the flavour is not diluted with excess cooking water, there is less need to add salt.

# Buckwheat with Sunflower Seeds

½ cup (90 g/3 oz) sunflower seeds
1 quantity cold Cooked Buckwheat
1 tablespoon soy sauce
freshly ground black pepper

Place the sunflower seeds into a saucepan and dry roast over a medium–high heat for 2–3 minutes. Add the buckwheat, cover and cook gently for 5 minutes. Season to taste with the soy sauce and pepper.
*Serves 4*

# Buckwheat and Hazelnut Pilaf

*Serve with tender crisp vegetables such as broccoli and carrots and surrounded by a colourful tasty sauce such as Tomato and Ginger Concasse (page 47).*

2 teaspoons oil
1 onion, diced finely
60 g (2 oz) chopped hazelnuts
2 celery stalks, diced finely
90 g (3 oz) mushrooms, chopped roughly
1 quantity cold Cooked Buckwheat (opposite)
1 tablespoon soy sauce
freshly ground black pepper

Heat the oil in a frying pan, skillet or wok and stir-fry the onion, hazelnuts and celery over a medium heat for 2–3 minutes. Stir in the mushrooms, cover and continue to cook for 5 minutes. Stir in the buckwheat, soy sauce and pepper to taste and heat through gently.
*Serves 4*

# Cooked Burghul Wheat

*Burghul, otherwise known as cracked wheat, is often used as the base for the ever popular Middle Eastern salad, tabbouleh salad. It can also be cooked quickly and served as an accompaniment to stews or used as a base for pilafs, burgers or stuffings.*

2 cups (375 g/12 oz) burghul wheat
2 cups (500 mL/16 fl oz) water

Place the burghul into a medium-sized saucepan and roast by shaking the pan over a medium–high heat for 2–3 minutes. Add the water and bring the mixture to the boil, stirring occasionally. Reduce the heat, cover and simmer gently, for 10–15 minutes. Remove the saucepan from the stove and allow to stand (covered if the burghul is dry, uncovered if the burghul is moist) for 5 minutes before fluffing the burghul up with a fork and serving.
*Makes about 4 cups*

# Basic Cooked Pulses

*We've been told forever that pulses—dried beans, peas and lentils—are good for us, but it is only recently that we have come to appreciate just how important these foods are for providing plenty of sustained energy—all the more to enjoy life with! Pulses are also easy to store, cheap to buy and can be whipped up into a myriad of tasty dishes from spicy braises and soups to luscious lasagnes. It's important to pre-soak pulses, both to ensure that they can be cooked in a reasonable time and to render them digestible. It's a good idea to soak whichever pulses you will need for the week as soon as you unpack your shopping. The pulses can then be drained and either cooked straight away or stored for later use. Simply place the amount of cooked pulses you would normally use for a meal in an airtight storage container and store in the refrigerator for 5–7 days, or in the freezer for several weeks.*

2 cups (375 g/12 oz) dried beans *or* peas *or*
    lentils, rinsed and drained
4 cups (1 litre/1¾ imp. pints) cold water
additional 4 cups (1 litre/1¾ imp. pints) water

Place the pulses and water in a container and cover with a lid. Set aside to soak for 6–8 hours or overnight. In warm weather, it's a good idea to place the container of soaking pulses in the refrigerator, to prevent the water from becoming warm and causing the pulses to ferment. Drain the soaking water completely and place the pulses in a saucepan and cover with the additional water. Bring the water to the boil, then boil the pulses for 10 minutes. This renders them more digestible as the prolonged intense heat helps destroy enzymes which inhibit their digestion. Reduce the heat and simmer, with the lid slightly ajar, until the pulses become quite tender.
*Makes about 4 cups*

# Quick Soak Pulses

*This is a life saver, or should I say a 'meal saver' for those times when you want to use pulses in a special recipe but have forgotten to pre-soak them.*

2 cups (375 g/12 oz) pulses, rinsed and drained
4 cups (1 litre/1¾ imp. pints) water
additional 4 cups (1 litre/1¾ imp. pints) water

Place the pulses in a stainless steel or enamel saucepan and add the water. Bring the mixture to the boil and boil for 3–5 minutes. Remove from the heat, cover and set aside for about 30 minutes. Drain the pulses. Add the fresh water and continue to cook as specified in the following recipes.

# Cooked Brown Lentils

*It's a great idea to have one or two containers of cooked lentils on standby in the refrigerator or freezer as, once cooked, they can be whipped up into quick meals such as burgers, soups and even lasagne.*

2 cups (375 g/12 oz) brown lentils, soaked
    overnight and drained
4 cups (1 litre/1¾ imp. pints) water
2 bay leaves *or* 1 bouquet garni

Place the lentils in a saucepan and add the water and bay leaves (or bouquet garni). Bring the mixture to the boil and boil steadily, uncovered, for 10 minutes. Reduce the heat and simmer the lentils for 30 minutes, or until tender. Drain excess liquid off and retain for use.
*Makes about 4 cups*

### Storing Pulses
It's wise to buy amounts of pulses you will use within a few months. The longer you store pulses, the tougher they become and the longer the cooking time becomes.

# Cooked Red Kidney Beans

*Tasty and substantial, red kidney beans are a common ingredient in Mexican cooking. The hot spicy character of Mexican cuisine gives red kidney beans quite a lift, making dishes like Refried Beans (page 45) and Chili Beans (page 45) as delicious as they are nutritious. I also like to add red kidney beans to lasagne, burgers and pizzas.*

2 cups (375 g/12 oz) red kidney beans, soaked
   overnight and drained
4 cups(1 litre/1¾ imp. pints) water

Place the red kidney beans in a saucepan and add the water. Bring the mixture to the boil, then boil steadily, uncovered, for 10 minutes. Reduce the heat and simmer the beans for 45–60 minutes, or until tender. Drain the excess liquid off and retain for use.
*Makes about 4 cups*

# Cooked Adzuki Beans

*Adzuki beans, otherwise known as red beans, are related to the soy bean. They are quite often used in Chinese and Japanese sweets as well as in a variety of savoury dishes.*

2 cups (375 g/12 oz) adzuki beans, soaked
   overnight and drained
4 cups (1 litre/1¾ imp. pints) water

Place the beans in a saucepan and add the water. Bring the mixture to the boil, then boil steadily, uncovered, for 10 minutes. Reduce the heat and simmer the beans for 40–45 minutes, or until tender. Drain excess liquid off and retain for use.
*Makes about 4 cups*

*Left: Red Bean Balls. Tinted with the rich red of tomato paste and red sweet peppers these tasty little morsels become a colourful treat. Oven baking rather than deep frying keeps their fat content to a minimum.*

# Red Bean Balls

*These versatile morsels are delicious served with a dipping sauce, dressing or dip for starters, or cooked gently in Quick Pasta Sauce (page 50) for 10 minutes and served with your favourite pasta or fresh crusty bread.*

½ quantity Cooked Adzuki Beans, drained
   thoroughly
½ red sweet pepper (capsicum), diced finely
6 spring onions (scallions), sliced finely
1 tablespoon soy sauce
2 garlic cloves, crushed (pressed)
1 teaspoon grated ginger
2 tablespoons tomato paste (purée)
1 cup (125 g/4 oz) quick-cooking oats
freshly ground black pepper

Using a food processor, mince the beans until a coarse meal is produced. Transfer the mixture to a bowl and add the remaining ingredients. Form the mixture into balls about the size of a walnut and place on a prepared baking sheet. Place the tray in the freezer for 10–15 minutes to allow the balls to harden. Brush the balls with a little oil and bake them in a hot oven (200°C/400°F) for 25 minutes.
*Makes about 24*

# Cooked Soy Beans

*Cooked soy beans are delicious added to stir-fries, soups, stews and casseroles or, using a food processor, you can grind them to a coarse meal and use them as a base for delicious and nutritious burgers such as Roasted Soy and Cashew Burgers (page 49).*

2 cups (375 g/12 oz) soy beans, soaked overnight and drained
4 cups (1 litre/1¾ imp. pints) water

Place the soy beans in a saucepan and add the water. Bring the mixture to the boil, then boil the beans steadily, uncovered, for 10 minutes. Reduce the heat and simmer the beans for at least 1 hour, or until tender. Drain the excess liquid off and retain for use.
*Makes about 4 cups*

# Cooked Chickpeas

*Chickpeas retain their shape well when cooked and can be used to create interesting salads and side dishes, not to mention delicious felafels. Houmus dip, a great partner for felafel, is also based on cooked chickpeas. I always like to have a container of cooked chickpeas nestling in my refrigerator or freezer just waiting to be transformed into a quick meal.*

1½ cups (280 g/9 oz) chickpeas (garbanzo beans), soaked overnight and drained
4 cups (1 litre/1¾ imp. pints) water

Place the chickpeas in a saucepan and add the water. Bring the mixture to the boil, then boil steadily, uncovered, for 10 minutes. Reduce the heat and simmer the chickpeas for 55–60 minutes, or until tender. Drain the excess liquid off and retain for use.
*Makes about 4 cups*

# Soy Ginger Balls

2 cups Cooked Soy Beans (opposite), ground to a coarse meal, *or* 2 cups (310 g/10 oz) okara (page 344)
1 teaspoon grated ginger
1 tablespoon soy sauce
3 garlic cloves, crushed (pressed)
8 spring onions (scallions), finely sliced
125 g (4 oz) tofu, drained and mashed
3 tablespoons peanut butter
2 tablespoons besan flour

Combine all the ingredients together. Form the mixture into balls about the size of a walnut and place on a prepared baking sheet. Place the sheet in the freezer for 10–15 minutes to harden the balls. Brush the balls with a little oil and bake in a hot oven (200°C/400°F) for 25 minutes.
*Makes about 24*

### Adding Salt

I do not add salt to cooked pulses. If you feel, however, you really need to add salt, do so at the end of the cooking time. Adding salt at the beginning of cooking toughens the pulses.

# Cooked Lima Beans

*Like cooked chickpeas, cooked lima beans retain their shape well, making them a good candidate for tasty salads, casseroles and stews. When preparing salads from lima beans add the dressing while they are still warm and you will be amazed at the flavour they absorb.*

2 cups (375 g/12 oz) lima beans, soaked overnight
  and drained
4 cups (1 litre/1¾ imp. pints) water

Place the lima beans in a saucepan and add the water. Bring the mixture to the boil, then boil steadily, uncovered, for 10 minutes. Reduce the heat and simmer the lima beans gently for 45–60 minutes, or until tender. Drain the excess liquid off and retain for use.
*Makes about 4 cups*

# Cooked Red Lentils

*Red split lentils do not need as much soaking or cooking time as brown lentils. They make a good foundation for lentil patties, tasty soups and spicy dahls.*

2 cups (375 g/12 oz) red split lentils
2 cups (500 mL/16 fl oz) water

Place the lentils in a container and rinse twice with plenty of cold water to remove dust and grit. Cover with the water and allow to stand for 1 hour. Drain the lentils completely, place them in a saucepan and just cover with cold water. Bring the water to the boil and boil for 5 minutes, removing any scum that rises to the top of the water. Reduce the heat and simmer the lentils until they are tender, about 10-15 minutes.
*Makes about 4 cups*

# Cooked Borlotti Beans

*Borlotti beans, an attractive pink or crimson speckled Italian variety of bean, become quite creamy in texture when cooked. They are particularly suitable for making delicious dips, and as they retain their shape quite well, they make wonderful additions to salads and are perfect for adding to minestrone soup.*

2 cups (375 g/12 oz) borlotti beans, soaked
  overnight and drained
4 cups (1 litre/1¾ imp. pints) water

Place the beans in a saucepan and add the water. Bring the mixture to the boil, then boil steadily, uncovered, for 10 minutes. Reduce the heat and simmer the beans for 45–50 minutes, or until tender. Drain the excess liquid off and retain it for use.
*Makes 4 cups*

# Cooked Quinoa

*A grain grown high in the Andes, quinoa is favoured by vegetarians because it is a complete protein food, while other grains contain incomplete protein.*

1 cup (185 g/6 oz) quinoa
2 cups (500 mL/16 fl oz) water *or* vegetable stock

Place the quinoa and the water (or stock) into a saucepan, cover and bring the mixture to the boil. Reduce the heat to a simmer and cook, covered, for 10–15 minutes. Turn off the heat and allow to stand for 5 minutes.
*Makes about 2 cups*

**Storage Tips**
Left-over freshly cooked pasta, pulses and grains can be stored in airtight containers in the refrigerator or freezer for later use. Make sure they are well drained because moist cooked, starchy foods can spoil very easily.

# Salads and Dressings

*The salads in this chapter are something to look forward to, created from crisp mixed greens, fresh seasonal vegetables, fragrant tropical fruits and cooked grains, legumes and nuts. And there is no shortage of light and lively dressings to transform the simplest of salads into a mouth-watering delight.*

# Spinach and Bocconcini Salad with Strawberries

*This is one of my favourite salads—as beautiful as it is simple! It is a luscious combination of tastes and textures and makes a wonderful first course as well as a refreshing accompaniment. As for all salads containing leafy vegetables, it is important to add the dressing just before you serve it, otherwise the leaves will become limp.*

16 young spinach leaves, washed and trimmed
3 tablespoons balsamic vinegar *or* Raspberry
    Vinegar (page 295)
1 teaspoon honey
2 teaspoons olive oil
cracked black pepper
375 g (12 oz) bocconcini cheese, drained and
    sliced
1 punnet (carton) ripe strawberries, hulled,
    washed and sliced

Tear the spinach into bite-size pieces or shred it finely. Place the vinegar and honey in a small bowl or cup and mix to dissolve the honey. Add the oil and black pepper and whisk the mixture with a fork or small whisk. Arrange the spinach on a serving plate and top with the bocconcini cheese slices. Arrange the strawberries on top of the cheese and just before serving, drizzle the dressing over the salad.
*Serves 4*

# Medley of Avocado, Tomato and Basil

*A salad of delightful contrasts in flavour and texture, the smooth creamy texture of avocados is offset by the crunch of the cucumber, with the distinctive flavour of fresh basil thrown in for good measure. Serve on its own as an eye-catching first course or side dish.*

2 medium sized avocados, peeled, pip removed,
    sliced crossways
juice of 1 lemon *or* lime
leaves from ½ butter lettuce, washed and shaken
    dry
3 ripe tomatoes, sliced
¼ red onion, sliced thinly
¼ medium-sized Lebanese (continental) cucumber,
    sliced
2 tablespoons balsamic vinegar *or* Herb Vinegar
    (page 296)
2 teaspoons apple cider vinegar
1 teaspoon honey
2 teaspoons olive oil
a pinch of sweet paprika
freshly ground black pepper
½ cup basil leaves, washed and shaken dry

Place the avocado slices on a plate and sprinkle with the lemon (or lime) juice to prevent them from discolouring. Using a clean dry tea towel, pat the lettuce leaves dry and place them on a serving platter or individual plates. Arrange the avocado and tomato slices on top and scatter the onion and cucumber over. Make a dressing by mixing the vinegars with the honey, olive oil, sweet paprika and pepper. Cut the basil into fine strips using kitchen scissors. Just before serving, sprinkle the basil and the dressing over the salad.
*Serves 4*

*Overleaf: Spinach and Bocconcini Salad with Strawberries. The white bocconcini and vibrant red berries provide a beautiful contrast to the backdrop of rich green young spinach leaves.*

# Spinach, Blue Cheese and Walnut Salad

*Blue cheese and walnuts make good partners at any time and in this dish the marriage is enhanced by the tender young spinach and sweet juicy tomatoes. Serve as an appetiser or as a side dish for a savoury flan such as Golden Onion Flan (page 57) or Antipasto Polenta (page 118).*

250 g (8 oz) young spinach leaves, washed and
    shaken dry
125 g (4 oz) blue vein cheese
125 g (4 oz) cherry tomatoes, cut in half
½ cup (60 g/2 oz) walnuts
1 quantity Balsamic Dressing (page 148)

Using a clean dry tea towel, pat the spinach dry. Arrange the spinach leaves on a serving plate and crumble the cheese over. Scatter the tomatoes and walnuts over. Just before serving, drizzle the dressing over the salad.
*Serves 4*

# Orange Dressed Pawpaw

*A tangy delight, especially good as a partner for cheese and greens or served in attractive glass dishes as a refreshing first course.*

1 large pawpaw (papaya), peeled, halved and pips
    removed
1 quantity Orange Sesame Dressing (page 139)
1 tablespoon finely sliced chives

Cut the pawpaw into large cubes and toss carefully with the dressing. Cover and place in the refrigerator for 1 hour if possible to chill the salad and allow the wonderful flavours to infuse. Just before serving, sprinkle with the chives.
*Serves 4*

# Melon and Ginger Salad

*The nectar-like flavour of preserved ginger adds character to this beautiful salad. Melons with firm sweet flesh like honeydew and rockmelon (cantaloupe) are particularly suitable.*

1 kg (2 lb) melon, peeled, pips removed, cut into
    cubes
3 tablespoons preserved ginger, chopped finely
juice of 2 lemons
2 teaspoons lightly flavoured oil such as
    grapeseed *or* safflower oil
3 tablespoons pine nuts *or* slivered almonds

Place the melon in a mixing bowl. Combine the remaining ingredients and spoon over the melon. Toss the salad carefully to prevent the melon from breaking up. Chill before serving.
*Serves 4*

# Pineapple Salad

*When pineapples are at their best, sweet and ripe yet firm in texture, celebrate with this simple salad which makes an appetising first course.*

250 g (8 oz) bean shoots
¼ large ripe pineapple, peeled and diced
3 tablespoons finely sliced chives
½ cup (60 g/2 oz) pine nuts, roasted (page 17)
½ cup (125 mL/4 fl oz) unsweetened pineapple
    juice
2 tablespoons lemon juice
1 teaspoon honey
2 garlic cloves, crushed (pressed)
¼ teaspoon cracked black pepper
additional 2 tablespoons finely sliced chives

Carefully combine the bean shoots, pineapple, chives and pine nuts. To prepare the dressing, place the pineapple juice, lemon juice, honey, garlic and pepper in a small bowl and whisk all the ingredients together using a fork or a wire whisk. Drizzle the dressing over the salad and toss all together carefully. Serve scattered with the additional chives.
*Serves 4*

# Summer Greens with Mango Vinaigrette

*A light, refreshing and colourful salad with a splash of tropical sunshine, this makes a stunning first course as well as an accompaniment to a main meal dish. Or serve it with a selection of your favourite fresh cheeses and breads. On a nutritional note, the fruity dressing is much lower in fat than traditional salad dressings and there is no need to add salt as the raspberry vinegar adds plenty of flavour.*

375 g (12 oz) salad greens such as butter lettuce, young spinach *or* dandelion leaves
1 small mango, peeled and sliced
6 edible blossoms such as nasturtiums *or* violets *or* marigolds
¼ red onion *or* 3 spring onions (scallions), finely sliced
1 quantity Mango Vinaigrette (page 145)

Carefully wash the salad greens and pat them dry with a clean tea towel. Retain two or three of the blossoms for garnishing the finished dish. Separate the petals from the remaining blossoms and scatter them over the greens. Toss the greens, mango slices, petals and sliced onion in a serving bowl. Just before serving, pour the dressing around the base of a serving bowl, arrange the the salad on top and decorate with the blossoms.
*Serves 4*

*Right: Summer Greens with Mango Vinaigrette. The crowning glory of this salad is the vinaigrette, simply prepared by combining the exquisite scent of fresh mangoes with the fruity tang of raspberry vinegar.*

# Pawpaw and Avocado Salad

*Although mostly treated like a vegetable, avocado is really a fruit so it is no wonder that it harmonises well with fruits such as pawpaw, strawberries and oranges. The zesty flavour of the lemon juice and fresh ginger in the dressing is offset by the sweetness of the preserved ginger scattered throughout the salad.*

1½–2 avocados, peeled, pip removed and sliced
½ pawpaw (papaya), pips removed, peeled and sliced
2 tablespoons chopped preserved ginger
1 quantity Lemony Ginger Dressing (page 148)

Arrange alternate slices of avocado and pawpaw on a serving plate and scatter the ginger over. Sprinkle with the dressing, cover and set aside for 10 minutes to allow the flavours to infuse.
*Serves 4*

# Cucumber Raita with Mint

*This refreshing dish makes a great tastebud tempter at the beginning of a meal, a welcome contrast to a hot spicy curry and a delicious addition to salad plates and sandwiches.*

1 medium-sized cucumber, peeled
1 cup (250 mL/8 fl oz) Greek Yoghurt (page 273)
3 garlic cloves, crushed (pressed)
1 tablespoon lemon juice
2 tablespoons finely sliced mint leaves
freshly ground black pepper
additional 1 tablespoon finely sliced mint leaves

Cut the cucumber in half lengthways and scoop out the seeds using a metal teaspoon. Dice the cucumber finely and place in a bowl. Combine with the yoghurt, garlic, lemon juice, mint and pepper. Place in a serving bowl and garnish with the additional mint leaves.
*Serves 4*

# Brie Salad

*An exciting collection of flavours and textures, this dish serves as a superb appetiser or a special side dish.*

½ quantity Bruschetta Shapes (page 36)
225 g (7 oz) mixed salad greens, washed and
  shaken dry
2 tomatoes, cut into thin wedges
4 spring onions (scallions), finely sliced
125 g (4 oz) Brie, cut in fine wedges
1 quantity Balsamic Dressing (page 148)
cracked black pepper

Cut the bruschetta into croutons or leave whole if preferred. Using a clean dry tea towel, pat the salad greens dry. Arrange the greens, tomatoes, spring onions, Brie and croutons in a serving bowl. Just before serving, pour the dressing over and sprinkle with the pepper.
*Serves 4*

# Pasta Salad with Avocado

*I especially like using shell pasta or spirals for salads because the delicious dressing can nestle in the pasta to make every mouthful a treat.*

3 cups (500 g/1 lb) cold Cooked Penne, Spiral *or*
  Shell Pasta (page 104)
1 quantity Lemon, Ginger and Soy Dressing
  (page 148)
1 red sweet pepper (capsicum), seeded and cut
  into strips
4 spring onions (scallions), sliced finely
½ cup chopped parsley
cracked black pepper
2 avocados, peeled, pip removed and sliced
juice of 1 lemon

Place the pasta, dressing, sweet pepper, spring onions, parsley and pepper in a bowl and combine carefully to avoid breaking up the pasta. Place the avocado slices on a plate and sprinkle them with the lemon juice to prevent them from discolouring. Just before serving, carefully toss the avocado through the salad.
*Serves 4*

# Salad with Wild Greens

*Once upon a time salad greens meant little more than lettuce. Nowadays we can choose from an exciting range of greens including the tender butter lettuce, attractive curly leafed bitter endive (frisée) and peppery arugula (rocket). And most salad mixes today sport delicious sweet young dandelion leaves picked before the plant flowers.*

250 g (8 oz) mixed greens such as dandelion
  leaves, curly endive (frisée), comfrey, mustard
  greens *or* sorrel
1 small Florence fennel bulb (finoccio), trimmed
  and sliced finely
2 tablespoons finely sliced chives
1 quantity Apple Cider Dressing (page 136)

Place the greens in a bowl and combine well with the fennel and chives. Just before serving, pour the dressing over and toss the salad carefully.
*Serves 4*

# Soy Pasta Salad

*Soy pasta has a distinctive flavour and retains its shape well, making it a good candidate for tasty salads.*

125 g (4 oz) green beans, sliced
125 g (4 oz) broccoli florets
3 cups (500 g/1 lb) cold Cooked Soy Pasta
  (page 104)
4 spring onions (scallions), sliced finely
125 g (4 oz) button mushrooms, sliced
1 quantity Lemon, Ginger and Soy Dressing
  (page 148)

Cook the beans (page 96) and the broccoli (page 85) until tender crisp then set them aside to cool. Meanwhile, place the pasta, spring onions and mushrooms in a bowl and pour the dressing over. Toss the salad to combine the ingredients well. When the beans and broccoli are cool, carefully toss them through the salad. Cover the bowl and set the salad aside to allow the flavours to infuse.
*Serves 4*

# Carnival Tomato Salad

*Simply a carnival of colours and flavours, this salad is especially delicious served with a selection of cheeses and moist wholemeal bread such as Pumpernickel (page 243).*

½ bunch spinach, washed, trimmed and shredded finely
375 g (12 oz) ripe tomatoes, sliced
¼ red onion, cut into thin rings
½ yellow or green sweet pepper (capsicum), cut into thin rings
1 quantity Balsamic Dressing (page 148)
cracked black pepper

Arrange the spinach on a serving plate and top with the tomatoes, onion and sweet pepper. Just before serving, drizzle the dressing over the salad and sprinkle it with the pepper.
*Serves 4*

# Roasted Tofu Salad

*This is a salad to really get your teeth into. The crisp and crunchy vegetables seem to spring to life when doused with the Japanese inspired flavours of the delicious dressing.*

1 carrot, cut into very thin matchsticks
125 g (4 oz) snow peas (mangetout)
1 quantity Ginger Roasted Tofu (page 37), sliced and cut into strips
1 quantity Lemon, Ginger and Soy Dressing (page 148)
4 lemon wedges

Blanch the carrot and snow peas by placing them in a heatproof bowl and covering with boiling water. Allow them to stand for 1 minute, then drain the water and plunge the vegetables into icy cold water. Drain the vegetables completely after 1 minute, then spread them out on a clean tea towel and pat them dry. Combine the vegetables with the tofu. Just before serving, toss lightly with the dressing. Place in a serving dish and decorate with the lemon wedges.
*Serves 4*

# Fennel Salad

*This crisp textured salad is delicious served on its own or makes a wonderful accompaniment to Baked Ricotta Cheese (page 34) or vegetable flans.*

2 Florence fennel bulbs (finoccio), trimmed and sliced
½ cup chopped parsley
1 red apple, diced
½ cup (90 g/3 oz) sultanas (golden raisins)
½ cup (60 g/2 oz) dry roasted peanuts
1 quantity Lemon and Honey Dressing (page 144)
1 tablespoon additional dry roasted peanuts

Place the fennel, parsley, apple, sultanas and peanuts in a bowl and combine all the ingredients well. Sprinkle the salad with the dressing and toss lightly. Serve sprinkled with the additional peanuts.
*Serves 4*

# Pineapple and Lemon Salad

*Light and tangy, this makes a refreshing accompaniment to hot spicy dishes, and is superb served on a hot summer's day with a salad of crisp greens and fresh crusty bread.*

1 kg (2 lb) fresh pineapple, peeled and cut into cubes
juice of 2 lemons
1 teaspoon honey
1 tablespoon finely sliced pineapple sage leaves
additional pineapple sage leaves for garnishing

Place the pineapple in a bowl. Combine the lemon juice, honey and sage leaves and pour the mixture over the pineapple. Combine all the ingredients thoroughly and serve scattered with the additional pineapple sage leaves.
*Serves 4*

# Amazing Tomato Salad

*The combination of the rich red of the ripe tomatoes and the vivid splash of colour from the dressing makes this salad a sight for sore eyes. An informal light meal of summer antipasto treats can be centred around this simple yet stunning dish.*

4 ripe tomatoes, sliced
1 quantity Crimson Dressing (page 145)
2–3 spring onions (scallions), sliced finely
cracked black pepper

Arrange the tomato slices on a plate and drizzle the dressing over. Scatter the spring onions over and sprinkle with the pepper.
*Serves 4–6*

# Golden Mango Slaw

*Cool crisp cabbage forms a nutritious and flavour-packed foundation for many a popular salad. This salad is no exception and I've found that children will happily crunch their way through a good sized serve. Dressed up with the tropical fragrance of mangoes, this salad is wonderful served chilled on a hot summer's day.*

¼ small cabbage, trimmed and finely shredded
2 celery stalks, diced finely
2 tablespoons finely sliced chives *or* 3–4 spring
  onions (scallions), sliced finely
1 quantity Mango Vinaigrette (page 145)
shredded celery leaves

Combine the cabbage, celery, chives and spring onions and drizzle the dressing over. Toss the salad to ensure that the dressing coats all the vegetables. Cover and chill for 30 minutes to allow the flavours to infuse. Serve decorated with the celery leaves.
*Serves 4*

*Right: Amazing Tomato Salad. The crimson dressing reinforces the sweet fruity flavour of the sun ripened tomatoes in this delightfully simple summer salad.*

# Vibrant Pumpkin Salad

*Cooked until tender crisp, pumpkin has a character of its own and its versatility is extended even further. The secret of the vitality of this salad lies in the dressing, an infusion of full bodied flavours from the wild tang of the apple cider vinegar to the distinctive flavour of the extra virgin olive oil.*

2 tablespoons apple cider vinegar
juice of 1 lemon
3 teaspoons extra virgin olive oil
2 garlic cloves, crushed (pressed)
¼ teaspoon cracked black pepper
1 teaspoon honey
1 quantity Basic Cooked Pumpkin (page 93) *or*
  Roast Pumpkin (page 84), sliced
1 red sweet pepper (capsicum), roasted (page 84)
  and cut into strips
½ cup chopped coriander *or* parsley
3 tablespoons finely sliced chives
2 tablespoons pepitas (pumpkin seeds) (page 345)

To prepare the dressing, combine the vinegar, lemon, oil, garlic, pepper and honey. Carefully toss the pumpkin, sweet pepper, coriander (or parsley) and chives together with the dressing. Place the salad in a serving dish and scatter the pepitas over.
*Serves 4–6*

# Avocados with Crimson Dressing

*A simple fresh dish perfect for a first course in winter or a salad accompaniment.*

2 avocados, peeled, cut in half, pips removed
1 quantity Crimson Dressing (page 145)
2 tablespoons finely diced red onion
cracked black pepper

Slice the avocado halves into fan shapes and arrange on a plate. Drizzle the dressing over and sprinkle with the onions and the pepper.
*Serves 4*

# Citrus Avocado Salad

*A light crispy salad for the cooler months when supplies of fresh salad vegetables are limited. Serve as a tasty first course or as an accompaniment to hearty bean or pasta dishes.*

2 avocados, peeled, pip removed, sliced
1 quantity Orange Vinaigrette (page 149)
1 grapefruit, peeled and sliced, pips removed
1 orange, peeled and sliced, pips removed
½ red onion, diced finely
90 g (3 oz) bean shoots
3 tablespoons chopped parsley
thin slivers of orange zest and additional bean
   shoots for decorating

Arrange the avocado slices on a plate and drizzle the dressing over to prevent them from discolouring. Place all the remaining ingredients in a bowl and combine them carefully to avoid breaking up the bean shoots. Just before serving, toss the avocado and dressing carefully through the salad. Top with the orange zest and additional bean shoots.
*Serves 4*

**Zesting Citrus Fruits**
To remove the zest from oranges and lemons, first wash the fruit in warm water. Using a vegetable peeler or a sharp serrated knife, pare very thin strips of zest from the skins of the fruit. Take care to avoid including the bitter white pith which lies just under the zest. To obtain very thin slivers, use a small sharp knife or kitchen scissors.

# Nasturtium and Tomato Salad

*This salad adds a blaze of colour and a burst of peppery flavour to a summer meal and is especially good served with a platter of cheese, fresh crusty bread and a selection of antipasto treats.*

500 g (1 lb) tomatoes, cut into wedges
½ red onion, cut into fine slivers
3 tablespoons chopped parsley
1 quantity Apple Cider Dressing (below)
petals of 8 nasturtium blossoms
additional nasturtium blossoms for garnishing

Place the tomatoes, onion and parsley in a bowl and mix them carefully. Drizzle the dressing over, sprinkle with the nasturtium petals and toss the salad lightly. Decorate with the additional blossoms and serve at once.
*Serves 4*

# Apple Cider Dressing

*This tangy dressing is wonderful drizzled on salads of crispy apples or pears or fresh ripe tomatoes. But don't stop there. Use it to liven up salads of crunchy bean shoots or add that special touch to salads sporting cooked beans or beetroot (beets).*

½ cup (125 mL/4 fl oz) apple cider
1 tablespoon apple cider vinegar
2 teaspoons honey
½ teaspoon ground mustard seeds
2 tablespoons finely sliced chives

Place all the ingredients in a small bowl and using a small wire whisk or a fork, whisk them all together to combine them thoroughly.
*Makes about ¾ cup (185 mL/6 fl oz)*

# Marinated Tomato Salad

*A simple salad spiked with the distinctive Mediterranean flavours of black olives and balsamic vinegar. Serve with crusty bread and sliced feta cheese or Baked Ricotta Cheese (page 34) for a light meal.*

500 g (1 lb) tomatoes, cut into wedges
½ cup black olives
125 g (4 oz) green beans, cooked until tender crisp (page 96) and sliced
4 spring onions (scallions), chopped
1 quantity Balsamic Dressing (page 148)
½ cup chopped parsley *or* coriander

Toss all the ingredients together, keeping some of the parsley (or coriander) for sprinkling on top. Cover the salad and set aside for 5–10 minutes if possible to allow the flavours to infuse.
*Serves 4*

# Marinated Mushroom Salad

250 g (8 oz) mushrooms, sliced
4 spring onions (scallions), sliced finely
⅓ cup chopped coriander
juice of 2 lemons
2 garlic cloves, crushed (pressed)
1 teaspoon honey
1 tablespoon extra virgin olive oil
1 tablespoon soy sauce
¼ teaspoon cracked black pepper
additional 3 tablespoons chopped coriander

Place the mushrooms, spring onions and coriander in a bowl and combine well. Place the lemon juice in a small bowl and using a fork or a small wire whisk, beat in the garlic, honey, oil, soy sauce and pepper. Drizzle the dressing over and toss the salad to combine the ingredients well. Cover and set aside to allow the flavours to infuse. Serve sprinkled with the additional coriander.
*Serves 4*

# Bocconcini Salad with Pomegranate

*The splash of vivid crimson from the luscious juice and seeds of the pomegranate and the refreshing flavour of fresh mint and tangy citrus juice makes this a dish to remember. Serve at the start of the meal to get the conversation going.*

1 pomegranate
juice of 1 lime *or* lemon
1 teaspoon honey
1 tablespoon olive oil
⅛ teaspoon cracked black pepper
2 tablespoons chopped mint leaves
375 g (12 oz) bocconcini cheese, sliced
2 cups (185 g/6 oz) shredded arugula (rocket) *or* young spinach leaves
pomegranate pips for garnishing

To soften the pomegranate and extract the juice and seeds, first warm it by placing it in a microwave-proof bowl and cooking on high for 30 seconds only. Allow to stand for 1 minute. Alternatively, place the pomegranate in a heatproof bowl, cover with boiling water and allow to stand for 2 minutes. When the skin is cool enough to handle, knead the pomegranate gently as this helps release the seeds and juice from the pith. Using a small sharp knife cut the pomegranate in half. Squeeze the fruit on a citrus juicer much as you would to remove the juice from lemons. Reserve the pips for garnishing the salad.

Combine the pomegranate juice, lime (or lemon) juice, honey, olive oil, pepper and mint. Place the bocconcini and the arugula (or spinach) in a bowl and toss carefully to combine. Place the salad on a serving platter, drizzle with the dressing and scatter the pomegranate pips over.
*Serves 4*

# Mushroom and Hazelnut Salad

250 g (8 oz) button *or* cap mushrooms, trimmed
    and sliced
½ red sweet pepper (capsicum), seeded and cut
    into thin strips
2 celery stalks, cut into thin strips
½ cup (60 g/2 oz) hazelnuts, roasted (page 17) and
    chopped roughly
1 quantity Lemony Pepper Dressing (page 149)
3 tablespoons sliced chives
125 g (4 oz) bean shoots
additional 2 tablespoons chopped roasted
    hazelnuts

Place the mushrooms, sweet pepper, celery and
hazelnuts in a bowl and drizzle the dressing over.
Toss the salad lightly and just before serving, add
the chives and the bean shoots and toss the salad
to combine all the ingredients well. Place the
salad in a serving dish and scatter the additional
hazelnuts over.
*Serves 4*

# Orange and Mint Salad

*Bursting with the tang of the oranges and the
freshness of the mint, this salad makes a wonderful
accompaniment to hot spicy dishes or can simply be
a stimulant for jaded appetites.*

4 oranges, peeled and sliced, pips removed
3 tablespoons finely sliced mint leaves
1 quantity Orange Sesame Dressing (opposite)
mint leaves

Arrange the orange slices, overlapping, on a
serving plate. Scatter the chopped mint over and
drizzle with the dressing. Serve decorated with
the mint leaves.
*Serves 4*

*Left: Mushroom and Hazelnut Salad. A superb
combination of contrasts in taste and texture. Place
the salad in a bowl lined with green leaves and add
a few stalks of asparagus if it is season.*

# Zucchini and Grape Salad

*The success of this salad relies on your choice of the
freshest young zucchini (courgettes) which have far
more flavour than their more mature counterparts.
The crisp texture and slightly sweet flavour of
young zucchini also makes them particularly
suitable for serving raw.*

500 g (1 lb) young zucchini (courgettes), trimmed
    and sliced
250 g (8 oz) seedless red grapes, washed, shaken
    dry, stalks removed
½ cup chopped parsley
1 quantity Lemon and Honey Dressing (page 144)

Place the zucchini, grapes and parsley in a bowl
and toss them together to combine them
thoroughly. Drizzle the dressing over and toss the
salad lightly. Cover and set the salad aside for
30 minutes to allow the flavours to infuse.
*Serves 4–6*

# Orange Sesame Dressing

3 tablespoons freshly squeezed orange juice
2 tablespoons lemon juice
1 teaspoon honey
2 teaspoons sesame oil
1 tablespoon finely sliced chives
freshly ground black pepper

Place all the ingredients in a small bowl and
using a small wire whisk or a fork, whisk them
together until they are well combined.
*Makes about ½ cup (125 mL/4 fl oz)*

**Orange Hints**
When shopping, choose firm oranges which
seem heavy for their size. To peel the oranges,
use a small sharp serrated stainless steel knife
and pare as much pith from the oranges at the
same time as the skin. Take care not to pare away
the juicy flesh.

# Avocado, Celery and Pineapple Salad

*Creamy and crunchy at the same time, this delicious salad is a showpiece of pretty pastel colours.*

juice of 2 lemons
1 teaspoon honey
2–3 teaspoons extra virgin olive oil
2 tablespoons finely sliced chives
2 medium-sized avocados, peeled, and sliced or diced
1 Granny Smith apple, diced or sliced
¼ ripe pineapple, peeled, sliced or diced
2 celery stalks, sliced finely on the diagonal
additional 2 tablespoons finely sliced chives

To prepare the dressing, place the lemon juice in a small bowl and using a fork or a small wire whisk, beat in the honey and oil, then stir in the chives. Arrange the avocados and apple on a serving plate and drizzle the dressing over. Scatter the pineapple and celery over and sprinkle with the additional chives. Serve at once.
*Serves 4*

# Sweet Potato and Sesame Salad

*The sweet nutty flavour of sweet potatoes goes well with roasted sesame seeds at any time, and in this dish the sesame flavour is also echoed in the dressing. The tang of the orange juice provides a real lift for this wonderful golden salad.*

1 kg (2 lb) orange sweet potatoes, peeled, roasted (page 93) and sliced
1 quantity Orange Sesame Dressing (page 139)
1 tablespoon sesame seeds, roasted (page 17)
2 tablespoons chopped chives

Arrange the sweet potato on a serving platter. Drizzle the dressing over and sprinkle with the sesame seeds and the chives. Serve warm or cold.
*Serves 4*

# Bean Shoot and Peanut Salad

*Laced with the sweet and sour flavour of the dressing and the scrumptious flavour of dry roasted peanuts, this salad is very satisfying. Serve accompanied by tender-crisp steamed seasonal vegetables and a tasty rice salad.*

½ cup (125 mL/4 fl oz) unsweetened pineapple juice
2 teaspoons honey
1 teaspoon grated ginger
2 garlic cloves, crushed (pressed)
1 tablespoon soy sauce
2 tablespoons rice vinegar *or* white wine vinegar
2 tablespoons finely sliced chives
125 g (4 oz) bean shoots
2 celery stalks, sliced finely on the diagonal
125 g (4 oz) snow peas (mangetout), sliced
4 spring onions (scallions), sliced finely
1 cup (155 g/5 oz) dry roasted peanuts
½ cup chopped parsley *or* coriander
additional 3 tablespoons dry roasted peanuts
additional 2 tablespoons finely sliced chives

To prepare the dressing, place the pineapple juice, honey, ginger, garlic, soy sauce and vinegar in a small bowl and combine them thoroughly. Stir in the chives. Place the bean shoots, celery, snow peas, spring onions, peanuts and parsley (or coriander) in a bowl and toss all the ingredients together lightly to combine. Drizzle the dressing over and toss lightly to ensure the vegetables and peanuts are coated with the dressing. Place in a serving bowl and decorate with the additional peanuts and the chives.
*Serves 4–6*

# Tabbouleh Salad

*It's no wonder that this dish, originating in the Middle East, has won fame across many cultures. The cracked wheat, plumped up and juicy and laced with the refreshing flavours of the mint and lemon juice makes this a very satisfying salad. But tabbouleh is more than a salad. It makes a great sandwich filling for fresh pita pocket bread and a wonderful stuffing for firm ripe tomatoes.*

1 cup (185 g/6 oz) burghul wheat, roasted as for nuts and seeds (page 17)
½ cup (125 mL/4 fl oz) water
2 cups chopped parsley
1 cup chopped coriander
4 tablespoon chopped mint leaves
½ cup (125 mL/4 fl oz) lemon juice
250 g (8 oz) tomatoes, diced
6 spring onions (scallions), sliced finely
freshly ground black pepper
1 tablespoon extra virgin olive oil
2 tablespoons shredded mint leaves

When the wheat is cold, place it in a bowl and stir the water through. Cover and set the wheat aside for 30 minutes to allow it to soften. Drain the excess moisture from the wheat and combine it thoroughly with the parsley, coriander, mint, lemon juice, tomatoes, spring onions, pepper and oil. Cover and set the salad aside for 1 hour if possible to allow the flavours to infuse. Serve decorated with the shredded mint leaves.
*Serves 6*

# Hot Potato Salad

*Warm cooked potatoes seem as though they are just lying in wait for a tasty dressing to come along. They absorb the flavour of dressings far more readily than cold potatoes. Serve this salad warm or chilled, but be sure to dress it while the potatoes are warm.*

500 g (1 lb) potatoes, scrubbed and baked until tender (page 81)
3 tablespoons finely sliced chives
1 quantity Herbed Yoghurt Dukkah (page 100)
additional finely sliced chives
freshly ground black pepper

Slice or dice the potatoes and place them in a bowl. Sprinkle them with the chives and pour the dukkah over. Toss the potatoes carefully to coat them evenly with the dukkah. Cover and set them aside for 10–15 minutes to allow the flavours to infuse. Place the salad in a serving dish and serve sprinkled with the additional chives and pepper.
*Serves 4*

# Hot Beetroot and Potato Salad

*An eye opener of a salad if ever I saw one. Not only does the potato absorb the wonderful full-bodied flavour of the beetroot but the colour as well.*

375 g (12 oz) beetroot (beets), peeled and diced
375 g (12 oz) potatoes, peeled and diced
½ red onion, diced finely
freshly ground black pepper
1 quantity Lemony Yoghurt Dressing (page 148)
1 tablespoon finely sliced chives

Cook the beetroot (page 93) and potatoes (page 93) until tender. Place the vegetables in a bowl, scatter over the onion and drizzle with the dressing. Toss the salad to coat the potatoes and beetroot with the dressing. Serve sprinkled with the chives.
*Serves 4*

# Avocado and Radicchio Salad

*Radicchio is a fascinating vegetable, with its characteristic bitter flavour and crimson streaked tender leaves. It is often added to salad mixes but I can understand why it is a much loved Italian vegetable in its own right. This delicious 'bitey' salad is great for the winter months which suit the growing conditions of radicchio.*

2 medium-sized avocados, peeled, pip removed, sliced
juice of 1 lime *or* lemon
1 small head of radicchio, leaves separated, washed and dried
125 g (4 oz) feta cheese, sliced
3 tablespoons finely sliced chives
additional 2 tablespoons finely sliced chives
1 quantity Raspberry Vinaigrette (page 149)

Arrange the avocado in a single layer on a plate and sprinkle it with the lemon juice to prevent it from discolouring. Carefully combine the avocado with the radicchio, feta cheese and chives. Place the salad on a serving platter and sprinkle with the chives. Just before serving, drizzle the dressing over, or serve with the dressing on the side.
*Serves 4*

**Serving Radicchio**
Radicchio is best served raw to capture the beauty of its vibrant colour. Although some people prefer to blanch or grill radicchio to soften the flavour, I prefer to serve it fresh combined with complimentary vegetables. Once cooked, radicchio's leaves become a disappointing muddy colour.

*Right: Avocado and Radicchio Salad. The characteristic salty flavour and crumbly texture of feta cheese complements the ripe avocado beautifully and the bitter edge of the radicchio marries well with both flavours.*

# Rice and Apricot Salad

½ cup (125 mL/4 fl oz) apricot nectar
1 tablespoon orange juice
2 tablespoons olive oil
2 spring onions (scallions), sliced finely
freshly ground black pepper
3 cups (500 g/1 lb) cold Cooked Brown Rice (page 109)
½ cup (60 g/2 oz) slivered almonds, roasted (page 17)
½ cup (60 g/2 oz) sliced dried apricots
½ cup chopped parsley *or* coriander
additional 1–2 tablespoons roasted slivered almonds

To prepare the dressing, combine the apricot nectar, orange juice, oil, spring onions and pepper. Place the rice, almonds, apricots and parsley (or coriander) in a bowl and drizzle the dressing over. Toss the salad to combine all the ingredients well and place in a serving bowl. Scatter with the additional almonds.
*Serves 4*

# Lima Bean and Tomato Salad

*Team up with a light salad of greens and fresh wholemeal rolls for a light yet satisfying meal.*

3 cups (500 g/1 lb) Cooked Lima Beans (page 125)
½ red onion, diced finely
1 quantity Lemon, Ginger and Soy Dressing (page 148)
250 g (8 oz) tomatoes, diced
1 cup chopped parsley
4 lemon wedges

Place the beans and the onions in a bowl and combine them well. Pour the dressing over and toss the salad to coat the beans and the onion. Cover and set the salad aside to marinate. Just before serving, toss the beans lightly with the tomatoes and parsley. Serve accompanied by the lemon wedges.
*Serves 4*

# Date and Pistachio Salad

*Light and fruity, this salad is inspired by the Middle Eastern tradition of combining grain dishes with dried fruit and nuts. Nutritionally speaking, this makes good sense because the complete protein contained in the nuts complements the incomplete protein of grain dishes. However the true beauty of this salad lies in the colour contrast of the vivid green pistachios and the golden glow of the saffron rice.*

½ cup (60 g/2 oz) shelled pistachio nuts
3 cups (500 g/1 lb) cold Saffron Rice (page 110)
6–8 fresh dates, pitted and sliced
3 tablespoons finely sliced chives
1 quantity Lemon and Honey Dressing (below)

Place the pistachios in a heatproof bowl and cover with boiling water. Allow the nuts to stand for 1–2 minutes, then drain them completely, cover with cold water and slide the skins off. Combine three quarters of the pistachios with the other ingredients and serve scattered with the remaining pistachios.
*Serves 4*

# Lemon and Honey Dressing

*This sweet dressing is wonderful drizzled on grain salads and complements fruit-based salads well.*

juice of 2 lemons
2 teaspoons cider vinegar
2 teaspoons honey
1 tablespoon olive *or* sesame oil

Place all the ingredients in a small bowl and whisk them together until well combined.
*Makes about ½ cup (125 mL/4 fl oz)*

# Avocado and Tahini Salad

2 avocados, peeled, pip removed, sliced
juice of 1 lemon
1 cup (90 g/3 oz) shredded spinach leaves
1 cup (90 g/3 oz) alfalfa sprouts
1 cup (90 g/3 oz) bean shoots
½ carrot, scrubbed, cut into thin matchsticks
4–5 spring onions (scallions), sliced finely
1 quantity Creamy Tahini Dressing
lemon wedges

Place the avocado slices on a plate and sprinkle with the lemon juice to prevent them from discolouring. Thoroughly combine the spinach, sprouts, bean shoots, carrots and spring onions. Add the avocado slices and toss the salad carefully to avoid breaking up the avocado slices. Spoon the dressing on top, and decorate with the lemon wedges.
*Serves 4*

# Creamy Tahini Dressing

*This light creamy dressing is tasty enough for dipping fresh vegetable crudités into. It also doubles as a sauce for tender-crisp cooked green vegetables.*

½ cup (125 mL/4 fl oz) plain yoghurt
2–3 tablespoons tahini
juice of 1 lemon
2 garlic cloves, crushed (pressed)
1 teaspoon grated ginger
2 teaspoons apple cider vinegar

Whisk all the ingredients together until smooth.
*Makes about 1 cup (250 mL/8 fl oz)*

# Crimson Dressing

*A simply stunning full-bodied dressing of incredible hue. Use it drizzled over ripe avocados, tomatoes or asparagus for a knockout salad.*

2 tablespoons Raspberry Vinegar (page 295)
2 tablespoons beetroot (beet) juice
1 tablespoon olive oil
1 tablespoon minced red onion
⅛ teaspoon cracked black pepper

Place all the ingredients in a screw-top jar and shake well to combine.
*Makes about ½ cup (125 mL/4 fl oz)*

# Mango Vinaigrette

*Fresh mangoes need little done to them—they are incredible just as they are. When combined with the ruby red of raspberry vinegar, the mango takes on a whole new character, becoming a rich sunset gold in colour and developing a glorious sweet flavour with a sharp tang lingering in the background. This vinaigrette was made for all manner of crispy salad greens.*

½ large or 1 small mango, peeled, pip removed and sliced
juice of 1 lemon *or* lime
1 garlic clove, crushed (pressed)
2 tablespoons Raspberry Vinegar (page 295)
1 tablespoon olive oil

Blend all the ingredients until smooth using a food processor or blender.
*Makes about 1 cup (250 mL/8 fl oz)*

# Quick Berry Dressing

*This is a delightfully fruity dressing for those who do not have berry vinegar on hand. It can be prepared in minutes yet is capable of transforming the simplest of salads into a gourmet delight. Try drizzling it over a salad of fresh greens scattered with avocado slices or fresh strawberries and sliced bananas and you will know what I mean.*

½ punnet (carton) strawberries, hulls removed, *or* raspberries
1 tablespoon honey
3 tablespoons white wine vinegar
juice of 1 lemon
¼ teaspoon cracked black pepper

Press the berries through a coarse sieve into a medium-sized bowl. Using a whisk, beat the honey, vinegar, lemon juice and pepper through and use as soon as possible.
*Makes about 1 cup (250 mL/8 fl oz)*

# Tofu Mayonnaise

*Tofu to the rescue again! This mayonnaise is low in fat, yet is not missing any of the flavour of regular mayonnaise. Great for topping crispy salads or for providing a creamy blanket for potato salad, Tofu Mayonnaise also serves as a dip for crisp vegetable sticks or as a sandwich spread instead of butter or margarine.*

250 g (8 oz) tofu, drained
1 tablespoon oil
2 tablespoons lemon juice
2 teaspoons apple cider vinegar
1 teaspoon honey
1 teaspoon grainy mustard
1 garlic clove, crushed (pressed)

Blend all the ingredients until smooth using a food processor. If not using at once, store in an airtight container in the refrigerator.
*Makes about 1½ cups (375 mL/12 fl oz)*

# Cauliflower and Peanut Salad

*A delicious and satisfying salad laced with the peanut and chili flavour of a good satay sauce. The dressing however is light and clear, enabling the wonderful contrasts in colour to shine through.*

½ small cauliflower, trimmed and cut into florets
125 g (4 oz) green beans, topped and tailed
3 spring onions (scallions), sliced finely
3 tablespoons chopped parsley
1 quantity Sweet Chili Dipping Sauce (page 97)
½ cup (60 g/2 oz) dry roasted peanuts
½ cup (125 mL/4 fl oz) Greek Yoghurt (page 273)
   *or* light sour cream (optional)
additional 2 tablespoons dry roasted peanuts
additional 2 tablespoons finely diced red sweet
   pepper (capsicum)

Cook the cauliflower (page 85) and the beans (page 96) until just tender-crisp and set them aside to cool. Add the spring onions, parsley and the dipping sauce and toss the salad to combine all the ingredients thoroughly. If using the yoghurt (or sour cream), spoon on top of the salad and serve scattered with the additional peanuts and the additional red sweet pepper.
*Serves 4–6*

*Left: Cauliflower and Peanut Salad. A dish for those who aren't afraid of turning up the heat with chili peppers.*

# Red Cabbage Slaw

*Sweet and vibrant, this salad is a summer delight. Serve with a selection of fruit and cheese and fresh crusty bread for a wonderful light meal.*

¼ red cabbage, trimmed, washed, chopped finely
2 celery stalks, diced finely
½ cup (60 g/2 oz) dried currants
1 quantity Raspberry Vinaigrette (page 149)
clumps of redcurrants for garnishing

Place the cabbage, celery and currants in a bowl and combine all the ingredients thoroughly. Pour the dressing over and toss through the salad to ensure it is well coated with the dressing. Cover and set aside for 30 minutes or so to allow the flavours to infuse. Toss the salad once more, then place it in a serving dish and serve decorated with the redcurrants.
*Serves 4–6*

# Apple Crunch Salad

*The dressing alone will get the conversation started, but the combination of the creamy textured avocados and the crisp apples will keep it going. Serve as a first course with fresh crusty bread or as an accompaniment to a simple main dish such as a terrine or flan.*

juice of 2 limes *or* lemons
2 teaspoons honey
3 tablespoons coconut cream (page 341)
2 red apples, sliced
2 avocados, peeled, pip removed and sliced
2 tablespoons finely sliced chives

To prepare the dressing, place the lime (or lemon) juice, honey and coconut cream in a bowl and whisk until the ingredients are well combined. Just before serving, arrange the apple and avocado slices on a serving plate and drizzle the dressing over.
*Serves 4*

# Balsamic Dressing

*This recipe is for those who appreciate a dressing that is sure to wake up even the sleepiest of taste buds. Balsamic vinegar, with its characteristic spicy tang, is the key ingredient.*

1–2 garlic cloves, crushed (pressed)
1 tablespoon extra virgin olive oil
1 tablespoon balsamic vinegar
3 tablespoons red wine vinegar
cracked black pepper

Place all the ingredients in a screw topped jar and shake well to combine.
*Makes about ½ cup (125 mL/4 fl oz)*

# Lemony Yoghurt Dressing

*This is a good all round dressing for popular salads like coleslaw, waldorf salad and potato salad. If you enjoy cooked beetroot (beets) as much as I do, then a simple salad can be conjured up by dousing warm or cold cooked beetroot in this dressing.*

¾ cup (185 mL/6 fl oz) plain yoghurt
2 tablespoons lemon juice
½ teaspoon finely grated lemon rind
1 teaspoon honey
freshly ground black pepper

Place all the ingredients in a small bowl and whisk them together to combine them thoroughly.
*Makes about 1 cup (250 mL/8 fl oz)*

# Lemon, Ginger and Soy Dressing

1 tablespoon sesame oil
juice of 2 lemons
1 teaspoon honey
1 teaspoon grated ginger
2 garlic cloves, crushed (pressed)
1 tablespoon soy sauce

Place all the ingredients in a small bowl and using a small wire whisk or a fork, whisk them together until they are well combined.
*Makes about ½ cup (125 mL/4 fl oz)*

# Lemony Ginger Dressing

*To appreciate the fresh tang of this simple yet flavour-packed dressing, prepare it just before you use it. I love to drizzle this concoction over crisp salad greens or sliced avocado and fruit combinations.*

1 teaspoon honey
2–3 teaspoons sesame oil
1 teaspoon grated ginger
juice of 2 lemons
1 tablespoon finely sliced chives

Place the honey and oil in a cup or a small bowl and using a fork, whisk them together to combine them well. Whisk in the ginger and lemon juice, then stir in the chives. Serve at once.
*Makes about ½ cup (125 mL/4 fl oz)*

# Cashew Cream Dressing

*A rich creamy dairy-free recipe, great for topping coleslaw or tender-crisp cooked green vegetables.*

½ cup (125 mL/4 fl oz) Basic Nut Cream (page 281) using cashew nuts
1 teaspoon honey
½ cup (125 mL/4 fl oz) freshly squeezed orange juice
1 tablespoon finely sliced spring onions (scallions) *or* chives

Place all the ingredients in a small bowl and whisk them together until well combined.
*Makes about 1 cup (250 mL/8 fl oz)*

# Lemony Pepper Dressing

*A lovely light and clear dressing superb for pouring over fresh salad greens, ripe avocados and tender-crisp cooked asparagus.*

4 tablespoons lemon juice
1 tablespoon olive oil
2 teaspoons honey
2 teaspoons apple cider vinegar
¼ teaspoon cracked black pepper

Place all the ingredients in a small bowl and using a small wire whisk or a fork, whisk them together until they are well combined.
*Makes about ½ cup (125 mL/4 fl oz)*

# Orange Vinaigrette

3 tablespoons freshly squeezed orange juice
2 tablespoons oil
2 garlic cloves, crushed (pressed)
1 teaspoon honey
2 tablespoons Orange Vinegar (page 295) *or* white wine vinegar
1 tablespoon finely sliced spring onions (scallions) *or* chives

Place all the ingredients in a screw-top jar and shake well to combine.
*Makes about ¾ cup (185 mL/6 fl oz)*

# Raspberry Vinaigrette

*This popular dressing adds a splash of colour and characteristic fruity flavour to salads and vegetable dishes.*

3 tablespoons Raspberry Vinegar (page 295)
1 tablespoon white wine vinegar
2 tablespoons olive oil
1 teaspoon honey
1 clove garlic, crushed (pressed)
freshly ground black pepper

Place all the ingredients in a screw-top jar and shake well to combine.
*Makes about ½ cup (125 mL/4 fl oz)*

# Pineapple Mint Dressing

½ cup (125 mL/4 fl oz) pineapple juice
1 teaspoon honey
2 tablespoons chopped mint leaves
cracked black pepper
2 teaspoons apple cider vinegar

Place all the ingredients in a screw-top jar and shake the jar well to combine all the ingredients.
*Makes about ¾ cup (185 mL/6 fl oz)*

# Thick Yoghurt Dressing

1 cup (250 mL/8 fl oz) Yoghurt Cheese (page 271)
½ teaspoon ground mustard seeds
1–2 garlic cloves, crushed (pressed)
3 tablespoons lemon juice
1 tablespoon balsamic vinegar
1 tablespoon sesame oil *or* olive oil
pepper *or* Tabasco Sauce

Whisk all the ingredients together until well combined. If not using at once, store in the refrigerator in an airtight container.
*Makes about 1½ cups (375 mL/12 fl oz)*

# Fruit and Desserts

*Fresh and fragrant like summer mangoes or delicately perfumed like poached winter quinces, fruit makes wonderful desserts and sauces. Whether your dream desserts be fresh and fruity parfaits, creamy cheesecakes, mousses and slices, or heart-warming old-time favourites like puddings and tarts, you will find plenty of sweet treats to please.*

# Baked Lemon Cheesecake

*This continental-style cheesecake seems like a dieter's sin, yet it is lower in fat and sugar than its traditional counterpart. Topped with luscious seasonal fruits, this is a treat that is hard to beat!*

¾ cup (125 g/4 oz) quick-cooking oats
½ cup (60 g/2 oz) ground almonds (almond meal)
2 tablespoons sugar
1 teaspoon ground cinnamon
60 g (2 oz) butter melted
2 egg whites, lightly beaten
1 kg (2 lb) ricotta cheese *or* cottage cheese
½ cup (125 g/4 oz) caster (superfine) sugar
4 tablespoons plain yoghurt
3 eggs
2 tablespoons plain (all-purpose) flour
rind and juice of 2 medium lemons
500g (1 lb) fresh berries such as raspberries,
   strawberries *or* loganberries

To prepare the crust, mix the oats, almonds, sugar and cinnamon then add the butter and egg whites. Mix until well combined, then press onto the bottom of a prepared springform pan (deep cake pan with removable base). Bake in a hot oven (200°C/400°F) for 10 minutes.

Meanwhile, blend all the remaining ingredients except the berries together until smooth. Pour filling on top of prepared crust. Bake in a hot oven (200°C/400°F) for 10 minutes then reduce the oven heat to 150°C/300°F and bake for a further 40 minutes. Turn the oven off and allow the cheesecake to cool in the oven. When cool, place in the refrigerator to chill before decorating with the fresh berries and serving.
*Serves 10–12*

### Uncracked Cheesecakes
Leaving baked cheesecakes in the oven allows them to cool gradually. Removing cheesecakes from the oven as soon as they are cooked can cause cracking because of the sudden change in temperature from warm oven to the kitchen.

# Passion Fruit Cheesecake

*An unmistakable taste of summer lingers in the nectarful flavour of passion fruit. A superb cheesecake to linger over at the end of a light meal, it is delicious served drizzled with Passion Fruit and Mango Sauce (page 180).*

1 cup (125 g/4 oz) wholemeal (whole-wheat) plain
   (all-purpose) flour
1 cup (90 g/3 oz) desiccated coconut
3 tablespoons brown sugar
60 g (2 oz) melted butter
2 tablespoons oil
500 g (1 lb) Yoghurt Cheese (page 271) *or* cream
   cheese
4 eggs, beaten
½ cup (90 g/3 oz) caster (superfine) sugar
2 tablespoons honey
½ cup (125 mL/4 fl oz) passion fruit pulp

To prepare the crust, place the flour, coconut and brown sugar in a bowl and make a 'well' in the centre. Add the melted butter and oil and combine thoroughly. Press the mixture onto the bottom of a prepared springform pan (deep cake pan with removable base) and bake in a hot oven (200°C/400°F) for 10 minutes.

To prepare the filling, beat the Yoghurt Cheese (or cream cheese), eggs and sugar until smooth, then stir in the honey and passion fruit pulp. Pour the mixture onto the prepared crust and bake in a hot oven (200°C/400°F) for 10 minutes, then reduce the heat to 160°C/325°F for 45 minutes. Allow to cool in the oven. Chill completely before serving.
*Serves 10–12*

*Overleaf: The exquisite flavours of mango and passion fruit cap off this popular Passion Fruit Cheesecake.*

# Loganberry Cheesecake

*Serve with fresh loganberries or ripe red strawberries alongside. It's doubtful that you will have any leftovers from this delightful cheesecake, but if you do, you can store individually wrapped slices in the freezer to be enjoyed at a later time.*

½ cup (60 g/2 oz) wholemeal (whole-wheat) plain (all-purpose) flour
⅔ cup (60 g/2 oz) desiccated coconut
¾ cup (90 g/3 oz) ground almonds (almond meal)
2 tablespoons soft brown sugar
2 egg whites, beaten
½ cup (125 mL/4 fl oz) apple juice
2 tablespoons honey
2 teaspoons pure agar agar powder (page 341)
1 punnet (carton) loganberries
3 tablespoons caster (superfine) sugar
500 g (1lb) Yoghurt Cheese (page 271) *or* cream cheese
1 cup (250 mL/8 fl oz) light (single) cream

To prepare the crust, mix the flour, coconut, almonds, sugar and egg whites until well combined, then press onto the bottom of a prepared springform pan (deep cake pan with removable base). Bake in a hot oven (200°C/400°F) for 20 minutes.

Place the apple juice, honey and agar agar powder in a small saucepan and bring to the boil. Reduce the heat and simmer, stirring, for 1 minute. Using a food processor, blend the loganberries, sugar, Yoghurt Cheese (or cream cheese) and cream until smooth, then, while the machine is still operating, pour the agar agar mixture down the feeder tube. Blend for 30 seconds, then pour immediately onto the prepared crust. Chill for 1 hour before slicing.
*Serves 10–12*

**A Quick Berry Sauce**
When fresh berries are unavailable you can use frozen berries with good results. A delicious sauce can also be made from frozen berries. Simply push 1 cup of thawed berries through a coarse sieve and whisk the purée with 1 tablespoon each of lemon juice and honey until all the ingredients are combined thoroughly.

# Lemon and Coconut Cheesecake

*This 'cheesecake' without the cheese is for those who are looking for a delectable dairy free dessert. The richness of this cheesecake arises from the coconut cream which reinforces the coconut flavour of the crust and blends beautifully with the lemon and honey.*

1 cup (90 g/3 oz) desiccated coconut
¾ cup (90 g/3 oz) almonds
2 tablespoons soft brown sugar
2 tablespoons low-flavoured oil
750 g (1½ lb) tofu, drained well
4 tablespoons honey
3 tablespoons caster (superfine) sugar
225 mL (7 fl oz) coconut cream
juice and finely grated rind of 2 lemons
slices of kiwi fruit and star fruit

To prepare the crust, place the coconut, almonds and brown sugar in a food processor and process until the texture resembles fresh breadcrumbs. While the processor is running, add the oil. Using moistened hands, press the mixture evenly over the bottom of a prepared springform pan (deep cake pan with removable base). Bake in a hot oven (200°C/400°F) for 10 minutes.

Meanwhile, to prepare the filling, place the tofu and honey in a food processor and blend until smooth. Add the sugar, coconut cream, lemon rind and juice and blend until all the ingredients are thoroughly combined. Pour the mixture onto the crust and bake the cheesecake in a hot oven (200°C/400°F) for 10 minutes. Reduce the heat and bake in a slow oven (150°C/300°F) for a further 40 minutes. Allow the cheesecake to cool in the oven. Chill for 1 hour before decorating with slices of the kiwi fruit and star fruit.
*Serves 10–12*

# Sweet Short Pastry

*Quick and easy to prepare and scrumptious to eat, this pastry can be prepared in a food processor or by hand. Either way, it is a no-fuss recipe that can be used for any sweet dish requiring pastry.*

1½ cups (185 g/6 oz) wholemeal (whole-wheat)
   plain (all-purpose) flour
1 teaspoon baking powder
1–2 tablespoons soft brown sugar
60 g (2 oz) butter, melted
1 tablespoon oil
about 2 tablespoons water

Sift the flour with the baking powder and stir in the sugar. Make a 'well' in the centre and add the butter, oil and water to the well. Gradually work in the dry ingredients and mix until a soft consistency is formed. Alternatively, place the flour, baking powder and sugar in a food processor and process for a few seconds. While the machine is operating, pour the butter and oil down the feeder tube. Add sufficient water to bring the mixture to a soft consistency. Turn out onto a lightly floured bench top and knead for a few seconds only. Use as required.
*Makes 1 pastry shell*

# Basic Pastry Shell

*Tarts are gaining popularity over pies because they can be sweet and delectable without the additional pastry that's put on the tops of pies. Pile your tarts with fresh or stewed fruits and for a more hearty winter dish try sprinkling a crumble topping over the fruit.*

1 quantity Sweet Short Pastry (above) *or* Sweet
   Coconut or Almond Pastry (page 157)
additional flour

Roll the pastry out to a 3 mm (⅛ in.) thickness and line the bottom and sides of a tart or flan tin (pie pan). Run a rolling pin over the edges of the tin to trim the edges. Bake in a moderately hot oven (190°C/375°F) for 20 minutes. Set aside to cool and use as required.
*Makes 1 pastry shell*

# Rhubarb and Strawberry Tart

*The combination of the rosy hue of the rhubarb and the rich red of the ripe strawberries makes this an eye-catching dessert. Serve simply with Vanilla Whip (page 181) or whipping (double) cream.*

2 cups stewed rhubarb (page 161)
1 teaspoon pure agar agar powder (page 341)
1 cold prepared pastry shell using Sweet Short
   Pastry
375 g (12 oz) strawberries, halved lengthways

Place the rhubarb and agar agar powder in a saucepan and bring the mixture to the boil, stirring. Reduce the heat and simmer for 1 minute. Remove from the stove and set aside to cool. Pour the rhubarb into the prepared pastry shell and arrange the strawberries on top. Pop the tart into the freezer for 10 minutes to chill the fruit quickly and prevent it from seeping into the crust.
*Serves 8–10*

**More Strawberry Flavour**
For an extra special dessert, drizzle individual serves of this tart with Fresh Berry Coulis (page 178) using strawberries.

*Right: Rhubarb and Strawberry Tart. The creamy texture of the rhubarb filling offsets the luscious juicy texture of the ripe strawberries beautifully.*

# Sweet Oatmeal Pastry Shell

*This quick and easy pastry contains much more fibre and less fat than conventional pastry, but has a wonderful flavour and texture. The other difference is that instead of rolling this pastry out as for conventional pastry it is pressed onto the bottom of the pan. As such it is not suitable for using to top pies; I use a crumble topping instead of pastry for the top.*

1 cup (125 g/4 oz) wholemeal (whole-wheat) plain (all-purpose) flour
1 teaspoon baking powder
1 cup (90 g/3 oz) rolled oats
1–2 tablespoons soft brown sugar
60 g (2 oz) butter, melted
1 teaspoon vanilla essence (extract)
1 tablespoon oil
about 2 tablespoons water

Sift the flour and baking powder and combine with the oats and sugar. Mix the melted butter, vanilla, oil and water and pour over the dry ingredients. Combine all the ingredients until a soft pastry is formed. Using moistened hands, press the pastry onto the sides and then the bottom of a flan tin (pie pan) that has been brushed with a little oil. Trim the edges and bake the pastry shell in a moderate oven (180°C/350°F) for 25–30 minutes.
*Makes 1 pastry shell*

### Using Water with Pastry
The amount of water specified for the pastry recipes is approximate because the absorption rate of wholemeal (whole-wheat) flours varies according to the amount of bran, wheatgerm and starch each contains.

# Lemon and Apple Tart

*Simple, light and positively delicious, this tart keeps well for a day or two in the refrigerator (that's if no one discovers it first!) and also freezes well. Golden delicious apples are my first choice for this tart as they retain their shape really well and need very little additional sweetening. Granny Smith apples are, however, a close second.*

1 cup (250 mL/8 fl oz) apple juice
2 tablespoons soft brown sugar or 1 tablespoon honey
1 tablespoon lemon juice
2 teaspoons finely grated lemon rind
1 kg (2 lb) golden delicious apples, peeled and sliced neatly
1 quantity Lemon Cream Cheese (page 186)
1 prepared Sweet Oatmeal Pastry Shell, cold

Place the apple juice, sugar (or honey), lemon juice and lemon rind in a saucepan and bring the mixture to the boil. Add the apples and simmer gently until just tender, about 15–20 minutes. Set the mixture aside to cool completely.

Meanwhile, using a spatula or a bread and butter knife, spread the Lemon Cream Cheese evenly over the bottom of the pastry shell. Drain the apple thoroughly, reserving the apple juice. Arrange the apple slices on top of the cream cheese. Return the apple juice to the saucepan and bring to the boil, then simmer uncovered until it turns to a syrupy consistency. Spoon the syrup over the apples and chill the tart before slicing.
*Serves 8–10*

# Sweet Coconut or Almond Pastry

1 cup (125 g/4 oz) wholemeal (whole-wheat)
  self-raising flour
⅔ cup (60 g/2 oz) desiccated coconut *or* ground
  almonds (almond meal)
1½ teaspoons baking powder
2 tablespoons soft brown sugar
2 tablespoons oil
about 4 tablespoons water

Place the flour, coconut (or ground almonds),
baking powder and sugar in a food processor and
process the mixture for 1 minute. Add the oil
while the processor is operating and continue to
process until the mixture resembles fresh
breadcrumbs. Add the water and continue to
process until a firm pastry is formed.
*Makes 1 pastry shell*

# Apricot Lattice Pie

*This is an all year round dessert. When fresh
apricots are unavailable, use Stewed Dried Apricots
(page 164) which make a delicious thick filling for
tarts and pies.*

1 quantity Sweet Short Pastry (page 154)
1 quantity Stewed Apricots (page 164), cold

Roll the pastry out to a 3 mm (⅛ in.) thickness
and press the pastry onto the bottom and the
sides of a pie dish. Trim the edges neatly. Take
the trimmings and knead them together lightly,
then form a rectangle of pastry and roll it out to a
6 mm (¼ in.) thickness. Using a pair of kitchen
scissors or a sharp knife, cut the pastry into
strips and set them aside on a floured board.

Drain the excess juice from the apricots and
spread them evenly over the bottom of the pastry
shell. Working quickly, arrange the strips of
pastry in a lattice pattern on top, moistening the
ends and pressing them down onto the crust.
Bake the pie in a moderate oven (180°C/350°F)
for 30–35 minutes.
*Serves 8–10*

# Pecan Tart

*Pecan tart is such a popular rich sweet dish that I
couldn't resist coming up with a lighter alternative
to suit today's taste buds. But never fear, the
caramel-like flavour of the traditional pecan tart
still prevails in this scrumptious tart which is a
treat for special occasions. Serve just as it is with
piping hot freshly brewed coffee or tea.*

250 g (8 oz) ricotta cheese *or* tofu
2 eggs, beaten
30 g (1 oz) butter, melted
2 tablespoons honey
3 tablespoons golden syrup (light treacle)
1 teaspoon vanilla essence (extract)
1 teaspoon ground cinnamon
1 prepared pastry shell using Sweet Almond
  Pastry (opposite)
1 cup (155 g/5 oz) pecan nuts

Blend the ricotta cheese (or tofu), eggs, butter,
honey, golden syrup, vanilla and cinnamon
together until smooth. Place the mixture in the
prepared pastry shell and arrange the pecan nuts
neatly on top. Bake the tart in a hot oven
(200°C/400°F) for 10 minutes, then reduce the
heat and cook in a moderate oven (180°C/350°F)
for 25–30 minutes. Set the tart aside to cool
before slicing.
*Serves 8–10*

# Date and Orange Tartlets

*Dates and oranges harmonise well to make a delectable filling for these individual tarts.*

1 quantity Sweet Almond Pastry (page 157)
375 g (12 oz) Yoghurt Cheese (page 271) *or* cream
  cheese, softened
1 tablespoon honey
2 teaspoons finely grated orange rind
8 fresh dates, pitted and sliced
2–3 oranges, peeled and sliced thinly
8 almonds

Roll the pastry out to a 3 mm (⅛ in.) thickness and line the bottoms and sides of 8 individual flan tins (pie pans). Prick the bottoms with a fork or a skewer to prevent excess rising. Bake in a moderately hot oven (190°C/375°F) for 15 minutes, then set them aside to cool. Combine the Yoghurt Cheese (or cream cheese), honey and orange rind until smooth then place the mixture into a piping (pastry) bag and pipe onto the individual pastry shells. Arrange alternate slices of dates and oranges neatly on top of the mixture and place an almond in the centre of each. Chill before serving.
*Makes 8 individual serves*

### Seasonal Variations

This recipe can be varied according to the seasonal fruit available. Have fun experimenting with poached peaches or apricots, and sprinkle roasted slivered almonds over to decorate.

# Fresh Fig Tartlets

*The sweet almond pastry forms a superb backdrop for these tartlets. The simple filling is a harmonious blend of ripe figs laced with the zesty flavour of preserved ginger nestling on a creamy crust of soft cheese. Serve warm as they are, or chilled with fresh strawberries on the side.*

1 quantity Sweet Almond Pastry (page 157)
375 g (12 oz) Yoghurt Cheese (page 271) *or* cream
  cheese, softened
4 large firm fresh figs, stems snipped off
3 tablespoons preserved ginger syrup
1 tablespoon honey
1 tablespoon lemon juice

Roll the pastry out to a 3 mm (⅛ in.) thickness and line the bottoms and sides of 8 individual flan tins (pie pans). Prick the bottoms with a fork or a skewer to prevent excess rising. Bake in a moderately hot oven (190°C/375°F) for 10 minutes then set aside to cool. Place the Yoghurt Cheese (or cream cheese) in a piping (pastry) bag and pipe a thin layer evenly over the bottom of each pastry shell. Using a small sharp knife, cut the figs into thin slices. Arrange the fig slices on top of the cheese. Combine the ginger syrup, honey and lemon juice, then drizzle the mixture over the figs. Bake in a moderately hot oven (190°C/375°F) for 10–12 minutes. Allow them to stand for 5 minutes before serving.
*Makes 8 individual serves*

### Ginger Syrup

If you do not have a pot of preserved ginger, substitute 2 tablespoons honey combined with ½ teaspoon ground ginger and 1 tablespoon apple juice for the ginger syrup.

*Right: Fresh Fig Tartlets. The beauty of these tartlets lies in their simplicity. The succulence and sweetness of sun ripened fresh figs laced with ginger is a taste sensation that's hard to beat.*

# Apricot Tart

*A light, lively and delicious alternative to rich tarts filled with confectioners' custard, this tart is great served as it is or with a swirl of Lemon Whip (page 168).*

1½ cups (375 mL/12 fl oz) apricot nectar
2 tablespoons arrowroot
2 egg yolks
1 prepared pastry shell using Sweet Almond Pastry (page 157)
1 quantity Stewed Apricots (page 164), drained
125 g (4 oz) strawberries, halved lengthways
125 g (4 oz) grapes, halved and seeded
1 cup (250 mL/8 fl oz) pure apple juice
¾ teaspoon pure agar agar powder (page 341)

Place the apricot nectar and the arrowroot in a saucepan and beat with a wire whisk to combine them well. Heat, stirring or whisking constantly until the mixture thickens, remove from the heat then whisk in the egg yolks. Return to the heat and cook very gently until the mixture thickens. Be sure not to overheat the mixture at this stage or the eggs may curdle. Set the custard aside to cool, then spread over the bottom of the pastry shell. Arrange the apricots, strawberries and grapes on top of the custard and place the tart in the freezer to chill for 10 minutes. Meanwhile, place the apple juice and the agar agar powder into a saucepan and bring the mixture to the boil, stirring constantly. Reduce the heat and simmer for 1 minute. Remove the mixture from the heat and allow to cool slightly before spooning carefully over the chilled tart. Chill the tart for 10 minutes before slicing.
*Serves 8–10*

# Poached Apples

2 cups (500 mL/16 fl oz) pure apple juice
½ cup (125 mL/4 fl oz) dessert wine
1 tablespoon honey
4–6 whole cloves
4 strips lemon zest
3 apples, peeled and cored

Place the apple juice, wine, honey, cloves and lemon zest in a saucepan and bring the mixture to the boil. Reduce the heat and simmer for 5 minutes. Add the apples and cook gently, without simmering, for 15–20 minutes. Alternatively, place the apples in an ovenproof dish and pour the apple juice mixture over. Cover and bake in a moderate oven (180°C/350°F) for 30–35 minutes.
*Serves 4*

# Apple Rolls

*A simply delicious partnership of harmonious fruity flavours encased in light crispy pastry. Wonderful served on their own or with a scoop of vanilla ice cream or Greek Yoghurt (page 273).*

3 apples, halved and poached
12 sheets phyllo pastry
⅓ cup (60 g/2 oz) raisins
30 g (1 oz) walnuts
1 tablespoon oil

Chill the apples and drain the poaching liquid completely (retain to add to cold drinks or sauces). Using 2 sheets of phyllo pastry for each roll, brush the top sheet with a little of the oil, top with an apple half and a few of the walnuts and raisins. Roll the apple up in the pastry, folding the side edges over the apple half to form a package. Brush the outside of the pastry with a little oil and place the roll on a prepared baking sheet. Continue with the remaining apples and pastry. Bake in a moderate oven (180°C/350°F) for 30–35 minutes.
*Serves 6*

# Poached Rhubarb

*Cook this very gently so that the stalks remain intact and are resplendent in the crimson tinged juice. Serve simply, topped with a scoop of Greek Yoghurt (page 273) or a generous dollop of whipping (double) cream.*

1 cup (250 mL/8 fl oz) dark grape juice
2–3 tablespoons honey
2 teaspoons lemon juice
1 cinnamon stick
1 bunch rhubarb, washed thoroughly, trimmed
    and cut into 2.5 cm (1 in.) lengths

Place the grape juice, honey, lemon juice and cinnamon stick in a medium-sized saucepan and bring the mixture to the boil. Reduce the heat and cook the syrup for 5 minutes. Remove the cinnamon stick and add the rhubarb. Cover and cook very gently for 10 minutes.
*Serves 4*

# Stewed Rhubarb

*Stewed rhubarb makes a full flavoured tangy filling for pies and tarts, a delicious light breakfast, or a dessert when served topped with yoghurt.*

1 bunch rhubarb, washed thoroughly and
    trimmed
½ cup (125 mL/4 fl oz) honey
1 tablespoon lemon juice

Cut the rhubarb into 1 cm (½ in.) slices and place it in a saucepan. Drizzle the honey over and sprinkle with the lemon juice. There is no need to add water because rhubarb contains a considerable amount of water which seeps out as it stews. Cover the saucepan and bring the mixture to the boil, then reduce the heat immediately and simmer, covered, for 10 minutes. If not using at once, store as for Stewed Apples (next recipe).
*Serves 4*

# Stewed Apples

*Stewed apples have a myriad of uses, so when apples are in season I usually make up a container of stewed apples and keep them in the refrigerator to be enjoyed with yoghurt and muesli in the morning or to make pies or crumbles for desserts. Fruit stewed in fruit juice also makes a nutritious snack for hungry children.*

500 g (1 lb) apples, peeled and sliced
1 cup (250 mL/8 fl oz) apple juice
2 thick slices of lemon

Place the apples in a saucepan, pour the apple juice over and tuck the lemon slices down the side of the apples. Cover and bring the mixture to the boil, then reduce the heat and simmer the apples for 15–20 minutes, depending upon the type of apples you are using. Remove the lemon slices if not using the apples at once, allow them to cool, then place them in a covered container and store in the refrigerator for up to 1 week.
*Serves 4*

**Sugar-Free Stewing**
There is generally no need to add sugar to stewed fruit. Instead, I prefer to cook fruit in pure fruit juice which adds more flavour to the fruit than merely sweetening it.

# Poached Peaches

*This is a simply prepared yet delectable dish based on fresh new season's peaches. Serve these on their own or with plain yoghurt, or for special occasions accompany with Amaretto Cream (page 181) or Amaretto and Honey Cream Ice Cream (page 322).*

3 cups (750 mL/24 fl oz) peach *or* apricot nectar
1 cup (250 mL/8 fl oz) sweet white wine
1 vanilla bean, slit open
6 small to medium-sized peaches
peach leaves to decorate

Place the peach (or apricot) nectar in a large saucepan with the white wine and vanilla bean. Bring the mixture to the boil slowly, then reduce the heat to a simmer and cook for 5 minutes with the lid on the pan. Remove the vanilla bean and store it for later use.

Place the peaches in the fruit juice mixture and bring to the boil. Reduce the heat and poach the peaches over a gentle heat until they are just tender. The length of cooking time will depend on the type and ripeness of the peaches, but usually 10 minutes is all that is needed. Set the peaches aside to cool, then carefully remove their skins. Serve at once, or allow to cool in the poaching liquid before chilling in the refrigerator. Arrange the peaches on serving plates and just before serving, spoon some of the poaching liquid over and decorate with peach leaves.
*Serves 6*

# Poached Loquats

*Loquats, with their crisp sweet flesh, are delicious peeled and eaten fresh or poached in flavoured syrups. In this simple yet superb dish they are steeped in a spiked orange syrup. Serve simply with a generous spoonful of yoghurt or whipping (double) cream.*

2 cups (500 mL/16 fl oz) pure orange juice
1–2 tablespoons honey
500 g (1 lb) loquats, washed and trimmed
3 strips orange zest *or* 2 tablespoons Orange Liqueur (page 329)

Place the orange juice and honey in a saucepan and bring the mixture to the boil. Add the loquats, reduce the heat and cook them very gently in the syrup for 5–10 minutes, depending on their ripeness. Carefully spoon the loquats into a serving bowl. Add the orange zest (or liqueur) to the syrup and bring it to the boil. Simmer the syrup, uncovered, for 10 minutes to reduce it. Remove the orange zest and spoon the syrup over the loquats. Cover and chill them for 1 hour before serving.
*Serves 4–6*

# Poached Plums

2 cups (500 mL/16 fl oz) pure dark grape juice
1 tablespoon honey
4 star anise
500 g (1 lb) blood plums

Place the grape juice, honey and star anise in a saucepan and bring the mixture to the boil. Add the plums and cook them gently until they are tender, about 12–15 minutes, depending upon the ripeness of the fruit. Remove the plums and carefully slide the skins off. Place the plums in a serving dish. Remove the star anise and spoon the liquid over the plums. Serve at once or cover and chill for 1 hour before serving.
*Serves 4–6*

*Left: With their rosy blush and translucent succulent flesh, it's no wonder that Poached Peaches are an old time favourite dessert.*

# Poached Fruit Medley

*This dish offers a blend of colours, tastes and textures with the star fruit adding a touch of the exotic. A light summer dessert perfect for serving with a scoop of vanilla ice cream or yoghurt or, for a special touch, serve it with Almond Nougat Ice Cream (page 321).*

2 cups (500 mL/16 fl oz) pure apple juice
1 tablespoon lemon juice
2 slices lemon
1 tablespoon honey
4 nectarines, halved and pips removed
4 apricots, halved and pips removed
2 star fruit, sliced thickly

Place the apple juice, lemon juice and slices and honey in a saucepan and bring the mixture to the boil. Add the apricots and nectarines and cook the fruit very gently for 5 minutes. Add the star fruit and continue to cook gently for 5 minutes. Remove the saucepan from the heat and allow the fruit to stand in the hot syrup for 10 minutes. Spoon the fruit into a serving dish and return the saucepan to the stove and simmer, uncovered, for 10 minutes to reduce and thicken the syrup. Allow the syrup to cool before pouring over the fruit. Chill the fruit for 1 hour before serving.
*Serves 4*

# Stewed Apricots

500 g (1 lb) apricots, halved and pips removed
1 cup (250 mL/8 fl oz) apricot nectar
2–3 pieces cinnamon stick *or* 2–3 star anise

Place the apricots in a saucepan and tuck the pieces of cinnamon stick (or star anise) underneath. Pour the apricot nectar over, cover and bring the mixture to the boil. Reduce the heat and simmer the apricots for 10–15 minutes, depending upon their size and ripeness. Remove the cinnamon stick (or star anise) before serving.
*Serves 4*

# Stewed Quinces

*The wonderful scent of ripe quinces lures me to buy them as soon as they are in season and the rosy hue of cooked quinces always amazes me. Stewed quinces can be enjoyed on their own or combined with their seasonal mates—apples and pears. I like to take the edge off the tartness of quinces by adding honey.*

3 cups (750 mL/24 fl oz) apple juice
4 quinces, peeled, cored and sliced
2–3 tablespoons honey
1 cinnamon stick

Place the apple juice in a medium sized saucepan and as soon as the quinces have been peeled and sliced, submerge them in the juice to help prevent them from discolouring. Add the honey and cinnamon stick, cover the saucepan and bring the mixture to the boil. Reduce the heat and simmer the quinces until they are tender, about 30–35 minutes. Remove the cinnamon stick and if not using at once, store the quinces in a covered container in the refrigerator for up to a week.
*Serves 4*

# Stewed Dried Apricots

*Stewed dried apricots are particularly good for whisking into yoghurt because they are so rich and thick.*

250 g (8 oz) dried apricots
2 cups (500 mL/16 fl oz) apricot nectar
2–3 pieces cinnamon stick

Place the apricots and apricot nectar in a bowl and soak for 1 hour (or overnight). Place the apricots mixture and cinnamon stick in a medium sized saucepan, cover and bring the mixture to the boil. Cook gently for 20–25 minutes. Remove the cinnamon stick before serving.
*Serves 4*

# Dried Fruit Compôte

*This is a delicious winter dish, without added sugar, the sweetness being derived from the dried fruit and fruit juice. Serve with a dollop of Greek Yoghurt (page 273) and a scattering of roasted almonds or hazelnuts.*

125 g (4 oz) dried apricots
125 g (4 oz) dried figs
125 g (4 oz) prunes
2 cups (500 mL/16 fl oz) pure apple juice
1 cinnamon stick

Place the fruit in a bowl and cover with the fruit juice. Allow to stand for several hours or overnight if possible. Place the fruit and the juice into a saucepan with the cinnamon stick. Cover the saucepan and bring the juice to the boil, then reduce the heat and cook the fruit gently until it is tender, about 15 minutes. Remove the cinnamon stick and serve.
*Serves 6*

# Stewed Dates

*Use as a filling for phyllo rolls, tarts or for topping cakes.*

250 g (8 oz) pitted dates, chopped
1 cup (250 mL/8 fl oz) fruit juice
1 teaspoon ground cinnamon
1 tablespoon lemon juice

Place all the ingredients in a saucepan and bring the mixture to the boil, stirring occasionally. Reduce the heat and simmer the mixture until the dates become pulpy. Use as it is or blend until smooth.
*Makes 2 cups (500 mL/16 fl oz)*

# Pears in Red Wine

*It really is no wonder that this dish is so popular. It is simply prepared and yet has a glorious flavour all of its own. Pears are perfect for poaching, readily absorbing the flavours and colour of the poaching syrup. Serve the pears in attractive glass bowls with a little of the syrup spooned over. I enjoy a dollop of Yoghurt Cheese (page 271) or light sour cream alongside because it provides a wonderful contrast in flavour, colour and texture.*

3 cups (750 mL/24 fl oz) red wine
2 tablespoons soft brown sugar
1–2 tablespoons honey
½ lemon, sliced
1 cinnamon stick
8 pears, peeled, stalks left on

Place the wine, sugar, honey, lemon and cinnamon stick in a saucepan and bring the mixture to the boil, stirring. Reduce the heat and simmer, without stirring, for 10 minutes. Add the pears and cook them gently until they become tender, about 15–20 minutes. Remove the cinnamon stick and lemon slices before serving.
*Serves 4*

**Peaches Too**
Try this recipe using peaches. I have great success using small clingstone peaches which retain their shape well. Experiment with different spices too, like whole cloves or star anise instead of the cinnamon stick.

# Mixed Berry Brioche

4 brioche
250 g (8 oz) cream cheese
½ cup (125 mL/4 fl oz) fruit juice
2 teaspoons honey *or* 1–2 tablespoons Strawberry
   Liqueur (page 328)
375g (12 oz) berries such as raspberries,
   blueberries and strawberries
fine slivers of orange zest to decorate

Using a small sharp serrated knife, slice the brioche open and pull out the centres leaving 6mm (¼ in.) thick crusts. Place the cheese in a piping (pastry) bag and pipe it into the brioche. Place the juice and honey (or liqueur) in a small bowl and using a small wire whisk or fork, combine them thoroughly. Place the berries in a bowl and pour the sauce over. Fold the berries carefully through the sauce to coat them completely. Pile the berries into the brioche and spoon a little of the juice over. Serve at once.
*Serves 4*

# Rhubarb Fool

*This is a delightful partnership of sweet and saucy rhubarb and tangy Yoghurt Cheese (page 271) topped with raspberries and a swirl of cream.*

500 g (1 lb) Yoghurt Cheese (page 271)
2 cups Stewed Rhubarb (page 161)
1 tablespoon honey
125 g (4 oz) raspberries
whipping (double) cream or Lemon Whip
   (page 168)

Using a wooden spoon, soften the cheese and stir in the rhubarb. Beat the mixture until smooth, pour it into individual serving glasses and place in the refrigerator to chill. Just before serving, top the mixture with the fresh raspberries. Use a piping (pastry) bag with a fluted nozzle (tube) to pipe a swirl of cream or lemon whip on top.
*Serves 4*

# Raspberry and Coconut Slice

*Rich and fruity, this is heavenly topped with whipping (double) cream or thick yoghurt and surrounded with fresh berries. Serve hot, warm or cold.*

1 cup (155 g/5 oz) quick-cooking oats
1 cup (125 g/4 oz) wholemeal (whole-wheat)
   self-raising flour
½ cup (125 g/4 oz) sugar
1 egg, beaten
4 tablespoons coconut cream (page 279)
few drops pure vanilla essence (extract)
½ cup (4 oz) wholemeal (whole-wheat) plain
   (all-purpose) flour
⅔ cup (60 g/2 oz) desiccated coconut
2 tablespoons sugar
additional 2 tablespoons coconut cream
2 punnets (cartons) raspberries
1–2 tablespoons honey

To prepare the crust, combine the oats, self-raising flour, sugar, egg, coconut cream and vanilla and press down onto the bottom of a prepared springform pan (deep cake pan with removable base). Bake in a moderate oven (180°C/350°F) for 20 minutes. To make the crumble topping, combine the plain flour, coconut, sugar and coconut cream. Combine the raspberries with the honey and spread them evenly over the crust. Sprinkle the crumble topping over. Bake in a hot oven (200°C/400°F) for 10 minutes.
*Serves 6*

*Right: Mixed Berry Brioche. Ready-made breads and pastries make whipping up stunning fruit desserts seem like child's play.*

# Apricot Yoghurt Slice

*Serve as it is or top with poached apricot halves and slices of kiwi fruit for an attractive colour contrast.*

1 cup (125 g/4 oz) wholemeal (whole-wheat) plain (all-purpose) flour

⅔ cup (60 g/2 oz) desiccated coconut

2 tablespoons soft brown sugar

60 g (2 oz) butter, melted

435 g (14 oz) Yoghurt Cheese (page 271)

1 cup (250 mL/8 fl oz) plain yoghurt

1 cup (125 g/4 oz) chopped dried apricots

3 tablespoons caster (superfine) sugar *or* 3 tablespoons honey

1 teaspoon vanilla essence (extract)

2 tablespoons plain (all-purpose) flour

Combine the self-raising flour, coconut and brown sugar and pour the melted butter over. Combine well and press onto the bottom of a prepared 20 cm (8 in.) square pan. Bake in a hot oven (200°C/400°F) for 10 minutes. Meanwhile, mix or blend all the remaining ingredients together until smooth. Pour filling on top of prepared crust. Bake in a hot oven (200°C/400°F) for 10 minutes then reduce the oven heat to 160°C/325°F and bake for a further 30 minutes. Turn the oven off and allow the slice to cool in the oven. When cool, place in the refrigerator to chill before slicing.

*Makes 12 slices*

# Lemon Whip

*It's great fun to place this mixture in a piping (pastry) bag with a fluted nozzle (tube). You can pipe swirls on top of desserts, cakes, slices and pancakes. In fact it can be used wherever you would normally use sweet whipping (double) cream.*

250 g (8 oz) Yoghurt Cheese (page 271) ricotta *or* cheese *or* cream cheese

1 teaspoon finely grated lemon rind

1 tablespoon honey

Using a food processor, blend all the ingredients together until smooth.

*Makes about 1 cup (250 mL/8 fl oz)*

# Yoghurt and Sultana Slice

*Serve as it is or decorate with swirls of Lemon Whip or whipping (double) cream and fresh berries for special occasions.*

¾ cup (125 g/4 oz) wholemeal (whole-wheat) self-raising flour

½ cup (60 g/2 oz) ground almonds (almond meal)

2 tablespoons soft brown sugar

1 teaspoon mixed spice*

60 g (2 oz) butter melted

2 tablespoons oil

435 g (14 oz) Yoghurt Cheese (page 271)

½ cup (125 g/4 oz) caster (superfine) sugar

½ cup (125 mL/4 fl oz) plain yoghurt

2 tablespoons plain (all-purpose) flour

½ cup (90 g/3 oz) sultanas (golden raisins)

2 cups Stewed Apples (page 161), drained

rind and juice of 1 lemon

To prepare the crust, mix the flour, almonds, brown sugar and mixed spice then add the butter and oil. Mix until well combined, then press onto the bottom of a prepared 20 cm (8 in.) cake pan. Bake in a hot oven (200°C/400°F) for 10 minutes. Meanwhile, mix or blend the cheese, sugar, yoghurt and flour together until smooth. Scatter the sultanas over the prepared crust and arrange the stewed apple on top. Spread the filling over the apples. Bake in a hot oven (200°C/400°F) for 10 minutes then reduce the oven heat to 150°C/300°F and bake for a further 40 minutes. Turn the oven off and allow the slice to cool in the oven. Chill before slicing and decorating.

*Makes 12 slices*

*Please refer to the mixed spice recipe in our Cook's Notes, page 8.

# Quick Mango Mousse

*The mango causes the yoghurt to set magically like a mousse. A quick no-fuss dessert perfect for celebrating mango season. Delicious topped with sliced bananas which have been tossed in fresh passion fruit pulp.*

2 cups (500 mL/16 fl oz) yoghurt
2 large *or* 3 small mangoes, peeled and sliced
1 tablespoon honey
1 tablespoon lemon juice

Using a food processor, blend the yoghurt, mango, honey and lemon juice until smooth. Place the mousse in individual serving glasses and chill thoroughly before serving.
*Serves 4*

# Quick Chocolate Mousse

*Serve with Vanilla Whip (page 181) and chopped roasted hazelnuts or almonds.*

90 g (3 oz) dark (semi-sweet) compound cooking chocolate
2 cups (500 mL/16 fl oz) milk
1 teaspoon vanilla essence (extract)
1 rounded teaspoon pure agar agar powder (page 341)
250 g (8 oz) cream cheese

Break the chocolate into pieces and place in a saucepan with the milk and vanilla. Sprinkle the agar agar powder over the top and bring the mixture to the boil, stirring constantly. Reduce the heat and simmer the mixture for 1 minute then remove from the stove and set aside until the steam stops rising from the surface. Place the cream cheese in a bowl and soften it using a wooden spoon. Gradually add the chocolate mixture and beat until well combined. Pour the mousse into individual glasses immediately and chill thoroughly before serving.
*Serves 6*

# Strawberry Mousse

*Serve on a bed of Fresh Berry Coulis (page 178) with a dollop of whipping (double) cream or yoghurt. A few strawberry leaves at the side look great too. Agar agar jells at room temperature so it is important to have the moulds ready before you start.*

1 punnet (carton) strawberries, washed, hulled
3 tablespoons orange juice
3 tablespoons caster (superfine) sugar
250 g (8 oz) Yoghurt Cheese (page 271) *or* cream cheese
2 tablespoons honey
1 cup (250 mL/8 fl oz) milk
1 teaspoon pure agar agar powder (page 341)

Place the strawberries, orange juice, caster sugar and Yoghurt Cheese (or cream cheese) in a food processor and blend the mixture until smooth. Place the honey, milk and agar agar powder in a small saucepan and bring the mixture to the boil, stirring constantly. Reduce the heat and continue to cook for 1 minute. Remove from the heat. With the food processor running, add the agar agar mixture and blend for 30 seconds. Pour the combined mixture quickly but carefully into 6 dariole moulds that have been rinsed with water (this prevents the mixture from sticking to the moulds). Chill the mousses well before serving.
*Serves 6*

### Alternative Ingredients
For a non-dairy alternative, use tofu instead of cream cheese and soy milk instead of cow's milk.

# Basic Crêpes

*Crêpes can be used to make many wonderful desserts.*

1 cup (125 g/4 oz) wholemeal (whole-wheat) plain
  (all-purpose) flour
1 egg
1¼ cups (310 mL/10 fl oz) milk
2 teaspoons oil for cooking

Using a food processor, blend the flour, egg
and milk for 1 minute. Allow to stand for
10–15 minutes before cooking, if possible, as this
will soften the starch grains in the flour and
produce lighter crisper crêpes. Heat a frying pan,
skillet or crêpe pan with a little of the oil until
quite hot. Stir the batter briskly and cook ¼
cupfuls at a time, rotating the pan to spread the
crêpes out thinly as you add the batter. Cook
until the first side is a light golden brown, about
1 minute, then flip the crêpe over and cook for
10 seconds only. Continue to cook the crêpes
until all the batter is used, brushing the pan with
oil as required. Stack the crêpes on a cake rack
topped with a clean dry tea towel.
*Makes 8*

# Basic Eggless Crêpes

*In this recipe, it is the besan flour that binds the
crêpe mixture together, the task usually performed
by eggs in pancake and crêpe batters. These
pancakes are easy to prepare and delicious to eat.
Soy milk can be used if you wish, making this a
dairy-free recipe as well.*

1 cup (125 g/4 oz) wholemeal (whole-wheat) plain
  (all-purpose) flour
2 tablespoons besan flour (page 341)
1 tablespoon oil
1½ cups (375 mL/12 fl oz) milk
additional 2 teaspoons oil for cooking

Using a food processor, blend the flours, oil and
milk for 1 minute. Allow the mixture to stand for
5–10 minutes to thicken. Cook as for Basic
Crêpes.
*Makes 8*

# Berry Crêpes

*This simply prepared dish of golden brown crêpes
encasing soft fresh cheese and topped with ripe red
berries and a luscious sauce makes a superb
summer dessert.*

375 g (12 oz) Yoghurt Cheese (page 271) *or* cream
  cheese, softened
8 crêpes
250 g (8 oz) berries such as raspberries,
  strawberries *or* loganberries
1 quantity Spiked Strawberry Sauce (page 180)

Spread the Yoghurt Cheese (or cream cheese)
over each crêpe and fold each into a neat fan
shape. Arrange 2 crêpes on each serving plate
and pile the berries on top. Spoon the sauce over
and serve at once.
*Serves 4*

# Hot Apple and Raisin Crêpes

*The sauce transforms these crêpes into a wonderful
indulgence for a special meal. For everyday menus,
simply replace this rich sauce with a light fruity
sauce such as Fresh Berry Coulis (page 178).*

1 quantity Stewed Apples (page 161), drained
8 crêpes
1 quantity Rum and Raisin Sauce (page 177)

Arrange a large spoonful of stewed apples at one
end of each crêpe. Fold the crêpes over the apple,
forming a package. Place the crêpes, ends tucked
under, on a prepared baking sheet. Cover with
aluminium foil and heat the crêpes in a moderate
oven (180°C/350°F) for 15 minutes.
Alternatively, cover and heat the crêpes in a
microwave oven on high for 5 minutes. Heat the
sauce before spooning it over the crêpes. Serve
immediately.
*Serves 4*

*Right: Crêpes. A favourite dish in all seasons,
crêpes make an especially luscious summer dessert
when partnered by fresh berries as in Berry Crêpes.*

# Peach and Passion Fruit Crumble

⅔ cup (60 g/2 oz) desiccated coconut
½ cup (60 g/2 oz) plain (all-purpose) flour
1 cup (90 g/3 oz) untoasted muesli
3 tablespoons soft brown sugar
2 tablespoons butter *or* oil
1 teaspoon vanilla essence (extract)
4 peaches, sliced
½ cup (125 mL/4 fl oz) passion fruit pulp

Prepare the crumble topping by placing the coconut, flour, muesli and sugar in a food processor. While the machine is operating, add the butter (or oil) and vanilla essence down the feeder tube. Place the peaches in one ovenproof dish or 6 moulds and spoon the passion fruit pulp over. Top with the crumble and bake in a moderate oven (180°C/350°F) for 20–25 minutes.
*Serves 6*

# Apricot and Almond Crumble

½ cup (60 g/2 oz) almonds
½ cup (60 g/2 oz) plain (all-purpose) flour
1 cup (90 g/3 oz) untoasted muesli
2 teaspoons ground cinnamon
½ cup (90 g/3 oz) soft brown sugar
2 tablespoons butter *or* oil
1 teaspoon vanilla essence (extract)
1 quantity Stewed Apricots (page 164)
4 tablespoons slivered almonds

Prepare the crumble topping by placing the almonds, flour, muesli, cinnamon and sugar in a food processor and processing until a coarse meal is produced. While the machine is operating, add the butter (or oil) and vanilla essence down the feeder tube. Combine the apricots and slivered almonds and place in one ovenproof dish or 6 moulds. Top with the crumble and bake in a moderate oven (180°C/350°F) for 20–25 minutes.
*Serves 6*

# Summer Fruit Crumble

½ cup (60 g/2 oz) almonds *or* hazelnuts
½ cup (60 g/2 oz) plain (all-purpose) flour
1 cup (90 g/3 oz) untoasted muesli
3 tablespoons soft brown sugar
2 tablespoons butter *or* oil
1 teaspoon vanilla essence (extract)
2 peaches, peeled and sliced
3 nectarines, sliced
3 apricots, sliced
2 bananas, peeled and sliced
1 cup (250 mL/8 fl oz) Fresh Berry Coulis (page 178)

Prepare the crumble topping by placing the almonds (or hazelnuts), flour, muesli and sugar in a food processor. While the machine is operating, add the butter (or oil) and vanilla essence down the feeder tube. Combine all the fruits and place in one ovenproof dish or 6 moulds. Drizzle the Fresh Berry Coulis over and sprinkle the crumble mixture over the top. Bake in a moderate oven (180°C/350°F) for 20–25 minutes.
*Serves 6*

# Apricot Whip

*Enjoy this delicious whip all year round.*

2 tablespoons water *or* sweet white wine
1 tablespoon honey
60 g (2 oz) dried apricots, chopped finely
250 g (8 oz) Yoghurt Cheese (page 271) *or* ricotta cheese

Place the water (or wine) and honey in a small saucepan and bring to the boil. Place the apricots in a small bowl and pour the honey mixture over. Cover and stand for 15 minutes, then chill completely. Using a blender, blend the Yoghurt Cheese (or ricotta cheese) until smooth. Add the apricot mixture and continue to blend for 30 seconds.
*Makes 1 cup (250 mL/8 fl oz)*

# Basic Waffles

*If you do not have a waffle maker, cook the mixture as for Basic Pancakes (page 266). It is worthwhile making a double quantity of this recipe as waffles freeze well. This way you will have a special dessert ready in minutes—frozen waffles can be thawed in the microwave oven, and toasted under a hot grill (broiler) for 30 seconds each side.*

1½ cups (185 g/6 oz) self-raising flour
2 eggs, separated
2 tablespoons sugar *or* 1 tablespoon honey
30 g (1 oz) butter, melted
1 cup (250 mL/8 fl oz) milk

Blend all the ingredients (except for the egg whites) together until smooth. Whisk the egg whites until they form soft peaks, then carefully fold them into the batter. Preheat the waffle iron according to the manufacturer's instructions. Brush both the surfaces with a little melted butter and cook ½ cupfuls of the batter at a time until the waffles are golden brown (about 3–5 minutes). Place the cooked waffles on a clean dry tea towel.
*Makes 6*

# Basic Eggless Waffles

1 cup (250 mL/8 fl oz) soy milk
125 g (4 oz) silken tofu
1 tablespoon oil
1½ cups (185 g/6 oz) self-raising flour
¼ teaspoon bicarbonate of soda (baking soda)
3 tablespoons caster (superfine) sugar
1 teaspoon vanilla essence (extract)

Blend all the ingredients together until smooth. Cook as for Basic Waffles.
*Makes 6*

# Apple and Raisin Waffles

*Serve piping hot straight from the waffle iron as a snack or top with Orange and Walnut Sauce (page 180) or Rum and Raisin Sauce (page 177) and ice cream for a heart-warming dessert.*

125 g (4 oz) tofu, mashed
1 tablespoon oil
2 tablespoons sugar *or* 1 tablespoon honey
1 cup (250 mL/8 fl oz) soy milk
1 apple, grated
⅓ cup (60 g/2 oz) raisins, chopped
1½ cups (185 g/6 oz) self-raising flour
1 teaspoon mixed spice*

Beat the tofu, oil, sugar (or honey) and milk together and stir in the apple and raisins. Sift the flour and spice and fold into the mixture. Cook as for Basic Waffles.
*Makes 6*

# Hazelnut Waffles

*Serve with a scoop of Yoghurt Cheese (page 271) and fresh or lightly poached fruit.*

⅔ cup (90 g/3 oz) hazelnuts
125 g (4 oz) tofu, mashed
1 cup (250 mL/8 fl oz) soy milk
2 tablespoons honey
1 teaspoon vanilla essence (extract)
¼ teaspoon bicarbonate of soda (baking soda)
1½ cups (185 g/6 oz) self-raising flour
1 teaspoon mixed spice*

Grind the hazelnuts to a fine meal using a food processor. Add the tofu, soy milk, honey and vanilla and blend all the ingredients together until smooth. Sift dry ingredients together, fold into the mixture. Cook as for Basic Waffles.
*Makes 6*

*Please refer to the mixed spice recipe in our Cook's Notes, page 8.

# Avocado Fruit Salad

*The rich creamy texture of avocado marries well with fresh fruit—after all it is a fruit although it is mostly served as a vegetable. Serve this colourful variety of fruits with a scoop of fruit sorbet for a refreshing dessert.*

1 medium avocado, peeled and diced
juice of 1 lime *or* lemon
½ ripe pineapple, peeled and diced
2 peaches, washed, pips removed and cut into
   large dice
1 punnet (carton) strawberries, washed and
   hulled

Place the avocado in a bowl and drizzle with the lime (or lemon) juice. Carefully combine the avocado with the remaining ingredients and chill before placing in individual serving glasses.
*Serves 4*

# Spiked Berry Cocktail

*Based on ripe summer berries at their peak, this cocktail is a wonderful infusion of flavours and looks stunning served in a glass serving bowl. Serve accompanied by a bowl of whipping (double) cream.*

1½ cups (405 mL/13 fl oz) apple juice
1 vanilla bean, slit in half
2 tablespoons white rum *or* kirsch *or* 1 teaspoon
   vanilla essence (extract)
1 punnet (carton) blackberries
1 punnet (carton) blueberries (bilberries)
1 punnet (carton) raspberries

Place the apple juice, vanilla bean, rum (or kirsch or vanilla) in a small saucepan. Bring the mixture to the boil, then reduce the heat and simmer for 5 minutes. Allow the syrup to cool then remove the vanilla bean. Arrange the berries in layers in a serving bowl or individual serving bowls and spoon the syrup over.
*Serves 6*

# Fig and Almond Yoghurt Parfait

*Scented honey (page 310) adds a special touch to this simply delicious dessert which can be whipped up in minutes all year round. When, however, fresh figs are at their best in the summer months, they are well worth using.*

2 cups (500 mL/16 oz) plain yoghurt
12 dried figs, sliced
4–6 tablespoons almonds, roasted (page 17)
2 tablespoons honey

Place the yoghurt, figs and almonds in consecutive layers in parfait glasses, finishing with a layer of almonds. Just before serving, drizzle the honey over.
*Serves 4*

# Passion Fruit Parfait

*The shape of sliced star fruit makes it a wonderful addition to any dessert, but here it is laced with the flavour of ripe passion fruit and the lemon and honey of the Lemon Whip.*

2 cups (500 mL/16 fl oz) plain yoghurt
½ cup (125 mL/ 4 fl oz) passion fruit pulp
   combined with 1–2 tablespoons honey
1 quantity Lemon Whip (page 168)
1 star fruit, sliced

Place the yoghurt in 4 parfait glasses and swirl the passion fruit pulp through. Pipe the Lemon Whip on top and stand the star fruit slices around the whip.
*Serves 4*

*Left: Avocado Fruit Salad. Radiating with summer sunshine, the creamy flesh of the avocado provides a built-in dressing for this salad.*

# Fruit Cocktail

1 large mango, peeled, pip removed, sliced
1 punnet (carton) strawberries, hulled and halved
4 tablespoons passion fruit pulp
½ honeydew melon, sliced, peeled and cut into
   chunks
1 quantity Lemon Whip (page 168)
strawberry leaves *or* mint sprigs

Place the mango, strawberries, passion fruit
pulp and honeydew in a bowl and combine
carefully. Cover and chill for 1 hour before
spooning into individual serving glasses. Place
the Lemon Whip in a piping (pastry) bag and
pipe a swirl of the mixture on top of each serve
and decorate with the strawberry (or mint)
leaves.
*Serves 4*

# Summer Pears

250 g (8 oz) Yoghurt Cheese (page 271) *or* cream
   cheese
1 teaspoon finely grated lemon rind
2 teaspoons honey
125 g (4 oz) cherries, pitted and chopped roughly
2 medium-sized crisp pears
juice of ½ lemon
2 tablespoons flaked (sliced) almonds
additional 4 small bunches cherries, stalks
   attached

Combine the Yoghurt Cheese (or cream cheese)
with the lemon rind and honey, then fold in the
cherries. Cut the pears in half lengthways and
remove the cores using a metal teaspoon. Brush
the cut surfaces with lemon juice to prevent
them from discolouring. Fill the cavities with the
cheese and cherry mixture and sprinkle with the
flaked almonds. Serve on individual plates with
the additional cherries on the side.
*Serves 4*

# Tropical Fruit Cocktail

*Pawpaw and ginger harmonise beautifully to make
this delectable dessert. Add a hint of romance by
setting a fragrant blossom alongside.*

1 large pawpaw (papaya)
1 quantity Ginger Sauce (below)
edible blossoms such as frangipani *or* rose petals

Cut the pawpaw in half and scoop out the pips
using a spoon. Slice and peel the fruit carefully to
avoid bruising it, then place it in a bowl and
drizzle with the chilled Ginger Sauce. Carefully
combine all the ingredients. Cover and chill
thoroughly. Just before serving, place the fruit in
individual serving glasses, spoon the sauce over
and decorate with the blossoms.
*Serves 4–6*

# Ginger Sauce

*This sauce is equally wonderful spooned over fresh
or poached peaches, pears or figs or any ripe
tropical fruit.*

3 tablespoons chopped preserved ginger
¼ teaspoon ground ginger
1 cup (250 mL/8 fl oz) apple juice
2–3 teaspoons honey

Place all the ingredients in a saucepan and bring
to the boil, stirring constantly. Reduce the heat
and cook gently, stirring occasionally, for
10 minutes. Serve at once if accompanying hot
fruit desserts or puddings or chill thoroughly
before serving over fresh fruit.
*Makes about 1 cup (250 mL/8 fl oz)*

# Sticky Date Puddings

1½ cups (225 g/7 oz) pitted chopped dates
1 cup (250 mL/8 fl oz) apple juice
1 teaspoon ground cinnamon
2 teaspoons mixed spice*
½ teaspoon bicarbonate of soda (baking soda)
1 cup (90 g/3 oz) ground almonds (almond meal)
1 cup (125 g/4 oz) wholemeal (whole-wheat)
  self-raising flour

Place the dates, apple juice, cinnamon and mixed spice in a small saucepan and bring the mixture to the boil, stirring occasionally. Remove from the heat and stir in the soda. Allow to cool to lukewarm and stir in the ground almonds and the flour. Place the mixture in prepared dariole moulds. Bake in a moderate oven (180°C/350° F) for 25 minutes.
*Makes 6*

# Rum and Raisin Sauce

*A delicious sauce to add a touch of indulgence to pancakes, waffles, ice cream, puddings or poached fruit.*

30 g (1 oz) butter
60 g (2 oz) soft brown sugar
2 tablespoons honey
½ cup (90 g/3 oz) raisons
3 tablespoons flaked (sliced) almonds
1–2 tablespoons white rum
½ cup (125 mL/4 fl oz) apple juice

Place all the ingredients in a saucepan and bring to the boil, stirring constantly. Reduce the heat and cook gently, stirring occasionally, for 10 minutes.
*Makes about 1 cup (250 mL/8 fl oz)*

*Please refer to the mixed spice recipe in our Cook's Notes, page 8.

# Pear and Ginger Puddings

2 medium pears, peeled, diced
2 tablespoons preserved ginger, diced
2 tablespoons syrup from preserved ginger
½ teaspoon bicarbonate of soda (baking soda)
1 tablespoon hot water
2 eggs, separated
1 cup (125 g/4 oz) self-raising flour
1 teaspoon mixed spice*

Combine the pears, ginger and syrup. Dissolve the soda in the hot water and add to the pear mixture. Beat the egg yolks and add to the pear mixture. Beat the egg whites until they form soft peaks and set aside. Sift the flour and spice and fold into the pear mixture with the egg whites. Place the mixture into prepared dariole moulds or muffin pans. Bake in a moderate oven (180°C/350°F) for 20 minutes.
*Makes 6*

# Rum and Raisin Puddings

1 cup (155 g/5 oz) raisins
3 tablespoons soft brown sugar
3 tablespoons white rum
½ cup (60 g/2 oz) ground almonds (almond meal)
2 eggs
½ cup (125 mL/4 fl oz) plain yoghurt
1 cup (125 g/4 oz) wholemeal (whole-wheat)
  self-raising flour
2 teaspoons mixed spice*

Place the raisins in a container with a lid and sprinkle with the sugar. Pour the rum over and cover. Set aside for several hours if possible. Combine the almonds, eggs and yoghurt and fold in the flour and spice. Add the rum and raisin mixture and mix well. Place the mixture into prepared dariole moulds. Cover with aluminium foil that has been brushed with a little oil. Steam for 25–30 minutes.
*Serves 6*

# Instant Pawpaw Mousse

*The sherbet undertones of this mousse provide an harmonious backdrop for the distinctive flavour of this luscious tropical fruit.*

2 cups (500 mL/16 fl oz) Greek Yoghurt
   (page 273)
½ large ripe pawpaw (papaya), peeled, pips
   removed and cut into chunks
1 tablespoon honey
½ cup (125 mL/4 fl oz) freshly squeezed orange
   juice
2 navel oranges, peeled and sliced
pulp of 4 passion fruit

Using a food processor, blend the yoghurt, pawpaw, honey and orange juice until smooth. Immediately place the mixture in individual serving glasses and chill thoroughly before serving topped with the orange slices and passion fruit.
*Serves 4*

# Mango and Strawberry Parfait

*Serve with whipping (double) cream or yoghurt and, for special occasions, accompany with freshly toasted waffles.*

1 quantity Quick Mango Mousse (page 169)
1 punnet (carton) strawberries, hulled and sliced
1 mango, peeled, pip removed and sliced
1 quantity Fresh Berry Coulis using strawberries
   *or* 1 quantity Spiked Strawberry Sauce
   (page 180)
2 kiwi fruit, peeled and sliced

Spoon consecutive layers of the Mango Mousse, strawberries, mango and Strawberry Coulis (or Spiked Strawberry Sauce) into parfait glasses. Chill thoroughly. Just before serving, top with the kiwi fruit.
*Serves 4*

*Right: Strawberry Yoghurt Parfait serves both as a special summer breakfast and a light and refreshing dessert.*

# Strawberry Yoghurt Parfaits

*Serve this eye-catching dessert on its own or, for special occasions, team up with freshly toasted Hazelnut Waffles (page 173), cut into 'wafflettes'.*

1 quantity Strawberry Yoghurt (page 273)
1 banana, sliced on the diagonal
2 kiwi fruit, peeled and sliced
1 punnet (carton) strawberries, hulls removed
1 tablespoon honey
juice of ½ lemon
2 cups (500 mL/16 fl oz) Greek Yoghurt
   (page 273)
4 strawberries, hulls left on

Spoon the strawberry yoghurt into 4 parfait glasses. Place the banana, kiwi fruit and strawberries in a bowl, sprinkle with the lemon juice and drizzle the honey over. Carefully fold the lemon and honey through the fruit. Arrange layers of the strawberry mixture and Greek Yoghurt on top of the strawberry yoghurt, finishing with a layer of strawberries. Top with a whole strawberry. Serve at once.
*Serves 4*

# Fresh Berry Coulis

*The sky's the limit with a beautiful sauce like this— but why not begin with drizzling it over yoghurt or ice cream, or even on fresh strawberries to double up on the luscious flavour.*

250 g (8 oz) berries such as strawberries,
   raspberries *or* blackberries, chopped
2 tablespoons caster (superfine) sugar *or*
   1 tablespoon honey
2 tablespoons lemon *or* lime juice

Using a food processor, purée the berries and combine with the sugar (or honey) and lemon (or lime) juice. Press the mixture through a sieve to remove the pips and pulp and produce a smooth sauce.
*Makes about 1½ cups (375 mL/12 fl oz)*

# Spiked Strawberry Sauce

1 punnet (carton) berries such as strawberries,
   raspberries *or* blackberries, chopped
2 tablespoons sugar *or* 1 tablespoon honey
2 tablespoon lemon *or* lime juice
1–2 tablespoons Strawberry Liqueur (page 328) *or*
   kirsch *or* Cointreau

If using strawberries, remove the hulls first.
Using a food processor, purée the berries and
combine with the sugar (or honey), lemon (or
lime) juice and liqueur.
*Makes about 1½ cups (375 mL/12 fl oz)*

# Passion Fruit and Mango Sauce

½ mango, peeled, pip removed and sliced
1 cup (250 mL/8 fl oz) fresh *or* unsweetened
   canned pineapple juice
½ cup (125 mL/4 fl oz) passion fruit pulp

Using a blender, purée the mango, then add the
pineapple juice and blend until smooth. Transfer
the sauce to a bowl and whisk the passion fruit
pulp through.
*Makes about 1½ cups (375 mL/12 fl oz)*

# Mango and Lime Coulis

*A superb combination of flavours, this sauce boasts
the sweet fragrance of ripe mango contrasted with
the unmistakable tang of lime juice.*

1 large ripe mango, peeled, pip removed and
   sliced
2 teaspoons honey (optional)
2 tablespoons lime juice

Using a blender, blend the mango slices until
creamy smooth, adding the honey if you feel the
mango could have been riper. Using a broad
wooden spoon, push the mango purée through a
sieve. Just before serving, whisk in the lime juice.
*Makes about 1 cup (250 mL/8 fl oz)*

# Kiwi Fruit Coulis

*Served alongside strawberry coulis or mango nectar,
this sauce provides a vibrant colour contrast,
transforming a simple dessert of lightly poached or
fresh fruit into a stunning dish.*

3–4 large ripe kiwi fruit, peeled and chopped
2 tablespoons sugar *or* 1 tablespoon honey
2 tablespoons lemon *or* lime juice

Mash the kiwi fruit and combine with the sugar
(or honey). Using a wooden spoon, press the
mixture through a sieve and whisk in the lemon
juice.
*Makes about 1 cup (250 mL/8 fl oz)*

# Orange and Walnut Sauce

*Sauces need not be rich and sinful, although it's
great to have some of these in your repertoire for
special occasions. Serve this glossy sauce warm or
hot.*

1 cup (250 mL/8 fl oz) freshly squeezed orange
   juice
1 cup (90 g/3 oz) walnuts
1–2 tablespoons honey
4 star anise
30 g (1 oz) butter

Place all the ingredients in a saucepan and bring
the mixture to the boil, stirring occasionally.
Reduce the heat and simmer, stirring
occasionally, for 10 minutes. Remove from the
heat and pick out the star anise.
*Makes about 2 cups (500 mL/16 fl oz)*

# Rich Chocolate Sauce

*Use this indulgent sauce to drizzle on top of cakes and ice cream or to surround freshly cooked moist winter puddings.*

60 g (3 oz) dark (semi-sweet) compound cooking chocolate
1–2 tablespoons liqueur *or* 1 teaspoon vanilla essence (extract) and 1½ tablespoons water
3 tablespoons light (single) cream

Break the chocolate into small pieces and place in a small saucepan with the liqueur (or vanilla and water) and bring to the boil. Stir until the chocolate dissolves. Remove from the heat and whisk in the cream.
*Makes about ¾ cup (185 mL/6 fl oz)*

# Vanilla Whip

250 g (8 oz) ricotta cheese *or* tofu, drained
1 teaspoon vanilla essence (extract)
1–2 tablespoons honey

Using a blender, blend the ricotta cheese (or tofu), vanilla and honey until smooth. Use at once or store in a covered container in the refrigerator for 1–2 days.
*Makes 1¼ cups (310 mL/10 fl oz)*

# Raspberry Cream

*This colourful cream is luscious yet it is low in fat due to the use of ricotta cheese or fresh Yoghurt Cheese (page 271) which has been made from nonfat plain yoghurt. Use ricotta cheese to obtain a 'fluffy' texture, or use Tofu or Yoghurt Cheese for a 'creamy' texture. Try it with fresh berries, lightly poached fruit or on top of freshly baked scones (biscuits).*

250 g (8 oz) ricotta cheese *or* tofu, drained, *or* Yoghurt Cheese (page 271)
1 tablespoon honey
125 g (4 oz) raspberries

Place all the ingredients in a food processor and blend for 1 minute. Serve at once or store in a covered container in the refrigerator for 1–2 days.
*Makes about 1½ cups (375 mL/12 fl oz)*

# Amaretto Cream

*This velvety smooth cream makes an especially delicious accompaniment for stone fruit such as peaches, nectarines, plums or apricots.*

225 mL (7 fl oz) light (single) cream
225 mL (7 fl oz) milk
2 tablespoons Amaretto liqueur

Place the cream, milk and Amaretto in a food processor or blender and blend only until the mixture becomes rich and creamy, about 10–20 seconds. Take care not to blend the mixture for too long or the texture of the cream will become buttery.
*Makes 2 cups (500 mL/16 fl oz)*

# Cakes and Cookies

*Here you will find delicious dessert cakes for special occasions and scrumptious cakes and muffins for every day. Many of the cakes are light and moist due to the aerating effect of egg whites; some contain ground nuts such as almonds and hazelnuts to provide moist, rich cakes without lashings of cream or butter. There are some surprises in store too.*

# Rich Chocolate Cake

*Enjoy this special occasion cake drizzled with Real Chocolate Icing (page 192) and accompanied by a bowl of whipping (double) cream and fresh berries.*

¾ cup (60 g/2 oz) almonds
¾ cup (185 g/6 oz) caster (superfine) sugar
½ cup (125 mL/4 fl oz) safflower oil
2 tablespoons coffee liqueur *or* strong brewed
   coffee
4 eggs, separated
½ cup (125 mL/4 fl oz) plain yoghurt
1½ cups (185 g/6 oz) self-raising flour
4 tablespoons cocoa powder
pinch salt

Place the almonds in a food processor and process until a fine meal is produced. Add the castor sugar, oil, liqueur (or coffee), egg yolks and yoghurt and process until well combined. Transfer to a mixing bowl. Sift the flour, cocoa powder and salt and fold into the mixture. Whisk the egg whites until they form soft peaks, then fold them into the cake mixture. Place in a prepared 20 cm (8 in.) cake pan and bake in a moderate oven (180°C/350°F) for 30–40 minutes, or until cooked when tested with a skewer.
*Serves 10–12*

**The Carob Alternative**
For a delicious alternative to chocolate, try using carob (page 341). Simply replace the cocoa powder with an equal amount of carob powder, but because carob powder contains a natural sugar, making it much sweeter than cocoa powder, you will need to reduce the sugar to ½ cup (125 g/4 oz).

*Overleaf: Laced with almonds, and encased in real chocolate icing, Rich Chocolate Cake is an ideal special occasions cake.*

# Chocolate Torte

*This chocolate torte tastes positively sinful. It is anything but free of chocolate, yet is free of both eggs and dairy products—enjoy!*

250 g (8 oz) tofu, drained
3 tablespoons oil
3 tablespoons soft honey
½ cup (90 g/3 oz) brown sugar
½ cup (125 mL/4 fl oz) soy milk
1 teaspoon vanilla essence (extract)
1 cup (125 g/4 oz) wholemeal (whole-wheat)
   self-raising flour
½ cup (60 g/2 oz) white self-raising flour
4 tablespoons cocoa powder
**double quantity Chocolate Cream (below)**
**1 quantity Real Chocolate Icing (page 192)**
**walnut halves *or* strawberries**

Using a food processor or blender, blend the tofu, oil, honey, sugar, milk and vanilla until smooth, then place the mixture in a bowl. Sift the flours and cocoa powder and fold into the mixture, then pour the mixture into a prepared 20 cm (8 in.) cake pan. Sprinkle the top with a little water and bake in a moderate oven (180°C/350°F) for 30 minutes, or until cooked when tested with a skewer. Leave the cake in the pan for 5 minutes then turn it out onto a cake rack. When cold, slice into three layers using a sharp serrated bread knife. Spread the chocolate cream filling on two of the layers. Place the third layer on top and spread the chocolate icing evenly over the top. Decorate with the walnut halves or the strawberries.
*Serves 10–12*

# Chocolate Cream

250 g (8 oz) cream cheese *or* tofu, drained
1 tablespoon honey
1 teaspoon vanilla essence (extract)
2 tablespoons cocoa powder

Using a food processor, blend all the ingredients together until smooth.
*Makes about 1 cup (250 mL/8 fl oz)*

# Quince Upside Down Cake

3 tablespoons slivered almonds
1 quantity Stewed Quinces (page 164), drained well
1 tablespoon soft brown sugar
½ cup (60 g/2 oz) whole almonds
additional ½ cup (90 g/3 oz) soft brown sugar
1½ cups (185 g/6 oz) self-raising flour
1 teaspoon baking powder
1 teaspoon mixed spice*
2 tablespoons oil
½ cup (125 mL/4 fl oz) plain yoghurt
2 eggs, separated

Brush the inside of a 24 cm (10 in.) cake pan with a little melted butter or oil and line the bottom with baking paper. Spread the slivered almonds on the bottom of the pan, arrange the quinces on top and sprinkle with the brown sugar. Place the whole almonds in a food processor and process until a fine meal is produced, then add the additional sugar, flour, baking powder and mixed spice. Combine well, then place the mixture into a bowl. Combine the oil, yoghurt and egg yolks and fold into the dry ingredients. Whisk the egg whites until they form soft peaks, then carefully fold them into the mixture. Spread the mixture evenly over the quinces, then bake in a moderate oven (180°C/350°F) for 30 minutes, or until cooked when tested with a skewer. Leave the cake in the pan for 3–5 minutes, then turn out onto a cake rack.
*Serves 12*

# Hazelnut Coffee Cake

*Serve drizzled with Real Chocolate Icing (page 192) and sprinkled with chopped and whole hazelnuts. A bowl of whipping (double) cream adds the final, fatal touch. Looks great cooked in a fluted ring pan if you have one.*

¾ cup (90 g/3 oz) hazelnuts
¾ cup (125 g/4 oz) soft brown sugar
½ cup (125 mL/4 fl oz) safflower oil
2 tablespoons coffee liqueur
4 eggs, separated
½ cup (125 mL/4 fl oz) strong espresso coffee
1½ cups (185 g/6 oz) self-raising flour
2 teaspoons ground cinnamon

Place the hazelnuts in a food processor and process until a fine meal is produced. Add the sugar, oil, liqueur, egg yolks and coffee and process until well combined. Transfer to a mixing bowl. Sift the flour and cinnamon and salt and fold into the almond mixture. Whisk the egg whites until they form soft peaks, then fold them into the cake mixture. Place in a prepared 24 cm (10 in.)cake pan and bake in a moderate oven (180°C/350°F) for 30–40 minutes, or until cooked when tested with a skewer.
*Serves 10–12*

# Vanilla Cream

*Great fun to pipe onto cakes and pancakes and to use as a cream filling.*

250 g (8 oz) cream cheese
2 teaspoons vanilla essence (extract)
1 tablespoon honey

Blend all the ingredients together until smooth.
*Makes about 1 cup (250 g/8 fl oz)*

*Please refer to the mixed spice recipe in our Cook's Notes, page 8.

# Tutti Fruity Layer Cake

*Moist and delectable, this fruit-filled cake is perfect for special occasions, and although it is unlikely that you will have any left, it does keep well in the refrigerator for a day or two.*

¾ cup (125 g/4 oz) almonds
¾ cup (185 g/6 oz) caster (superfine) sugar
½ cup (125 mL/4 fl oz) safflower oil
finely grated rind of 1 lemon
4 eggs, separated
½ cup (125 mL/4 fl oz) plain yoghurt
1½ cups (185 g/6 oz) self-raising flour
double quantity Lemon Cream Cheese (below)
1 mango, peeled, pip removed, sliced
1 punnet (carton) strawberries, hulls removed
3 kiwi fruit, peeled and sliced
2–3 teaspoons pure icing sugar

Place the almonds in a food processor and process until a fine meal is produced. Add the sugar, oil, lemon rind, egg yolks and yoghurt and process until well combined. Transfer to a mixing bowl and fold in the flour. Whisk the egg whites until they form soft peaks, then fold them into the cake mixture. Place in a prepared 24 cm (10 in.) cake pan and bake in a moderate oven (180°C/350°F) for 30–40 minutes, or until cooked when tested with a skewer. When cold, cut the cake into 3 layers. Spread each layer with the Lemon Cream Cheese Topping. Top the bottom layer with the whole strawberries, the second layer with the sliced kiwi fruit and the top layer with mango slices. Dust the cake lightly with the icing sugar.
*Serves 10–12*

# Lemon or Orange Cream Cheese

250 g (8 oz) cream cheese
1 teaspoon finely grated lemon *or* orange rind
1 tablespoon honey

Blend all the ingredients together until smooth.
*Makes about 1 cup (250 g/8 oz)*

# Pineapple and Coconut Dessert Cake

*This cake has a texture rather like the moist semolina cakes I remember enjoying with freshly brewed coffee at continental cake shops. Serve simply with whipping (double) cream or Vanilla Whip (page 181).*

5 unsweetened canned pineapple rings, drained
1 tablespoon soft brown sugar
1 cup (90 g/3 oz) desiccated coconut
1 cup (125 g/4 oz) self-raising flour
2 teaspoons baking powder
1 teaspoon mixed spice*
225 g (7 oz) tofu *or* ricotta cheese, drained and mashed
2 tablespoons honey
2 tablespoons oil
additional ½ cup (90 g/3 oz) soft brown sugar
225 mL (7 fl oz) coconut cream

Brush the inside of a 24 cm (10 in.) cake pan with a little melted butter or oil and line the bottom with baking paper. Arrange the pineapple slices on top and sprinkle them with the brown sugar. Place the coconut in a food processor and process until a fine meal is produced, then add the flour, baking powder and mixed spice. Put in a bowl. Using a food processor or blender, blend the tofu (or ricotta cheese), honey, oil, sugar and coconut cream and combine well. Mix the dry and liquid ingredients together well. Spread evenly over the pineapple slices in the prepared pan. Bake in a moderate oven (180°C/350°F) for 40 minutes, or until cooked when tested with a skewer.
*Serves 10*

*Please refer to the mixed spice recipe in our Cook's Notes, page 8.

*Right: Tutti Fruity Layer Cake. Generous layers of tantalising fresh fruits nestle in a lemon scented cream cheese filling.*

# Chocolate Coconut and Date Cake

*This moist chocolate cake is enriched with coconut cream rather than butter or milk. Serve it plain or dress it up by icing it with Chocolate and Date Cream (below) and piping stars of Vanilla Whip (page 181) around the outside.*

250 g (8 oz) tofu, drained
225 mL (7 fl oz) coconut cream
3 tablespoons honey
½ cup (90 g/3 oz) soft brown sugar
½ cup (125 mL/4 fl oz) soy milk
2 cups (250 g/8 oz) wholemeal (whole-wheat) self-raising flour
4 tablespoons cocoa powder
1 cup (155 g/5 oz) chopped pitted dates

Using a food processor or blender, blend the tofu, coconut cream, honey, sugar and milk until smooth, then place the mixture in a bowl. Sift the flour and cocoa powder and fold into the mixture with the dates. Pour the mixture into a prepared 20 cm (8 in.) cake pan and bake in a moderate oven (180°C/350°F) for 30 minutes, or until cooked when tested with a skewer.
*Serves 12*

# Chocolate and Date Cream

*A luscious chocolate topping laced with the full fruity flavour of dates. This topping does not contain any added sugar, yet it's surprisingly sweet.*

1 cup (155 g/5 oz) chopped pitted dates
1 tablespoon cocoa powder
½ cup (125 mL/4 fl oz) water

Place all the ingredients into a small saucepan and bring the mixture to the boil, stirring occasionally. Reduce the heat to a simmer and cook, covered, until the dates become pulpy. Using a food processor, blend the mixture until smooth.
*Makes about 1 cup (250 mL/8 fl oz)*

# Apple and Ginger Cake

60 g (2 oz) butter, softened
1 tablespoon oil
2 tablespoons honey
3 tablespoons soft brown sugar
2–3 eggs, separated
2 green apples, diced
2 teaspoons finely grated lemon rind
½ cup (125 mL/4 fl oz) plain yoghurt
2–3 tablespoons crystallised (candied) ginger
2 cups (250 g/8 oz) wholemeal (whole-wheat) self-raising flour
1 teaspoon mixed spice*
1 quantity Lemon and Ginger Cream (below)
additional 1–2 tablespoons chopped crystallised (candied) ginger

Beat the butter, oil, honey, sugar and egg yolks together and stir in the apples, lemon rind, yoghurt and ginger. Sift the flour and spice and fold into the apple mixture. Whisk the egg whites until they form soft peaks and carefully fold into the mixture. Place in a prepared 20 cm (8 in.) cake pan and bake in a moderate oven (180°C/350°F) for 35 minutes. When cold, spread the Lemon and Ginger Cream over and scatter with the additional crystallised ginger.
*Serves 12*

# Lemon and Ginger Cream

250 g (8 oz) cream cheese
1 teaspoon finely grated lemon rind
1 tablespoon finely chopped crystallised (candied) ginger
2–3 teaspoons honey
¼ teaspoon ground ginger

Blend all the ingredients together until smooth.
*Makes about 1 cup (250 mL/8 fl oz)*

*Please refer to the mixed spice recipe in our Cook's Notes, page 8.

# Banana and Walnut Cake

*This is a cake for a special occasion. To prepare an everyday version, simply prepare half the quantity given and cook the cake in a loaf pan.*

225 g (7 oz) walnuts
60 g (2 oz) self-raising flour
1 teaspoon baking powder
3 eggs, separated
½ cup (125 g/4 oz) soft brown sugar
2 tablespoons oil
1 teaspoon vanilla essence (extract)
4 ripe bananas, mashed
double quantity Vanilla Cream (page 185)
½ cup (60 g/2 oz) chopped walnuts

Place the walnuts, flour and baking powder into a food processor and process until a fine meal is produced. Whisk the egg whites until they form soft peaks. Beat the egg yolks, sugar, oil, vanilla and bananas together and fold in the walnut and flour mixture. Carefully fold in the egg whites and place in two prepared sandwich tins (layer cake pans) which have been lined with baking parchment. Bake in a moderate oven (180°C/350°F) for 30–40 minutes, or until cooked when tested with a skewer. When the cakes are cold sandwich them together with half the vanilla cream. Spread the remaining cream over the top of the cake and decorate with the chopped walnuts.
*Serves 10*

# Plum Pudding Cake

*Serve in thin wedges on its own, or surrounded by Plum and Raspberry Sauce (below) with whipping (double) cream alongside.*

1½ cups Poached Plums (page 163), pips removed
3 cups (475 g/15 oz) mixed dried fruit (fruit cake mix)
2 eggs, beaten, *or* 2 tablespoons oil
1 teaspoon vanilla essence (extract)
3 tablespoons soft brown sugar
1 cup (155 g/5 oz) semolina
1 cup (125 g/4 oz) wholemeal (whole-wheat) self-raising flour, sifted
2 teaspoons mixed spice*

Using a food processor, blend the plums until smooth, or push them through a sieve. Add the mixed fruit, eggs (or oil), vanilla and sugar and beat in the semolina. Sift the flour and spice then fold it into the fruit mixture. Pour the mixture into a prepared ring cake pan and bake in a moderate oven (180°C/350°F) for 45 minutes.
*Serves 8–10*

# Plum and Raspberry Sauce

*Rich and fruity, this sauce makes a superb accompaniment for dessert cakes and puddings. It's also a great sauce for drizzling over ice cream or yoghurt.*

1 cup Poached Plums (page 163), pips removed
½ punnet (carton) raspberries
2 teaspoons honey (optional)

Using a food processor, blend the plums until smooth then add the raspberries and honey.
*Makes about 1½ cups (375 mL/12 fl oz)*

*Please refer to the mixed spice recipe in our Cook's Notes, page 8.

# Apple Crumble Slice

*This is a really scrumptious slice absolutely bursting with apples. Be sure to allow it to stand for a few hours before serving as the apple filling 'softens' the crust beautifully.*

2 cups (185 g/6 oz) untoasted muesli
1 cup (125 g/4 oz) wholemeal (whole-wheat)
   self-raising flour
3 tablespoons soft brown sugar
1 teaspoon ground cinnamon
1 teaspoon mixed spice*
⅔ cup (185 mL/6 fl oz) yoghurt
2 tablespoons oil
½ cup (60 g/2 oz) almonds
1 cup (3 oz) untoasted muesli
½ cup (60 g/2 oz) wholemeal (whole-wheat) plain
   (all-purpose) flour
additional 1 teaspoon ground cinnamon
1½ tablespoons honey
1 tablespoon oil
double quantity of Stewed Apples (page 161)
   excess juice drained

To prepare the crust, combine the muesli, flour and sugar, cinnamon and mixed spice. Combine the yoghurt and oil and mix into the dry ingredients. Spread the mixture onto the bottom of a prepared 20 cm (8 in.) square cake pan and bake in a moderate oven (180°C/350°F) for 20 minutes. To prepare the crumble topping, place the almonds in a food processor or blender and process to a coarse meal. Add the muesli, flour and cinnamon and continue to process, adding the honey and oil as the machine is operating. Arrange the apples on top of the crust and sprinkle the crumble mixture over. Return to the oven and bake for a further 20 minutes. When cold, cut into 12 squares.
*Serves 12*

# Raspberry Slice

*Delectable as it is or served with whipping (double) cream or Vanilla Whip (page 181).*

1 cup (90 g/3 oz) desiccated coconut
1 cup (125 g/4 oz) wholemeal (whole-wheat)
   self-raising flour
3 tablespoons caster (superfine) sugar
60 g (2 oz) butter, melted
1/2 teaspoon vanilla
2 punnets (cartons) raspberries
double quantity Fresh Berry Coulis (page 178),
   using raspberries

Combine the coconut, flour and sugar then add the butter and vanilla, mixing thoroughly. Press the mixture onto the bottom of a prepared 20 cm (8 in.) square cake pan and bake in a moderate oven (180°C/350°F) for 20 minutes. When cold, cut into fingers or squares and arrange the raspberries on top. Just before serving, drizzle the Raspberry Coulis over.
*Serves 12*

**A Butter Substitute**
125 g (4 oz) tofu combined with 2 tablespoons oil can be used instead of the butter.

*Please refer to the mixed spice recipe in our Cook's Notes, page 8.

*Right: Raspberry Slice. The distinctive sharp flavour of raspberries harmonises well with the coconut shortcake base.*

# Chocolate Almond Slice

*This scrumptious slice can be served as it is or, for special occasions, ice with Real Chocolate Icing (below) and top with almonds.*

1 cup (90 g/3 oz) ground almonds (almond meal)
1 cup (90 g/3 oz) desiccated coconut
2 tablespoons cocoa powder
½ cup (60 g/2 oz) wholemeal (whole-wheat) self-raising flour
3 tablespoons soft brown sugar
2 tablespoons honey
60 g (2 oz) butter, melted
2 tablespoons oil
1 teaspoon vanilla essence (extract)

Mix the almonds, coconut, cocoa powder, flour and sugar. Combine the honey, butter, oil and vanilla and pour over the dry ingredients. Combine well and press the mixture down into a prepared square baking tin. Bake in a hot oven (200°C/400°F for 20 minutes. Allow to cool before icing or slicing.
*Serves 12*

# Real Chocolate Icing

*An indulgent topping and the finishing touch for the very best of cakes and slices. While on the topic of indulging, why not go the whole way and spike this topping? Simply replace the vanilla with a tablespoon or two of coffee liqueur (page 333).*

225 g (7 oz) dark (semi-sweet) compound chocolate
½ cup (125 mL/4 fl oz) light (single) cream *or* soy milk
1 teaspoon pure vanilla essence (extract)

Melt the chocolate (page 206) and whisk in the cream and vanilla. Use while still warm.
*Makes about 1½ cups (375 mL/12 fl oz)*

# Date Loaf

*Simply delicious sliced and spread with a little butter, Yoghurt Cheese (page 271) or cream cheese.*

60 g (2 oz) butter
2 tablespoons honey
1 cup (155 g/5 oz) chopped pitted dates
½ cup (125 mL/4 fl oz) fruit juice
1½ cups (185 g/6 oz) wholemeal (whole-wheat) self-raising flour
1 teaspoon mixed spice*

Place the butter, honey, dates and fruit juice in a saucepan and bring the mixture to the boil. Reduce the heat and cook gently for 2 minutes. Remove the mixture from the stove and set it aside to cool to lukewarm. Sift the flour and spice together and fold it into the date mixture. Spoon the mixture into a prepared loaf pan. Bake in a moderate oven (180°C/350°F) for 30–35 minutes.
*Makes 1 loaf*

# Banana Loaf

*An all-time favourite, this loaf keeps well for a day or two, and should you wish to keep it any longer, it freezes well too.*

3 very ripe bananas, mashed
3 tablespoons soft brown sugar
1 teaspoon vanilla essence (extract)
3 tablespoons oil
2 eggs, beaten
½ teaspoon bicarbonate of soda (baking soda) dissolved in 2 tablespoons boiling water
2 cups (250 g/8 oz) wholemeal (whole-wheat) self-raising flour
2 teaspoons mixed spice*

Combine the bananas, sugar, vanilla, oil, eggs and soda mixture thoroughly. Sift the flour and the spice and fold into the banana mixture. Place the mixture into a prepared loaf pan. Bake in a moderate oven (180°C/350°F) for 40–45 minutes.
*Makes 1 loaf*

*Please refer to the mixed spice recipe in our Cook's Notes, page 8.

# Blueberry Muffins

*Muffins of any type make great treats and are wonderful served straight from the oven when you have the time to enjoy a leisurely brunch.*

2 tablespoons melted butter *or* oil
3 tablespoons honey
1 egg, beaten
½ cup (125 mL/4 fl oz) plain yoghurt
1 teaspoon vanilla essence (extract)
1½ cups (185 g/6 oz) self-raising flour, sifted
1 punnet (carton) blueberries (bilberries)

Place the butter (or oil), honey, egg, yoghurt and vanilla in a bowl. Using a wire whisk or a wooden spoon beat all the ingredients together to combine them thoroughly. Beat the flour into the mixture then carefully fold in the blueberries. Place the mixture in prepared muffin pans. Bake the muffins in a moderate oven (180°C/350°F) for 25–30 minutes.
*Makes 12*

Frozen Blueberries
Thawed frozen blueberries can be used with excellent results if you cannot obtain fresh ones.

# Quick Banana Muffins

2 tablespoons melted butter *or* oil
3 tablespoons honey
1 egg, beaten
1 teaspoon vanilla essence (extract)
½ cup (125 mL/4 fl oz) plain yoghurt
2–3 ripe bananas, mashed
1½ cups (185 g/6 oz) self-raising flour
¼ teaspoon bicarbonate of soda (baking soda)

Beat the butter (or oil), honey, egg, vanilla, yoghurt and banana together. Sift the flour with the soda and fold into the banana mixture. Place in prepared muffin tins pans and bake in a moderate oven (180°C/350°F) for 25–30 minutes.
*Makes 12*

# Ready When You Are Muffins

*The beauty of this recipe is that you can cook the prepared mixture exactly when you need it. Once prepared, the mixture can be stored in a covered container in the refrigerator for 2–3 weeks! The mixture can be taken straight from the refrigerator, popped into prepared muffin pans and baked in a matter of 25 minutes.*

½ cup (125 mL/4 fl oz) oil
½ cup (90 g/3 oz) soft brown sugar
3 tablespoons honey
2 eggs, beaten
½ cup (125 mL/4 fl oz) fruit juice
2 cups (500 mL/16 fl oz) thin plain yoghurt *or* buttermilk
2 cups (250 g/8 oz) wholemeal (whole-wheat) plain (all-purpose) flour
2 teaspoons mixed spice*
1 teaspoon ground cinnamon
1½ teaspoons bicarbonate of soda (baking soda)
1 cup (90 g/3 oz) rolled oats
1 cup (90 g/3 oz) untoasted muesli
1 cup (155 g/5 oz) sultanas (golden raisins)

Combine the oil, sugar, honey, eggs, fruit juice and yoghurt (or buttermilk). Sift the flour, spices and soda and beat into the mixture. Add the oats, muesli and sultanas and mix well. If possible, cover and set the mixture aside for 1 hour before baking to allow the dry ingredients to soften. Place the mixture into prepared muffin pans. Bake in a moderately hot oven (190°C/375°F) for 15 minutes.
*Makes 24*

*Please refer to the recipe for mixed spice in our Cook's Notes, page 8.

# Peachy Galettes

*Life can be rosier than the blush of a peach when you serve these delicious light galettes as a dessert or a snack. These galettes are sweet and moist yet contain very little fat.*

½ cup (125 mL/4 fl oz) hot water
1 tablespoon sugar
½ cup (125 mL/4 fl oz) cold water
7 g (¼ oz) active dried yeast
2½ cups (310 g/10 oz) plain (all-purpose) flour
½ cup (60 g/2 oz) ground almonds (almond meal)
additional plain (all-purpose) flour
4 teaspoons honey
8 canned or poached peach halves, drained
1 quantity Sticky Bun Glaze (page 252)

Follow the method for Basic Bread (page 244), adding the ground almonds to the flour before combining it with the yeast mixture. After the first kneading, roll the dough out to a 6 mm (¼ in.) thickness and cut out 6–8 rounds using a large round cutter or a saucer traced with a knife. Place the rounds of dough on prepared baking sheets and drizzle ½ teaspoon of honey over each one. Top each with a peach half and allow to stand in a warm place for 15–20 minutes. Bake in a hot oven (200°C/400°F) for 20 minutes. Brush with Sticky Bun Glaze as soon as you remove them from the oven.
*Makes about 8*

### Pastry Galettes
Traditional galettes made from pastry are unfortunately high in fat, but they are nice for special occasions. Prepare the galettes as above, replacing the yeast dough with 2 sheets of prepared puff pastry, each cut into 4 rounds or squares. Omit the Sticky Bun Glaze which can make pastry soggy.

*Left: Whether prepared the traditional way using puff pastry base as pictured, or using a light yeast dough, Peachy Galettes make a popular brunch dish or snack.*

# Apricot Coconut Galettes

*Serve as they are or with a scoop of Greek Yoghurt (page 273) or Yoghurt Cheese (page 271) and Fresh Berry Coulis (page 178).*

½ cup (125 mL/4 fl oz) hot water
1 tablespoon sugar
½ cup (125 mL/4 fl oz) cold water
7 g (¼ oz) active dried yeast
½ cup (45 g/1½ oz) desiccated coconut
2 cups (250 g/8 oz) plain (all-purpose) flour
additional plain (all-purpose) flour
4 tablespoons Zesty Apricot Spread (page 309) *or* apricot jam
24 canned or poached apricot halves, drained
1 punnet (carton) strawberries *or* blackberries, hulled
Passion Fruit Glaze (below)

Follow the method for Basic Bread (page 244), adding the coconut to the flour before combining it with the yeast mixture. After the first kneading, roll the dough out to a 6 mm (¼ in.) thickness and cut out 8 rounds using a large round cutter or a saucer traced with a knife. Place the rounds of dough on prepared baking sheets. Using a pastry brush, spread the apricot spread (or jam) evenly over the dough. Arrange the apricot halves on top then cover the trays and allow the galettes to stand in a warm place for 15–20 minutes. Bake in a hot oven (200°C/400°F) for 20 minutes. Remove the galettes from the oven and immediately arrange the strawberries (or blackberries) on top and brush generously with Passion Fruit Glaze.
*Makes 8*

# Passion Fruit Glaze

3 tablespoons honey
3 tablespoons passion fruit pulp
½ cup (125 mL/4 fl oz) fruit juice

Place all the ingredients in a small saucepan and bring the mixture to the boil, stirring. Reduce the heat and simmer for 2–3 minutes. Use while hot.
*Makes about ¾ cup (185 mL/6 fl oz)*

# Basic Wholemeal Scones

*Scones (biscuits), warm and steamy from the oven make a great accompaniment to soups and are all-round favourites accompanied by a pot of berry jam and a bowl of whipping (double) cream. Served cold, they are great spread with savoury dips and topped with slices of fresh tomato and chopped fresh herbs.*

1 cup (125 g/4 oz) wholemeal (whole-wheat)
    self-raising flour
1 cup (125 g/4 oz) white self-raising flour
1 cup (250 mL/8 fl oz) milk
30 g (1 oz) butter, melted
additional plain (all-purpose) flour

Sift the flours together and make a 'well' in the centre. Add the milk and butter and mix to a soft dough. Knead lightly for 1 minute only. Roll out to 18 mm (¾ in) thickness and cut into desired shapes using a scone cutter or sharp knife. Place on a prepared baking sheet and brush the tops with a little milk. Bake in a hot oven (200° C/400° F) for 10–12 minutes.
*Makes about 12*

# Pumpkin Scones

1 cup (125 g/4 oz) wholemeal (whole-wheat)
    self-raising flour
1 cup (125 g/4 oz) white self-raising flour
1 teaspoon mixed spice*
1 cup (250 g/8 oz) mashed pumpkin
30 g (1 oz) butter, melted
3–4 tablespoons milk
additional plain (all-purpose) flour

Prepare and cook as for Basic Wholemeal Scones, adding the pumpkin to the flour with the butter and adding enough milk to form a soft dough.
*Makes about 12*

**A Herbal Twist**
For delicious herbed pumpkin scones (biscuits), simply add 3 tablespoons finely sliced chives to the flour before combining it with the butter.

# Date Scones

*Great served straight from the oven with a little butter, or allow to cool, split in half and pipe Lemon or Orange Cream Cheese (page 186) on top.*

1 cup (125 g/4 oz) wholemeal (whole-wheat)
    self-raising flour
1 cup (125 g/4 oz) white self-raising flour
¾ cup (125 g/4 oz) roughly chopped pitted dates
1 tablespoon soft brown sugar
¾ cup (225 mL/7 fl oz) milk
30 g (1 oz) butter, melted
additional plain (all-purpose) flour

Prepare and cook as for Basic Wholemeal Scones, adding the dates and sugar to the flour before combining with the remaining ingredients.
*Makes about 18*

# Beetroot Scones

*These vibrant coloured scones (biscuits) are great spread with light cream cheese and topped with Low-Sugar Berry Jam (page 309).*

1 cooked beetroot (beet) (page 93), peeled and
    chopped
1 tablespoon honey
30 g (1 oz) butter, melted
¾ cup (185 mL/6 fl oz) milk
1 cup (125 g/4 oz) wholemeal (whole-wheat)
    self-raising flour
1 cup (125 g/4 oz) white self-raising flour
additional plain (all-purpose) flour

Using a food processor or blender, purée the beetroot, then add the honey, butter and milk and blend the mixture until smooth. Transfer the mixture to a bowl and work the two flours in to form a soft dough. Continue as for Basic Wholemeal Scones.
*Makes about 18*

*Please refer to the recipe for mixed spice in our Cook's Notes, page 8.

# Wholemeal Rock Cakes

2 cups (250 g/8 oz) wholemeal (whole-wheat)
   self-raising flour
1 teaspoon mixed spice*
1 cup (155 g/5 oz) mixed dried fruit (fruit cake
   mix)
3 tablespoons soft brown sugar
60 g (2 oz) butter, melted
2 tablespoons oil
1 egg, beaten
3 tablespoons milk

Mix the flour, mixed spiced, dried fruit and
sugar and make a 'well' in the centre. Beat the
butter, oil, egg and milk together until creamy
and pour into the 'well'. Gradually work the dry
ingredients into the centre, so that a rough
dough is produced. Place heaped tablespoonfuls
of the mixture onto prepared baking sheets and
bake in a moderately hot oven (190°C/375°F) for
15–20 minutes.
*Makes about 12*

# Apple and Raisin Rock Cakes

2 cups (250 g/8 oz) wholemeal (whole-wheat)
   self-raising flour
1 teaspoon finely grated lemon rind
1 cup (155 g/5 oz) raisins
1 large green apple, diced
3 tablespoons soft brown sugar
60 g (2 oz) butter, melted
2 tablespoons oil
1 egg, beaten
3 tablespoons milk

Mix the flour, lemon rind, raisins and apple and
make a 'well' in the centre. Beat the sugar, butter,
oil, egg and milk together until creamy and pour
into the 'well'. Gradually work the dry
ingredients into the centre, so that a rough
dough is produced. Place heaped tablespoonfuls
of the mixture onto prepared baking sheets and
bake in a moderately hot oven (190°C/375°F) for
15–20 minutes.
*Makes about 12*

# Banana and Walnut Rock Cakes

2 cups (250 g/8 oz) wholemeal (whole-wheat)
   self-raising flour
1 teaspoon mixed spice*
1 cup (125 g/4 oz) chopped walnuts
2 ripe bananas, mashed
3 tablespoons soft brown sugar
60 g (2 oz) butter, melted
2 tablespoons oil
1 egg, beaten
1 teaspoon vanilla essence (extract)

Mix the flour, spice and walnuts and make a
'well' in the centre. Beat the banana, sugar, butter,
oil, egg and vanilla together until well combined
and pour into the 'well'. Gradually work the dry
ingredients into the centre, so that a rough
dough is produced. Place heaped tablespoonfuls
of the mixture onto prepared baking sheets and
bake in a moderately hot oven (190°C/375°F) for
15–20 minutes.
*Makes about 12*

# Lemon and Coconut Buttons

1¾ cups (225 g/7 oz) wholemeal (whole wheat)
   self-raising flour
⅔ cup (60 g/2 oz) desiccated coconut
½ cup (125 g/4 oz) caster (superfine) sugar
60 g (2 oz) butter, melted
1 tablespoon oil
1 egg, beaten
finely grated rind and juice of 1 lemon

Mix the flour, coconut and the sugar. Beat the
butter, oil, egg, lemon rind and juice together
and thoroughly combine with the dry
ingredients. Form the mixture into balls about
the size of a walnut, place on prepared baking
sheets and bake in a moderate oven
(180°C/350°F) for 10–12 minutes.
*Makes about 20*
*Please refer to the recipe for mixed spice in our
Cook's Notes, page 8.

# Peanut Clusters

*These scrumptious cookies are fairly bursting with peanuts. They are delicious served with freshly brewed coffee at the end of a light meal.*

30 g (1 oz) butter, melted
3 tablespoons oil
½ cup (90 g/3 oz) soft brown sugar
1 teaspoon vanilla essence (extract)
1 egg, beaten
1 cup (155 g/5 oz) dry roasted peanuts
1 cup (125 g/4 oz) self-raising flour

Beat the butter, oil, sugar, vanilla and egg until creamy, then gradually mix in the peanuts and the flour. Place tablespoonfuls of the mixture onto prepared baking sheets and bake in a moderate oven (180°C/350°F) for 15–20 minutes.
*Makes about 18*

# Coconut Munchies

*These sweet golden cookies are a delightful accompaniment for pineapple-based desserts and fruit salads. Or just eat them straight from the jar.*

60 g (2 oz) butter, softened
2 tablespoons oil
2 tablespoons honey
3 tablespoons soft brown sugar
1 teaspoon vanilla essence (extract)
1 egg, beaten
1 cup (90 g/3 oz) desiccated coconut
1 cup (125 g/4 oz) wholemeal (whole-wheat) self-raising flour

Beat the butter, oil, honey, sugar, vanilla and egg until well combined then add the coconut and flour. Mix well and place tablespoonfuls of the mixture onto prepared baking sheets. Bake in a moderate oven (180°C/350°F) for 12–15 minutes.
*Makes about 24*

# Honey Ginger Nuts

60 g (2 oz) butter, melted
2 tablespoons oil
3 tablespoons soft brown sugar
3 tablespoons honey
1 cup (125 g/4 oz) wholemeal (whole-wheat) self-raising flour
1 cup (125 g/4 oz) white self-raising flour
2 teaspoons ground ginger
¼ teaspoon bicarbonate of soda (baking soda)

Beat the butter, oil, sugar and honey until creamy. Sift the flours, ginger and soda and thoroughly combine with the butter mixture. Form the mixture into balls about the size of a walnut and place on prepared baking sheets. Bake in a moderate oven (180°C/350°F) for 10–12 minutes.
*Makes about 20*

# Sesame Cookies

60 g (2 oz) butter
2 tablespoons oil
½ cup (125 g/4 oz) caster (superfine) sugar
1 egg, beaten
½ teaspoon vanilla
1 cup (125 g/4 oz) sesame seeds
1 cup (125 g/4 oz) wholemeal (whole-wheat) plain (all-purpose) flour
½ cup (60 g/2 oz) white self-raising flour

Beat the butter, oil, sugar, egg and vanilla together until creamy, then beat in the sesame seeds. Sift the flours and add to the mixture. Form the mixture into balls about the size of a walnut and place on prepared baking sheets. Bake in a moderate oven (180°C/350°F) for 15–20 minutes. Cool on a cake rack and store in an airtight container.
*Makes about 24*

*Right: Peanut Clusters, Coconut Munchies and Honey Ginger Nuts. Built on a foundation of wholemeal flour and containing less fat and sugar, these cookies are as nutritious as they are scrumptious.*

# Amaretto Cookies

1 cup (155 g/5 oz) almonds
½ cup (60 g/2 oz) rice flour
¾ cup (125 g/4 oz) soft brown sugar
2 tablespoon honey
60 g (2 oz) butter, melted
1 tablespoon Amaretto liqueur
additional 18 almonds for topping the cookies

Using a food processor, process the almonds until a fine meal is produced. Transfer the almond meal to a bowl and add the rice flour and sugar. Mix the honey, butter and liqueur and pour over the dry ingredients. Work all the ingredients together to combine thoroughly. Form the mixture into small balls and place on a prepared baking sheet. Press an almond on top of each cookie. Bake in a moderate oven (180°C/350°F) for 12–15 minutes. Cool on a cake rack and store in an airtight container.
*Makes about 18*

# Chocolate Chip Cookies

1 cup (125 g/4 oz) wholemeal (whole-wheat)
    self-raising flour
½ cup (60 g/2 oz) plain (all-purpose) flour
⅔ cup (60 g/2 oz) desiccated coconut
3 tablespoons caster (superfine) sugar
60 g (2 oz) chocolate chips
60 g (2 oz) butter, melted
2 tablespoons oil
1 egg, beaten

Combine the flours, coconut, sugar and chocolate chips. Whisk the butter, oil and egg together and gradually work into the dry ingredients. Form the mixture into balls about the size of a walnut and place on a prepared baking sheet. Bake in a moderate oven (180°C/350°F) for 20 minutes. Cool on a cake rack and store in an airtight container.
*Makes about 15–18*

# Carrot and Spice Cookies

1 carrot, trimmed, scrubbed and grated
2 tablespoons honey
3 tablespoons soft brown sugar
3 tablespoons fruit juice
1 cup (90 g/3 oz) rolled oats
1 cup (125 g/4 oz) wholemeal (whole-wheat)
    self-raising flour
1 teaspoon bicarbonate of soda (baking soda)
2 teaspoons mixed spice*

Combine the carrot, honey, brown sugar and fruit juice thoroughly, then stir in the oats. Sift the flour, soda and spice together and gradually add to the carrot mixture, mixing thoroughly. Place tablespoonfuls of the mixture on prepared baking sheets. Bake in a moderate oven (180°C/350°F) for 20–25 minutes. Cool on a cake rack and store in an airtight container.
*Makes about 18*

# Sunflower Cookies

60 g (2 oz) butter
2 tablespoons oil
3 tablespoons soft brown sugar
2 tablespoons honey
3 tablespoons orange juice
1 cup (125 g/4 oz) hulled sunflower seeds
1½ cups (185 g/6 oz) wholemeal (whole-wheat)
    plain (all-purpose) flour
1 teaspoon bicarbonate of soda (baking soda)

Beat the butter, oil, sugar and honey together until creamy, then add the orange juice and sunflower seeds. Sift the flour and soda and fold into the mixture. Form the mixture into balls about the size of a walnut and place on prepared baking sheets leaving about 3 cm (1¼ in.) space between to allow for spreading. Bake in a moderate oven (180°C/350°F) for 20 minutes. Cool on a cake rack and store in an airtight container.
*Makes about 24*

*Please refer to the recipe for mixed spice in our Cook's Notes, page 8.

# Pineapple Cream

*A delightful tangy cream for piping on top of cakes and desserts to add a touch of summer sunshine.*

250 g (8 oz) cream cheese *or* ricotta cheese
3 tablespoons well-drained, crushed pineapple
2 teaspoons honey

Blend all the ingredients together until smooth.
*Makes about 1 cup (250 mL/8 fl oz)*

# Coffee Cream Topping

250 g (8 oz) cream cheese
1 tablespoon honey
1 teaspoon instant coffee
1 teaspoon vanilla essence (extract)

Blend all the ingredients together until smooth.
*Makes about 1 cup (250 mL/8 fl oz)*

**Decorating Ideas**
For a decorative touch, use a piping (pastry) bag with a fluted nozzle (tube) to pipe swirls or rosettes of whipping (double) cream on top of cakes and desserts.

# Coconut Cream Cheese

*This topping is especially good for topping or filling moist wholemeal (whole-wheat) carrot, banana or pineapple cakes.*

250 g (8 oz) Yoghurt Cheese (page 271) *or* cream cheese
1 tablespoon lemon juice
1 tablespoon honey
4 tablespoons desiccated coconut

Place the cheese in a bowl and soften it with a wooden spoon. Gradually add the honey and beat the mixture until it becomes creamy. Add the lemon juice and continue to beat the mixture as you gradually add the coconut.
*Makes about 1 cup (250 mL/8 fl oz)*

# Honey and Walnut Cream

*Delicious spread on top of apple cakes, or use it to fill spice cakes.*

250 g (8 oz) cream cheese, softened
1 tablespoon honey
2 tablespoons chopped walnuts
¼ teaspoon ground cinnamon

Combine all the ingredients.
*Makes about 1 cup (250 mL/8 fl oz)*

# Creamy Ginger Topping

*Wonderful used as a topping for cakes, for filling pitted fresh dates or on crispy pears.*

250 g (8 oz) cream cheese
1 tablespoon syrup from preserved ginger, *or* ¼ teaspoon ground ginger combined with 1 tablespoon honey

Soften the cream cheese and beat until smooth with the ginger syrup (or ginger and honey).
*Makes about 1 cup (250 mL/8 fl oz)*

# Creamy Date Topping

4 tablespoons chopped pitted dates
3 tablespoons boiling water
few drops vanilla essence (extract)
250 g (8 oz) cream cheese *or* Yoghurt Cheese (page 271)

Place the dates in a small bowl and cover with the boiling water. Allow to stand for 5–10 minutes. Place the date mixture, vanilla and cheese into a food processor and blend until smooth.
*Makes about 1½ cups (375 mL/12 fl oz)*

# Confections

*These delicious confections include something for everyone. There are simple fruit combinations—some 'au naturel' and some dipped or nestled in chocolate or toffee—scrumptious fruit and nut bars for after school snacks, succulent fresh and dried fruits adorned with swirls of creamy fillings, and delectable fruit and cheese balls to add that final touch to fruit and cheese platters.*

# Stuffed Strawberries

*These look wonderful served with slices of kiwi fruit (Chinese gooseberry) or slivers of honeydew melon. Use large berries with a firm sweet flesh.*

12 large strawberries, hulls removed
1 quantity Spiked Strawberry Cream (below)
slivers of honeydew melon

Cut the strawberries into 4 from the stalk end down, but do not cut right through. Place the cream in a piping (pastry) bag and pipe it into the cavities of each strawberry. Serve surrounded by the honeydew melon.
*Serves 4–6*

**Berry Care**
Buy strawberries just before you plan to use them. Although they can be stored in a covered container in the refrigerator for several days, they seem to lose that bright fresh look of freshly picked berries. It's also important to wash or wipe over berries just before use—wet or damp berries spoil very rapidly.

# Spiked Strawberry Cream

*This cream is perfect for piping on top of a variety of fruit desserts, mousses and even crêpes and pancakes, but piped into fresh berries it makes a stunning sweet treat.*

250 g (8 oz) Yoghurt Cheese (page 271) *or* cream cheese, softened
2 teaspoons honey
1–2 tablespoons Strawberry Liqueur (page 328)

Place the cheese in a bowl and, using a wooden spoon, beat in the honey until the mixture becomes creamy. Add the liqueur and continue to beat the mixture until it becomes velvety smooth.
*Makes about 1 cup (250 mL/8 fl oz)*

*Overleaf: Savoured with a glass of your favourite dessert wine, Lemon and Ginger Figs make a simple yet wonderful finale to a special meal.*

# Lemon and Ginger Figs

*There's something about new season's figs that inspires preparing simple yet delicious dishes. Fresh figs are wonderful served 'au naturel' but this dish is a great way to dress up figs simply.*

6 large fresh figs, washed, patted dry, stems snipped
1 quantity Lemon and Ginger Cream (page 188)
3 tablespoons slivered almonds, roasted (page 17)
fine slivers of lemon zest

Cut the figs in half lengthways and place on serving plates. Place the Lemon Ginger Cream into a piping (pastry) bag and carefully pipe attractive swirls on top of the figs. Decorate with the slivered almonds and lemon zest and chill thoroughly before serving.
*Serves 6*

# Figs with Almond Cream

*The vibrant colour of fresh ripe strawberries with their hulls attached provides a wonderful colour and texture contrast for sweet almond cream and plump juicy figs. Serve as a dessert with freshly brewed coffee.*

8 fresh figs, washed, patted dry, stems snipped
1 quantity Basic Nut Cream (page 281) using almonds
8 strawberries, hulls left on

Cut the figs into 4 from the stalk end down, but do not cut right through. Place the almond cream into a piping (pastry) bag and pipe the mixture into the cavities and top with a whole unhulled strawberry.
*Serves 4*

**Washing Figs**
All soft fruits should be washed carefully just before using, but in the case of figs, with their fragile skins, it is especially important—ripe figs are extremely perishable, especially when the skins are damp.

# Apricots with Hazelnut Cream

*These are simply prepared but look and taste terrific.*

6 ripe apricots, halved and pips removed
1 quantity Basic Nut Cream (page 281) using
   hazelnuts
6 whole strawberries, hulls left on, *or* 6 hazelnuts

Arrange the apricots on a serving plate. Place the hazelnut cream into a piping (pastry) bag and pipe small swirls into the cavities of the apricots. Top each swirl with a strawberry (or a hazelnut) and chill thoroughly before serving.
*Serves 4–6*

# Stuffed Prunes

*These can be prepared well ahead of time and stored in a covered container in the refrigerator or even the freezer.*

12 pitted prunes
½ quantity Lemon *or* Orange Cream Cheese
   (page 186)
12 large dried apricot halves
12 pecan nuts *or* almonds

Using a small sharp knife, slice the prunes down the middle and open the flesh out slightly. Place the cream cheese in a piping (pastry) bag and pipe rosettes into the cavities of the prunes. Top each with 2 dried apricot pieces and 1 pecan nut (or almond). Chill the prunes thoroughly before serving.
*Serves 4–6*

# Ginger Steeped Prunes

*Serve as an after dinner treat with cups of piping hot freshly brewed tea.*

12 pitted prunes
12 almonds
2 tablespoons preserved ginger syrup *or*
   ½ teaspoon ground ginger combined with
   2 tablespoons honey

Place the almonds in the cavity of the prunes. Place the prunes in a bowl and drizzle the ginger syrup (or honey mixture) over. Mix carefully to coat the prunes evenly with the syrup. Cover and allow to marinate for 1 day in the refrigerator.
*Makes 12*

# Stuffed Dates

*These can be prepared a day before needed and stored, covered, in the refrigerator. In summer, serve with fresh berries for a burst of colour.*

12 fresh dates
250 g (8 oz) light cream cheese
2 teaspoons honey
1 teaspoon finely grated lemon rind
12 pecan nuts
ground cinnamon

Cut the dates in half lengthways and remove the pips. Blend the cream cheese, honey and lemon rind until smooth and place in a piping (pastry) bag. Pipe swirls of the mixture into the cavities of the dates and top with the pecans. Dust with cinnamon and serve.
*Makes 12*

### Date Storage
When fresh dates are at their best, you can stash some away in your freezer for later use. If you have missed your chance to buy a reasonable amount when they are in season, you can use dried table dates. These are large and plump and can be stored in an airtight jar for eating plain as a snack or for using in confections.

# Melted Chocolate

*There is quite a variety of chocolates on the market. For special confections, it really is worthwhile to buy the very best quality chocolate you can afford—you will definitely notice the difference.*

**250 g (8 oz) dark (semi-sweet) chocolate, broken into pieces about 2.5 cm (1 in.) square**

To use the microwave method, place the chocolate in a microwave-proof bowl and microwave on medium-high for 2 minutes, stirring every 40 seconds.

To melt the chocolate on top of the stove, place 2 cups of water in the bottom of a double boiler and bring to the boil. Place the chocolate in the top of the double boiler and place on top of the base. Allow the chocolate to heat through, stirring occasionally, until it melts.

# Liqueur Chocolate

*Chocolate spiked with liqueur is a real treat as it is. Spoon it into confectioners' papers as soon as it has been prepared. I also like to use it for dipping quality fresh and dried fruit into, or even for drizzling over special occasion cakes.*

**250 g (8 oz) dark (semi-sweet) chocolate**
**2 tablespoons liqueur (pages 327–9)**

Melt the chocolate as specified above and stir in the liqueur. Use as required.
*Makes about 10–12 chocolates*

# Dried Apricot and Strawberry Dips

*What a wonderful way to enjoy the best of both worlds—fresh and dried fruits are recommended for good health, and I highly recommend chocolate for good eating and good fun!*

**12 whole dried apricots**
**12 strawberries, hulls left on**
**90 g (3 oz) dark (semi-sweet) chocolate**

Open out the apricots and place the strawberries inside so that the strawberries protrude slightly. Place the apricots on a plate and put in the freezer for 5–10 minutes. Meanwhile, melt the chocolate. Holding onto the strawberries, dip the apricots in the chocolate so that the chocolate reaches halfway up the sides. Allow to set.
*Serves 4–6*

# Cherry Dips

*A simple yet stunning after dinner treat.*

**12 pairs luscious-looking cherries**
**125 g (4 oz) dark (semi-sweet) chocolate**

Place the cherries on a plate and put in the freezer for 5–10 minutes. Meanwhile, melt the chocolate. Holding onto the cherry stalks, dip the cherries in the chocolate so that it reaches halfway up the sides. Allow to set.
*Makes 12*

**Freezing Fruit**
Partially freezing fruit first speeds the setting process. Chocolate sets more quickly on cold fruit.

*Right: Dried Apricot and Strawberry Dips. Enjoy the natural sweetness of fresh and dried fruit with a touch of rich dark chocolate.*

# Chocolate Cloaked Strawberries

*An ever popular finale to a special meal.*

12 strawberries, hulls left on
12 toothpicks (cocktail sticks)
125 g (4 oz) dark (semi-sweet) chocolate

Place the toothpicks in the hull end of the strawberries. Place on a plate and put in the freezer for 5–10 minutes. Meanwhile, melt the chocolate (page 206). Holding onto the toothpicks, dip the strawberries into the chocolate so that the chocolate reaches halfway up the sides. Allow to set.
*Makes 12*

# Banana Balls

*A great way to use up nicely ripened bananas, which is actually the way bananas should be when we eat them. Oats are high in dietary fibre and are a good source of iron. Added to fruit balls like these, they firm up the mixture well without the expense and fat content of nuts.*

2 ripe bananas, mashed
1 teaspoon vanilla essence (extract)
1 tablespoon honey
2 cups (185 g/6 oz) quick-cooking oats
⅔ cup (60 g/2 oz) desiccated coconut

Combine the bananas, vanilla, honey and oats. Form the mixture into small balls about the size of a walnut and roll in the desiccated coconut.
*Makes about 12*

# Walnut and Honey Cheese Balls

*A delicious addition to a fruit and cheese plate.*

250 g (8 oz) Yoghurt Cheese (page 271) *or* cream cheese
1 tablespoon honey
⅔ cup (90 g/3 oz) walnuts, chopped
additional ½ cup (60 g/2 oz) finely chopped walnuts

Combine the cheese, honey and walnuts thoroughly. Form the mixture into small balls and roll in the additional chopped walnuts.
*Makes about 12*

# Cheese and Apricot Balls

*Serve surrounded by fresh fruit and nuts for a delightful snack or an after dinner treat served with coffee or tea.*

250 g (8 oz) Yoghurt Cheese (page 271) *or* cream cheese
1 tablespoon honey
125 g (4 oz) dried apricots, chopped finely
⅔ cup (60 g/2 oz) desiccated coconut

Combine the cheese, honey and apricots thoroughly. Allow to stand for 30 minutes, if possible, to thicken. Form the mixture into small balls about the size of a walnut and roll in the desiccated coconut.
*Makes about 12*

# Banana and Raisin Balls

*These are popular with children and are always enjoyed when we're picnicking outdoors or hiking.*

1 ripe banana, mashed
1 teaspoon vanilla essence (extract)
1½ cups (250 g/8 oz) raisins, chopped finely
⅔ cup (90 g/3 oz) walnuts, chopped
1⅓ cups (125 g/4 oz) desiccated coconut

Combine the banana, vanilla, raisins and walnuts and add enough coconut to bring the mixture to a soft dough consistency. Form the mixture into small balls about the size of a walnut and roll in the remaining desiccated coconut. If not using at once, store in an airtight container in the refrigerator.
*Makes about 12*

### Time Saver
It is well worthwhile preparing double quantities of fruit or cheese based balls as they can be stored in small containers in the freezer for several weeks and used as required.

# Seed Balls

*A portable energy-filled snack. Seeds are very nutritious, containing dietary fibre, protein, vitamins and minerals.*

125 g (4 oz) sesame seeds, roasted (page 17)
125 g (4 oz) sunflower seeds, roasted (page 17)
2 tablespoons honey
1 teaspoon vanilla essence (extract)
1⅓ cups (125 g/4 oz) desiccated coconut

Grind the seeds to a coarse meal using a food processor. Place the meal into a bowl and add the honey and vanilla. Combine well, adding enough coconut to bring the mixture to a dough-like consistency. Form the mixture into small balls about the size of a walnut and roll in the remaining desiccated coconut.
*Makes about 12*

# Date and Apricot Balls

*Delicious served with a platter of sliced crisp pears or nashi fruit.*

1⅔ cups (250 g/8 oz) chopped pitted dates
1 cup (125 g/4 oz) finely chopped dried apricots
1 tablespoon honey
1 cup (90 g/3 oz) wheatgerm
⅔ cup (60 g/2 oz) desiccated coconut

Combine the dates, apricots and honey and add enough wheatgerm to bring the mixture to a soft dough consistency. Form the mixture into small balls about the size of a walnut and roll in the desiccated coconut.
*Makes about 12*

### Chopping Dried Fruit
Dried fruit is easy to chop if you have a food processor—simply drop the fruit down the feeder tube while the processor is operating with the metal chopping blade. One word of caution, however. Make sure that pitted dates have actually had every single pip removed. Otherwise your machine will be labouring as it attempts to chop the rock hard pips.

# Spiked Apricot Balls

*A real treat with a cup of freshly brewed coffee or tea.*

1 cup (125 g/4 oz) chopped dried apricots
2 tablespoons fruit liqueur (pages 327–9) *or* sherry
1 tablespoon honey
60 g (2 oz) almonds, chopped
250 g (8 oz) cream cheese
60 g (2 oz) ground almonds (almond meal)
⅔ cup (60 g/2 oz) desiccated coconut

Combine all the ingredients thoroughly. Form the mixture into small balls about the size of a walnut and roll in the desiccated coconut.
*Makes about 12*

# Fig and Ginger Balls

*Ginger makes a harmonious partner for figs and this recipe is a delightful way to enjoy the two flavours. These are great added to a cheese platter.*

250 g (8 oz) dried figs, chopped finely
2 tablespoons finely chopped preserved ginger
1–2 tablespoons honey
¾ cup (125 g/4 oz) ground almonds (almond meal)
⅔ cup (60 g/2 oz) desiccated coconut

Combine all the ingredients thoroughly. Form the mixture into small balls about the size of a walnut and roll in the desiccated coconut.
*Makes about 12*

# Sunflower Bars

2 cups (185 g/6 oz) quick-cooking oats
1 cup (125 g/4 oz) sunflower seeds
½ cup (60 g/2 oz) sesame seeds
⅔ cup (60 g/2 oz) desiccated coconut
½ cup (90 g/3 oz) soft brown sugar
60 g (2 oz) butter, melted
3 tablespoons oil
1 teaspoon vanilla essence (extract)

Place the oats, seeds, coconut and sugar in a bowl and mix well. Whisk the butter, oil and vanilla together and pour over the dry ingredients. Combine well and press the mixture down into a prepared 20 cm (8 in.) square cake pan. Bake in a moderate oven (180°C/350°F) for 20–25 minutes. Leave in the pan until cold, then cut into bars. Store in an airtight container if not using at once.
*Makes 15–18*

# Chocolate Chip Muesli Bars

*The ingredients in most muesli bars are bound together with a butterscotch mixture, rather high in fat and sugar. I only use mixtures like these for real toffee or nut brittle mixes which are obviously 'extra' type foods. Muesli bars contain such nutritious ingredients that I endeavour to keep the fat and sugar to a minimum so they can be enjoyed as an energy-laden snack, just the thing for taking on a hike or a picnic.*

1 cup (90 g/3 oz) untoasted muesli
2 cups (185 g/6 oz) rolled oats
1 cup (90 g/3 oz) desiccated coconut
90 g (3 oz) chocolate chips
3 tablespoons oil
3 tablespoons soft brown sugar
1 teaspoon vanilla essence (extract)
2 egg whites, beaten

Place the muesli, oats, coconut and chocolate chips in a bowl and combine. Whisk the oil, brown sugar, vanilla and egg whites together and pour over the dry ingredients. Combine well and press the mixture down into a prepared 20 cm (8 in.) square baking pan. Bake in a moderate oven (180°C/350°F) for 20–25 minutes. Leave in the tin until cold, then cut into squares, wedges or fingers. Store in an airtight container if not using at once.
*Makes 15–18*

*Left: Chocolate Chip Muesli Bars. Based on unsweetened muesli and rolled oats with a fair spattering of chocolate chips, this recipe is a great way to stretch your chocolate enjoyment further.*

# Date Bars

*Dates are such a great natural sweetener that only a minimum of honey is needed to sweeten these scrumptious bars.*

250 g (8 oz) pitted dates, chopped finely
1 cup (90 g/3 oz) rolled oats *or* rolled wheat
1 cup (90 g/3 oz) desiccated coconut
2 tablespoons honey
2 tablespoons oil
60 g (2 oz) butter, melted
½ cup (125 mL/4 fl oz) fruit juice
½ cup (60 g/2 oz) wholemeal (whole-wheat)
  self-raising flour
1 teaspoon mixed spice*
½ teaspoon bicarbonate of soda (baking soda)

Place the dates, oats (or wheat) and coconut into a bowl and mix well. Combine the honey, oil, butter and fruit juice and add to the dry mixture. Sift the flour, mixed spice and soda and combine thoroughly with the date mixture. Press the mixture into a prepared 20 cm (8 in.) square cake pan. Bake in a moderate oven (180°C/350°F) for 25–30 minutes. Allow to cool in the tin. When completely cold, cut into bars.
*Makes about 12*

### Storing Date Bars

Date Bars keep quite well stored in an airtight container in the pantry for a few days, and they freeze well too.

# Apricot Muesli Bars

2 cups (185 g/6 oz) rolled oats
1 cup (90 g/3 oz) wheatgerm
1 cup (125 g/4 oz) chopped dried apricots
1 cup (90 g/3 oz) desiccated coconut
2 teaspoons mixed spice*
2 tablespoons oil
½ cup (90 g/3 oz) soft brown sugar
1 teaspoon vanilla essence (extract)
2 egg whites

Place the oats, wheatgerm, apricots, coconut and mixed spice in a bowl and combine. Whisk the oil, sugar, vanilla and egg whites together and pour over the dry ingredients. Combine well and press the mixture down into a prepared 20 cm (8 in.) square cake pan. Bake in a moderate oven (180°C/350°F) for 20–25 minutes. Leave in the tin until cold, then cut into bars. Store in an airtight container if not using at once.
*Makes 15–18*

# Raisin and Nut Bars

*These bars are both delicious and easy to prepare. This is a no-bake recipe, great for hot summer months when you don't want to heat up the kitchen with a hot oven.*

125 g (4 oz) raisins, chopped finely
125 g (4 oz) pitted dates, chopped finely
½ cup (125 mL/4 fl oz) apricot nectar
1 cup Basic Nut Butter (page 280) using cashew
  nuts *or* Peanut Butter (page 281)
3 cups (280 g/9 oz) quick-cooking oats
1 teaspoon mixed spice*

Combine the raisins, dates, apricot nectar and cashew (or peanut) butter. Add the oats and spice and mix thoroughly. Press the mixture firmly into a prepared 20 cm (8 in.) square cake pan. Cover and refrigerate for 2 days before cutting into small bars.
*Makes about 24*

*Please refer to the recipe for mixed spice in our Cook's Notes, page 8.

# Fruit Salad Bars

*A nutritious and delicious snack food, these bars are based on dried fruits and nuts and have a relatively small amount of added sugar in the form of honey.*

125 g (4 oz) dried apricots, chopped finely
125 g (4 oz) dried pears, chopped finely
125 g (4 oz) dried peaches, chopped finely
125 g (4 oz) raisins, chopped finely
3 tablespoons honey
2 tablespoons fruit juice
1 cup (90 g/3 oz) wheatgerm
⅔ cup (60 g/2 oz) desiccated coconut

Combine all the ingredients thoroughly and press the mixture firmly into a prepared 20 cm (8 in.) square cake pan. Cover and refrigerate for 2 days before cutting into small bars.
*Makes about 24*

# Unbaked Apricot Bars

1 cup (125 g/4 oz) finely chopped dried apricots
3 tablespoons Basic Nut Butter (page 280) using almonds
3 tablespoons honey
⅔ cup (60 g/2 oz) quick-cooking oats
1 cup (90 g/3 oz) wheatgerm

Combine all the ingredients thoroughly and press the mixture firmly into a prepared 20 cm (8 in.) square cake pan. Cover and refrigerate for 2 days before cutting into small bars.
*Makes about 24*

### Hand Mixing

When making confections that use nut butters, it's often best to mix ingredients by hand. The heat from your hands will help to soften the nut butter and ensure the ingredients are thoroughly combined.

# Butterscotch Almonds

2 cups (250 g/8 oz) almonds
½ cup (125 mL/4 fl oz) honey
60 g (2 oz) butter
1 teaspoon vanilla essence (extract)

Place the honey and butter into a small saucepan and heat gently, stirring. Simmer the mixture gently for 10 minutes, taking care that it does not burn. When it is ready, the mixture should be a light golden brown colour. Meanwhile, spread the almonds out evenly over the bottom of a prepared 20 cm (8 in.) square cake pan. Pour the mixture over the almonds so that they are half submerged and set aside until the mixture has set. Place the tin out of the reach of children because it will become very hot immediately the butterscotch is added. When completely cold, turn the butterscotch out onto a wooden board and cut into squares.
*Makes about 36 squares*

# Sesame Brittle

60 g (2 oz) butter
1 tablespoon oil
3 tablespoons honey
3 tablespoons soft brown sugar
125 g (4 oz) sesame seeds, roasted (page 17)

Place the butter and oil in a small saucepan and heat gently until the butter melts. Add the honey and brown sugar and stir over the heat only until the sugar dissolves. Cook the toffee gently, without stirring for 10 minutes, taking care that the mixture does not boil. Stir in the sesame seeds and immediately pour the mixture into a prepared 20 cm (8 in) square cake pan. Set the toffee aside to cool and when the mixture has become brittle, turn it out onto a wooden board. Using a sharp knife, cut into squares or rough pieces.
*Makes about 36 pieces*

# Honey Pop

*To ease the conscience, serve this honey toffee-laced popcorn accompanied by a colourful platter of fresh ripe fruits, and enjoy it all. A delicious party treat for all ages.*

30 g (1 oz) butter
1 tablespoon oil
½ cup (125 g/4 oz) popping corn
3 tablespoons honey

Place the butter and the oil in a heavy based saucepan and melt over a medium heat. Add the popping corn and shake the pan to ensure the corn is evenly coated with the butter and oil. Place the lid on the pan and cook over a medium-high heat, shaking the pan occasionally to allow all the corn to come in contact with the heat. When the popping sound has ceased, drizzle the honey over the popcorn to coat it evenly. Stir the honey through the popcorn over a low–medium heat for 1–2 minutes so that the honey caramelises on the surface of the hot pan. Take care not to overheat the honey or it will burn. Tip the popcorn into a heatproof bowl and set aside to cool slightly before serving. (Otherwise the hot honey coating can burn unsuspecting fingers and tongues.)
*Serves 4–6*

# Hazelnut, Raisin and Apricot Rock

*Creamy milk chocolate is generally preferred by children (and some adults) to the sharp tasting dark (semi-sweet) chocolate. Choose for yourself!*

1 cup (125 g/4 oz) hazelnuts
1 cup (125 g/4 oz) dried apricots
1 cup (155 g/5 oz) raisins
250 g (8 oz) milk chocolate melts or dark (semi-sweet) chocolate

Combine the hazelnuts, apricots and raisins and spread out on the bottom of a prepared dish or cake pan. Melt the chocolate (page 206) and pour over the hazelnut mixture. Allow to set, then chop into rough pieces.
*Makes about 36 pieces*

# Rum and Raisin Rock

*If I were you, I would be sure to make this with dark (semi-sweet) chocolate—it is laced with rum so it's a good idea to discourage the children from devouring it when your back is turned! Instead, keep this delectable chocolate to serve at the conclusion of a special dinner or afternoon tea.*

2 cups (375 g/12 oz) seeded raisins
2 tablespoons white rum
250 g (8 oz) dark (semi-sweet) chocolate

Place the raisins into a small bowl and sprinkle with the rum. Cover and set aside to soak for 15 minutes. Spread the raisins out in a prepared dish or cake pan. Melt the chocolate (page 206) and pour over the raisins. Allow to set, then chop into rough pieces.
*Makes about 36 pieces*

*Right: Energy packed Hazelnut, Raisin and Apricot Rock. Enjoy it when you are exercising outdoors and you can put the extra energy to good use!*

# Coconut Roughs

2 tablespoons chopped raisins
2 tablespoons chopped glacé cherries
1 cup (90 g/3 oz) desiccated coconut
125 g (4 oz) milk chocolate melts

Combine the raisins, cherries and coconut together well. Melt the chocolate (page 206) and stir in the dry ingredients. Mix well and place dessertspoons of the mixture on a prepared baking sheet. Place the tray in the refrigerator until the chocolates have set, then arrange them on a serving plate.
*Makes about 18*

# Chocolate Apricot Delights

12 large dried apricots
1 quantity Liqueur Chocolate (page 206) using Apricot Liqueur (page 329)
12 hazelnuts

Arrange the apricots on a plate and place in the freezer for 5 minutes. Meanwhile, prepare the liqueur chocolate. Spoon a little of the chocolate on top of each apricot and top each one with a hazelnut.
*Makes 12*

# Fruit and Choc Balls

½ cup (60 g/2 oz) almonds, chopped
½ cup (125 g/4 oz) raisins, chopped finely
60 g (2 oz) chocolate chips
250 g (8 oz) ricotta cheese *or* cream cheese
½ cup (60 g/2 oz) ground almonds (almond meal)
⅔ cup (60 g/2 oz) desiccated coconut

Combine the chopped almonds, raisins, chocolate chips and cheese and add enough ground almonds to bring the mixture to a soft dough consistency. Form the mixture into small balls about the size of a walnut and roll in desiccated coconut.
*Makes about 12*

# Chocolate Raisin Balls

*These are a real sweet treat, chocolaty and fruity at the same time. Great for young and old.*

60 g (2 oz) milk chocolate melts
90 g (3 oz) tofu, drained and mashed
2 teaspoons vanilla essence (extract)
1 cup (155 g/5 oz) chopped seeded raisins
⅔ cup (60 g/2 oz) desiccated coconut
additional 2–3 tablespoons ground almonds (almond meal) *or* ground hazelnuts *or* desiccated coconut

Melt the chocolate (page 206) and stir in the remaining ingredients except for the additional coconut, if using. Form the mixture into small balls about the size of a walnut and roll them in the additional coconut. Place the balls on a plate, cover and chill for 1 hour before serving.
*Makes about 12*

# Quick Glacé Strawberries

*A small platter of these superb strawberries makes an eye-catching dish to serve with coffee and liqueur at the end of a special meal. They also make a simply stunning finishing touch to fresh and dried fruit platters, special cakes and desserts. Choose firm sweet berries with vibrant green hulls for the best result.*

1 punnet (carton) strawberries
½ cup (125 mL/4 fl oz) apple juice
2 teaspoons sugar
½ teaspoon pure agar agar powder (page 341)
toothpicks (cocktail sticks)

Wipe the strawberries over with a slightly damp cloth but do not wash them. Place them on a plate, insert toothpicks in the hull and pop them into the freezer for 5 minutes. Meanwhile, place the apple juice, sugar and agar agar powder in a small saucepan and bring the mixture to the boil, stirring. Reduce the heat and simmer the mixture for 1 minute, stirring, then remove from the heat and pour the mixture into a heatproof bowl. When the steam stops rising from the top of the mixture take the strawberries, one by one, and dip them into it, swizzling the toothpick to ensure that the whole berry is coated. The jelly should set very quickly, so once it is firm place the strawberries on a clean dry plate and continue until all the berries are coated. If not using them at once, store in the refrigerator.
*Serves 4–6*

### Sealing Strawberries

Chilling the strawberries in the freezer assists in the quick preparation of this dish. The cold berries cause the agar agar jelly to set almost immediately. The jelly coating improves the keeping properties of the berries remarkably well because they are sealed off from the oxygen in the air. They will keep well in the refrigerator for 2–3 days.

# Dried Fruit Pinwheels

*A simple combination of dried fruits of carnival colours, perfect for serving simply as they are, for a light sweet treat, or for topping a platter of dried fruits and cheeses.*

155 g (5 oz) large dried pears
⅔ cup (90 g/3 oz) dried apricots
¼ teaspoon oil

Place the pears, cut side down, on a wooden board and soften by rolling a rolling pin over several times, applying firm pressure. Place a 24 cm (9 in.) length of plastic wrap (cling film) on the board and arrange the pears, cut side up, overlapping slightly so that a rectangle of pears is formed. Place the apricots on top, overlapping them slightly. Using the rolling pin that has been brushed with the oil to prevent the fruit from sticking, apply firm even pressure as you run the rolling pin over the apricots several times. The pears and the apricots should now be adhering to one another. Roll the fruit up, keeping the plastic wrap on the outside of the roll, then twist the ends of the wrap to keep the fruit rolled up tightly. Place the roll in the refrigerator for 1 hour before slicing into pinwheels using a large sharp knife.
*Makes about 10 pinwheels*

### Moistening Dried Fruit

Make sure you use moist dried pears and apricots. If the fruit has dried out excessively during storage, you can soften it up nicely by placing it in a steamer insert over boiling water for 1 minute. Remove from the heat and spread the fruit out on a clean tea towel to dry for a minute or two, then use as required.

# Drinks

*Here you will find a collection of ideas for many delicious concoctions, including chilled drinks to refresh you on hot summer days, quick juices to put a spring in your step and soothing night caps to coax you off to sleep at night. Explore the limitless possibilities and combinations for punches, smoothies, yoghurt-based lassis, shakes and granitas—'Cheers!'*

# Watermelon Wonder

*Fresh watermelon juice is perfect for serving on hot summer days, just when watermelons are at their peak. Strawberries, a seasonal mate, add sweetness and colour to this beautiful drink.*

1 kg (2 lb) watermelon pieces, rind removed
8 strawberries, hulls removed
2 cups crushed ice
additional strawberries

Run the watermelon and strawberries through a juice extractor. Serve at once over crushed ice, decorated with the additional strawberries.
*Serves 2*

# Pineapple and Ginger Pick-Me-Up

*The distinctive flavour of fresh root ginger packs quite a punch in this truly refreshing drink. Be sure to buy firm fresh ginger and store it in the vegetable crisper of your refrigerator to retain its freshness.*

2.5 cm (1 in.) piece root ginger
1 kg (2 lb) pineapple, peeled
1–2 teaspoons honey (optional)
crushed ice

Using a sharp serrated stainless steel knife, cut the pineapple in lengthways slices. This will make it easier to insert into the feeder tube of a juice extractor. First run the whole piece of ginger through a juice extractor, then the pineapple slices. If using honey, whisk it through the drink before pouring it into glasses. Serve at once over plenty of crushed ice.
*Serves 2*

*Overleaf: Whether whipped up from milk, like Strawberry and Banana Smoothie (page 224), or purely from fruit, like Mango and Passionfruit Delight (page 221), freshly prepared fruit drinks simply burst with vitality.*

# Carrot and Celery Juice

*Carrot juice is incredibly sweet, luscious on its own or with ice to dilute its rich flavour, but celery adds a welcome burst of flavour.*

4 medium carrots, sliced
2 celery stalks, sliced
4 ice cubes

Run the carrots and celery through a juice extractor and serve at once over the ice cubes.
*Serves 2*

# Carrot, Apple and Beetroot Juice

*The colour alone is incredible, but the richness of the flavour makes this a drink with a difference. Beetroot (beet) is a good source of vitamins A and C and also contains iron and potassium, so enjoy it fresh once in a while and you will see there is much more to beetroot than the canned pickled variety with which we're all familiar.*

1 medium carrot, scrubbed and sliced
4 medium Granny Smith apples, washed and
    sliced
1 beetroot (beet), trimmed and peeled *or* scrubbed
    and sliced
4 ice cubes

Run the carrot, apples and beetroot through a juice extractor and serve at once over the ice cubes.
*Serves 2*

**Using a Juice Extractor**
To make fresh juices using a juice extractor, simply wash the fruit and vegetables well and cut into pieces that can fit into the feeder tube. There is no need to peel most fruits, the exceptions of course being pineapple and melons like watermelon, honeydew and rockmelon (cantaloupe).

# Mango and Passion Fruit Delight

*A delicious tropical drink, perfect for an afternoon pick-me-up.*

1 mango, peeled, pip removed and sliced
2 teaspoons honey
2 cups (500 mL/16 fl oz) fresh *or* unsweetened
    canned pineapple juice
pulp of 2–3 passion fruit
about 1 cup crushed ice

Using a blender, purée the mango, honey and pineapple juice until smooth. Whisk the passion fruit through the crushed ice and pour it into 2 glasses. Top up with the mango and pineapple mixture.
*Serves 2*

# Cashew and Pineapple Whirl

*A tasty and substantial drink, wonderful for serving with a cereal-based breakfast such as muesli and yoghurt for a nutritious start to the day.*

½ cup cashew nuts
2 cups (500 mL/16 fl oz) fresh *or* unsweetened
    canned pineapple juice
2 teaspoons honey
about ½ cup crushed ice

Using a blender, grind the cashews to a fine meal. Add one of the cups of pineapple juice and blend until smooth. Add the remaining pineapple juice, honey and ice and blend for 30 seconds. Serve at once.
*Serves 2*

# Honeydew Heaven

*If you don't have a juice extractor to make fresh pineapple juice, you can still go to heaven—simply use unsweetened canned pineapple juice!*

435 g (14 oz) ripe honeydew, peeled, pips
    removed and sliced
1 cup (250 mL/8 fl oz) fresh *or* unsweetened
    canned pineapple juice
1 cup (250 mL/8 fl oz) chilled buttermilk
2 teaspoons honey
about ½ cup crushed ice

Using a food processor, blend all the ingredients together until smooth. Serve at once.
*Serves 2*

# Apricot and Hazelnut Whirl

*Enjoy this as a nutritious breakfast when on the run.*

½ cup (60 g/2 oz) hazelnuts
2 teaspoons honey
3 ripe apricots, sliced, *or* 6 dried apricots, finely
    chopped
2 cups (500 mL/16 fl oz) chilled milk
about ½ cup crushed ice

Using a blender, chop the hazelnuts until a fine meal is produced. Add the honey, apricots and milk and blend until smooth. Add enough crushed ice to bring the drink to the desired consistency and continue blending for 10–20 seconds. Serve at once.
*Serves 2*

# Pineapple and Lemon Zinger

*The sharp distinctive flavour of lemon thyme and the tang of fresh lemon adds quite a lift to pineapple juice, making this an especially refreshing drink for hot summer days.*

4 ice cubes
thin slices of lemon
2 sprigs lemon thyme
3 cups (750 mL/24 fl oz) fresh *or* unsweetened
    canned pineapple juice
juice of 1 lemon

Place the ice cubes, lemon slices and the thyme sprigs into 2 glasses. Combine the pineapple and lemon juice and pour over the ice. Swizzle the drink and serve at once.
*Serves 2*

# Rosemary Refresher

*Rosemary, with its strong yet pleasant aroma, packs a real punch in this drink, even after a brief immersion!*

2 teaspoons honey
2 cups (500 mL/16 fl oz) fresh *or* unsweetened
    canned pineapple juice
juice of 1 lemon
about 1 cup crushed ice
2 sprigs rosemary, leaves only
4 ice cubes

Place the honey in a jug and blend with a tablespoon or two of boiling water to thin. Whisk or shake all the other ingredients until thoroughly combined. Place 2 ice cubes in each glass. Strain the drink and pour over the ice.
*Makes 2 tall glasses*

*Left: Pineapple and Lemon Zinger. A touch of lemon brings out the sweetness of the pineapple juice and the zesty flavour of lemon thyme gives both you and the drink a real lift.*

# Double Trouble Redcurrant Juice

*This is a colourful drink to serve special friends on a hot summer's day.*

1 punnet (carton) redcurrants, washed and stalks
    removed
about 2 cups crushed ice *or* 8 ice cubes
4 cups (1 litre/1¾ imp. pints) pure apple and
    blackcurrant juice

Retain 4 clumps of redcurrants for decoration and place the ice in 4 glasses. Using a blender, whiz the redcurrants and juice together for 10 seconds or so. Strain the juice and pour it over the ice. Decorate the glasses with the clumps of redcurrants and serve at once.
*Serves 4*

# Pina Colada

*With the first sip, this concoction seems to be a pleasantly smooth drink and it's then that the full bodied flavour of the rum greets the taste buds. A great drink to serve when guests arrive as a conversation starter.*

3 cups (750 mL/24 fl oz) chilled fresh *or*
    unsweetened canned pineapple juice
2 teaspoons honey
3 tablespoons coconut cream
2 tablespoons white rum
about 1 cup crushed ice
swizzle sticks decorated with fresh fruit

Using a blender, blend the pineapple juice, honey and coconut cream until foamy. Add the rum and ice and blend for 10 seconds. Serve immediately, with the fruity swizzles.
*Serves 2*

**Swizzle Sticks**
Bamboo skewers or satay sticks laced with fresh fruit make stunning swizzles to give even the simplest of concoctions a festive touch and a burst of colour.

# Banana Smoothie

*Breakfast in seconds—smoothies are the real 'fast 'foods', both to prepare and to drink.*

1 banana, sliced
2 teaspoons honey
2 cups (500 mL/16 fl oz) chilled milk
few drops vanilla essence (extract)
about ½ cup crushed ice

Using a food processor, blend the banana and honey together until smooth. Add the milk, vanilla and ice and blend for 30 seconds. Serve at once.
*Serves 2*

### Energy and Fibre
Adding a tablespoon or so of wheatgerm or muesli to fruit and milk smoothies before blending the ingredients together will provide for longer lasting energy as well as additional dietary fibre.

# Banana and Mango Smoothie

*Spicy and icy, this makes a wonderfully refreshing drink for a hot summer's day.*

1 cup sliced mango
1 banana, sliced
2 teaspoons honey
pinch ground cinnamon (optional)
2 cups (500 mL/16 fl oz) chilled milk
about ½ cup crushed ice

Using a food processor, purée the mango, banana, honey and cinnamon. Add the milk and ice and blend for 30 seconds. Serve at once.
*Serves 2*

# Pawpaw and Banana Smoothie

*My advice for drinking fresh juices and smoothies at once should really be heeded here—the pawpaw causes the drink to set if it's left to stand for too long! To be on the safe side, serve this delicious drink with a parfait spoon.*

1 cup chopped pawpaw (papaya)
1 banana, sliced
2 teaspoons honey
2 cups (500 mL/16 fl oz) chilled milk
about ½ cup crushed ice

Using a food processor, blend the pawpaw, banana and honey together until smooth. Add the milk and ice and continue blending until the mixture becomes quite foamy. Serve at once.
*Serves 2*

# Strawberry and Banana Smoothie

1 banana, sliced
8 ripe strawberries, hulls removed
2 cups (500 mL/16 fl oz) chilled milk
1–2 teaspoons honey
about ½ cup crushed ice

Using a food processor, purée the banana and strawberries, then add the milk, honey and ice and blend all together until smooth. Serve at once.
*Serves 2*

### Milk Varieties
Use any type of milk your heart desires, but remember, if you are really listening to your heart, to use low-fat varieties of milk (or occasionally try combinations based on nuts and ice instead). Whichever milk you use, make sure it is icy cold. Don't forget buttermilk and yoghurt either; they will add a welcome tang to your favourite fruity drinks.

# Avocado and Banana Surprise

*Surprisingly creamy and delicious, this filling drink is wonderful served with a light salad of fruit and greens.*

1 banana, sliced
½ small avocado, peeled, pip removed and sliced
2 teaspoons honey
few drops vanilla essence (extract)
2 cups (500 mL/16 fl oz) chilled milk
about ½ cup crushed ice

Using a food processor, blend the banana, avocado and honey together until smooth. Add the milk and ice and blend for 30 seconds. Serve at once.
*Serves 2*

# Pineapple and Avocado Smoothie

*The tropical touch of fresh ripe pineapple offsets the richness of avocado to make this a creamy delight, without the use of milk.*

2 cups (500 mL/16 fl oz) fresh *or* unsweetened canned pineapple juice
1 small *or* half medium avocado, pip removed and sliced
2 teaspoon honey
about ½ cup crushed ice

Using a food processor, blend all the ingredients together until smooth, adding enough ice to achieve the desired consistency
*Serves 2*

# Crimson Velvet

*The combination of the tang of fresh berries and yoghurt and the rich sweetness of grenadine makes this is a truly remarkable drink.*

1 cup raspberries *or* loganberries
2 tablespoons plain yoghurt
2 tablespoons grenadine syrup *or* 3 teaspoons honey
2 cups (500 mL/16 fl oz) milk
about ½ cup crushed ice

Using a food processor, blend the berries, yoghurt and grenadine (or honey) together until smooth. Add the milk and ice and blend until foamy.
*Serves 2*

# Peach and Almond Smoothie

*A delightful dairy-free drink laced with the light milky flavour of almonds.*

⅓ cup (60 g/2 oz) almonds
1 medium peaches, peeled, pip removed and sliced
1 cup (250 mL/8 fl oz) apricot nectar
1 cup (250 mL/8 fl oz) chilled water
About ½ cup crushed ice

Using a blender, grind the almonds to a fine meal then add the peach and the apricot nectar. Blend until smooth then add the milk and ice and blend for 30 seconds
*Serves 2*

**Using Canned Peaches**
Although you won't achieve the tang characteristic of fresh peaches, peaches canned in their own juice are great for making smoothies.

# Thick Mango Smoothie

*So thick and creamy you can eat it with a spoon! In fact this smoothie makes a wonderful summer dessert so I suggest you serve it with parfait spoons.*

1 ripe mango, peeled, pip removed and sliced
2 teaspoons honey
2 cups (500 mL/16 fl oz) chilled milk
about ½ cup crushed ice
1–2 scoops vanilla ice cream

Using a blender, blend the mango and honey together until smooth. Add the milk and ice and blend for 30 seconds, then add the ice cream and blend for a further 10 seconds. Serve at once.
*Serves 2*

# Dark Grape Lassi

*A lassi is a chilled drink based on yoghurt and often containing fruit or fruit juice. Much loved in India, these drinks are very refreshing in hot weather.*

2 cups (500 mL/16 fl oz) dark grape juice
1 cup (250 mL/8 fl oz) plain yoghurt
about ½ cup crushed ice *or* 4 ice cubes

Using a blender, blend all the ingredients together until well combined. Alternatively, place all the ingredients in a large jar and shake vigorously until the mixture becomes foamy. Serve at once.
*Serves 2*

# Strawberry Fluff

*It's the addition of the yoghurt that makes this a light fluffy drink. Sweetened by the ripe strawberries and the fruit juice, there is no need for added sugar.*

8–10 strawberries, hulls removed
1 cup (250 mL/8 fl oz) plain yoghurt
2 cups (500 mL/16 fl oz) chilled apple and
   blackcurrant juice
about ½ cup crushed ice

Using a blender, blend the strawberries and yoghurt together until smooth. Add the fruit juice and blend until the mixture is light and fluffy. Add the ice and blend for a few seconds, then serve at once.
*Serves 2*

**Using Honey**
Honey is suggested for sweetening many of the recipes. If the fruit you are using, however, is beautifully ripe, or you usually do not add sweetening to your fruit drinks, the honey can be omitted. I suggest using honey with fruit drinks as, to my mind, it complements fruity flavours well.

# Apricot Lassi

*This quick drink can be enjoyed all year round, but in summer it looks wonderful decorated with a swizzle stick laced with slices of fresh apricots and ripe red strawberries.*

2 cups (500 mL/16 fl oz) apricot nectar
2 teaspoons honey
1 cup (250 mL/8 fl oz) plain yoghurt
about ½ cup crushed ice

Using a blender, blend all the ingredients together until well combined. Alternatively, place all the ingredients in a large jar and shake vigorously until the mixture becomes foamy. Serve at once.
*Serves 2*

*Right: Strawberry Fluff and Apricot Lassi. These yoghurt-based drinks sweetened with fresh fruit and fruit juice make great pick-me-ups all year round.*

# Carob and Honey Shake

*Carob, often used as an alternative to chocolate, does have a chocolate-like flavour but I prefer to regard it as a delicious ingredient in its own right. It has its own distinctive character after all. Fruity and spicy, it makes a wonderful flavouring for hot and cold drinks.*

1 tablespoon carob powder
2 teaspoons honey
1–2 tablespoons boiling water
2 cups (500 mL/16 fl oz) chilled milk
about ½ cup crushed ice
2–4 ice cubes

Place the carob and honey in a cup and blend to a thick syrup with the water. Place the ice cubes in 2 glasses. Place the milk and crushed ice in a large jar and add the carob mixture. Shake all the ingredients together until fluffy and pour into the glasses. Serve at once.
*Serves 2*

### Smoothies and Shakes

While smoothies are based on fruit and milk or juice combinations, and require a blender or food processor for their preparation, shakes can be made using a large screw topped jar or bottle.

# Mocha Shake

2 teaspoons cocoa powder
1 tablespoon boiling water
4 teaspoons honey
2 cups (500 mL/16 fl oz) chilled milk
½ cup (125 mL/4 fl oz) chilled espresso coffee
few drops vanilla essence (extract)
1 tablespoon skim milk powder
4 ice cubes

Place the cocoa powder in a cup and blend to a smooth paste with the boiling water and the honey. Place the remaining ingredients in a large jar and shake vigorously until the drink becomes light and fluffy. Serve at once.
*Serves 2*

# Special Iced Coffee Parfaits

*The vanilla-laced ice cubes and ice cream chill this drink beautifully and take the edge off the strong coffee flavour. Serve as a refreshing snack on summer afternoons with friends or as a light dessert. Be sure to serve with parfait spoons to scoop up all the ice cream.*

3 cups (750 mL/24 fl oz) chilled low-fat milk
1 cup (250 mL/8 fl oz) chilled strong espresso coffee
4 milk ice cubes
2 scoops vanilla ice cream
shaved chocolate *or* cracked chocolate-coated coffee beans

Shake the milk, coffee and ice cubes together. Place the ice cream into 2 parfait glasses and pour the coffee mixture over. Sprinkle with shaved chocolate or scatter with the coffee beans and serve at once.
*Serves 2*

### Making Milk Ice Cubes

Milk ice cubes are great to have on hand for adding to smoothies and shakes. Simply combine milk and vanilla essence well and pour into ice cube containers. Freeze and store the ice cubes in a freezer bag until required.

# Pineapple Punch

*Pineapple sage leaves impart even more pineapple flavour to this delicious punch and, along with the star fruit, provide the garnish at the same time.*

2 cups (500 mL/16 fl oz) pineapple juice
1 cup (250 mL/8 fl oz) apple juice
juice of 1 lemon
1 cup crushed ice
1 star fruit, washed and sliced
½ lemon, sliced thinly
8 pineapple sage leaves, sliced finely

Combine the pineapple, apple and lemon juices. Just before serving, place the ice, star fruit, lemon slices and sage leaves in a punchbowl or jug. Pour the juices over and serve at once.
*Serves 4*

# Strawberry Wine

1 punnet (carton) chilled strawberries, hulls removed and halved
½ cup (125 mL/4 fl oz) pure apple juice
2 tablespoons grenadine syrup
½ cup crushed ice
3 cups (750 mL/24 fl oz) chilled sparkling white wine
4 additional strawberries, sliced

Using a blender, purée the strawberries. Add the apple juice and blend for 10–20 seconds. Using a wooden spoon, press the purée through a coarse sieve. Place the strawberry purée in a jug and combine with the grenadine, ice and wine. Whisk the mixture briefly to combine all the ingredients and immediately pour into 4 glasses. Top with the sliced strawberries and serve at once.
*Serves 4*

# Citrus Fruit Punch

*Tangy and refreshing, this punch can be made in the colder months when citrus fruits are at their best. In summer, the punch can be adorned with edible blossoms such as honeysuckle, nasturtium, frangipani or marigold.*

1 orange, washed and sliced thinly
1 lemon, washed and sliced thinly
1 grapefruit, peeled, pith and pips removed and sliced thinly
12 ice cubes
3 cups (750 mL/24 fl oz) freshly squeezed orange juice
juice of 2 lemons
2 cups (500 mL/16 fl oz) mineral water
2–3 teaspoons honey
1–2 tablespoons boiling water

Place the sliced oranges, lemons, grapefruit and ice in a punch bowl or jug. Combine the orange and lemon juices and the mineral water. Place the honey in a cup and blend to a syrup with the boiling water. Stir the honey through the fruit juice and adjust the flavour, adding a little more honey if necessary. Pour the punch over the fruit and ice and serve at once.
*Serves 4–6*

Fruit Juices
To obtain the best result when making fruit drinks, use freshly squeezed juices or commercial 'pure fruit juice/no added sugar' varieties of juice. If adding fruit, use the freshest of fruit, or fruit canned in its own juice.

# Apricot Fruit Cup

*The colour of this superb punch reminds me of the rosy hue of a summer sunrise. Summer is also reflected in the flavour and aroma of summer fruits and blossoms.*

8–10 ice cubes
4 scented geranium leaves
4 scented geranium blossoms
1 punnet (carton) ripe strawberries, hulls removed and halved
4 cups (1 litre/1¾ imp. pints) apricot nectar
1 cup (250 mL/8 fl oz) sweet white wine *or* apple juice
2 cups (500 mL/16 fl oz) mineral water
additional sliced strawberries

Place the ice, geranium leaves and blossoms in a large jug or punch bowl. Using a blender, purée the strawberries then add the apricot nectar and blend for 20–30 seconds. Strain the mixture though a sieve and pour into the punch bowl. Just before serving, stir the wine (or apple juice) and mineral water through, and add sliced strawberries to decorate.
*Serves 4–6*

# Herbed Punch

*Icy cold brews brimming with edible blossoms and new season's fruits and herbs are refreshing on hot summer days.*

2 cups (500 mL/16 fl oz) well-infused herb tea
3 cups (750 mL/24 fl oz) pure unsweetened fruit juice
1 lemon, sliced
8 ice cubes
4 mint sprigs
½ cup edible blossoms such as lavender, borage *or* camomile

Combine the herb tea and fruit juice. Just before serving, place the lemon, ice cubes, mint sprigs and blossoms in a punchbowl or jug and pour the tea mixture over. Serve at once.
*Serves 4*

# Double Mint Cooler

*It's worthwhile making a double quantity of this as any remaining cooler can be popped in the refrigerator for an instant pick-me-up.*

2–3 peppermint tea bags
2 cups (500 mL/16 fl oz) boiling water
2 teaspoons honey
4 mint sprigs, leaves only
8 ice cubes

Infuse the tea bags in the boiling water and allow to stand for 20 minutes. Remove the tea bags and stir in the honey. Place the mint leaves and ice cubes in a jug and pour the peppermint tea over.
*Serves 2*

**Freezing Mint**
While your garden is sporting copious mint plants, pick some sprigs and freeze them in ice cubes—these are great added to pure fruit juices, herb teas and fruit punches.

# Strawberry Punch

4 ice cubes
1 cup strawberries, sliced
8–10 mint leaves, sliced finely
2 cups (500 mL/16 fl oz) apple and blackcurrant juice
1 cup (250 mL/8 fl oz) mineral water
125 g (4 oz) redcurrants, snipped into small clumps
4 mint sprigs

Place the ice cubes into a jug and top with the strawberries and the mint. Combine the fruit juice and the mineral water and pour over. Give the drinks a swizzle and serve topped with the redcurrants and the mint sprigs.
*Serves 4*

*Right: Scented with geranium leaves and blossoms, Apricot Fruit Cup makes a great aperitif. Enjoy it uplifted with wine or purely as a fruit-based drink.*

# Lemon Apple Punch

*What a welcome sight a jug of chilled punch is for those who return home hot and tired! For just those occasions, have a jug of this refreshing punch lurking in the refrigerator—it is easily prepared in the morning and, by evening, all the flavours have infused beautifully.*

2 lemon-scented tea bags
½ lemon, washed well and sliced thinly
1 cinnamon stick
2 teaspoons honey
2 cups (500 mL/16 fl oz) boiling water
1 cup (250 mL/8 fl oz) apple juice
8 ice cubes

Place the tea bags in a heatproof jug with the lemon slices, cinnamon stick and honey. Pour the boiling water over, then cover and set aside to cool slightly. Remove the teabag, add the apple juice and stir the punch well. Cover the jug and store in the refrigerator for several hours. Serve over the ice cubes.
*Serves 4*

# Tropical Fruit Punch

12 ice cubes
1 mango, peeled, pip removed and diced or chopped finely
4 cups (1 litre/1¾ imp. pints) fresh or unsweetened canned pineapple juice
½ cup (125 mL/4 fl oz) passion fruit pulp
juice of 2 limes
2 cups (500 mL/16 fl oz) mineral water
edible blossoms such as frangipani

Place the ice cubes in a punch bowl or jug. Using a blender, purée the mango, then add the pineapple juice and blend for 20 seconds. Strain the mixture through a coarse sieve, then combine with the passion fruit pulp, lime juice and mineral water. Pour the punch over the ice and mix briefly. Float the blossoms on top and serve at once.
*Serves 4*

# Pineapple and Date Delight

*Naturally sweetened by the dates, this is a wonderful drink to enjoy on busy summer days when you need to be on your toes but do not have the desire to eat a substantial meal. I usually like to follow this drink with some soft fruits and a handful of almonds.*

2 fresh dates, pitted *or* 2 tablespoons chopped pitted dates
2 cups (500 mL/16 fl oz) fresh *or* unsweetened canned pineapple juice
½ cup crushed ice

Using a blender, purée the dates, then add half of the pineapple juice and blend until smooth. Add the remaining pineapple juice and ice and blend for a further 10 seconds.
*Serves 2*

**A Creamier Version**
For a wonderful creamy drink, replace half a cup of the pineapple juice with half a cup of plain yoghurt.

# Honey and Lemon Bubbly

*Bubbles galore—mineral water adds a welcome fizz to pure fruit drinks, and for those of you with lemon trees that periodically brim with lemons, this recipe is a delight.*

4 ice cubes
juice of 4 lemons
4 teaspoons honey
2 cups (500 mL/16 fl oz) mineral water
swizzle sticks sporting lemon twists

Place the ice cubes into 2 glasses. Combine the lemon juice, honey and mineral water and pour over the ice. Serve with the swizzles.
*Serves 2*

# Lemon-Scented Water

*Scented water is refreshing and although it is easily prepared it is quite a treat. Leaving the water to stand allows the flavours from the lemon to infuse thoroughly.*

1 lemon, washed and sliced thinly
4 cups (1 litre1¾ imp. pints) water

Place the lemon in a jug and pour the water over. Allow to stand in the refrigerator for at least 1 hour but preferably all day or overnight.
*Serves 2–4*

### Refreshing Water

Water is the most refreshing drink of all. Many of us have unfortunately become used to drinking sweetened drinks all the time, which not only allows excess sugar and 'empty kilojoules' to creep into our diets but can cause dental caries. It's a good idea to start including a tall glass or two of water in our diets each day, increasing to 8 glasses per day over time.

# Grape Juice Granita

*To prepare your own granita concoctions, three quarters fill serving glasses with crushed ice and pour freshly extracted juices over the top. Serve immediately. And remember, it's good to serve granitas with a parfait spoon both to swizzle and to scoop! Or, for a special occasion, try topping the ice up with a fruity liqueur (pages 327–9).*

4 cups (1 litre/1¾ imp. pints) dark grape juice
2 small bunches of dark grapes

Pour 3 of the 4 cups of the grape juice into ice cube freezer trays and allow 2 hours for it to freeze. Crush the ice cubes  and place the ice in 2 tall glasses. Pour the remaining grape juice over, swizzle through and serve, at once, arranging a bunch of grapes on the side of each glass.
*Serves 2*

# Prune and Lemon Granita

*Prune juice is such a sweet flavoursome drink that it can well be diluted with plenty of ice, as it is in this delicious granita.*

3 cups (750 mL/24 fl oz) prune juice
juice of 1 lemon
2 cups crushed ice
swizzles with lemon twists

Combine the prune juice with the lemon juice and ice and place the mixture in a freezer container and freeze for 1½ hours. Break up the ice crystals that have formed on the sides of the container. Place the ice in 2 tall glasses, swizzle through and serve at once.
*Serves 2*

# Orange and Mango Granita

*This is such a simply prepared drink yet one that is superb to serve. The only trick is remembering to allow time for the orange juice ice cubes to freeze.*

2 cups (500 mL/16 fl oz) pure orange juice
½ large ripe mango, peeled, pip removed and sliced
additional 1 cup (250 mL/8 fl oz) pure orange juice
swizzle laced with orange twists and strawberries

Pour the orange juice into 2 ice cube freezer trays and allow 2 hours to freeze. Crush the ice cubes and place the ice in 2 tall glasses. Blend the mango and orange juice and strain through a coarse sieve. Pour the juice over the ice, swizzle through and serve at once.
*Serves 2*

### To Crush Ice

To crush ice, place ice cubes in a clean tea towel, draw up the ends and thrash the bench—just about as good as bread-making for releasing pent up emotions or tension!

# Strawberry Liqueur Granita

*I like to serve this at the end of a summer meal instead of coffee or tea. In winter, you can still enjoy the taste of summer, captured in the strawberries used to make this delicious liqueur.*

1½ cups (375 mL/12 fl oz) apple and blackcurrant
  juice
2 tablespoons grenadine syrup
½ cup (125 mL/4 fl oz) Strawberry Liqueur
  (page 328)
4 strawberries, hulls removed and sliced

Place the apple and blackcurrant juice in an ice cube tray and allow 2 hours to freeze completely. Crush the ice cubes and place the ice in 2 glasses. Top each serve with 1 tablespoon grenadine syrup, pour the liqueur over and scatter the strawberries over. Serve at once.
*Serves 2*

# Spiked Apricot and Peach Granita

*Peach liqueur has a wonderful smooth flavour, very easy to drink, so watch out! I like to dilute its impact on the senses with the complementary sweetness of apricot nectar and the crushed ice, cooling down both you and the drink.*

2½ cups (625 mL/20 fl oz) apricot nectar
1 cup (250 mL/8 fl oz) apricot nectar
4 tablespoons Peach Liqueur (page 328)
6 strawberries, sliced

Freeze half the apricot nectar in ice cube trays for 2 hours, placing the remaining juice in the refrigerator to use when assembling the drinks. Just before serving, crush the apricot nectar ice cubes and spoon the crushed ice into 2 glasses. Pour ½ cup apricot nectar over each serve. Top each serve with 2 tablespoons of the liqueur and scatter the strawberries over. Serve at once.
*Serves 4*

# Spiked Apple and Berry Granita

*The fruit ice cubes are the key to the success of this wonderful drink—so remember to make them beforehand. The distinctive colour and flavour of the Raspberry Ratafia and the fresh raspberries does the rest.*

1¼ cups (310 mL/10 fl oz) apple and blackcurrant
  juice
½ cup (125 mL/4 fl oz) Raspberry Ratafia
  (page 328)
2–3 tablespoons raspberries

Place the juice in an ice cube tray and allow 2 hours to freeze completely. Crush the ice cubes and place the ice in 2 glasses. Top each serve with 3 tablespoons of the Raspberry Ratafia and scatter with the raspberries. Serve at once.
*Serves 2*

# Chinese Green Tea

*Chinese tea is a wonderful refresher served at the beginning of the meal and in between courses.*

1 teaspoon green tea
4 cups (1 litre/1¾ imp. pints) boiling water

Warm the tea pot before you begin, as you would do for all tea-making. Add the tea and top with freshly boiled water. Allow to stand for 5 minutes before serving.
*Serves 2–4*

**Herbal and Green Teas**
Chinese green tea is a great standby when entertaining as it does not become bitter after standing and, like herb teas, is just as delicious served warm as it is piping hot, unlike standard teas.

*Left: Strawberry Liqueur Granita. Serving liqueurs as granitas allows you to savour their rich flavour as long drinks.*

# Lemon Soother

*A good bedtime drink, or a soothing drink to treat yourself to at the end of a long hard day.*

2 teaspoons honey
juice of 2 lemons
4 slices lemon
2 teaspoons lemon thyme leaves
1 camomile tea bag
2 cups (500 mL/16 fl oz) water

Place 1 teaspoon honey, half the lemon juice and 2 slices of lemon in each of two coffee mugs. Place the thyme, tea bag and water in a small saucepan and bring the mixture to the boil. Remove from the stove and allow to stand for 5 minutes. Strain into the coffee mugs. Stir and serve at once.
*Serves 2*

# Hot Cinnamon Nightcap

2 cups (500 mL/16 fl oz) skim milk
1 cinnamon stick
2 teaspoons honey

Place the milk and cinnamon stick into a small saucepan and heat the mixture gently. Remove before the milk reaches boiling point. Remove the cinnamon stick and stir in the honey.
*Serves 2*

# Star Anise and Apricot Nectar

2 cups (500 mL/16 fl oz) apricot nectar
1/2 cup (125 mL/4 fl oz) water
2 star anise
2 teaspoons honey

Place the apricot nectar, water and star anise into a small saucepan and heat the mixture gently to boiling point. Remove from the heat, cover and allow to stand for 5–10 minutes. Remove the star anise and stir in the honey.
*Serves 2*

# Mulled Apple and Cinnamon

2 cups (500 mL/16 fl oz) pure apple juice
1 cup (250 mL/8 fl oz) water
1 cinnamon stick
2–3 whole cloves
2 teaspoons honey
4 lemon slices

Place the apple juice, water, cinnamon stick and cloves into a small saucepan and heat gently. Place 1 teaspoon of honey and two lemon slices in each of 2 mugs. Remove the cinnamon stick and cloves and pour the remaining liquid over the lemon slices and honey.
*Serves 2*

# Camomile Night Cap

*Hot herby brews are reminiscent of grandma's home remedies and are great for nurturing yourself and loved ones. If sleep eludes you, a cup of camomile or other soothing herb tea can work wonders. Try also infusing hot teas with lemon, orange or lime slices.*

2 teaspoons loose camomile tea *or* 2 tea bags
½ cinnamon stick, crushed
2 cups (500 mL/16 fl oz) boiling water
1–2 teaspoons honey

Place the tea (or tea bag) and cinnamon stick into a small tea pot or jug. Pour over the boiling water, cover and allow to infuse for 5–10 minutes. Strain, sweeten with honey if desired and serve at once.
*Serves 2*

# Milk and Molasses Nightcap

*Do be sure to buy de-bittered molasses which has a rather caramel-like flavour, really delicious with warm milk. It is available from health food stores and some supermarkets. Take care not to buy crude molasses which has an overpowering flavour.*

2 teaspoons de-bittered molasses (black treacle)
2 cups (500 mL/16 fl oz) milk

Place the molasses into 2 mugs. Heat the milk almost to boiling point, then pour over the molasses. Stir briskly and enjoy.
*Serves 2*

**Teeth Care**
When enjoying soothing sweetened drinks as nightcaps, remember to give your teeth a once over to avoid dental caries.

# Spiced Milk

*Star anise is one of my favourite spices—I enjoy the waft of its wonderful scent as I open up the airtight jar I store it in. Star anise blends well with cinnamon to give an exotic flavour to this soothing drink.*

2 cups (500 mL/16 fl oz) milk
2 star anise
1 cinnamon stick
2 teaspoons honey

Place the milk, star anise and cinnamon stick into a small saucepan and heat the mixture gently. Remove before the milk reaches boiling point. Remove the star anise and cinnamon stick and stir in the honey.
*Serves 2*

# Special Hot Chocolate

*The vanilla and honey add a special touch to hot chocolate which can be enjoyed all year round, but especially during the cooler months when it can be sipped as you curl up in front of a heater, perhaps with a good book!*

3 cups (750 mL/24 fl oz) milk
3 teaspoons cocoa powder
2 teaspoons honey
½ cup (125 mL/4 fl oz) water
few drops vanilla essence (extract)

Heat the milk gently. Meanwhile, place the cocoa powder and honey into a cup and blend to a smooth paste, adding the water gradually. When the milk is hot, whisk in the cocoa mixture. Cook gently, stirring, for 1 minute. Whisk the vanilla through and serve.
*Serves 2*

# Mexican-Style Hot Chocolate

*The burst of cinnamon flavour makes this drink a winner.*

3 cups (750 mL/24 fl oz) milk
½ cinnamon stick
3 teaspoons cocoa powder
2 teaspoons honey
2 tablespoons boiling water
2 teaspoons grated milk chocolat
additional 2 cinnamon sticks

Place the milk and ½ cinnamon stick in a saucepan and heat gently. Meanwhile, place the cocoa powder and honey into a cup and blend to a smooth paste, adding the water gradually. When the milk is hot, whisk in the cocoa mixture. Heat gently, stirring, for 1 minute. Remove the cinnamon stick and strain the mixture into a jug. Pour into 2 mugs, sprinkle with shaved chocolate and serve with cinnamon sticks as swizzles.
*Serves 2*

# Part Two: How to Make Your Own

*Investing a little time and effort in whipping up a batch of homemade delights such as oven-fresh bread, sweet or spicy succulent preserves, juicy sprouts and delectable liqueurs pays good dividends. You will only have to reach as far as your pantry shelf to add a touch of the exotic to both daily and special occasion meals.*

# Planning

I make no apologies for the time some of these recipes take to prepare and/or mature; the preparation procedures are very simple, we simply need to learn the rules of the 'waiting game'. The first time I made Strawberry Liqueur (page 328) I found it hard to set the berries aside to macerate for a few days, not because I wanted to get my hands on the liqueur, but because I was impatient to decant it into its beautiful bottle. I had been used to whipping up quick recipes and being rewarded with stunning results right there and then. But I'm learning. . .

Many of us claim that we are far too busy to prepare anything but the obligatory meal here and there, and that whipping up homemade bread, breakfast mixes and the like is simply out of the question. I understand that it is often difficult to fit the preparation of these 'extras' into the busy schedules of those who leave home every day to work. But if you enjoy cooking, why not win back some time on the weekends or during holidays to stock up the pantry?

I often set a day or two aside to do just that, and I really make the best use of my time by having several homemade delights growing, brewing, baking or setting at the same time! For example, when you are pre-heating the oven to cook bread, don't waste energy (both your own and the oven's). Pop a tray or two of muesli in so that it can be toasting at the same time. Sprouts are wonderful to have growing in the background —they only need to be rinsed 2–3 times a day. And why not whip up some yoghurt while you're at it? Once the starter culture has been whisked

*Overleaf: Having a ready stock of flavour-packed and colourful concoctions like fragrant vinegars, oils and preserves can provide inspiration for exploring your own creativity with food.*

through the milk, the yoghurt can be popped into its insulated container and tucked away in a warm corner of your kitchen. You won't need to give it any more attention until it is time to pop it in the refrigerator to chill. In between times, cut some feta into slices or cubes and submerge it in extra virgin olive oil, adding an array of fresh and dried herbs as you go. Then it will be perfect to serve with the fresh crusty bread that is soon to emerge from your oven!

If you're like me and have family and friends you don't seem to be able to spend as much time with as you would like, invite them over to laugh and talk while you make pasta, tofu or bread together. It's a wonderful way to spend time with one another and you both get to share the goodies you've had fun preparing. I recently had the pleasure of a very fruitful afternoon spent with my husband and sister, each with our own task of peeling garlic, plucking basil leaves from their stalks and blanching and peeling tomatoes. At the end of the day we had produced several jars of fresh pesto sauce and a copious amount of pasta sauce.

I enjoy these cooking sprees immensely, but it doesn't end there. Throughout the year I prepare for the summer harvests of soft fruit and berries, tomatoes and basil. One way to do this is to take up the hobby of jar and bottle collecting. When shopping I'm always on the lookout for beautiful or unusual bottles, perfect for decanting fragrant vinegars, oils and liqueurs. It doesn't take long for the word to get out that you are a 'preserving and bottling freak'. When my friends and family visit, the tinkling of distant chimes can be heard as they approach the front door—or is it the bag of bottles and jars they have in tow?

## Shopping

Harvesting your own crops or buying fruits and vegetables in bulk when they are at their peak freshness must be a prerequisite for preserving and bottling. At no other time is it as important to use quality seasonal produce. It makes good sense economically speaking, but it also ensures the time you have invested will be rewarded with a variety of superb preserves to enjoy throughout the year. Sweet juicy sun ripened **tomatoes** can be blanched and peeled (page 77) and bottled whole or as purée for use during the colder months when tomatoes are out of season. And **mango** season just never seems to be long enough, so be sure to buy up big when the price is right and preserve their sweet nectar-like flavour for use in salsas, desserts and ice creams. **Fresh herbs** can be purchased in bulk, dried and stored in airtight jars, or chopped and frozen. **Berry fruits** not only make exquisite jams, sauces, vinegars and ice creams, but they can be frozen just as they are and whipped up into delectable dishes to serve all year round. If you make **yoghurt and fresh cheeses** regularly, it is worthwhile purchasing plenty of cartons of ultra heat treated milk—it is cheaper to buy in bulk, has a prolonged shelf life and will be there just when you get the urge for a cooking spree.

## Preparation Tips

**Fresh mangoes** can be peeled and the flesh sliced off the pip, using a sharp serrated knife. You can have mangoes all year round by freezing the flesh. To keep the slices separate, spread them out in an even layer on trays and pop the trays in the freezer. Once frozen, the mango slices can be transferred to a freezer container or freezer bag. Seal and label the container/s and return to the freezer. **Berries** can be frozen the same way so that when you come to use them you can select exactly the amount of loose berries you need, rather than chopping your way through an ice cube of frozen berries. **Whole tomatoes** can also be washed, patted dry and popped into freezer bags as they are. Freeze until required and then plunge them into warm water. As the tomatoes thaw, the skins (which have burst during the freezing process) can be easily removed. As they continue to thaw, place the tomatoes in a bowl so that you can collect and use any juices that are released.

When **citrus fruits** are at their best, thin strips of zest can be pared from the skin and popped into a freezer bag and frozen, as is, or cut into slivers first. Grated orange and lemon rind can also be frozen, and remains crumbly and easy to measure out and use even when frozen. It's also handy to have orange, lemon and lime slices in the freezer for use in herb teas and fruit punches.

**Fresh parsley** can be chopped and placed in small freezer containers or bags, and like grated orange and lemon rind, it retains a crumbly texture even when frozen, making it easy to use.

Drying **chilies** is easy. All you have to do is string them up and hang them in your kitchen. They make an eye-catching decoration as they are drying. Bouquets of **fresh herbs** can be dried the same way. Once they have become quite crumbly, they can be packed into airtight jars for later use. Chilies can also be added to foods preserved under oil, to add flavour and to provide a stunning garnish.

## Sterilising Bottles and Jars

It is important to sterilise the bottles and jars you are going to store preserves in. (Make sure you use glass bottles and jars that withstand heat.) There are several ways to sterilise bottles and jars. Here are two simple ways I use. For the 'on top of the stove' method, simply place the jars on a trivet in a large boiling pan and cover them completely with water. Cover the pan, bring the water to the boil and keep it boiling for 20 minutes. Using long-handled tongs, carefully remove the jars from the hot pan, empty them of water and stand them on wooden boards to allow the remaining water to evaporate. For the oven method, place the jars on a baking sheet and heat in a slow oven (150°C/300°F) for 30 minutes. Take care when handling the hot jars and remember the basic rule—place hot preserves in hot jars and cold preserves in cold jars.

## Labelling Preserves

Whether you are popping an extra loaf or two of bread in a freezer bag or freshly prepared jam or chutney in jars, always remember to place an appropriate label on the container. Otherwise you could be in for a big surprise, like when you take what you think is a sweet fruit bread from the freezer only to discover that it really is olive bread. Or you bite into your toast topped with what you're sure is apricot conserve, only to discover that it is hot mango chutney! Record the name of the contents and the date it was made on the label. And it's not a bad idea to jot down the number of serves a freezer container of prepared food holds. It's also good to get into the habit of rotating the contents of your pantry and/or freezer so that the foods which have been stored for the longest time are placed at the front of the shelf and used first.

# Pumpernickel Bread

*Dark, moist and very tasty, this bread makes a wonderful accompaniment for Pumpkin Soup (page 33). It makes a compatible partner for all manner of cheeses and is especially good sliced thinly and topped with Gruyère cheese.*

1 cup (250 mL/8 fl oz) hot water

1 teaspoon sugar

1 cup (250 mL/8 fl oz) cold water

15 g (½ oz) active dry yeast

3 cups (375 g/12 oz) rye flour

1 cup (125 g/4 oz) wholemeal (whole-wheat) plain (all-purpose) flour

¼ teaspoon salt (optional)

3 cups (375 g/12 oz) sprouted wheat (page 257)

4 tablespoons debittered molasses (page 344)

1 tablespoon oil

Combine the hot water with the sugar in a small bowl. Add the cold water and whisk the yeast through using a fork. Set aside for 5 minutes. Meanwhile, combine the flours, salt and sprouted wheat and make a 'well' in the centre. Pour the yeast mixture, molasses and oil into the 'well' and combine all the ingredients thoroughly. Place into 2 prepared bread pans. Cover and set aside to prove (rise) for 1–1¼ hours. Bake in a hot oven (210°C/425°F) for 30 minutes. Place the loaves on a cake rack to cool.
*Makes 2 loaves*

### Developing Flavour

It's best to make this bread the day before you wish to use it. This allows the flavour of the bread to develop. As soon as the bread is cold, wrap it in a clean dry tea towel, then pop it in a plastic (polythene) bag. If you wish to keep the bread for more than a day or two, it's best to store it in the refrigerator.

---

# Breads

*Is any aroma from the kitchen more inviting than that of freshly baked bread? If there is one, I have yet to discover it! Try your hand (literally) at making a basic loaf to start with then enjoy experimenting with the myriad of ingredients that can be incorporated— golden polenta, sprouted grains, roasted seeds and nuts, puréed vegetables and succulent dried fruits.*

# Pistachio Bread

*This superb golden bread interspersed with the vibrant green pistachios makes a colourful accompaniment to soup or an antipasto meal.*

½ cup (125 mL/4 fl oz) hot water

1 teaspoon sugar

¾ cup (225 mL/7 fl oz) cold water

7 g (¼ oz) active dry yeast

1½ cups (185 g/6 oz) plain (all-purpose) flour

1½ cups (185 g/6 oz) wholemeal (whole-wheat) plain (all-purpose) flour

¼ teaspoon salt

1 teaspoon ground turmeric

1 cup (125 g/4 oz) shelled pistachio nuts

¼ teaspoon freshly ground black pepper

Follow the method for Basic Bread (page 244), adding the turmeric and pistachios to the flours before combining it with the yeast mixture. After the first kneading, form the dough into 1 round loaf and place on prepared baking sheets. Cover and set aside in a warm place for 45 minutes. Brush the top with a little warm water and bake in a hot oven (210°C/425°F) for 30 minutes.
*Makes 1 loaf*

*Left: A touch of turmeric provides the colour to Pistachio Bread, while the pistachios add a burst of flavour and a delightful texture contrast.*

# Basic Bread

¾ cup (225 mL/7 fl oz) hot water
1 teaspoon sugar
2 cups (500 ml /16 fl oz) cold water
15 g (½ oz) active dry yeast
6 cups (750 g/1½ lb) plain (all-purpose) flour
¼ teaspoon salt (optional)
additional plain (all-purpose) flour

Place the hot water into a bowl, add the sugar and stir until it is dissolved. Add the cold water, whisk the yeast through and set the mixture aside until a 'sponge' forms on top of the mixture. This usually takes about 5 minutes. Meanwhile, sift the flour and salt into a large bowl and make a 'well' in the centre. Pour the yeast mixture into the 'well' and work the flour in gradually until a ball of soft dough is formed. Turn the dough out onto a lightly floured surface and knead for about 10 minutes, sprinkling the surface with additional flour as required. You will know the dough is sufficiently kneaded when it springs back immediately when pressed gently with your fingers. Place the dough in a clean warm bowl, cover and place it in a warm location until the dough doubles in size. This usually takes about 45 minutes.

'Punch down' the dough and knead for about 2–3 minutes. Divide the mixture in half, shape each half into one loaf and place the dough in prepared bread pans. Cover the pans and place them in the warm location again. Allow them to stand until they double in size once more; again this should take about 45 minutes. Brush the tops of the loaves with a little warm water and bake them in a hot oven (210°C/425°F) for 30 minutes or until they turn golden brown and give a 'hollow' sound when tapped. Turn the loaves out onto a cake rack to cool.
*Makes 2 loaves*

# Wholemeal Bread

1 cup (250 mL/8 fl oz) hot water
1 teaspoon sugar
2 cups (500 mL/16 fl oz) cold water
15 g (½ oz) active dry yeast
6 cups (790 g/ 1½ lb) wholemeal (whole-wheat) plain (all-purpose) flour
¼ teaspoon salt (optional)
additional wholemeal (whole-wheat) plain (all-purpose) flour
sesame *or* poppy seeds for topping

Follow the method for Basic Bread up until you are ready to bake the loaves. Brush the tops of the loaves with a little warm water and sprinkle them with the sesame or poppy seeds. Bake in a hot oven (210°C/425°F) for 30 minutes.
*Makes 2 loaves*

# Sprouted Wheat Bread

1 cup (250 mL/8 fl oz) hot water
1 teaspoon sugar
1 cup (250 mL/8 fl oz) cold water
15 g (½ oz) active dry yeast
3 cups (375 g/12 oz) wholemeal (whole-wheat) plain (all-purpose) flour
3 cups (375 g/12 oz) white plain (all-purpose) flour
2 cups (185 g/6 oz) sprouted wheat (page 257)
¼ teaspoon salt (optional)
additional wholemeal (whole-wheat) plain (all-purpose) flour
rolled wheat flakes for topping

Follow the method for Basic Bread, adding the sprouted wheat to the flour before adding the yeast mixture. Brush the tops of the loaves with a little warm water and sprinkle them with the rolled wheat flakes. Bake in a hot oven (210°C/425°F) for 30 minutes.
*Makes 2 loaves*

# Cheese and Gherkin Bread

*This tasty bread does not need any topping. Simply serve it hot, steamy and tasty as soon as it is turned out of the pan.*

½ cup (125 mL/4 fl oz) hot water
1 teaspoon sugar
1 cup (250 mL/8 fl oz) cold water
7g (¼ oz) active dry yeast
1 cup (125 g/4 oz) plain (all-purpose) flour
2 cups (250 g/8 oz) wholemeal plain (all-purpose) flour
155 g (5 oz) tasty cheese, grated
125 g (4 oz) gherkins, sliced or diced
additional white plain (all-purpose) flour

Follow the method for Basic Bread (page 244), adding the cheese and gherkins to the flour before combining it with the yeast mixture. After the first kneading, form the dough into 2 round loaves and place on prepared baking sheets. Cover and set aside in a warm place for 45 minutes. Brush the tops with a little warm water and bake in a hot oven (210°C/425°F) for 30 minutes. Allow to cool slightly then place on cake racks to cool.
*Makes 2 loaves*

# Tomato Bread

½ cup (125 mL/4 fl oz) hot water
1 teaspoon sugar
½ cup (125 mL/4 fl oz) cold water
7 g (¼ oz) active dry yeast
2 cups (250 g/8 oz) white plain (all-purpose) flour
1 cup (125 g/4 oz) wholemeal (whole-wheat) plain (all-purpose) flour
½ cup (125 mL/4 fl oz) tomato paste (purée)
½ cup (60 g/2 oz) additional white plain (all-purpose) flour

Prepare the dough as for Basic Bread (page 244), adding the tomato paste to the flour with the yeast mixture.
*Makes 1 loaf*

# Basil Bread

*Aromatic and moist, this bread is delectable topped with wafers of Jarlsberg cheese or thick slices of ripe red tomatoes and cracked black pepper. It also makes a delightful accompaniment for hot or chilled soups.*

½ cup (125 mL/4 fl oz) hot water
1 teaspoon sugar
1 cup (250 mL/8 fl oz) cold water
7 g (¼ oz) active dry yeast
2 cups (250 g/8 oz) white plain (all-purpose) flour
1 cup (125 g/4 oz) wholemeal (whole-wheat) plain (all-purpose) flour
¼ teaspoon salt (optional)
1 cup finely chopped basil leaves
½ cup (60 g/2 oz) additional white plain (all-purpose) flour

Prepare the dough as for Basic Bread (page 244), adding the basil to the flour before adding the yeast mixture.
*Makes 1 loaf*

# Tomato and Basil Twist

*This superb bread is a perfect marriage of harmonious and universally popular flavours.*

1 quantity Tomato Bread dough (opposite)
1 quantity Basil Bread (above)

After the first proving of the dough, cut each piece of dough in half. Roll each of the four pieces of dough into long 'sausages' and place each 'sausage' of Tomato Bread next to a 'sausage' of Basil Bread. Twist the furthest ends together and tuck them under the dough. Twist the two 'sausages' together and tuck the end pieces under the dough. Place the 'twists' into 2 prepared bread pans and bake as for Basic Bread (page 244).
*Makes 2 loaves*

# Rye Bread

¾ cup (225 mL/7 fl oz) hot water
1 teaspoon sugar
2 cups (500 mL/16 fl oz) cold water
15 g (½ oz) active dry yeast
2 cups (250 g/8 oz) wholemeal (whole-wheat)
  plain (all-purpose) flour
2 cups (250 g/8 oz) rye flour
2 cups (250 g/8 oz) white plain (all-purpose) flour
¼ teaspoon salt (optional)
additional wholemeal (whole-wheat) plain
  (all-purpose) flour
sesame *or* poppy seeds for topping

Follow the method for Basic Bread (page 244)
up until you are ready to bake the loaves. Brush
the tops of the loaves with a little warm water
and sprinkle them with the sesame or poppy
seeds. Bake in a hot oven (210°C/425°F) for 30
minutes.
*Makes 2 loaves*

# Top Knot Rolls

½ cup (125 mL/4 fl oz) hot water
1 tablespoon sugar
¾ cups (225 mL/7 fl oz) cold water
7 g (¼ oz) active dry yeast
3 cups (375 g/12 oz) white plain (all-purpose)
  flour
additional white plain (all-purpose) flour

Prepare the dough as for Basic Bread (page 244)
up until after the first proving (rising). Divide
the mixture into 18 rolls. Cut a small piece of
dough from each roll and set aside. Shape each
roll into a round, tucking the ends underneath.
Place the round of dough in prepared muffin
pan, and brush the tops with a little warm water.
Shape the additional small pieces of dough into
small balls and, tucking the ends under, place
firmly on top of the rounds. Cover the rolls and
place them in a warm location again for about 45
minutes. Brush the tops of the rolls with a little
warm water and bake them in a hot oven
(210°C/425°F) for 15 minutes.
*Makes about 18 rolls*

# Foccacia

*Slice fresh from the oven and top with your
favourite salad vegetables, cheese or antipasto
delights. After it has cooled, toast both sides of the
bread to crisp it up just before serving.*

½ cup (125 mL/4 fl oz) hot water
2 teaspoons sugar
¾ cups (225 mL/7 fl oz) cold water
7 g (¼ oz) active dry yeast
2½ cups (310 g/10 oz) white plain (all-purpose)
  flour
½ cup (60 g/2 oz) gluten flour (page 343)
¼ teaspoon salt (optional)
additional white plain (all-purpose) flour
2 tablespoons sesame *or* poppy seeds

Follow the method for Basic Bread (page 244)
up until you are ready for the first proving
(rising). Divide the mixture in half and place
each piece of dough on a prepared baking sheet
and shape into flat ovals about 2 cm (⅞ in.) thick.
Cover the loaves and place them in a warm
location for about 45 minutes. Brush the tops of
the loaves with a little warm water and sprinkle
them with sesame or poppy seeds. Bake the
loaves in a hot oven (210°C/425°F) for 30
minutes.
*Makes 2 loaves*

## Brushing Dough
Brushing yeast doughs before baking results in
golden brown bread with a slightly shiny surface.
Warm water or milk are usually used.

*Right: Have fun creating interesting shapes from
yeast dough such as Top Knot Rolls and
flavoursome colourful bread such as Pumpkin Bread
(page 248).*

# Grainy Mustard Bread

1 cup (250 mL/8 fl oz) hot water

1 teaspoon sugar

1 cup (250 mL/8 fl oz) cold water

15 g (½ oz) active dry yeast

2 tablespoons grainy mustard

2 cups (250 g/8 oz) plain (all-purpose) flour

2 cups (250 g/8 oz) wholemeal (whole-wheat)
   plain (all-purpose) flour

1 cup (125 g/4 oz) grated tasty (mature cheddar)
   cheese

additional plain all-purpose flour

Follow the method for Basic Bread (page 244), adding the grainy mustard and the cheese to the flour before combining. After the first kneading, form the dough into 2 round loaves and place on prepared baking sheets. Cover and set aside in a warm place for 45 minutes. Brush the tops with a little warm water and bake in a hot oven (210°C/425°F) for 30 minutes. Allow to cool slightly then place on cake racks to cool.
*Makes 2 loaves*

# Pumpkin Bread

*Pumpkin bread develops a really good crust, dark golden brown and crunchy, but its true beauty is revealed upon slicing. The texture of the bread is moist and light.*

3 tablespoons hot water

1 teaspoon sugar

½ cup (125 mL/4 fl oz) cold water

7 g (¼ oz) active dry yeast

1 cup (250 g/8 oz) cooked mashed pumpkin

1½ cups (185 g/6 oz) plain (all-purpose) flour

1½ cups (185 g/6 oz) wholemeal (whole-wheat)
   plain (all-purpose) flour

additional plain all-purpose flour

2 teaspoons poppy seeds

Follow the method for Basic Bread (page 244), adding the pumpkin to the flour with the yeast mixture. Before baking, brush the loaf with a little warm water and sprinkle the poppy seeds over.
*Makes 1 loaf*

# Olive Bread

*This bread is so delicious that it will be eaten as soon as it emerges from the oven! That's why this recipe is for two loaves—enjoy one now and pop one in the freezer for later.*

1 cup (250 mL/8 fl oz) hot water

1 teaspoon sugar

1 cup (250 mL/8 fl oz) cold water

15 g (½ oz) active dry yeast

2 cups (250 g/8 oz) plain (all-purpose) flour

2 cups (250 g/8 oz) wholemeal (whole-wheat)
   plain (all-purpose) flour

1 cup (155 g/5 oz) pitted black olives

1 cup (155 g/5 oz) stuffed olives

additional plain all-purpose flour

Follow the method for Basic Bread (page 244), adding the olives to the flour before combining it with the yeast mixture. After the first kneading, form the dough into 2 round loaves and place on prepared baking sheets. Cover and set aside in a warm place for 45 minutes. Brush the tops with a little warm water and bake in a hot oven (210°C/425°F) for 30 minutes. Allow to cool slightly then place on cake racks to cool.
*Makes 2 loaves*

### Advancing to Wholemeal

Wholemeal (whole-wheat) flour is recommended for the additional nutrients it provides. If you prefer a somewhat lighter textured bread than 100% wholemeal, try using half white flour and half wholemeal flour to begin with and, over time, gradually increase the ratio of wholemeal flour to white flour.

# Cheese and Chive Pinwheels

½ cup (125 mL/4 fl oz) hot water
2 teaspoons sugar
1 cup (250 mL/8 fl oz) cold water
7 g (¼ oz) active dry yeast
1½ cups (185 g/6 oz) wholemeal (whole-wheat) plain (all-purpose) flour
3 tablespoons gluten flour (page 343)
1 cup (125 g/4 oz) white plain (all-purpose) flour
additional wholemeal (whole-wheat) plain (all-purpose) flour
1½ cups (185 g/6 oz) grated tasty (mature cheddar) cheese
4 tablespoons finely sliced chives
freshly ground black pepper

Prepare the dough as for the method for Basic Bread (page 244) to the point of shaping the loaves. Shape the dough into a 23 x 28 cm (9 in. x 11 in.) rectangle and scatter the cheese, chives and pepper evenly over the dough, leaving a 3 cm (1¼ in.) strip of dough uncovered along the long edge furthest from you. Brush the uncovered strip of dough with a little warm water and using a firm even pressure, roll each piece of dough into a roll, beginning with the edge closest to you. Using a large sharp knife, cut the roll into about 18 'pinwheels'. Place the pinwheels on prepared baking sheets allowing 3 cm (1¼ in.) space between each one to allow for expansion. Cover the pinwheels and place them in a warm location for about 45 minutes. Bake in a hot oven (210°C/425°F) for 15 minutes or until they turn golden brown.
*Makes about 18 pinwheels*

### Serving Pinwheels
Laced with your choice of flavours, pinwheels make great accompaniments for piping hot soups or hotpots. Serve them hot and aromatic, straight from the oven, or crisp them up for a few minutes in a hot oven just before serving.

# Garlic Pinwheels

½ cup (125 mL/4 fl oz) hot water
2 teaspoons sugar
1 cup (250 mL/8 fl oz) cold water
7 g (¼ oz) active dry yeast
2 cups (250 g/8 oz) wholemeal (whole-wheat) plain (all-purpose) flour
1 cup (125 g/4 oz) white plain (all-purpose) flour
additional wholemeal (whole-wheat) plain (all-purpose) flour
2 teaspoons oil
*Garlic Butter:*
45 g (1½ oz) butter
1 tablespoon oil
4 garlic cloves, crushed (pressed)
¼ teaspoon cracked black pepper

Prepare the dough as for the method for Basic Bread (page 244) to the point of shaping the loaves. Shape and bake as for Cheese and Chive Pinwheels, topping with the garlic butter instead of the cheese and chives.
*Makes about 18 pinwheels*

# Sweet Pepper Pinwheels

½ cup (125 mL/4 fl oz) hot water
2 teaspoons sugar
1 cup (250 mL/8 fl oz) cold water
7 g (¼ oz) active dry yeast
1½ cups (185 g/6 oz) wholemeal (whole-wheat) plain (all-purpose) flour
3 tablespoons gluten flour (page 343)
1 cup (125 g/4 oz) white plain (all-purpose) flour
additional wholemeal (whole-wheat) plain (all-purpose) flour
2 teaspoons oil
2 red sweet peppers (capsicums), seeded, diced
1 large onion, diced finely
½ teaspoon sweet paprika
freshly ground black pepper

Prepare the dough as for the method for Basic Bread (page 244) to the point of shaping the loaves. Shape and bake as for Cheese and Chive Pinwheels, topping with the sweet pepper, onion and paprika instead of the cheese and chives.
*Makes about 18 pinwheels*

# Polenta and Sunflower Seed Rolls

*These golden brown rolls have a sweet, nutty flavour of their own. Especially delicious served straight from the oven with a bowl of hot soup.*

1 cup (250 mL/8 fl oz) hot water
2 teaspoons sugar
2 cups (500 mL/16 fl oz) cold water
7 g (¼ oz) active dry yeast
1 1/2 cup (310 g/10 oz) polenta
1½ cups (310 g/10 oz) white plain (all-purpose) flour
1½ cups (310 g/10 oz) wholemeal (wholewheat) flour
½ cup (60 g/2 oz) gluten flour (page 343)
¼ teaspoon salt (optional)
1 cup (155 g/5 oz) toasted sunflower seeds (page 18)
additional white plain (all-purpose) flour

Combine the hot water and sugar in a small bowl. Add the cold water and whisk the yeast using a fork then set aside for 5 minutes. Meanwhile, combine the polenta, flours, salt and sunflower seeds and make a 'well' in the centre. Pour the yeast mixture into the well and, using a wooden spoon, beat the mixture for 1 minute until a stiff batter is formed. Place the mixture in prepared muffin pans, cover and set aside to prove for 45 minutes. Bake them in a hot oven (210°C/425°F) for 15–20 minutes or until they turn golden brown and give a 'hollow' sound when tapped. Place the rolls on a cake rack if not using at once.
*Makes about 18 rolls*

**Locations for Proving**
Over the years I have discovered many a suitable warm location for proving (rising) yeast doughs. They range from the kitchen near a warm oven to warm draught-free nooks and crannies in the garden! (I do enclose the bowl in a large dark coloured plastic (polythene) bag first, to keep unwanted visitors out and to keep warmth and moisture in!)

# Fruit and Nut Bread

*Delicious sliced thinly and spread with light cream cheese or butter, or served with a colourful platter of seasonal fruits. Leave the fruit and nuts whole in this bread.*

¾ cup (225 mL/7 fl oz) hot water
1 tablespoon sugar
1 cup (250 mL/8 fl oz) cold water
7 g (¼ oz) active dry yeast
1 cup (125 g/4 oz) wholemeal (whole-wheat) plain (all-purpose) flour
1 cup (125 g/4 oz) rye flour
2 cups (250 g/8 oz) white plain (all-purpose) flour
1 cup (155 g/5 oz) dried apricots
½ cup (75 g/2½ oz) pitted dates
½ cup (75 g/2½ oz) dried figs
½ cup (60 g/2 oz) walnuts
additional wholemeal (whole-wheat) plain (all-purpose) flour
poppy seeds for topping

Follow the method for Basic Bread (page 244) until the stage of the first proving. Shape the dough into 2 round loaves and place on a prepared baking sheet. Cover the bread and place it in a warm location for about 45 minutes. Brush the tops of the loaves with a little warm water and sprinkle them with poppy seeds. Bake in a hot oven (210°C/425°F) for 30 minutes or until the loaf turns golden brown and gives a 'hollow' sound when tapped. Place the loaf on a cake rack to cool.
*Makes 2 loaves*

*Right: Naturally sweetened with dried apricots, figs and dates, Fruit and Nut Bread is terrific toasted for breakfast.*

# Sweet Potato Bread

½ cup (125 mL/4 fl oz) hot water
2 teaspoons sugar
1 cup (250 mL/8 fl oz) cold water
7 g (¼ oz) active dry yeast
2 cups (250 g/8 oz) wholemeal (whole-wheat) plain (all-purpose) flour
2 cup (250 g/8 oz) white plain (all-purpose) flour
¼ teaspoon salt (optional)
1 cup (250 g/8 oz) cooked mashed sweet potato
1 cup (125 g/4 oz) walnuts
1 cup (155 g/5 oz) raisins
additional wholemeal (whole-wheat) plain (all-purpose) flour
poppy seeds for topping

Follow the method for Basic Bread (page 244) up to the stage of the first proving, adding the sweet potato, walnuts and raisins to the flour and yeast mixture. Shape the dough into 2 round loaves, cover and allow to stand in a warm place for about 45 minutes. Brush the tops of the loaves with a little warm water, sprinkle with poppy seeds and bake in a hot oven (210°C/425°F) for 30 minutes.
*Makes 2 loaves*

# Coconut Bread

½ cup (125 mL/4 fl oz) hot water
1 teaspoon sugar
½ cup (125 mL/4 fl oz) cold water
7 g (¼ oz) active dry yeast
1½ cups (185 g/6 oz) plain (all-purpose) flour
1 cup (125 g/4 oz) wholemeal (whole-wheat) plain (all-purpose) flour
½ cup (45 g/1½ oz) desiccated coconut

Follow the method for Basic Bread (page 244), adding the coconut to the flour before combining it with the yeast mixture. After the first kneading, form the dough into 1 loaf and place on a prepared baking sheet. Cover and set aside in a warm place for 45 minutes. Brush the top with a little warm water and bake in a hot oven (210°C/425°F) for 30 minutes.
*Makes 1 loaf*

# Hot Cross Buns

½ cup (125 mL/4 fl oz) hot water
1 teaspoon sugar
½ cup (125 mL/4 fl oz) cold water
7 g (¼ oz) active dry yeast
1½ cups (185 g/6 oz) plain (all-purpose) flour
1 cup (125 g/4 oz) wholemeal (whole-wheat) plain (all-purpose) flour
1 cup (155 g/5 oz) mixed dried fruit (fruit cake mix)
½ cup (60 g/2 oz) white plain (all-purpose) flour
4 tablespoons cornflour (cornstarch)
4 tablespoons water
Sticky Bun Glaze (below)

Follow the method for Basic Bread (page 244), adding the fruit to the flour before combining with the yeast. After the first proving, punch the dough down and knead for 1 minute on a lightly floured surface. Cut the dough into 12 pieces and knead each piece for 30 seconds. Form each piece of dough into a bun by tucking the outside edge under the bun and placing it immediately on a prepared baking sheet. Cover and set aside for about 45 minutes or until the buns double in size. Combine the additional flour and cornflour and gradually add the water, beating until a smooth batter is produced. Place the batter in a piping (pastry) bag and pipe crosses on top of the buns. Bake in a hot oven (200°C/400°F) for 20 minutes. Remove the buns from the oven and using a pastry brush, brush with the Sticky Bun Glaze immediately.
*Makes 12 buns*

# Sticky Bun Glaze

½ cup (125 mL/4 fl oz) fruit juice
1 tablespoon honey
½ teaspoon pure agar agar powder (page 341)

Place the fruit juice and honey in a small saucepan and sprinkle the agar agar powder on top. Bring the mixture to the boil, stirring, then reduce the heat and simmer for 1 minute.

# Wheat Tortillas

2 cups (250 g/8 oz) wholemeal (whole-wheat)
  plain (all-purpose) flour
2 cups (250 g/8 oz) wholemeal (whole-wheat)
  flour
1 teaspoon baking powder
1–2 tablespoons oil
½ cup (125 mL/4 fl oz) warm water

Sift the flour and baking powder and make a
'well' in the centre. Add the oil and gradually mix
in all the water. The mixture should be a soft
dough consistency. Turn the dough out onto a
lightly floured surface and knead lightly. Form
into 8 balls of dough and roll each ball out to a
6mm (¼ in.) circle. Cook in a heavy frying pan
over a medium–high heat for 1 minute on the
first side and for about 10 seconds on the other
side. As you make the tortillas, stack them under
a clean dry tea towel to prevent them from
drying out.
*Makes 8*

# Pita Pocket Bread

*Serve warm with a tasty dip, or slice, open and pile
delicious sandwich fillings inside.*

½ cup (125 mL/4 fl oz) hot water
1 teaspoon sugar
1 cup (250 mL/8 fl oz) cold water
7 g (¼ oz) active dry yeast
1 tablespoon oil
3 cups (375 g/12 oz) plain (all-purpose) flour
additional plain (all-purpose) flour
1–2 teaspoons oil

Prepare as for Basic Bread (page 244) up until
the first proving (rising). Form into 10 balls of
dough and roll each ball out to a 6mm (¼ in.)
circle. Set aside for 15–20 minutes. Meanwhile,
place 3 oven sheets in the oven and preheat for
5 minutes. Brush with oil and carefully arrange
the rounds of dough on top. Bake in a very hot
oven (230°C/450°F) for 2–3 minutes. Remove
from the oven and place on a clean dry tea towel.
Cover with another tea towel.
*Makes 12*

# Wholemeal Damper

*Damper, a type of Australian quick bread, was
traditionally whipped up and baked in the great
outdoors over a camp fire. But don't worry if you
would like to try damper and you're fresh out of
camp fires, because it can also be whipped up and
baked in the average home oven. Damper is a great
recipe for children to try their hand at as it is very
simply prepared and is usually cooked before the
attention span wears out! Serve hot straight from
the oven as a snack or as an accompaniment to a
selection of antipasto dishes or a tasty vegetable
hotpot.*

3 cups (375 g/12 oz) wholemeal (whole-wheat)
  self-raising flour
a pinch of salt
1½ cups (405 mL/13 fl oz) water
1 tablespoon oil
additional plain (all-purpose) flour

Place the flour and salt into a bowl and make a
'well' in the centre. Combine the water and oil
and pour it into the 'well'. Gradually incorporate
all the flour into the mixture. The dough should
not be too dry, rather like scone (biscuit) dough.
Turn the dough out onto a lightly floured surface
and knead it lightly for 1 minute only, adding a
little of the additional flour as required. Form the
dough into a round loaf and place on a prepared
baking sheet. Using a large sharp knife, slash a
cross into the top of the loaf. Bake in a hot oven
(200°C/400°F) for 35–40 minutes or until
cooked when tested with a skewer.
*Serves 6*

# Basic Sprouts

*For those like me, who get a kick out of producing homemade goodies, you are in for a real adventure when it comes to discovering the range of 'sproutables'—from the ever popular mung beans and alfalfa sprouts to wheat and chick pea (garbanzo bean) sprouts—even raw almonds can be sprouted, and are well worth trying.*

½ cup (90 g/3 oz) dried beans *or* seeds *or* grain *or* nuts
2 cups (500 mL/16 fl oz) cold water

Pick over the beans to remove any split or damaged ones as these will not sprout, and can spoil and contaminate the rest of the batch. Wash the beans in cold water then drain and place them in a container and cover with cold water. Set the container aside for 8–10 hours or overnight. In warmer months, place the container in the refrigerator while the beans are soaking to prevent the water from becoming warm and the beans beginning to ferment. Drain the beans, then rinse and drain them again thoroughly. Rinse the beans with cool water at least morning and night and always drain thoroughly.

When tiny leaves develop on the sprouts, spread them out in a colander or on a non-metallic tray and place them in a location where they are in indirect sunlight (direct sunlight or a hot location will cause the sprouts to shrivel and dry out after all the nurturing they have so far received!) The leaves should turn green after 3–6 hours of indirect sunlight. Refresh the sprouts in cold water and drain them thoroughly. If you are not going to use them at once, place them in a bowl or a container, cover and store in the refrigerator for up to 1 week.

### Sprouting Containers
Special sprouting containers are available at health food stores. However, you can improvise by using a wide necked-glass jar covered with a piece of muslin held on with an elastic band for a 'flow-through ventilation lid'.

# Sprouted Seeds and Grains

*There is something very satisfying about witnessing the transformation of a handful of dried beans, seeds or grains into a brimming bowlful of succulent green-leafed sprouts in only a matter of days. And that's not all—then you get to have the fun of throwing them into all manner of dishes including salads, sandwiches, stir-fries, stuffed vegetables, terrines, breads and cakes.*

# Alfalfa Sprouts

*Ever popular in salads and sandwiches, alfalfa sprouts have a refreshing flavour reminiscent of sweet young peas. When sprouted, alfalfa seeds yield about 10 times their initial measure.*

2½ tablespoons alfalfa seeds
1 cup (250 mL/8 fl oz) cold water

Follow the method for Basic Sprouts, rinsing the seeds morning and night. Alfalfa sprouts take 5–7 days to mature, depending upon temperature.
*Makes about 2 cups sprouts*

# Sprouted Almonds

1 cup (155 g/5 oz) almonds
4 cups (1 litre/1¾ imp. pints) cold water

Follow the method for Basic Sprouts, rinsing the nuts 3–4 times a day if possible. Sprouted almonds take about 7 days to mature.
*Makes about 2 cups sprouts*

*Left: A surprising variety of seeds and grains can be converted into succulent sprouts, like Sprouted Lentils (page 256), Alfalfa Sprouts and Chick Pea Sprouts (page 256).*

# Chick Pea Sprouts

*Use in stir-fries, soups and casseroles. Chick pea (garbanzo bean) sprouts yield about twice their initial measure. They require more frequent rinsing than most other sproutables, about 4 times daily. If not including in cooked dishes, chick pea sprouts need to be steamed for 3–4 minutes to render them digestible. They are best grown on their own and extra care should be taken to drain them thoroughly after rinsing as they have a tendency to become mouldy.*

1 cup (225 g/7 oz) chick peas (garbanzo beans)
4 cups (1 litre/1¾ pints) cold water

Follow the method for Basic Sprouts (page 255), rinsing 4 times a day if possible. Chick pea sprouts take about 3 days to mature.
*Makes about 2 cups sprouts*

### To Prevent Spoilage

Make sure the sprouts are not sitting in water or they will spoil rapidly and become mouldy. It's also important that there is adequate air circulation at all times. Leave the sprouting jar near the sink or where you will notice it, so you will remember to rinse the sprouts in cold water several times a day.

# Sprouted Lentils

*Use in salads, stir-fries and soups, added at the end of the cooking time. Do not use split lentils, only brown or green whole lentils. Sprouted lentils yield about 5–6 times their initial measure.*

⅓ cup (60 g/2 oz) brown lentils
2 cups (500 mL/16 fl oz) cold water

Follow the method for Basic Sprouts (page 255), rinsing the lentils 3 times a day if possible. Lentil sprouts take about 4–5 days to mature.
*Makes about 2 cups sprouts*

# Mung Bean Sprouts

*Use in salads and sandwiches and add at the very end of the cooking time to stir-fries, vegetable dishes and soups. Mung bean sprouts yield about 4 times their initial measure.*

½ cup (90 g/3 oz) mung beans
2 cups (500 mL/16 fl oz) cold water

Place the beans in a container and cover with the water. Set aside to soak for 8–10 hours or overnight, then drain the water completely. Spread a clean dry tea towel out on a non-metallic tray and sprinkle the beans over. Sprinkle with cold water until the tea towel becomes damp, but not wet. Cover with the clean damp tea towel and set aside, sprinkling with a little cold water twice a day and covering each time with a damp tea towel. Once you see tiny leaves forming on the sprouts, leave the tray uncovered for 1 day in indirect sunlight so that the leaves turn pale green. Mung bean shoots take about 4–5 days to mature.
*Makes about 2 cups sprouts*

### Tray Method

Mung beans are best sprouted by the tray method to ensure that long sprouts develop. If they are too cramped during their growth, mung bean sprouts become curly!

# Fenugreek Sprouts

*Fenugreek has a 'curry like' flavour. After all, fenugreek seeds are a common ingredient in curry mixtures. Use fenugreek sprouts as an additional ingredient in salads, sandwiches and even soups. It's best to eat the sprouts soon after the tiny leaves have formed and have just turned green because over-mature sprouts develop a bitter taste. Fenugreek seeds yield about 8 times their initial measure.*

3 tablespoons fenugreek seeds
2 cups (500 mL/16 fl oz) cold water

Follow the method for Basic Sprouts (page 255), rinsing the seeds 3 times a day. Fenugreek sprouts take about 4–5 days to mature.
*Makes about 2 cups sprouts*

# Sprouted Rye

*Use in breads, cakes and muffins. Sprouted rye yields about 4 times its initial measure.*

½ cup (90 g/3 oz) rye
2 cups (500 mL/16 fl oz) cold water

Follow the method for Basic Sprouts (page 255), rinsing the rye 2–3 times a day. Sprouted rye takes about 4–5 days to mature.
*Makes about 2 cups sprouts*

### Storing Sprouts

Store mature sprouts in a closed container in the warmest part of the refrigerator. Never store when they have not been thoroughly drained, or they will spoil rapidly.

# Sprouted Wheat

*Sprouted wheat is delicious added to salads, stuffed vegetables, bread and cakes. It has a remarkably sweet nutty flavour, and when added to cakes and loaves, the usual amount of sugar can be reduced. Sprouted wheat makes a welcome addition to wholemeal bread. Sprouted Wheat Bread (page 244) has an interesting moist chewy texture. Sprouted wheat yields about 3–4 times its initial measure.*

½ cup (90 g/3 oz) wheat
2 cups (500 mL/16 fl oz) cold water

Follow the method for Basic Sprouts (page 255), rinsing the wheat 3 times a day. Sprouted wheat takes about 4 days to mature.
*Makes about 2 cups sprouts*

# Soy Bean Sprouts

*Use in stir-fries, taco and pasta sauces and sweet and sour vegetables to start with, and then experiment with favourite dishes of your own. Soy bean sprouts yield about 4–5 times their initial measure. Soy bean sprouts need to be steamed for 2–3 minutes before eating. Roasted, they make a delicious snack (page 261).*

½ cup (90 g/3 oz) soy beans
2 cups (500 mL/16 fl oz) cold water

Follow the method for Basic Sprouts (page 255), rinsing the beans 4 times a day if possible. Soy bean sprouts take about 4–5 days to mature.
*Makes about 2 cups sprouts*

### Detecting Mould

When the wheat sprouts are mature, they develop small white fluffy roots which can be mistaken for mould, so look carefully before you become dismayed and throw them out—mouldy sprouts have an unmistakable musty aroma.

# Cauliflower and Fenugreek Soup

*An aromatic soup. The flavour of the curry paste is echoed by the fenugreek sprouts which have been blended with the soup, and again by the fresh sprout garnish.*

2 teaspoons oil
1 onion, chopped
1 tablespoon curry paste
½ cauliflower, trimmed and chopped
2 cups (500 mL/16 fl oz) vegetable stock
½ cup fenugreek sprouts (page 257)
½ cup chopped coriander
freshly ground black pepper
additional fenugreek sprouts for garnishing

Place the oil in a saucepan and stir-fry the onion and curry paste for 2 minutes. Add the cauliflower and stock and bring the mixture to the boil. Reduce the heat and simmer for 15 minutes, or until the cauliflower is tender. Using a food processor or blender, blend the soup until smooth with the fenugreek sprouts. Reheat the soup gently, stir in the coriander and season to taste with the pepper. Serve topped with a small clump of the additional sprouts.
*Serves 4*

# Sprout Salad with Blue Vein Dressing

2 cups mung bean sprouts (page 256)
1 cup alfalfa sprouts (page 255)
1 cup (90 g/3 oz) chopped spinach leaves
½ cucumber, halved lengthways, seeds removed and sliced
1 quantity Blue Vein Dressing (right)
8 cherry tomatoes, cut into quarters

Combine the sprouts, spinach and cucumber. Place in individual serving bowls and top each serve with a generous dollop of the dressing and scatter with the cherry tomatoes.
*Serves 4*

# Nasturtium and Lentil Salad

*The peppery flavour of nasturtiums complements the lentils and the tang of the lemon dressing sets this salad off beautifully.*

3 cups (375 g/12 oz) sprouted lentils (page 256)
3 tablespoons finely sliced chives
3 tablespoons finely shredded nasturtium leaves
1 quantity Lemony Pepper Dressing (page 149)
Petals of 6–8 nasturtium blossoms

Combine the lentils, chives and nasturtium leaves. Just before serving, toss lightly with the dressing and scatter the nasturtium petals over.
*Serves 4*

### Advantages of Sprouts

Sprouts score well nutritionally speaking as they are high in dietary fibre and, apart from nut sprouts, contain only traces of fat. When eaten in significant amounts, they are a good source of vitamin C, and are a great stand-by for times when the range of fresh vegetables is limited.

# Blue Vein Dressing

90 g (3 oz) blue vein cheese
2 teaspoons balsamic vinegar
¼ teaspoon cracked black pepper
½ cup (125 mL/4 fl oz) plain yoghurt

Using a blender, blend all the ingredients until smooth.
*Makes about 1 cup (250 mL/8 fl oz)*

*Right: Sprouted lentils can liven up your menu all year round. Add a splash of cheery colour with summer blossoms, as shown in Nasturtium and Lentil Salad.*

# Orange and Sprout Salad

*This salad is a wonderful marriage of flavour and texture contrasts. The sweet fruity flavour of the sprouted wheat is offset by the slightly bitter edge of the endive and the tang of the orange dressing. And the succulent orange slices are contrasted by the crisp texture of the bean sprouts and celery.*

½ cup (90 g/3 oz) raisins *or* sultanas
1 quantity Orange Sesame Dressing (page 139)
2 cups (250 g/8 oz) sprouted wheat (page 257)
1 celery stalk, washed, trimmed and sliced thinly
1 large orange, peeled and sliced, pips removed
90 g (3 oz) mung bean sprouts (page 256)
90 g (3 oz) curly endive (frisée) leaves, washed
    and torn into large bite-size pieces
3 spring onions (scallions), sliced finely
cracked black pepper

Place the raisins into a small bowl and cover with the dressing. Set aside to soak for 15 minutes, if possible, to soften and flavour the raisins. Toss the raisins with the wheat, celery, orange slices, bean sprouts, endive and spring onions. Place the salad in a serving dish and sprinkle with the pepper.
*Serves 4*

# Spinach and Sprouted Wheat Salad

2 cups (250 g/8 oz) sprouted wheat (page 257)
1 cup (155 g/5 oz) dry roasted peanuts
½ cup (90 g/3 oz) sultanas (golden raisons)
1 quantity Lemony Ginger Dressing (page 148)
2 cups (185 g/6 oz) shredded spinach

Place the wheat, peanuts and sultanas in a bowl. Drizzle the dressing over and toss the salad to combine all the ingredients thoroughly. Cover and set aside and just before serving, toss the spinach through.
*Serves 4*

# Fruity Sprout Salad

*The surprisingly sweet flavour of the sprouted wheat harmonises well with the fruit. Prepare this luscious salad just before you serve it, piled into cups of butter lettuce.*

2 cups (185 g/6 oz) mung bean sprouts (page 256)
225 g (7 oz) peeled pineapple, cut into slivers
2 bananas, peeled and sliced on the diagonal
½ cup (90 g/3 oz) sultanas (golden raisins)
3 tablespoons shredded coconut
1 quantity Lemony Ginger Dressing (page 148)

Carefully combine the bean sprouts, pineapple, bananas, sultanas and coconut. Drizzle the dressing over and serve at once.
*Serves 4*

# Beetroot and Chick Pea Salad

*Having sprouted chick peas on hand is a real time-saver. Dried chick peas take over an hour to cook even after they have been soaked, but chick pea sprouts only need 10 minutes steaming to render them tender and very edible.*

2 cups (250 g/8 oz) chick pea (garbanzo bean)
    sprouts (page 256)
2 medium beetroot (beets), cooked (page 93),
    peeled and diced
1 quantity Lemony Yoghurt Dressing (page 148)
2 tablespoons finely sliced chives

Steam the sprouts for 10 minutes, then set aside to cool to lukewarm. Toss the beetroot and sprouts with the dressing. Place the salad in a serving dish and serve sprinkled with the chives.
*Serves 4*

# Chick Pea Salad

*The warm sprouts readily absorb the full-bodied flavour of the dressing.*

3 cups (500 g/1 lb) chick pea (garbanzo bean) sprouts (page 256)
2 tomatoes, diced
1 stick celery, diced
3 spring onions (scallions), sliced finely
½ cup chopped coriander
1 quantity Balsamic Dressing (page 148)

Steam the sprouts for 10 minutes. Meanwhile, combine the tomatoes, celery, spring onions and coriander together. Pour the dressing over the warm chick peas, then add the vegetable mixture. Toss the salad lightly and serve.
*Serves 4*

# Sprouted Lentil Salad

*Serve with warm pita bread and a selection of tasty dips.*

2 tablespoons olive oil
2 teaspoons cumin seeds
1 teaspoon minced chili peppers
2 garlic cloves, crushed (pressed)
juice of 1 lemon
2 tomatoes, diced
1 teaspoon honey
3 cups (375 g/12 oz) sprouted lentils (page 256)
1 cup chopped coriander

Heat the oil in a frying pan, skillet or wok and add the cumin seeds, chili and garlic and stir-fry the mixture over a medium–high heat for 2 minutes. Remove from the heat and grind to a paste using a mortar and pestle. Place the lemon juice, tomato and honey in a bowl and stir in the spices mixture. Add the lentils and coriander and toss the salad to combine all the ingredients thoroughly.
*Serves 4*

# Spicy Potato Salad

4 medium potatoes, cooked (page 93) and sliced
2 tablespoons roasted sesame seeds (page 17)
¼ teaspoon cracked black pepper
3 spring onions (scallions), sliced finely on the diagonal
3 tablespoons fenugreek sprouts (page 257)
1 cup (250 mL/8 fl oz) plain yoghurt
4 tablespoons chopped coriander

Arrange the potato slices, overlapping them on a serving platter. Sprinkle with the sesame seeds and pepper and scatter the spring onions and sprouts over. Spoon the yoghurt onto the centre of the platter and sprinkle all with the coriander.
*Serves 4*

# Roasted Soy Snacks

*These tasty beans can be eaten as a satisfying and tasty snack, much the same as we eat roasted nuts. They are also scrumptious added to salads and stir-fries.*

1 tablespoon soy sauce
1 tablespoon oil
2 garlic cloves, crushed (pressed)
2 teaspoons honey
4 cups (500 g/1 lb) soy bean sprouts (page 257)

Combine the soy sauce, oil, garlic and honey and drizzle over the sprouts. Toss the sprouts to coat them with the mixture. Spread the sprouts out on a prepared baking sheet and bake in a moderately hot oven (190°C/375°F) for 25–30 minutes. Allow to cool on the baking sheet.
*Makes 4 cups*

# Quick Apple and Raisin Breakfast Mix

*This is easy to make and does not need an oven. The aroma emanating from the coconut as it is toasting will really entice even the most avid breakfast refuser!*

2½ cups (250 g/8 oz) rolled oats
⅔ cup (60 g/2 oz) desiccated coconut
1 cup (60 g/2 oz) puffed wheat
½ cup (60 g/2 oz) sunflower seeds
½ cup (90 g/3 oz) chopped raisins
½ cup (30 g/1 oz) chopped dried apples

Place the oats, coconut, puffed wheat and sunflower seeds in a large heavy-based frying pan, skillet or saucepan and dry roast by stirring over medium heat for 6–8 minutes, or until the mixture becomes a light golden brown. Remove from the heat and combine with the raisins and apples. Allow to cool, then store in airtight jars until ready to use.
*Makes about 5 cups*

# Apple and Sultana Muesli

1½ cups (125 g/4 oz) rolled oats
2 tablespoons wheat germ
1 tablespoon dessicated coconut
3 tablespoons almonds
3 tablespoons sultanas (golden raisins)
2 apples, skin left on and grated
1½ cups (375 mL/12 fl oz) milk *or* yoghurt

Combine all the ingredients thoroughly. Cover and chill for 10–15 minutes to allow the oats to soften and absorb the juice from the apples. Place the muesli in 2 serving bowls and serve at once.
*Serves 2*

*Left: Quick Apple and Raisin Breakfast Mix and Apricot Granola are nutritious alternatives to commercial varieties often laden with added sugar, fat and even salt.*

# Mueslis and Breakfast Mixes

*Why not dive into the following breakfast mixes, ranging from old-fashioned hot porridge to fruity granolas and wholemeal pancakes which need only be topped up with fresh fruit and yoghurt. Get yourself off to a great start to the day!*

# Apricot Granola

*This is a delicious mix with a softer texture than regular granolas. Serve with a generous spoonful of Greek Yoghurt (page 273) and top up with low-fat milk and fresh fruit in season.*

1 cup okara (page 344) or coarsely ground cooked soy beans
2 cups (185 g/6 oz) rolled oats
1 cup (90 g/3 oz) unprocessed bran
⅔ cup (60 g/2 oz) shredded coconut
3 tablespoons fruit juice
2–3 teaspoons honey
½ cup (60 g/2 oz) finely chopped dried apricots

Combine the okara (or soy beans), oats, bran and coconut. Place the fruit juice and honey in a cup or small bowl and whisk together using a fork. Pour the juice mixture over the dry ingredients and mix through using your hands. Spread the mixture out on baking sheets and bake in a moderate oven (180°C/350°F) for 25–30 minutes or until golden brown, shaking the baking sheets occasionally during cooking to ensure even browning. Remove from the oven and allow to cool on the baking sheets. Place in storage containers with the dried apricots and shake to mix.
*Makes about 5 cups*

# Basic Toasted Muesli

*Many toasted muesli mixes contain a considerable amount of added sugar and oil, but I think this is completely unnecessary. I like to sweeten the mixes with fruit juice and dried fruit, but if you are used to the commercial sweet mixes, add the optional honey at first, then when your taste has adapted to less sweet foods, try it without the honey. These mixes are also delicious eaten straight out of the jar as a snack.*

3 cups (280 g/9 oz) rolled oats
1 cup (30 g/1 oz) puffed wheat
⅔ cup (60 g/2 oz) desiccated coconut
½ cup (125 mL/4 fl oz) fruit juice
2–3 teaspoons honey (optional)
½ cup (90 g/3 oz) sultanas (golden raisins)

Combine the oats, wheat and coconut, then mix in the fruit juice (and honey, if using). Spread the mixture out on baking sheets and bake in a moderate oven (180°C/350°F) for 25–30 minutes or until golden brown, shaking the baking sheets occasionally during cooking to ensure even browning. Remove from the oven and allow to cool on the baking sheets. Place in storage containers with sultanas and shake to mix.
*Makes 5 cups*

**Dieting Tip**
Recent research indicates that those of us who consume a breakfast rich in dietary fibre are less likely to overeat later in the day and tend to consume less fat during the day as well—so here is another good reason to dive into the muesli barrel rather than a cup of coffee. Oh, and next time you want to catch up with family and friends, why not lure them over to share a scrumptious breakfast with you—it might even spur them on to see breakfast in a new light.

# Apple and Cinnamon Toasted Muesli

3 cups (280 g/9 oz) rolled oats
1 cup (90 g/3 oz) unprocessed bran
1 teaspoon ground cinnamon
½ cup (60 g/2 oz) chopped almonds
1 cup (250 g/8 fl oz) apple juice
1 tablespoon honey (optional)
½ cup (30 g/1 oz) chopped dried apples

Combine the oats, bran, cinnamon, almonds, apple juice (and honey, if using). Spread the mixture out on baking sheets and bake in a moderate oven (180°C/350°F) for 25 minutes. Allow to cool on the baking sheets and then combine with the apples. When completely cold, store in airtight jars.
*Makes 5 cups*

# Toasted Sesame Muesli

3 cups (280 g/9 oz) rolled oats
1 cup (90 g/3 oz) unprocessed bran
1 cup (30 g/1 oz) puffed wheat
4 tablespoons sesame seeds
½ cup (125 mL/4 fl oz) fruit juice
1 tablespoon honey (optional)
½ cup (90 g/3 oz) sultanas (golden raisins)

Combine the oats, bran, wheat and sesame seeds. Combine the fruit juice (and honey, if using) and pour it over the dry ingredients. Continue as for Basic Toasted Muesli (above).
*Makes about 5 cups*

# Toasted Apricot and Almond Muesli

*Fresh fruit makes a great summer partner for muesli. A dollop of yoghurt (page 272) or nut cream (page 281) is the icing on the cake!*

3 cups (280 g/9 oz) rolled oats
1 cup (90 g/3 oz) unprocessed bran
½ cup (60 g/2 oz) chopped almonds
1 cup (250 mL/8 fl oz) apricot nectar
1 tablespoon honey (optional)
½ cup (60 g/2 oz) chopped dried apricots

Combine the oats, bran, almonds, nectar (and honey, if using). Spread the mixture out on baking sheets and bake in a moderate oven (180° C/350°F) for 25 minutes. Allow to cool on the baking sheets and then combine with the apricots. When completely cold, store in airtight jars.
*Makes about 5 cups*

# Toasted Fruit Salad Muesli

2 cups (185 g/6 oz) rolled oats
1 cup (30 g/1 oz) puffed rice *or* corn
½ cup (60 g/2 oz) wheat germ
½ cup (60 g/2 oz) unprocessed bran (rice, barley *or* wheat)
⅔ cup (30 g/1 oz) shredded coconut
½ cup (125 mL/4 fl oz) fruit juice
½ cup (90 g/3 oz) dried fruit salad pieces

Place the oats, puffed rice or corn, wheat germ, bran and coconut into a large bowl and combine well. Pour the fruit juice over and rub the mixture through with your hands to coat as much of the mixture with the fruit juice as possible. Spread the mixture out on baking sheets and bake in a moderate oven (180°C/350°F) for 30 minutes or until golden brown. Remove from the oven and allow to cool on the baking sheets. Place in storage containers with the fruit salad pieces and shake to mix.
*Makes about 5 cups*

# Fruity Okara

*Delicious eaten as a snack straight from the jar or eaten with milk or yoghurt for a delicious breakfast with a difference.*

3 tablespoons fruit juice
2–3 teaspoons honey
½ teaspoon mixed spice*
3 cups (155 g/5 oz) okara (page 344)
½ cup (90 g/3 oz) sultanas (golden raisins)
½ cup (60 g/2 oz) chopped dried apricots

Combine the fruit juice, honey and spice. Place the okara in a bowl and sprinkle the fruit juice mixture over. Spread the mixture out on a prepared baking sheet. Bake in a slow oven (150°C/300°F) until the mixture is dry and crumbly (about 1–1½ hours). Allow the okara to cool completely, then mix with the sultanas and apricots before storing in an airtight jar.
*Makes about 4 cups*

# Roasted Okara with Almonds

3 tablespoons fruit juice
2–3 teaspoons honey
3 cups (500 g/1 lb) okara (page 344)
1 cup (125 g/4 oz) roughly chopped almonds

Combine the fruit juice and honey. Place the okara and the almonds in a bowl and sprinkle the fruit juice mixture over. Spread the mixture out on a prepared baking sheet. Bake in a slow oven (150°C/300°F) until the mixture is dry and crumbly (about 1–1½ hours). Allow the okara to cool completely before storing in an airtight jar.
*Makes about 4 cups*

*Please refer to the recipe for mixed spice in our Cook's Notes, page 8.

# Basic Pancakes

1½ cups (185 g/6 oz) wholemeal (whole-wheat)
  self-raising flour
1 cup (250 mL/8 fl oz) milk
1 egg
1 tablespoon honey *or* 1½ tablespoons sugar
1 teaspoon butter *or* margarine

Place all the ingredients in a food processor and
blend for 1 minute. Allow the mixture to stand
for 5–10 minutes if possible to allow the starch
grains in the flour to soften. Place tablespoonfuls
of the mixture in a moderately hot frying pan or
skillet that has been brushed with the butter (or
margarine). Cook until bubbles start to form,
then flip the pancakes over and cook for a
further 1–2 minutes. Remove from the pan and
cover with a tea towel until required.
*Makes about 18*

### Fluffy Pancakes
Try using plain yoghurt or buttermilk instead of
milk for light fluffy pancakes.

# Banana Pancakes

2 ripe bananas, mashed
½ teaspoon bicarbonate of soda (baking soda)
1 tablespoon hot water
1 egg
1–2 tablespoons sugar
1 cup (125 g/4 oz) wholemeal (whole-wheat)
  self-raising flour
½ teaspoon ground cinnamon
½ cup (125 mL/4 fl oz) yoghurt *or* milk
1 teaspoon butter (*or* margarine)

Prepare and cook as for Basic Pancakes (above).
*Makes about 18*

*Right: Packed with the goodness of wholemeal flour
and fresh fruit, Apple and Muesli Pancakes and
Banana Pancakes make a great weekend breakfast
or brunch.*

# Apple and Muesli Pancakes

*Serve hot topped with a scoop of Yoghurt Cheese
(page 271) and drizzled with a little honey.
Delicious and moist served cold for a snack too.*

1 cup (125 g/4 oz) wholemeal (whole-wheat)
  self-raising flour
1 cup (90 g/3 oz) muesli
1 teaspoon mixed spice*
1 egg
1 tablespoon honey
¾ cup (225 mL/7 fl oz) milk
1 apple, grated
1 teaspoon butter *or* margarine

Mix the flour with the muesli and the spice and
make a 'well' in the centre. Combine the egg,
honey, milk and apple and pour into the 'well'.
Gradually work the dry ingredients in and beat
the mixture with a wooden spoon for
1–2 minutes. Cook as for Basic Pancakes.
*Makes about 12*

# Eggless Pancakes

*The tofu and the oil replace the egg in this pancake
mix, a great recipe to have on hand for when you
are out of eggs.*

125 g (4 oz) tofu, drained and mashed
1 tablespoon oil
1 tablespoon honey
1 cup (250 mL/8 fl oz) soy milk
vanilla essence (extract)
1½ cups (185 g/6 oz) wholemeal (whole-wheat)
  self-raising flour
1 teaspoon butter *or* margarine

Prepare and cook as for Basic Pancakes
(opposite).
*Makes about 12*

*Please refer to the recipe for mixed spice in our
Cook's Notes, page 8.

# Buckwheat Pancakes

*These flavoursome pancakes are delicious served with honey and fresh fruit. Serve them individually or serve them stacked and drizzled with Fresh Berry Coulis (page 178) and Yoghurt Cheese (page 271) for a summer treat, or top with Dried Fruit Compôte (page 165) for a warming winter breakfast.*

½ cup (60 g/2 oz) buckwheat flour
1 cup (125 g/4 oz) wholemeal (whole-wheat) self-raising flour
1 teaspoon baking powder
1 egg, beaten
1 tablespoon honey
1½ cups (375 mL/12 fl oz) thin plain yoghurt *or* buttermilk
1 teaspoon butter *or* margarine

Prepare and cook as for Basic Pancakes (page 266).
*Makes about 18*

# Creamed Rice

2 cups (310 g/10 oz) cooked rice such as jasmine *or* basmati rice
2 cups (500 mL/16 fl oz) milk
2 teaspoons honey
a few drops vanilla essence (extract)

Place the rice and milk in a small saucepan and bring the mixture to the boil, stirring. Reduce the heat and simmer for 15–20 minutes, stirring occasionally. Stir in the honey and vanilla.
*Serves 2*

# Fruity Creamed Rice

1 quantity cold Creamed Rice (above)
150 g (5 oz) canned pineapple, chopped
2 tablespoons sultanas (golden raisins)
additional 2 tablespoons chopped pineapple

Add the pineapple and sultanas to the rice and serve topped with the additional pineapple.
*Serves 2*

# Buckwheat Porridge

*Buckwheat porridge has a wonderful distinctive flavour. Try it drizzled with a little honey or topped with sliced banana.*

½ cup (90 g/3 oz) buckwheat
2 cups (500 mL/16 fl oz) water
½ cup (125 mL/4 fl oz) milk

Place the buckwheat in a saucepan and dry roast over a medium heat for 3 minutes. Add the water and bring the mixture to the boil, stirring. Cover and cook, stirring occasionally, for 15 minutes. Stir in the milk and reheat gently.
*Serves 2*

**Sweetening Porridge**
If you wish to sweeten porridge, stir in a little honey or chopped dried fruit at the same time as the milk.

# Creamed Fruity Semolina

*Although you may not have wonderful memories of semolina, the raisins and almonds in this recipe really give the semolina a lift. Serve on a cold morning for a delicious and satisfying start to the day.*

4 tablespoons semolina
2 cups (500 mL/16 fl oz) milk
2 tablespoon chopped almonds
3 tablespoons chopped raisins
additional chopped raisins and almonds

Place the semolina and milk in a small saucepan and bring the mixture to the boil. Reduce the heat and simmer, stirring, for 5 minutes. Stir in the almonds and raisins and serve topped with the additional chopped raisins and almonds.
*Serves 2*

# Porridge

*Serve drizzled with a teaspoon of honey or with chopped raisins and almonds. A great start to a winter's day.*

1½ cups (125g/4 oz) rolled oats
3 cups (750 mL/24 fl oz) water

Place the oats and water in a small saucepan and bring the mixture to the boil, stirring. Reduce the heat and simmer, covered, for 5–10 minutes (depending on how long it takes you to have a shower!).
*Serves 2*

### Reducing Cooking Times
Soaking grains such as oats the night before allows them to soften and greatly reduces the cooking time.

# Microwave Porridge

*This is a good trick for avoiding a porridge-coated saucepan! You can cook and serve the porridge from the same bowl, and while you're at it, make sure it is a good-sized bowl to allow for the porridge which bubbles and expands during cooking.*

⅓ cup (30 g/1 oz) rolled oats
⅔ cup (180 mL/6 fl oz) hot water

Microwave on high for 1 minute. Stir, then cook on high for 30 seconds.
*Serves 1*

### Even Faster Porridge
Starting off this porridge with hot water from a kettle keeps the cooking time to a minimum.

# Fruity Polenta

*A quick and easy way to enjoy polenta.*

1 cup (250 mL/8 fl oz) water
1 cup (250 mL/8 fl oz) milk
3 tablespoons fine polenta (cornmeal)
2 teaspoons honey
2 tablespoons sultanas (golden raisins)

Place the water and milk in a saucepan and bring it to the boil. Add a continuous stream of polenta from your hand while stirring constantly with the other. Cook, stirring, for 5–10 minutes. Stir the honey through, scatter the sultanas over and serve.
*Serves 2*

# Oat and Polenta Porridge

*This recipe is wonderful for introducing the uninitiated to polenta.*

1 cup (90 g/3 oz) rolled oats
4 cups (1 litre/1¾ imp. pints) water
½ cup (90 g/3 oz) fine polenta (cornmeal)

Place the oats and water in a small saucepan and bring the mixture to the boil, stirring. While boiling, add the polenta in a thin continuous stream from your hand, and continue to boil, stirring, for 5 minutes.
*Serves 2*

# Wheat Grain Porridge

*Soak the wheat grain in the water the night before to considerably reduce the cooking time, or use sprouted wheat (page 257) for a quick cooked sweet porridge.*

1 cup (225 g/7 oz) wheat grain
2 cups (500 mL/16 fl oz) water

Place the wheat and water in a saucepan and bring the mixture to the boil. Reduce the heat and simmer for 1 hour, stirring occasionally.
*Serves 2*

# Basic Cottage Cheese

*Cottage cheese is very versatile and can be used to make a wide range of dishes from dips and spreads to cheesecakes, mousses and dessert toppings.*

2 quarts (2 litres/3¼ imp. pints) skim milk
2 tablespoons lemon juice, strained

Bring the milk to the boil, then stir in the lemon juice. When curds and whey begin to form, remove the saucepan from the heat and set aside for 10–15 minutes. Pour the mixture into a sieve lined with muslin which has been propped on top of a bowl to catch the whey as it drains from the curds. (Whey is rich in minerals and protein and can be used in drinks instead of buttermilk and also in soups and sauces.) Fresh cottage cheese keeps for 4–5 days in the refrigerator.
*Makes about 500 g (1 lb)*

# Panir

*Of Indian origin, panir is also known as fresh curd cheese. It is prepared in much the same way as cottage cheese, but panir is pressed under a heavy weight to remove as much whey as possible and to set it into a very firm curd. The cheese can then be sliced or cut into cubes and added to salads, curries, braises and stir-fries.*

3 quarts (3 litres/4¾ imp. pints) milk
4 tablespoons strained lemon juice

Place the milk in a large saucepan and bring it to the boil. Stir in the lemon juice, then cover, checking that curds have started to form after 2–3 minutes (if not, simply stir in an additional tablespoon of strained lemon juice). Cover and allow to stand for 10 minutes. Spoon the curds into a sieve (or colander) lined with muslin placed on top of a bowl. Fold the cloth over the cheese and place a plate on top. Place a heavy weight such as a jar of dried beans on top of the plate and set the cheese aside for 1–1½ hours. Turn the cheese out of the sieve and, if not using at once, store in an airtight container in the refrigerator.
*Makes about 500 g (1 lb)*

# Yoghurt, Buttermilk and Fresh Cheeses

*I really enjoy making yoghurt and fresh cheeses. Perhaps what's so fascinating is the fact that with very little effort on my part, a common food like milk can take on such a diversity of shapes, tastes and textures. The flavour of these foods is especially wonderful too, smooth with just a mildly sharp edge.*

# Yoghurt Cheese

*Served with savoury or sweet accompaniments, this is a truly versatile cheese. It can be made from full cream milk, reduced fat milk or skim milk. It is wonderful used as a base for sauces, dressings, quick fruit whips and instant mousses. It can be rolled into balls and served with other cheeses in cheese platters or served with fresh fruit or fruit preserved or canned in its own juice. A scoop of Yoghurt Cheese also makes a great topping for hot sweet or savoury pancakes or even nachos (page 45).*

2 quarts (2 litres/3¼ imp. pints) plain yoghurt
  (page 272)

Pour the yoghurt into a sieve lined with muslin which has been propped on top of a bowl. Pull up the ends of the cloth and twist. Secure with a rubber band and hang above a bowl to collect the whey for about 8 hours. (I usually do this overnight when the kitchen is cool.)
*Makes about 500 g (1 lb)*

*Left: Panir, ready for eating, and Yoghurt Cheese in the making. The satisfying firm texture of panir makes it a great cheese for slicing while the moist creamy texture and tangy edge of Yoghurt Cheese makes it a wonderful substitute for cream cheese in many recipes.*

# Basic Plain Yoghurt

*Yoghurt is a cultured milk which has been converted into a semi-solid consistency by lactic acid producing bacteria in the starter culture. These 'friendly' bacteria convert lactose (milk sugar) into lactic acid which causes the milk to set. Natural acidopholous yoghurt makes a good starter culture for yoghurt. Do not use sweetened or fruit yoghurts as the fruit will interfere with the yoghurt-making process. 'Yoghurt-like desserts' not only bear little resemblance to yoghurt but do not contain living bacteria. It's very economical to make your own yoghurt so you can have plenty on hand to whip up some delicious drinks, desserts and toppings, dressings, ice creams, cakes, pancakes and waffles.*

**4 cups (1 litre/1¾ imp. pints) milk**
**1½ tablespoons plain yoghurt**

Place the milk in a saucepan and heat to boiling point. Remove the saucepan from the heat and set aside to cool to a little warmer than body heat, actually about 43°C (110°F). If you do not have a thermometer, submerge a clean finger in the milk and if you can keep it comfortably submerged to the count of 10, it is not too hot.

Place the yoghurt in a clean dry container or jar and gradually add the milk, whisking the mixture constantly. Cover the container immediately and place in your chosen warm cosy location. Allow to stand, undisturbed, for 4–5 hours, then chill in the refrigerator until ready to use.
*Makes 4 cups (1 litre/1¾ imp. pints)*

### Keeping Yoghurt Warm
To keep yoghurt warm during the incubation time use a yoghurt maker or wide mouthed thermos flask. I have often used clean dry jars which need only be sealed, wrapped in one or two thick tea towels and then covered completely with a plastic (polythene) bag. In cooler weather you need to 'rug up' your yoghurt with an extra tea towel and allow it to incubate in a warm area of your kitchen. You can, of course, buy special yoghurt makers from cookware shops.

# Low-Fat Plain Yoghurt

*I've found that using a mixture of skim milk and full cream milk is the most successful for making yoghurt for general use. Try experimenting with both skim milk yoghurt and full cream yoghurt and a blend of the two. It is certainly worthwhile in terms of keeping the intake of saturated fats as low as possible. I seem to have hit a happy medium with my family and friends by combining about 2 parts skim milk with 1 part full cream milk.*

**2½ cups (625 mL/1 imp. pint) skim milk**
**1½ cups (375 mL/12 fl oz) full cream milk**
**1½ cups non fat plain yoghurt**

Follow the method for Basic Plain Yoghurt (opposite).
*Makes 4 cups (1 litre/1¾ imp. pints)*

# Nonfat Plain Yoghurt

*Skim milk can be used on its own very successfully to make delicious yoghurt. Adding skim milk powder to the milk before adding the yoghurt results in a thicker yoghurt. And remember, before you use that last tablespoon or so of yoghurt, keep it to start your next batch off with.*

**4 cups (1 litre/1¾ imp. pints) skim milk**
**2--3 tablespoons skim milk powder (optional)**
**1½ tablespoons nonfat plain yoghurt**

Follow the method for Basic Plain Yoghurt (opposite), whisking the skim milk powder (if using) into the milk at the same time as the yoghurt.
*Makes 4 cups (1 litre/1¾ imp. pints)*

### Using UHT Milk
If you wish to shorten the preparation time, use UHT milk which does not need to be brought to the boil as it has been sterilised during the heat treatment. Simply heat the milk to the correct temperature and proceed as for the basic method.

# Greek Yoghurt

*Greek Yoghurt is luscious and thick and great to dollop on top of desserts and cakes instead of cream. It can also be used as a sour cream substitute. Greek Yoghurt can be prepared from full cream, low fat or nonfat yoghurt.*

6 cups (1.5 litres/2½ imp. pints) plain yoghurt

Pour the yoghurt into a sieve (or colander) lined with muslin which has been propped on top of a bowl. Cover and allow to stand for about 4 hours.
*Makes about 4 cups (1 litre/1¾ imp. pints)*

# Fruit Yoghurt

*Plain yoghurt can be sweetened with low-sugar jams or spreads such as Low-Sugar Berry Jam (page 309) and Zesty Apricot Spread (page 309). Fruit should not be added before the yoghurt is incubated as the fruit will interfere with the yoghurt-making process.*

3 cups (750 mL/24 fl oz) yoghurt
2 tablespoons low-sugar jam (page 309)
1 cup sliced *or* chopped fresh fruit, *or* fruit preserved *or* canned in juice

Whisk the jam and fruit through the yoghurt and serve.
*Makes 4 cups (1 litre/1¾ imp. pints)*

# Passion Fruit Yoghurt

2 cups (500 mL/16 fl, oz) Greek Yoghurt (above) *or* Yoghurt Cheese (page 271)
1 tablespoon honey
4 tablespoons passion fruit pulp

Whisk the yoghurt and honey together until well combined, then stir in the passion fruit pulp. Chill the yoghurt thoroughly before serving.
*Makes about 2½ cups (625 mL/1 imp. pint)*

# Thick Mango Yoghurt

*If you wish to make fruit yoghurt using fresh fruit only, it's best to use Greek Yoghurt to counteract the addition of juice from fruit which often causes yoghurt to become runny. This yoghurt has a luscious thick texture and if you wish to make a fruit yoghurt with a 'mousse-like' texture, you can even use Yoghurt Cheese (page 271) instead of the Greek Yoghurt.*

2 cups (500 mL/16 fl oz) Greek Yoghurt (opposite)
1 large mango, peeled, pip removed, diced

Combine the yoghurt and the mango well and chill before serving.
*Makes about 2½ cups (625 mL/1 imp. pint)*

# Strawberry Yoghurt

*The true flavour of fresh strawberries really shines through in this delicious yoghurt which serves as a refreshing summer breakfast or dessert. If the strawberries are very sweet and ripe, there will be no need to add any honey.*

1 punnet (carton) strawberries, hulled and sliced
2 cups (500 mL/16 fl oz) Greek Yoghurt (opposite)
2–3 teaspoons light-tasting honey

Fold the strawberries carefully through the yoghurt and chill thoroughly before serving.
*Makes about 3 cups (750 mL/24 fl oz)*

# Buttermilk

*Buttermilk is wonderful to have on hand to use in drinks such as smoothies and in hot or cold soups, dressings, sauces, cakes, pancakes, waffles and even in bread.*

3½ cups (875 mL/28 fl oz) UHT skim milk
5 tablespoons buttermilk

Place the milk in a saucepan and heat to 35°C (95°F). (When using UHT milk, it is not necessary to boil the milk first.) Place the buttermilk in a wide mouthed Thermos flask or yoghurt maker, then pour the skim milk over, whisking to thoroughly combine the ingredients. Cover, set aside and do not disturb for 4–5 hours. Chill and store in an airtight container in the refrigerator for up to 1 week.
*Makes 4 cups (1 litre/1¾ imp. pints)*

# Crème Fraîche

*Although it is devilishly rich, I have no conscience about dolloping crème fraîche onto cakes and desserts for special occasions— enjoy! I must admit though, I have most often made it especially to make Coeur à la Crème.*

1¾ cups (440 mL/14 fl oz) whipping (double) cream
4 tablespoons buttermilk

Heat the cream to boiling point. Remove the saucepan from the heat and allow the cream to cool. Whisk in the buttermilk and pour immediately into a preheated wide mouthed Thermos flask or yoghurt maker. Cover and set aside in a location where it will not be disturbed for 6–8 hours. Chill and store in the refrigerator for up to 1 week.
*Makes about 2 cups (500 mL/16 fl oz)*

# Coeur à la Crème

*This is a beautifully romantic dish to bestow upon loved ones, including yourself. Serve decorated with fresh berries, Fresh Berry Coulis (page 178) or Spiked Strawberry Sauce (page 180).*

2 cups (500 mL/16 fl oz) Greek Yoghurt (page 273)
1 cup (250 mL/8 fl oz) Crème Fraîche (opposite)
few drops pure vanilla essence (extract)

Place the yoghurt into a bowl and fold in the crème fraîche and vanilla. Place into individual heart shaped moulds which have been lined with small squares of muslin. Fold the cloth over the cheese mixture and stand the moulds on a plate to catch the whey as it drains. Refrigerate overnight, turn out and decorate.
*Serves 4*

# Light Sour Cream

*Sour cream and crème fraîche are used in cooking to enrich sauces because, when they are heated, they don't curdle as readily as regular cream. I recommend using this sour cream, which contains all the flavour but only half the fat.*

1¾ cups (440 mL/14 fl oz) UHT reduced fat cream
4 tablespoons buttermilk

Place the cream and the buttermilk in a saucepan and whisk briefly. Heat to 50°C (86°F), then remove from the heat and pour the mixture into a preheated wide mouthed Thermos flask or yoghurt maker. Set aside and do not disturb for 24 hours. Chill and store in an airtight container in the refrigerator for 1 week.
*Makes about 2 cups (500 mL/16 fl oz)*

**Preheating Thermos Flasks**
Simply fill with boiling water, stand for 1 minute, then drain completely before using.

*Left: Creamy and delectable, Coeur à la Crème makes a stylish dessert that can be prepared well ahead of time.*

# Herbed Cheese Balls

*Serve as part of an antipasto dish with a selection of fresh and pickled vegetables and fresh crusty bread or rolls. To preserve under oil, see 'Preserves' (page 299).*

250 g (8 oz) Yoghurt Cheese (page 271)
½ cup finely chopped herbs such as coriander, parsley *or* chives

Form the cheese into small balls and roll in the herbs. Use at once or store in a covered container in the refrigerator for up to 1 week.
*Makes about 12*

# Sesame Seed Cheese Balls

250 g (8 oz) Yoghurt Cheese (page 271)
3 tablespoons finely sliced chives
freshly ground black pepper
½ cup (60 g/2 oz) sesame seeds, roasted (page 17)

Combine the cheese, chives and pepper and form the mixture into small balls. Roll the balls in the sesame seeds and, if not using them at once, store them in a covered container in the refrigerator for up to 1 week.
*Makes about 20 balls*

# Cheese and Paprika Balls

250 g (8 oz) Yoghurt Cheese (page 271)
3 tablespoons finely chopped red sweet pepper (capsicum)
¼ teaspoon cracked black pepper
1 tablespoon sweet paprika
½ cup finely chopped parsley

Combine the cheese, sweet pepper and pepper, then form the mixture into small balls. Roll the balls in the paprika and parsley mixture. Use at once or store in a covered container in the refrigerator.
*Makes about 12*

# Walnut and Cheese Balls

*Delicious served with an array of fresh seasonal fruit and salad greens.*

250 g (8 oz) Yoghurt Cheese (page 271) *or* light cream cheese
90 g (3 oz) walnuts, chopped finely
1 tablespoon fruit liqueur
½ cup (60 g/2 oz) ground almonds (almond meal)
additional finely chopped walnuts

Combine the cheese, walnuts, liqueur and almonds and form into balls about the size of a walnut. Roll in the additional finely chopped walnuts and serve.
*Makes about 12*

# Spicy Sunflower Seed Balls

2 teaspoons oil
1 teaspoon finely sliced chili peppers
2 garlic cloves, crushed (pressed)
1 teaspoon grated ginger
½ cup sunflower seeds, roasted (page 17)
250 g (8 oz) Panir (page 271)
additional 2 tablespoons roasted sunflower seeds

Heat the oil in a saucepan and stir the chilies, garlic, ginger and sunflower seeds over a medium–high heat for 2 minutes. Place the Panir in a bowl, add the spicy sunflower seed mixture and combine well. Form the mixture into balls about the size of a walnut. Place on a serving plate and sprinkle with the additional sunflower seeds.
*Makes about 12*

# Prune and Almond Cheese

*A delightful blend of flavours, this cheese is wonderful served with a platter of fresh red and green grapes.*

250 g (8 oz) cream cheese
90 g (3 oz) pitted prunes, chopped
2 teaspoons honey
½ cup (60 g/2 oz) finely chopped almonds

Combine the cheese with the prunes and honey and set the mixture aside for 1–2 hours to become firm. Form the mixture into small balls and roll in the chopped almonds.
*Makes about 12*

# Spiked Fruit Cheese

*Serve with a platter of fresh seasonal fruit and crackers or fresh crusty bread.*

3 tablespoons chopped dried apricots
3 tablespoons chopped raisins
1–2 tablespoons sherry *or* fruit liqueur
  (pages 327–9)
250 g (8 oz) cream cheese *or* ricotta cheese

Place the dried fruit in a small bowl and sprinkle with the sherry (or liqueur). Cover and set aside for 1–2 hours. Add the cheese and combine carefully to prevent breaking the fruit up. Place the mixture into one medium or several small muslin-lined moulds. Fold the cloth over the cheese mixture and place a plate on top. Set aside for 1–2 hours.
*Serves 4*

# Hazelnut and Apricot Cheese

250 g (8 oz) ricotta cheese *or* Yoghurt Cheese
  (page 271)
60 g (2 oz) hazelnuts, roasted (page 17) and
  chopped
60 g (2 oz) dried apricots, chopped
2 teaspoons honey
dried apricots and hazelnuts to decorate

Combine all the ingredients and press into muslin lined moulds or form the mixture into small balls. Set aside for 1 hour before serving to enable the flavours to infuse and the texture to become firm.
*Serves 4–6*

# Cottage Cheese Whip

*Great for topping Baked Jacket Potatoes (page 81) instead of Sour Cream.*

250 g (8 oz) cottage cheese (page 271)
1 cup (250 mL/8 fl oz) plain yoghurt
2 tablespoons lemon juice
freshly ground black pepper

Using a food processor or blender, blend all the ingredients together until smooth.
*Serves 6–8*

# Basic Nut Milk

*Nut milks make wonderful drinks. Whipped up in seconds, they are delicious just as they are, or sweetened with a little honey or fresh fruit. Lightly flavoured nuts such as almonds, cashews, hazelnuts, Brazil nuts or peanuts are usually used because stronger tasting nuts such as walnuts and pecan nuts produce milk with a rather overpowering flavour. Use only the freshest of nuts for the best result, choosing raw nuts rather than roasted.*

*Nut milks are light yet satisfying and provide added variety in our diets, especially for those people who do not consume dairy products. It's a good idea to have a supply of nut milk frozen in ice block trays so they can be added to smoothies, dessert creams and salad dressings just when you need them. The bonus is that the nut milk ice blocks chill the drinks and creams while they are being prepared, so there is no need to add ice.*

½ cup (60 g/2 oz) nuts such as almonds, cashews, hazelnuts, Brazil nuts *or* peanuts
2 cups (500 mL/16 fl oz) chilled water *or* fruit juice

Place the nuts or seeds into a blender and blend to a smooth paste with a little water (or fruit juice). Add enough water to bring the mixture to the required consistency. Prop a muslin-lined sieve over a bowl and pour the mixture in. Pull up the ends of the cloth and twist to extract the maximum amount of liquid. (Set the pulp aside to use later in burgers and patties, cakes, loaves, bread, muesli and crumble toppings.) Use the milk at once if possible, but if not, store in an airtight container in the refrigerator for a day or two. As nut milk separates upon standing, it must be shaken vigorously before use.
*Makes 2 cups (500 mL/16 fl oz)*

*Left: Coconut Cream and Coconut Milk in the making. Use these to enrich your favourite spicy vegetable dishes, cakes and desserts and even grain dishes.*

# Nut Milks, Nut Butters and Creams

*Quickly and simply prepared, nut milks, butters and creams can be added to all manner of scrumptious dishes such as light and refreshing drinks, dips, dressings, sauces, soups, casseroles, sandwich spreads and dessert toppings. The benefit of making your own? Once you've tasted the wonderful sweet nutty flavour of these freshly prepared foods, you'll never need to ask again.*

# Coconut Cream

*I enjoy using coconut cream to provide fragrance and a rich texture to recipes as an alternative to cream.*

185 g (6 oz) fresh coconut flesh, peeled
1 cup (250 mL/8 fl oz) boiling water

Using a vegetable peeler, peel the dark skin from the coconut flesh. Using a large sharp knife, cut the coconut flesh into small pieces. Using a blender, chop the coconut to produce a coarse meal. While the machine is operating, gradually add the boiling water. Blend for 2 minutes. Prop a muslin-lined sieve over a bowl and pour the mixture in. Pull up the ends of the cloth and twist to extract the maximum amount of liquid. Pour the liquid into an airtight container, cover and refrigerate. After 45 minutes or so, the cream will rise to the top and can be scooped off with a spoon. Retain the coconut milk.
*Makes about ½ cup (125 mL/4 fl oz)*

# Coconut Milk

185 g (6 oz) coconut, flesh grated *or* the pulp
  remaining after making coconut cream
1¼ cups (310 mL/10 fl oz) boiling water

Place the coconut flesh in a heatproof bowl and
pour the boiling water over. Cover and set aside
to soak until it is cool. Strain the milk from the
flesh as for Coconut Cream (page 279).
*Makes about 1¼ cups (310 mL/10 fl oz)*

# Carob and Almond Milk

½ cup (60 g/2 oz) almonds
2 cups (500 mL/16 fl oz) chilled water
3 teaspoons carob powder
2 teaspoons honey
a few drops vanilla essence (extract)
½ cup crushed ice

Using a blender, grind the almonds until a fine
meal is produced. Add half of the water and
continue to blend until the mixture becomes
quite creamy. Add the carob powder, honey,
vanilla essence and ice and blend for 30 seconds.
Add enough of the remaining water to bring the
milk to the desired consistency. Serve at once.
*Makes 2 tall glasses*

# Sesame and Sunflower Milk

*Seeds can be used to make light and refreshing
concoctions.*

⅓ cup (2 oz) hulled sesame *or* sunflower seeds
2 cups (500 mL/16 fl oz) chilled water
1 teaspoon honey
few drops vanilla essence (extract)

Place the seeds in a blender or food processor
and grind to a meal. Gradually add the water,
honey and vanilla and follow the method for
Basic Nut Milk (page 279).
*Makes 2 cups (500 mL/16 fl oz)*

# Banana Cashew Milk

*This is a wonderfully quick breakfast drink. If you
are 'on the run' grab a piece of fresh fruit as you
pass by the fruit bowl and you will have plenty of
energy to start the day on the right foot.*

½ cup (60 g/2 oz) cashew nuts
1 cup (250 mL/8 fl oz) chilled water
2 teaspoons honey
1 banana, sliced
1 cup crushed ice
1 cup (250 mL/8 fl oz) apple juice

Using a blender, grind the cashew nuts until a
fine meal is produced. Add the water and
continue to blend until the mixture becomes
quite creamy. Add the honey, banana, ice and
apple juice and blend for 30 seconds. Serve at
once.
*Makes 2 tall glasses*

# Basic Nut Butter

*Nut butters are usually made from dry roasted nuts
because this way the oils are extracted more easily
to form a moist paste. To savour the scrumptious
flavour of freshly prepared nut butters, prepare
only the amount you will use within a week or
two, and store the butters in the refrigerator until
ready to use.*

2 cups (250 g/8 oz) almonds *or* cashew nuts *or*
  hazelnuts, dry roasted (page 17)
2–3 tablespoons oil

Place the nuts into a blender and grind to a fine
meal. While the machine is operating, add the oil
very gradually until a paste forms. Take care not
to add too much oil.
*Makes about 1 cup (250 g/8 oz)*

# Peanut Butter

*Peanut butter is an all round favourite as a spread for sandwiches and hot toast, but why stop here—it can also be whipped up into quick sauces and dips such as Scrumptious Peanut Dip (page 22).*

2 cups (250 g/8 oz) peanuts, dry roasted (page 17)
2–3 tablespoons oil

Follow the method for Basic Nut Butter (page 280).
*Makes about 1 cup (250 g/8 oz)*

# Basic Nut Creams

*The nuts most suitable for making nut creams are almonds, cashews and peanuts due to their mild flavour. Stronger tasting nuts such as walnuts and pecan nuts produce creams with a rather overpowering flavour.*

1 cup (125 g/4 oz) almonds *or* cashew nuts,
   hazelnuts *or* peanuts
½ cup (125 mL/4 fl oz) water *or* fruit juice

Remove the skins from the nuts by rubbing off (peanuts) or by blanching. Using a blender or food processor, grind the nuts to a meal, then gradually add the liquid. Blend the mixture until a smooth cream is produced.
*Makes about ¾ cup (225 mL/6 fl oz)*

### Blanching Nuts
To blanch nuts, place them in a heatproof bowl and completely cover with boiling water. Set aside for 5 minutes, then drain the nuts and rinse with cold water. The skins should now slide off the nuts quite easily.

# Soy Nut Cream

*Nut cream is delectable as it is, and when further enriched with soy milk rather than water or fruit juice it becomes quite exquisite. I use this cream as a base for tantalising dressings for vegetables and salads.*

1 cup (125g/4 oz) almonds *or* cashew nuts,
   hazelnuts *or* peanuts, blanched
½ cup (125mL/4 fl oz) soy milk

Using a blender or food processor, grind the nuts to a meal, then gradually add the soy milk. Blend the mixture until a smooth cream is produced.
*Makes about ¾ cup (225 mL/6 fl oz)*

# Sweet Cashew Cream

*A light fluffy cream, this is heavenly dolloped onto all manner of desserts or even toasted muesli (page 264) for an indulgent breakfast. Simply pour a little nonfat milk around the muesli then top with a generous dollop of cashew cream. To top it off, scatter fresh strawberries over.*

1 cup (125 g/4 oz) raw cashew nuts
½ cup (125 mL/4 fl oz) pure apple juice
1–2 teaspoons honey

Follow the method for Basic Nut Cream (opposite).
*Makes about 1⅓ cups (305 mL/10 fl oz)*

### Obtaining Coconut Flesh
To remove the coconut flesh from its shell, pierce the coconut and drain the liquid away. Place the coconut in a moderate oven (180°C/350°C) and roast for 25 minutes. Set the coconut aside until it is cool enough to handle. Break the shell with a mallet or hammer. Prise the flesh away from the shell. It should come away quite easily as the shell expands and the flesh shrinks during the roasting process.

# Basic Tofu

*Tofu is generally readily available to most of us, but if you cannot obtain it, or if you simply wish to save money and/or enjoy the additional benefits of homemade tofu such as a supply of okara (page 344) and whey (page 284), as I quite often do, then the effort is really worthwhile. This tofu has a firm texture due to the use of nigari (page 344) and the homemade soy milk. Firm-textured tofu is great for adding to stir-fries, for roasting and grilling, and for making ever popular burgers.*

2 cups (435 g/14 oz) dried soy beans, washed
3 quarts (3 litres/4¾ imp. pints) water
2 teaspoons nigari (page 344), dissolved in
    3 tablespoons water

Place the beans in a large container and cover with 2 litres of the water. Cover and allow to stand overnight or for 10–12 hours. (In warm weather, place the container in the refrigerator to prevent the beans from fermenting.) Using a food processor or blender, process the beans and the soaking liquid together (in batches) for about 1 minute, adding the additional 1 litre of water along the way. At this stage the mixture looks creamy and foamy, rather like soap suds!

Place the mixture in a large heavy-based boiler or preserving pan and bring it to the boil, stirring occasionally with a long handled spoon to prevent the mixture from catching on the bottom of the pan. Reduce the heat and simmer for 15 minutes, taking care that the mixture does not boil over. (If it threatens to boil over and the 'foam' is rising above the sides of the saucepan, quickly sprinkle the foam with a little cold water, and set the pan aside from the heat. Reduce the heat and continue to simmer the mixture.)

Pour the mixture through a large sieve which has been lined with a muslin and placed over a large heatproof bowl (or another boiler). Allow the pulp (okara) to cool slightly, then don rubber gloves and pull the ends of the muslin up, twist and secure with a rubber band. Twist the cloth tightly to remove as much liquid (soy milk) as possible. (Now you will know why you needed rubber gloves.) Set the okara aside to use later and pour the soy milk back into the original boiler.

# Tofu and Soy Products

*Soy foods such as soy beans, soy milk, tofu and tempeh are economical sources of protein, are easier to prepare than most people realise and have amazing potential. And yet, they are one of the most under-rated foods I can think of.*

Heat the soy milk to just below boiling point (about 80°C/175°F) then remove the boiler from the heat. Stir the milk briskly in a circular fashion and pour the nigari mixture in. Cover and set the mixture aside for 5 minutes to allow the curds to form. (If this does not happen, dissolve an additional ½ teaspoon nigari in 1 tablespoon water and stir into the mixture.)

Line a colander or large sieve with a clean dry piece of muslin and place over a large bowl to collect the whey. Carefully pour the mixture into the colander and fold the muslin over the tofu. Cover with a plate and place a 1 kg (2 lb) weight such as a large jar of dried beans or honey on top to press out as much whey as possible.

Allow the tofu to stand for 1 hour then unwrap it and place it in a container with enough cold water to cover. Place the lid on the container and store in the refrigerator. If not using in a day, drain the water off each day, replace with cold fresh water and refrigerate.
*Makes about 750 g (1½ lb) tofu, plus about 4 cups (1 litre/1¾ imp. pints) okara and 4 cups (1 litre/1¾ imp. pints) whey*

**Curdling Milk**
Lemon juice can also be used to curdle the milk, in much the same way as panir is made (page 271). You will need to use ½ cup (125 mL/4 fl oz) strained lemon juice for the Basic Tofu recipe.

*Left: Tofu, soy milk, pre-soaked soy beans and okara. Tofu, a nutritious protein-packed food, is prepared from soy milk in much the same way as fresh cheese is prepared from cow's milk.*

# Quick Tofu

*I say 'quick' because many of the steps in the method for Basic Tofu (page 283) can be omitted when you commence the process with ready-made soy milk. Keep cartons of UHT soy milk in your pantry for your next tofu-making session. Unfortunately you will not score the bonus points of the okara, but you will have the whey to use as well as the tofu. This tofu has a ricotta cheese-like consistency, rather similar to silken tofu (page 346) and is especially suitable for making cheesecakes, dips, cakes, pancakes and waffles.*

3 quarts (3 litres/4¾ imp. pints) soy milk
2 teaspoons nigari dissolved in 3 tablespoons
    water

Place the soy milk into a large saucepan and heat to just below boiling point (about 80°C/175°F) then remove the pan from the heat. Stir the milk briskly in a circular fashion and pour the nigari mixture in. Cover and set the mixture aside for 5 minutes to allow the curds to form. (If this does not happen, dissolve an additional ½ teaspoon nigari in 1 tablespoon water and stir into the mixture.)

Line a colander or large sieve with a clean dry piece of muslin and place over a large bowl to collect the whey. Carefully pour the mixture into the colander and fold the cloth over the tofu. Now proceed as for Basic Tofu (page 283).

**Uses for Whey**
Whey is one of the by-products of the tofu-making process. Like the whey produced from the regular cheese-making process, the whey from soy milk contains valuable minerals; it can be used as vegetable stock in soups, casseroles and sauces, and is actually a spectacular cleaning reagent! The soy lecithin present actually dissolves oil and acts as a detergent—yes, you can even wash dishes with this stuff! Or, firm fruits like apples and pears can be wiped over with a cloth dipped in whey, to help remove any residue of pesticides or wax.

# Frozen Tofu

*The first time I froze tofu I thought I had ruined it, and promptly threw it in the bin. After all, freezing tofu changes its nature, but I didn't suspect that it would look like a washing up sponge! And this is in fact what it does look and behave like—the texture becomes stringy and tough and it is dispersed with tiny air pockets, just like a sponge. But I later discovered that this has its benefits. It becomes much more absorbent and develops a chewy texture, making it a suitable ingredient for casseroles, stews or vegetable soups and textured vegetable protein (page 285). However, pre-frozen tofu is not suitable for deep frying as it absorbs heaps of oil, and the texture renders it unsuitable for dips, dressings and cheesecakes.*

**Tofu as required, well drained**

Place the tofu into a freezer bag and freeze. When you are ready to use it, thaw it and squeeze out any liquid. Chop the tofu finely and use as required.

# Parboiled Tofu

*Pre-cooking tofu this way helps it to retain its shape when added to stir-fries and braises. It is perfect for serving as an appetiser with each serve accompanied by a small bowl of dipping sauce (pages 96–7).*

500 g (1 lb) firm tofu, drained
4 cups (1 litre/1¾ imp. pints) vegetable stock *or*
    water

Place the vegetable stock (or water) in a saucepan and bring it to the boil. Add the tofu bit by bit and simmer it for 3–5 minutes. Remove the tofu, using a slotted spoon, and serve immediately or set aside to use as required later.
*Serves 4–6*

# Textured Vegetable Protein (TVP)

*This tasty TVP will reconstitute to serve 4 people.*

750 g (1½ lb) tofu, frozen, thawed, liquid removed
2 tablespoons soy sauce
freshly ground black pepper
oil

Depending on the texture required, chop finely, shred or cut the tofu into small cubes. Place in a bowl and sprinkle with the soy sauce and pepper. Combine well and spread the mixture out on a prepared baking sheet. Bake in a moderately slow oven (170°C/325°F) until the mixture is dry and crumbly (about 45 minutes–1 hour). Allow the TVP to cool completely before storing in an airtight jar.
*Makes 2 cups (150 g/5 oz)*

# Spicy Textured Vegetable Protein (TVP)

*To reconstitute the TVP, place in a bowl and cover with boiling water (1 part water:1 part TVP), cover and allow to stand for 10 minutes.*

750 g (1½ lb) tofu, frozen, thawed, liquid removed
2 tablespoons soy sauce
2 teaspoons sesame oil
3 garlic cloves, crushed (pressed)
1 teaspoon grated ginger
1 teaspoon honey
freshly ground black pepper

Depending on the texture required, chop finely, shred or cut the tofu into small cubes and place in a bowl. Combine the soy sauce, sesame oil, garlic, ginger, honey and pepper and sprinkle over the TVP. Combine well and spread the mixture out on a prepared baking sheet. Bake in a moderately slow oven (170°C/325°F) until the mixture is dry and crumbly (about 45 minutes–1 hour). Allow the TVP to cool completely before storing in an airtight jar.
*Makes 2 cups (550 g/5 oz)*

# Mediterranean-Style TVP

*This delicious ingredient is a result of my experimenting and having fun with some of my favourite flavours which, as if you didn't know them already, are garlic, basil and tomato with a touch of olive oil. To reconstitute the TVP, place in a bowl and cover with boiling water (1 part water:1 part TVP), cover and allow to stand for 10 minutes.*

750 g (1½ lb) tofu, frozen, thawed, liquid removed
2 tablespoons tomato paste (purée)
2 teaspoons olive oil
3 garlic cloves, crushed (pressed)
2 teaspoons dried basil
1 teaspoon honey
2–3 teaspoons balsamic *or* white wine vinegar
freshly ground black pepper

Depending on the texture required, chop finely, shred or cut the tofu into small cubes and place in a bowl. Combine the tomato paste, olive oil, garlic, basil, honey, vinegar and pepper and sprinkle over the TVP. Combine well and spread the mixture out on a prepared baking sheet. Bake in a moderately slow oven (170°C/325°F) until the mixture is dry and crumbly (about 45 minutes–1 hour). Allow the TVP to cool completely before storing in an airtight jar.
*Makes 2 cups (150 g/5 oz)*

# Marinated Tofu

500 g (1 lb) tofu, drained
½ cup (125 mL/4 fl oz) vegetable stock
2 tablespoons mirin (page 343)
3 spring onions (scallions), sliced finely
2–3 garlic cloves, crushed (pressed)
2 teaspoons sesame oil
2 tablespoons chopped herbs
cracked black pepper
1 teaspoon honey
1 teaspoon grated ginger

Cut the tofu into desired shapes and spread out on a large plate. Combine the remaining ingredients and pour over the tofu. Cover and set aside to marinate for at least 1 hour and up to 24 hours in the refrigerator. Drain the tofu and use as required.
*Serves 4*

# Tofu Paprika

*Serve with a tasty relish, dip or dressing and some crisp salad greens.*

375 g (12 oz) tofu, drained
1 tablespoon white miso (page 343) *or* soy sauce
½ cup (60 g/2 oz) wholemeal (whole-wheat) plain (all-purpose) flour
1 tablespoon sweet paprika
½ cup (125 mL/4 fl oz) peanut oil

Cut the tofu into 6 mm (¼ in.) slices and brush with the miso (or soy sauce). Combine the flour and paprika and dip the tofu slices in the mixture. Place the coated tofu slices in the freezer to chill. Meanwhile, heat the oil in a frying pan, skillet or wok. Fry the tofu slices until golden brown, then drain well on brown paper.
*Serves 4*

*Right: Marinated Tofu, a great way to lace this versatile ingredient with whatever flavours your heart desires. Chili peppers, garlic and ginger give this otherwise bland food a real lift.*

# Spicy Grilled Tofu

2 teaspoons oil
2 spring onions (scallions), sliced finely
1 tablespoon finely sliced chili peppers
1 tablespoon curry powder
4 tablespoons coconut cream
375 g (12 oz) tofu, drained, sliced thickly

Place the oil, spring onions, chilies and curry powder into a small saucepan and stir them over a medium heat for 2–3 minutes. Remove from the heat and stir in the coconut cream. Place the tofu slices on a plate and brush both sides generously with the coconut cream mixture. Allow to stand for 10 minutes if possible. Grill (broil) for 5 minutes on each side.
*Serves 4*

# Tiny Tofu Parcels

*These make a delightful appetiser served with a tasty chutney (page 305) and Cucumber Raita (page 130).*

225 g (7 oz) firm tofu, drained well
1 quantity Quick Satay Sauce (page 99)
9 sheets phyllo pastry
a little sesame oil
sesame seeds

Cut the tofu into about 18 rectangles and place them in a bowl with the Quick Satay Sauce. Toss the ingredients together to coat the tofu well. Cut the phyllo sheets in half crossways, stack on top of one another and position the sheets with the shortest sides opposite you. Place each piece of tofu on the end of the phyllo closest to you. Taking a single sheet of phyllo, fold the two long sides over the tofu and roll the tofu up to form small parcels. Place the parcels on a prepared baking sheet. Brush the parcels lightly with oil and sprinkle with sesame seeds. Bake in a hot oven (200°C/400°F) for 15 minutes or until the parcels become golden brown.
*Serves 4–6*

# Spicy Tofu

*This tasty tofu is especially good for tossing through stir-fried vegetables and salads and even makes a tasty sandwich filling.*

500 g (1 lb) tofu, drained
1–2 tablespoons sesame oil
3 garlic cloves, crushed (pressed)
1 tablespoon chopped thyme
1 teaspoon ground cumin
2 teaspoons ground coriander

Cut the tofu into 6 mm (¼ in.) slices and place a single layer on a plate. Combine the oil, garlic, thyme, cumin and coriander. Using a pastry brush, brush the spice mixture over both sides of the tofu slices. Place the tofu on a prepared baking sheet and bake in a hot oven (200°F/400°F) for 20 minutes.
*Serves 4–6*

# Tofu Foccacia Bake

*Serve piping hot with a tasty sauce such as Chili and Garlic Sauce (page 99) or Fresh Mango Salsa (page 99) alongside.*

8 slices foccacia
2 tablespoons tahini, *or* peanut butter
1 quantity Ginger Roasted Tofu (page 37)
1 red sweet pepper (capsicum), roasted (page 84)
   and cut into strips
cracked black pepper
finely sliced chives

Spread the tahini (or peanut butter) on the foccacia slabs. Top with the Ginger Roasted Tofu and arrange the sweet pepper strips in a lattice pattern on top. Sprinkle with the pepper and place on a prepared baking sheet. Bake in a hot oven (200°C/400°F) for 10 minutes. Decorate with the chives.
*Serves 4*

# Tofu and Sesame Balls

*Serve with a tasty dipping sauce (pages 96–7) or reheat gently in Sweet and Sour Sauce (page 100) or Quick Pasta Sauce (page 90).*

375 g (12 oz) tofu, drained, mashed
3 garlic cloves, crushed (pressed)
1 teaspoon grated ginger
1 tablespoon white miso (page 343)
½ cup (60 g/2 oz) soy flour
2 teaspoons oil
½ cup (60 g/2 oz) sesame seeds

Combine the tofu, garlic, ginger and miso and then add enough soy flour to bring the mixture to a soft dough consistency. Form the mixture into balls about the size of a walnut. Place the oil and the sesame seeds into two separate bowls and coat the tofu balls, first with the oil, then with the seeds. Place the balls on a prepared baking sheet and bake in a hot oven (200°C/400°F) for 20–25 minutes.
*Makes about 18 balls*

**Serving Hint**
Individual frittatas are easy to serve and look wonderful. Simply divide the mixture between 4 small ovenproof dishes and bake for 20 minutes.

# Roasted Okara

*Like TVP, okara has a satisfying texture, but its milky flavour and tender texture make it suitable for a range of dishes across the menu, from breakfast mixes to pâtés, cakes and bread. Try this recipe so you will have a supply of flavoured okara at your fingertips. To reconstitute the okara for use in savoury dishes, place in a bowl and cover with boiling water (1 part water:1 part okara), cover and allow to stand for 10 minutes.*

4 cups (800 g/1¾ lb ) okara (page 344)
1 teaspoon oil
2 tablespoons soy sauce

Combine the okara with the oil and the soy sauce. Spread the mixture out on a prepared baking sheet. Bake in a moderately slow oven (170°C/325°F) until the mixture is dry and crumbly (about 45 minutes–1 hour). Allow the okara to cool completely before storing in an airtight jar.
*Makes about 4 cups (300 g/10 oz)*

# Curry Flavoured Okara

*This is wonderful to have on hand for quick meals. There is no need to roast spices first for they are already waiting in this spicy okara to leap into your favourite stir-fry of seasonal vegetables. Simply place the okara in a bowl and cover with boiling water (1 part water:1 part okara), cover and allow to stand while you are whipping up the vegetables.*

1 tablespoon curry paste
1 tablespoon soy sauce
2 tablespoons coconut cream
4 cups (800 g/1¾ lb) okara (page 344)

Mix the curry paste, soy sauce and coconut cream, then combine with the okara. Spread the mixture out on a prepared baking sheet. Bake in a moderately slow oven (170°C/325°F) until the mixture is dry and crumbly (about 45 minutes–1 hour). Allow the okara to cool completely before storing in an airtight jar.
*Makes about 4 cups (300 g/10 oz)*

# Soy and Ginger Balls

*Delicious served with Sweet and Sour Sauce (page 100) and a side dish of noodles or rice.*

2 cups (435 g/14 oz) cooked soy beans (page 124), ground to a pulp, *or* 2 cups okara (page 344)
2 teaspoons grated ginger
2 teaspoons honey
1 tablespoon soy sauce
2 garlic cloves, crushed (pressed)
about 2 tablespoons besan flour (page 341)
freshly ground black pepper

Place all the ingredients except the besan flour into a food processor and combine. Add enough besan flour to bring the mixture to a moist dough consistency. Form the mixture into balls about the size of a walnut and place on a prepared baking sheet. Brush the tops of the balls with a little oil, then bake them in a hot oven (200°C/400°F) for 15 minutes.
*Makes about 18 balls*

# Okara Felafels

*Serve with Tofu Houmus (page 22), wedges of tomato and a salad of crisp greens.*

2 cups (400 g/13 oz) okara or cooked ground soy beans
2 teaspoons oil
1 large onion, chopped finely
3 garlic cloves, crushed (pressed)
¼ teaspoon chili powder
1 tablespoon ground cumin
½ teaspoon turmeric powder
¼ teaspoon cracked black pepper
1 cup chopped parsley
½ cup (60 g/2 oz) sesame seeds
additional 2 tablespoons oil

Combine all the ingredients except for the sesame seeds and **additional** oil. Form the mixture into balls the size of a walnut and brush lightly with the oil. Roll the balls in the sesame seeds and place on a prepared baking sheet. Bake in a hot oven (200°F/400°F) for 20 minutes.

# Basic Pasta Dough

*In my opinion, freshly made pasta has a wonderful melt-in-the mouth texture that just cannot be mimicked by dried pasta, and it really is quite simple to make. I prepare the fresh pasta dough an hour or two ahead of time, then cover and refrigerate it until just before meal time.*

3 tablespoons semolina
2 cups (250 g/8 oz) plain (all-purpose) flour
3 eggs, beaten
additional plain (all-purpose) flour

Place the semolina and flour in a bowl and make a 'well' in the centre. Add the eggs and gradually work in the flour and semolina to form a soft dough. Turn the mixture out onto a floured surface and knead well for 10 minutes, adding additional flour as required. Cover the dough with a damp tea towel and set aside to rest for 5 minutes or place in a covered container in the refrigerator until required. Using a rolling pin or pasta machine, roll the dough out very thinly. Cut into the desired shape and dry or cook.
*Serves 4*

### Wholemeal Pasta

Wholemeal (whole-wheat) pasta dough is simply prepared. Omit the semolina in the Basic Pasta Dough recipe and use wholemeal (whole-wheat) plain (all-purpose) flour instead of plain (all-purpose) white flour.

# Spinach Pasta Dough

½ cup puréed cooked spinach
2 eggs, beaten
3 tablespoons semolina
2 cups (250 g/8 oz) wholemeal (whole-wheat)
   plain (all-purpose) flour
additional plain (all-purpose) flour

Whisk the spinach and the eggs together. Place the semolina and flour in a bowl and make a 'well' in the centre. Add the spinach mixture and gradually work in the flour and semolina to form a soft dough. Continue as for Basic Pasta (above).
*Serves 4*

## Pasta

*Making your own pasta is great fun. It is not only fascinating to see the pasta emerge, but fresh pasta only takes a few minutes to cook and can be laced with your very own favourite flavours. Pasta is easy to make and some types such as gnocchi, tortelli and lasagne do not require a pasta machine, so why not get started now?*

# Sweet Pepper Pasta Dough

1 red sweet pepper (capsicum), roasted (page 84)
2 eggs, beaten
3 tablespoons semolina
2 cups (250 g/8 oz) plain (all-purpose) flour
additional plain (all-purpose) flour

Using a food processor or blender, blend the sweet pepper and eggs together until smooth. Place the semolina and flour in a bowl and make a 'well' in the centre. Add the sweet pepper mixture and gradually work in the flour and semolina to form a soft dough. Continue as for Basic Pasta (opposite).
*Serves 4*

# Basic Fettucine

1 quantity pasta dough, such as basic pumpkin, wholemeal (whole-wheat) *or* spinach

Roll the dough out very thinly and using a pasta machine, sharp knife or kitchen scissors, cut the dough into ribbons 6 cm (¼ in.) wide. Cook the fettucine at once, or set it aside to dry.
*Serves 4*

*Left: Red Pepper, Spinach and Pumpkin Pasta in the making. Try cooking all these varieties of pasta together for a carnival of colour.*

# No Egg Pasta Dough

*This is a very easy pasta to prepare, requiring less working and kneading than egg-based pasta. Tofu pasta also cooks very quickly and has a particularly light texture, making it an excellent dough for making lasagne.*

2 cups (250 g/8 oz) plain (all-purpose) flour
225 g (7 oz) tofu, drained and mashed well
2 tablespoons oil
a little water
additional plain (all-purpose) flour

Place the flour in a bowl and make a 'well' in the centre. Add the tofu and the oil and work the flour in gradually until a soft dough is formed, adding a little water if needed. Turn the dough out onto a floured surface and knead for 3–5 minutes. Proceed as for Basic Pasta Dough (page 291).
*Serves 4*

# Pumpkin Pasta Dough

*This attractive golden pasta is great served with a light pasta sauce and a salad of leafy greens.*

1 cup (280 g/9 oz) puréed cooked pumpkin
  (page 93)
1 egg, beaten
1 cup (155 g/5 oz) semolina
1½ cups (250 g/8 oz) wholemeal (whole-wheat)
  plain (all-purpose) flour
additional plain (all-purpose) flour

Whisk the pumpkin and the egg together. Place the semolina and flour in a bowl and make a 'well' in the centre. Add the pumpkin mixture to the well and gradually work in the flour and semolina to form a soft dough. Proceed as for Basic Pasta Dough (page 291).
*Serves 4*

# Beetroot Pasta Dough

1 beetroot (beets), cooked (page 93), peeled and
  chopped
1 egg, beaten
3 tablespoons semolina
2 cups (250 g/8 oz) plain (all-purpose) flour
additional plain (all-purpose) flour

Using a food processor or blender, blend the beetroot and egg together until smooth. Place the semolina and flour in a bowl and make a 'well' in the centre. Add the beetroot mixture to the well. and gradually work in the flour and semolina to form a soft dough. Turn the mixture out onto a floured surface and knead well for 10 minutes, adding additional flour as required. Cover the dough with a damp tea towel and set aside to rest for 5–10 minutes. Using a rolling pin or pasta machine, roll the dough out very thinly. Cut into the desired shape and cook at once, or set aside to dry.
*Serves 4*

# Wholemeal Lasagne Dough

3 cups (375 g/12 oz) wholemeal (whole-wheat)
  plain (all-purpose) flour
freshly ground black pepper
2 eggs, beaten
1 tablespoon olive oil
½ cup (125 mL/4 fl oz) warm water
additional flour

Place the flour in a bowl, sprinkle with the pepper and make a 'well' in the centre. Whisk the eggs, oil and water together and add to the well. Gradually work in the flour until a soft dough is formed. Knead for 5 minutes. Cover and set aside for 30 minutes if possible. Roll the dough out thinly on a floured surface and cut into sheets according to the size of your lasagne dish. Assemble the lasagne with your favourite piping hot sauce in between the layers of pasta and cook at once in a moderate oven (180°C/350°F) for 40 minutes.
*Serves 6*

# Spinach and Walnut Tortelli

*This tortelli is particularly tasty and makes an eye-catching appetiser or light main meal served doused in Pesto Sauce (page 97) and on a bed of Tomato Concasse (page 101).*

60 g (2 oz) ricotta cheese
1–2 cloves garlic, crushed (pressed) (optional)
4 tablespoons cooked puréed spinach
2 tablespoons finely chopped walnuts
freshly ground black pepper
1 quantity Pumpkin Pasta Dough (page 292)

Combine the ricotta cheese, garlic, spinach, walnuts and pepper together thoroughly. Roll the pasta dough out thinly into 2 rectangles. Place a teaspoonful of the filling at 2.5 cm (1 in.) intervals in rows along one rectangle of dough. Using a pastry brush, brush a little water all around the filling. Place the remaining rectangle of dough on top and press it down firmly around the filling. Using a decorative scone or biscuit (cookie) cutter, cut the dough around the filling to form the tortelli.
*Makes about 36 medium–large tortelli*

### Shaping Gnocchi

Gnocchi can be shaped by rolling the dough into small balls the size of a marble or by shaping pieces of the dough using fluted gnocchi boards which are available at cookware shops. I especially like to place the dough in a large piping (pastry) bag with a fluted nozzle and pipe long strips of the dough onto a lightly floured wooden board, then cut the dough at the desired intervals according to the size you wish to make.

# Basic Gnocchi

*This dough makes light fluffy gnocchi which is lower in fat due to using ricotta or tofu rather than the traditional eggs. Gnocchi should be cooked just before serving.*

250 g (8 oz) ricotta cheese *or* tofu, drained
30 g (1 oz) grated Parmesan cheese
1 egg, beaten
4 tablespoons soy flour
1 cup (125 g/4 oz) potato flour
a little grated nutmeg
additional plain (all-purpose) flour

Place the ricotta cheese (or tofu), Parmesan and egg into a food processor and blend until smooth. While the processor is operating, add the soy flour, potato flour and nutmeg and process for 30 seconds. Turn the dough out onto a floured surface and knead for 30 seconds only, or until a soft dough is formed. Form the mixture into small balls about the size of a small marble.
*Serves 4*

# Pumpkin Gnocchi

½ cup (125 g/4 oz) cooked mashed pumpkin
  (page 93)
250 g (8 oz) ricotta cheese *or* tofu, drained
1 egg
⅛ teaspoon freshly ground black pepper
1½ cups (185 g/6 oz) plain (all-purpose) flour
a little additional plain (all-purpose) flour

Place the pumpkin, ricotta cheese (or tofu), egg and pepper in a food processor and blend until smooth. Gradually add the flour until a soft dough is formed, then turn the dough out onto a floured surface. Form into desired shapes as for Basic Gnocchi (above).
*Serves 4*

# Basic Fruit Vinegar

*Fruit vinegars not only add zest to dressings and sauces, but a carnival of colour as well. The ruby red of raspberry vinegar or the warm gold of orange vinegar can be splashed on avocados and mangoes, transforming simply beautiful fruits into eye-catching appetisers or salads.*

**250 g (8 oz) fruit, left whole *or* sliced, depending on the fruit**
**4 cups (1 litre/1¾ imp. pints) vinegar**

Place the fruit in a large sterilised jar and pour the vinegar on top. Seal and set aside to marinate in a warm location for at least 2 weeks. It's best to choose a location where you will see it, not only because the vibrant coloured fruits and fresh herbs marinating is a sight for sore eyes, but also because you will remember to shake the jar occasionally to assist with extracting the juice from the flavouring medium. Prop a muslin-lined sieve over a large bowl and pour the mixture in. Pull up the ends of the cloth and twist continuously until as much liquid as possible is extracted from the fruit. Discard the fruit. Pour the vinegar into attractive bottles with airtight lids.
*Makes 4 cups (1 litre/1¾ imp. pints)*

# Raspberry Vinegar

*No wonder this is an old-time favourite! The colour is incredible, as is the rich fruity flavour. It's spectacular added to tomato salads (page 134) and drizzled on top of avocados for a change from lemon juice.*

**1 punnet (carton) raspberries**
**4 cups (1 litre/1¾ imp. pints) white wine vinegar**

Follow the method for Basic Fruit Vinegar.
*Makes 4 cups (1 litre/1¾ imp. pints)*

*Left: Steeping fresh seasonal fruits, herbs and spices in quality vinegars and oils is a great way to capture the flavours of the seasons in your cooking.*

# Vinegars and Oils

*Flavoured vinegars and oils are wonderful to have on hand so that full-flavoured dressings and sauces can be whipped up in seconds. Much of the depth of flavour during prolonged cooking can be replaced in an instant. These wonderful ingredients are a must.*

# Orange Vinegar

*This is delicious with honey and sesame oil in dressings and wonderful drizzled on freshly sliced mangoes and pawpaw for instant remarkable salads. Try using it also in Orange Vinaigrette (page 149) and Orange Sesame Dressing (page 139).*

**4 cups (1 litre/1¾ imp. pints) white wine vinegar**
**3 tablespoons sugar**
**1 teaspoon whole cloves**
**1 cinnamon stick**
**3 oranges, washed and sliced thinly**

Place the vinegar, sugar, cloves and cinnamon stick in a saucepan and bring the mixture to the boil. Reduce the heat and simmer for 5 minutes. Remove from the heat and stir in the oranges. Cover and set aside to cool. Place the oranges and liquid into a sterilised jar and proceed as for Basic Fruit Vinegar (opposite).
*Makes 4 cups (1 litre/1¾ imp. pints)*

### Choosing a Vinegar

It's important to use white wine vinegar rather than distilled vinegar. After all, if you are using good quality fruit and you are bothering to prepare and bottle the vinegars and oils in the first place, make the effort really worthwhile—the difference in flavour is remarkable.

# Strawberry Vinegar

*Strawberry vinegar harmonises especially well with fresh salad greens and avocados, but for a treat try sprinkling it over sliced fresh bocconcini cheese and dusting it all with cracked black pepper. For a special decorative effect, place clumps of redcurrants in the bottle when preparing the vinegar.*

2 punnets (cartons) strawberries, washed and
    sliced
4 cups (1 litre/1¾ imp. pints) white wine vinegar

Follow the method for Basic Fruit Vinegar (page 295).
*Makes 4 cups (1 litre/1¾ imp. pints)*

# Basic Herb Vinegar

*Choose quality fresh herbs for making these special vinegars, all the better if you grow your own.*

1 cup (90 g/3 oz) fresh herbs
4 cups (1 litre/1¾ imp. pints) white wine vinegar
fresh herbs for decorating

Place the herbs in attractive sterilised bottles and pour the vinegar over carefully. Top with non-metallic lids and set aside to marinate for at least 2 weeks. Prop a muslin-lined sieve over a large bowl and pour the mixture in. Pull up the ends of the cloth and twist continuously until as much liquid as possible is extracted from the herbs. Discard the herbs. Place the fresh herbs in attractive bottles and carefully pour the vinegar over. Seal with airtight lids.
*Makes 4 cups (1 litre/1¾ imp. pints)*

### Storing Garlic Oil
It's best to store garlic oil in a cool dark place, even in the refrigerator, if not using within 1–2 weeks as garlic can spoil when stored at room temperature for too long. If you store it in the refrigerator, do not be dismayed if the oil becomes cloudy and solidifies—it will resume its golden liquid state once brought back to room temperature.

# Thyme Vinegar

*Especially good for dressing up tender crisp carrots, fennel and sweet peppers (capsicums), thyme vinegar also adds a flavour boost to marinades and sauces. The garlic softens the distinctive thyme flavour beautifully.*

1 cup (90 g/3 oz) fresh thyme
4 garlic cloves, peeled and sliced
4 cups (1 litre/1¾ imp. pints) white wine vinegar

Place the thyme and garlic in attractive sterilised bottles and pour the vinegar over carefully. Seal and set aside to marinate for at least 2 weeks. Remove the herbs and pour the vinegar into decorative bottles with a fresh stem of thyme.
*Makes 4 cups (1 litre/1¾ imp. pints)*

# Tarragon Vinegar

*Great for greens, both crispy salads and vibrant short-cooked broccoli, cabbage, spinach and silverbeet. Also great with warm cooked beetroot.*

1 cup (90 g/3 oz) fresh tarragon
3 bay leaves
4 cups (1 litre/1¾ imp. pints) white wine vinegar

Place the tarragon and bay leaves in attractive sterilised bottles and pour the vinegar over carefully. Seal and set aside to marinate for at least 2 weeks.
*Makes 4 cups (1 litre/1¾ imp. pints)*

# Chili Vinegar

*This vinegar is for the courageous! Try it added to salad dressings or dipping sauces.*

90 g (3 oz) fresh red and green chili peppers
4 cups (1 litre/1¾ imp. pints) white wine vinegar

Place the chilies in attractive sterilised bottles and pour the vinegar over carefully. Seal and set aside to marinate for at least 2 weeks.
*Makes 4 cups (1 litre/1¾ imp. pints)*

# Rosemary Vinegar

90 g (3 oz) fresh rosemary
1 tablespoon black peppercorns
4 cups (1 litre/1¾ imp. pints) white wine vinegar

Place the rosemary and peppercorns in attractive sterilised bottles and pour the vinegar over carefully. Seal and set aside to marinate for at least 2 weeks.
*Makes 4 cups (1 litre/1¾ imp. pints)*

# Basic Flavoured Oil

*It's a good idea to use extra virgin olive oil or other cold pressed oils as the base for your flavoured oil. The final flavour really is superior. If the budget cannot be stretched to meet the cost of these more expensive oils, do be sure to choose the best quality oil you can afford and do be sure to choose mono-unsaturated oil such as rape seed (colza) oil.*

1 cup (30 g/1 oz) fresh *or* dried herbs *or* spices
2 cups (500 mL/16 fl oz) olive oil

Place the herbs in attractive sterilised bottles and pour the oil over carefully. Seal and set aside to marinate for at least 2 weeks.
*Makes 2 cups (500 mL/16 fl oz)*

# Garlic Oil

*The great thing about making garlic oil is that you always have peeled garlic on hand, as well as the flavoured oil, for when you are in a hurry. If you use up all of the garlic, simply replace it with additional peeled garlic cloves.*

30 g (1 oz) garlic cloves, peeled
2 cups (500 mL/16 fl oz) olive oil

Place the garlic in attractive sterilised bottles and pour the oil over. Seal and set aside to marinate. It's not necessary to wait for 2 weeks for the garlic flavour to infuse—2 days is enough to get it started.
*Makes 2 cups (500 mL/16 fl oz)*

# Chili Oil

*This is a stunning oil, both in appearance and in the flavour kick it adds! For the weak-kneed, I recommend that the seeds are removed from the chilies. It's great added to Indian and Mexican dishes, but remember to serve these dishes with a jug of chilled water!*

6 fresh red and green chili peppers
2 cups (500 mL/16 fl oz) olive oil

Place the chilies in attractive sterilised bottles and pour the oil over carefully. Seal and set aside to marinate for at least 2 weeks.
*Makes 2 cups (500 mL/16 fl oz)*

# Pasta Oil

*If you cook pasta dishes regularly, this is a great oil to have on standby—the flavour is already in the oil, so all you need to do is stir-fry chopped onions and tomatoes in mere teaspoons of the oil to enjoy authentic pasta sauce flavours!*

30 g (1 oz) garlic cloves, peeled
30 g (1 oz) basil leaves, sliced
30 g (1 oz) oregano
4 cups (1 litre/1¾ imp. pints) olive oil

Place the garlic, basil and oregano in attractive sterilised bottles and pour the oil over. Seal and set aside to marinate for a day or two.
*Makes about 4 cups (1 litre/1¾ imp. pints)*

### Recycling Bottles
Ornamental bottles are available at cookware shops and department stores but remember recycling is the way to go—do keep an eye open for bottles that olive oil, maple syrup, wine, spirits and liqueurs come in—some look marvellous with fragrant vinegars and oils in them, topped with a cork.

# Marinated Sun-dried Tomatoes

*Sun-dried tomatoes are wonderful as part of an antipasto spread but can also be used as a sandwich filling, added to sauces and even popped on top of pizzas. The oil the tomatoes are submerged in is delicious in dressings too!*

125 g (4 oz) sun-dried tomatoes
2 teaspoons preserved capers
½ teaspoon black peppercorns
2–3 bay leaves *or* sprigs of dried oregano
about 1 cup (125 mL/8 fl oz) extra virgin olive oil

Place the tomatoes in a small heatproof bowl and cover with boiling water. Allow to stand for 1 minute, then drain the tomatoes thoroughly and spread them out on a clean dry tea towel. (You can keep the soaking liquid for adding to stock or soup.) When dry, place the tomatoes in a clean dry jar, sprinkling the layers with the capers, peppercorns and bay leaves (or oregano). Pour on enough olive oil to completely submerge the tomatoes, then seal the jar. Store in a cool, dark place.
*Makes 1 x 250 g (8 oz) jar*

# Marinated Feta Salad

*This tasty blend of antipasto delights can be prepared well ahead of time, and taken straight to the table in the jar.*

500 g (1 lb) feta cheese, drained well and cut into
    cubes *or* thick slices
1 cup black and green olives, drained
1 red sweet pepper (capsicum), roasted and cut
    into strips
3 sprigs rosemary
3 teaspoons black peppercorns
virgin olive oil

Arrange all the ingredients except the oil, in layers in a jar. Pour the oil over completely submerging the ingredients. Seal and store in a cool, dark place.
*Makes 2 x 500 g (1 lb) jars*

# Preserves

*I really do enjoy stocking up the larder with simple preserves, and arranging them in a burst of colour on my kitchen shelves—jars of summer fruits submerged in pure fruit juice and vacuum sealed make a spectacular display as well as a great way to extend and vary the menu all year round. Remember, too, there is something very special about giving a beautiful jar of preserves to family members and friends as a gift.*

# Spicy Marinated Olives

250 g (8 oz) olives
4 tablespoons diced pickled peppers, drained well
3–4 chili peppers sliced, seeds discarded
2 teaspoons cumin seeds
1 teaspoon coriander seeds
2 garlic cloves, sliced finely
about 1 cup (250 mL/8 fl oz) virgin olive oil

Place all the ingredients except for the olive oil in a bowl and toss together to combine thoroughly. Place the mixture in a 375 g (12 oz) jar and pour the olive oil over until the olives are completely submerged, then seal the jar.
*Makes about 1 x 375 g (12 oz) jar*

**Things under oil**
When you serve 'things under oil', do it in style, Mediterranean style that is. You will not need to use butter or margarine, just fresh crusty bread and fresh sun-ripened vegetables.

*Left: Preserving your favourite ingredients under oil such as the feta cheese, olives, herbs and roasted peppers used in Marinated Feta Salad means that you will have tasty tidbits on hand for quick meals. The oil can later be used to conjure up tasty dressings and sauces.*

# Pickled Red Grapes

*The ruby red of the grapes is echoed by the vibrant berry vinegar, making this a stunning dish. Serve with Brie or Camembert, tender salad greens and crusty bread for a wonderful appetiser or afternoon snack with friends.*

2 kg (4 lb) red seedless grapes, removed from stalks
1 cup (250 mL/8 fl oz) Raspberry *or* Strawberry Vinegar (pages 295 and 296)
1 cup (250 mL/8 fl oz) white wine vinegar
4 tablespoons sugar
1 cinnamon stick, broken into 3 pieces
10 whole cloves

Wash the grapes and pat dry. Place in sterilised jars. Place the remaining ingredients in a saucepan and bring the mixture to the boil. Reduce the heat and simmer for 10 minutes. Remove from the heat and strain over the grapes. Allow to cool before sealing the jars.
*Makes 4 about x 500 g (1 lb) jars*

# Pickled Beetroot

2 kg (4 lb) beetroot (beet), scrubbed and cooked (page 93)
2 cups (500 mL/16 fl oz) white wine vinegar
2 cups (500 mL/16 fl oz) cider vinegar
1 cup (250 mL/8 fl oz) water
½ cup (90 g/3 oz) soft brown sugar
1 teaspoon whole cloves
1 teaspoon black peppercorns

Slice, dice or cut the beetroot into matchsticks and place in sterilised jars. Place the remaining ingredients in a saucepan and bring the mixture to the boil. Reduce the heat and simmer for 10 minutes then remove from the heat and set aside to cool. Strain the liquid then pour over the beetroot, covering it completely. Seal.
*Makes about 5 x 500 g (1 lb) jars*

# Pickled Carrots

1 kg (2 lb) carrots, scrubbed *or* peeled
2 cups (500 mL/16 fl oz) white wine vinegar
60 g (2 oz) sugar
1 teaspoon dill seeds
½ teaspoon whole cloves
1 cinnamon stick
1 teaspoon black peppercorns

Cut the carrots into fancy shapes. Cook until tender-crisp (page 93) then pack into sterilised jars. Place the remaining ingredients in a saucepan and bring the mixture to the boil, then reduce the heat and simmer for 10 minutes. Strain the liquid and pour over the carrots. Allow to cool before sealing the jar.
*Makes about 3 x 500 g (1 lb) jars*

**Preserving under Oil**
Use extra virgin olive oil or virgin olive oil for preserving under oil. Olive oil is a mono-unsaturated oil and therefore recommended for good health. Extra virgin olive oil is cold pressed, which has its own benefits (page 344). Be sure to prepare amounts of 'things under oil' that you are likely to consume within the next two months, especially if you will be opening the jar regularly.

# Pickled Red Cabbage

*Pickled red cabbage makes a tasty and colourful addition to an antipasto spread and can also be served as a side vegetable or condiment.*

3 kg (6 lb) red cabbage, trimmed and chopped finely
1 tablespoon salt
2 cups (500 mL/16 fl oz) white wine vinegar
2 cups (500 mL/16 fl oz) cider vinegar
1 cup (250 mL/8 fl oz) water
½ cup (90 g/3 oz) soft brown sugar
1 teaspoon whole cloves
2 teaspoons star anise
1 teaspoon black peppercorns

Place the cabbage in a large non-metallic bowl and sprinkle the salt over. Toss so that the salt covers as much cabbage as possible. Cover the bowl and allow the cabbage to stand for 1 day or overnight. Rinse the cabbage with cold water and drain it thoroughly, then repeat the rinsing procedure twice to remove as much salt as possible. Drain the cabbage well and spread it out on a clean dry towel. When dry, pack it into sterilised jars. Place the remaining ingredients in a saucepan and bring the mixture to the boil. Reduce the heat and simmer for 10 minutes then remove from the heat and set aside to cool. Strain the liquid then pour over the cabbage, covering it completely. Seal the jars when cold.
*Makes about 6 x 500 g (1 lb) jars*

# Sun-dried Tomato Pâté

90 g (3 oz) sun-dried tomatoes
1 teaspoon finely sliced chili peppers
3 tablespoons sweet sherry
½ cup (60 g/2 oz) cashews, roasted (page 17)
1 tablespoon olive oil

Blend all the ingredients until smooth in a food processor. If not using at once, place in a clean dry jar and cover with a layer of olive oil. Store in the refrigerator.
*Makes about 1 cup (250 g/8 oz)*

# Roasted Sweet Pepper Pâté

1 large red sweet pepper (capsicum), roasted (page 84)
30 g (1 oz) sun-dried tomatoes
3 garlic cloves, crushed (pressed)
¼ teaspoon cracked black pepper
3 tablespoons sweet sherry
½ cup (60 g/2 oz) almonds, roasted (page 17)
1 tablespoon olive oil

Blend all the ingredients until smooth in a food processor. If not using at once, place in a clean dry jar and cover with a layer of olive oil. Store in the refrigerator.
*Makes about 1 cup (250 g/8 oz)*

# Olive Paste

*Delicious spread on top of toasted crusty bread and topped with slices of sun-ripened tomatoes.*

1 cup pitted black olives
2–3 garlic cloves, crushed (pressed)
freshly ground black pepper
2 tablespoons extra virgin olive oil
2 teaspoons finely grated lemon rind or chopped Preserved Lemon (page 302)

Blend all the ingredients until smooth in a food processor. If not using at once, place in a clean dry jar and cover with a layer of olive oil. Store in the refrigerator.
*Makes about 1 cup (250 g/8 oz)*

# Pickled Fennel

*Delicious served with cheese and salad greens and fresh crusty bread.*

6 Florence fennel bulbs (finocchio), trimmed and
    cut into thin wedges
1 white onion, cut into thin rings
1 red sweet pepper (capsicum), roasted (page 84)
    and cut into strips
2 cups (500 mL/16 fl oz) white wine vinegar
3 tablespoons sugar
2 teaspoons celery seeds
1 teaspoon mustard seeds
1 teaspoon black peppercorns

Combine the fennel, onion and sweet pepper and pack into hot sterilised jars. Place the vinegar, sugar, celery seeds, mustard seeds and peppercorns in a saucepan and bring the mixture to the boil. Reduce the heat and simmer for 10 minutes. Strain the liquid and pour over the fennel. Allow the pickles to cool before sealing.
*Makes about 2 x 500 g (1 lb) jars*

# Pickled Figs

*These succulent morsels develop a superb flavour after languishing in the spice-laden pickling medium. Wonderful served with antipasto.*

2 kg (4 lb) figs
1½ cups (405 mL/12 fl oz) white wine vinegar
1 cup (250 mL/8 fl oz) apple juice
4 tablespoons soft brown sugar
2 teaspoons star anise
1 cinnamon stick, broken into pieces

Wash the figs, pat dry and snip off their stems. Prick several times with a needle then place in sterilised jars. Place the remaining ingredients in a saucepan and bring the mixture to the boil. Reduce the heat and simmer for 10 minutes. Remove from the heat and strain over the figs. Allow to cool before sealing the jars.
*Makes about 4 x 500 g (1 lb) jars*

*Right: Preserved Lemons, a wonderful ingredient to have on hand for injecting flavour into soups, stews, salads, sauces and dressings.*

# Pickled Sultana Grapes

*Sweet, zesty and tangy all at once, the flavour of summer is captured in these beautiful grapes to be enjoyed all year round.*

2 kg (4 lb) sultana grapes, removed from stalks
2 cups (500 mL/16 fl oz) Orange Vinegar
    (page 295)
4 tablespoons sugar
6 strips orange zest

Wash the grapes and pat them dry. Place in sterilised jars. Place the remaining ingredients in a saucepan and bring the mixture to the boil. Reduce the heat and simmer for 10 minutes. Remove from the heat and strain over the grapes. Allow to cool before sealing the jars.
*Makes about 4 x 500 g (1 lb) jars*

# Preserved Lemons

*Otherwise known as Moroccan lemons, and used in Middle Eastern dishes, the skin of preserved lemons becomes tender and tangy. Adding just a little of the diced skin to salads, soups, sauces, casseroles and curries provides quite a flavour burst. They are great in dressings too, combined with extra virgin olive oil and black pepper and served with tomatoes and broccoli. I also like to preserve limes this way and add them to curries.*

10 lemons, washed and dried
4 tablespoons rock salt
8–10 bay leaves
2 teaspoons black peppercorns
2 cups (500 mL/16 fl oz) lemon juice

Cut the lemons into wedges and sprinkle them with the salt. Pack the lemons in sterilised jars with the bay leaves and black peppercorns and pour the lemon juice over. Seal and allow to stand for 4–6 weeks before using. These lemons keep unopened without refrigeration for up to 1 year. Once the jar has been opened, the lemons should be stored in the refrigerator.
*Makes 1 large jar*

# Spiced Redcurrants

*These make a wonderful garnish all year round, but especially when you miss redcurrants in winter! Great added to salads or as a garnish for cheese or fruit platters or tofu dishes.*

1 cup (250 mL/8 fl oz) apple and blackcurrant juice
½ cup (125 mL/4 fl oz) white wine vinegar
½ cup (90 g/3 oz) sugar
1 teaspoon whole cloves
2 punnets (cartons) redcurrants, washed and patted dry
1 cup (250 mL/8 fl oz) Raspberry *or* Strawberry Vinegar (pages 295 and 296)

Place the juice, white wine vinegar, sugar and cloves in a small saucepan and bring the mixture to the boil, stirring until the sugar has dissolved. Remove from the heat, add the raspberry vinegar. Place the redcurrants in sterilised jars and pour the mixture over the currants and seal when cool.
*Makes about 2 x 250 g (8 oz) jars*

# Beetroot and Apple Relish

2 teaspoons oil
2 large onions, diced
3 green apples, diced
3 medium-sized beetroot (beets), cooked, peeled and diced
1 cup (155 g/5 oz) chopped raisins
1 cup (250 mL/8 fl oz) white wine vinegar
90 g (3 oz) soft brown sugar
½ teaspoon salt

Heat the oil in a frying pan, skillet or wok and stir-fry the onions and apples for 2–3 minutes. Add the remaining ingredients and cook over a medium-high heat, stirring, for 20–25 minutes. Place the mixture in hot sterilised jars and allow to cool completely before sealing.
*Makes about 3 x 500 g (1 lb) jars*

# Spicy Eggplant Relish

2 teaspoons olive oil
2 onions, diced
3 cloves garlic, crushed (pressed)
1 teaspoon yellow mustard seeds
1 teaspoon finely minced chili peppers
4 medium eggplants (aubergines), diced
juice of 1 lemon
3 tomatoes, peeled and diced
2 teaspoons honey
½ cup (125 mL/4 fl oz) white wine vinegar
1 tablespoon balsamic vinegar

Heat the oil in a frying pan, skillet or wok and stir-fry the onions, garlic, mustard seeds and chili peppers for 2–3 minutes. Add the eggplant, lemon juice and tomatoes and stir-fry over a medium–high heat for 10 minutes. Add the honey and white wine vinegar and continue to cook, stirring occasionally, for 20–25 minutes. Stir in the balsamic vinegar. Pour the relish into hot sterilised jars and allow to cool completely before sealing.
*Makes about 5 x 500 g (1 lb) jars*

# Fresh Mango Relish

1 ripe mango, peeled, pip removed, sliced
4 fresh dates, pitted and sliced
½ cucumber, halved lengthways, seeds removed and sliced
4 spring onions (scallions), sliced finely on the diagonal
1 tablespoon finely chopped preserved ginger
1 teaspoon finely chopped chili peppers
freshly ground black pepper

Combine all the ingredients thoroughly and place in an airtight container. Store in the refrigerator for up to 1 week.
*Makes about 1½ cups (375 g/12 oz) jar*

# Tomato and Apple Chutney

1½ kg (3 lb) tomatoes, diced
1 kg (2 lb) apples, diced
1 kg (2 lb) onions, diced
½ teaspoon salt
1 cup (250 mL/8 fl oz) white wine vinegar
1 cup (155 g/5 oz) soft brown sugar
2 teaspoons mustard seeds
2 teaspoons grated ginger
1 teaspoon cracked black pepper

Place all the ingredients in a large saucepan and bring the mixture to the boil. Reduce the heat and simmer for 1 hour. Pour the chutney into hot sterilised jars and allow to cool completely before sealing.
*Makes about 5 × 500 g (1 lb) jars*

**Buying Seasonal Foods**
If you invest time in preserving foods, you can enjoy buying bulk quantities of ripe seasonal fruits and vegetables without worrying about over-stretching the food budget as seasonal foods are much cheaper.

# Apricot Chutney

2 kg (4 lb) ripe apricots, pips removed and sliced
2 cups (310 g/10 oz) sultanas (golden raisins)
1 kg (2 lb) onions, diced
½ teaspoon salt
1 cup (250 m/8 fl oz) white wine vinegar
½ cup (90 g/3 oz) soft brown sugar
2 teaspoons mustard seeds
2 teaspoons grated ginger
1 teaspoon cracked black pepper

Place all the ingredients in a large saucepan and bring the mixture to the boil. Reduce the heat and simmer for 1 hour. Pour the chutney into hot sterilised jars and allow to cool completely before sealing.
*Makes about 6 × 500 g (1 lb) jars*

# Peach Chutney

2 kg (4 lb) ripe peaches, diced
2 cups (310 g/10 oz) chopped pitted dates
1 cup (155 g/5 oz) sultanas (golden raisins)
3 onions, diced
1 cup (155 g/5 oz) soft brown sugar
½ teaspoon salt
2 teaspoons grated ginger
2 teaspoons mustard seeds
1 teaspoon cracked black pepper
1 cup (250 mL/8 fl oz) apricot nectar
1 cup (250 mL/8 fl oz) white wine vinegar

Place all the ingredients in a large saucepan and combine them well. Bring the mixture to the boil, reduce the heat and simmer until the chutney is thick, about 45 minutes–1 hour. Pour the chutney into hot sterilised jars and allow to cool completely before sealing.
*Makes about 6 × 500 g (1 lb) jars*

# Cranberry Sauce

1½ kg (3 lb) cranberries
3 onions, chopped
1 cup (250 mL/8 fl oz) apple juice
1 cup (155 g/5 oz) soft brown sugar
1 cup (250 mL/8 fl oz) white wine vinegar
1 teaspoon salt
2 teaspoons mixed spice*
¼ teaspoon freshly ground black pepper

Place all the ingredients in a large saucepan and bring the mixture to the boil. Reduce the heat and simmer for 1 hour. Pour the sauce into hot sterilised jars and allow to cool completely before sealing.
*Makes about 5 × 250 g (8 oz) jars*

*Please refer to the recipe for mixed spice in our Cook's Notes, page 8.

# Pears in Apple and Blackcurrant Juice

3 kg (6 lb) pears, peeled, halved and cored
6 cups (1.5 litres/2½ imp. pints) apple and
  blackcurrant juice
24 whole cloves

Pack the pears into sterilised jars with the cloves and fill nearly to overflowing with the fruit juice. Seal the tops of the jars and place them on a trivet in a preserving pan or extra large saucepan with at least 2.5 cm (1 in.) water covering the tops. Bring the water to the boil and boil continuously for 20 minutes, topping up as necessary with boiling water. Leave the jars standing in the water until it is cool. Remove the jars, dry them completely and attach a label with contents and date. Store in a cool dark place such as the bottom of the pantry or a cupboard away from any heat source such as the oven or heater.
*Makes 2 x 2 kg (4 lb) jars*

# Quinces in Apple Juice

3 kg (6 lb) quinces, peeled and sliced
6 cups (1.5 litres/2½ imp. pints) apple juice
3 cinnamon sticks, halved
24 whole cloves

Pack the quinces into sterilised jars with the cinnamon sticks and cloves and fill nearly to overflowing with the apple juice. Seal the tops of the jars and continue as for Pears in Apple and Blackcurrant Juice (above).
*Makes 3 x 1 kg (2 lb) jars*

**Blanching Peaches**
Place the peaches on a large boiler and cover completely with boiling water. Allow to stand for 2 minutes, then drain the water completely. Cover with icy cold water and remove the skins.

# Peaches in Apricot Nectar

3 kg (6 lb) peaches, blanched and peeled
9 cups (2 litres/4 imp. pints) apricot nectar
4 whole cloves

Pack the peaches into large wide-necked the sterilised jars with the cloves and fill nearly to overflowing with the apricot nectar. Seal the tops of the jars and continue as for Pears in Apple and Blackcurrant Juice (opposite).
*Makes 3 x 2 kg (4 lb) jars*

# Plums in Dark Grape Juice

3 kg (6 lb) blood plums
flavouring spices *or* citrus zest
8 cups (2 litres/3¼ imp. pints) dark grape juice

Pack the plums and spices or zest into sterilised jars and fill nearly to overflowing with the grape juice. Seal the tops of the jars and continue as for Pears in Apple and Blackcurrant Juice (opposite).
*Makes 4 x 1 kg (2 lb) jars*

**Choosing appropriate jars**
The size of the jars and the amount of fruit juice required varies considerably when bottling fruit. For example, whole fruit requires large wide-necked jars to fit the fruit in and to make serving easier. Whole fruit doesn't pack down in jars as well as sliced fruit so more fruit juice is required to fill.

*Right: Bottled fruit such as Peaches in Apricot Nectar can be used to add variety and interest to your menus all year round. Fruit can be simply and nutritiously preserved in fruit juice or fruit nectar which contains much less sugar than the syrups traditionally used for fruit bottling.*

# Plum Jam

*Many jam recipes call for 3 cups (750 g/1½ lb) sugar to be used per 1 kg (2 lb) fruit. To modify this recipe in keeping with today's lighter approach to eating, I have reduced the amount of sugar and have added pure fruit juice to the mixtures instead of water. I hope you enjoy the delicious jams that the following recipes produce as much as I do. Even though the sugar content has been reduced, this jam will keep for up to 12 months in a cool dry cupboard or pantry.*

**2 kg (4 lb) blood plums, sliced, pips removed**
**½ cup (125 mL/4 fl oz) dark grape juice**
**4 cups (1 kg/2 lb) sugar**

Place all the ingredients into a large saucepan and bring the mixture slowly to the boil, stirring occasionally until the sugar dissolves. Boil the mixture, uncovered, for 25–30 minutes. When the jam seems to be thickening, test to see if it has jelled. Set aside to cool slightly and spoon the mixture into hot sterilised jars. Allow to cool before wiping jars over, sealing and labelling.
*Makes about 6 cups*

# Strawberry Jam

*I make this delicious jam at the height of summer when strawberries are ripe, red and juicy, and cheap as well.*

**8 punnets (cartons) strawberries, hulls removed**
**1 cup (250 mL/8 fl oz) apple juice**
**juice of 2 lemons**
**4 cups (1 kg/2 lb) sugar**

Place all the ingredients into a large saucepan and bring the mixture slowly to the boil. Boil the mixture, uncovered, for 25–30 minutes. When the jam seems to be thickening, test to see if it has jelled. Set aside to cool slightly and spoon the mixture into hot sterilised jars. Allow to cool before wiping jars over, sealing and labelling.
*Makes about 6 cups*

# Apple and Raspberry Jam

*One of the highlights of summer for us is taking a picnic lunch to our favourite berry farm and picking baskets of ripe red raspberries to take home and enjoy. There's usually a story behind the jars of jam prepared from berries picked by family and friends—and it's good fun (and often a good laugh) to reminisce while enjoying the jam in the cooler months.*

**5 punnets (cartons) raspberries**
**4 apples, peeled, cored and diced**
**2 cups (435 g/14 oz) sugar**
**juice of 2 lemons**

Place the berries and apples into a large saucepan and bring the mixture slowly to the boil. Reduce the heat and simmer, covered, for 40 minutes. Stir in the sugar and lemon juice and bring the mixture to the boil once more, stirring only until the sugar dissolves. Reduce the heat and simmer the jam for 10–15 minutes but having tested to see if the jam has jelled after 10 minutes. Set the jam aside to cool slightly, then spoon the mixture into hot sterilised jars. Allow the jam to cool completely before sealing, wiping the jars over and labelling.
*Makes about 5 cups*

**Jelling**
To test if jam has jelled, first check to see if the jam has thickened. If it has, immediately remove the jam from the heat. Have a saucer on stand by, chilling in the freezer. Take a teaspoonful of the jam and drop it onto the chilled saucer. Place the saucer in the freezer for several minutes. If the jam has become a 'spreading' consistency upon cooling, it is ready to pour into the jars. If it still looks quite runny, return the jam to the stove and continue to cook until it jells when tested.

# Low-Sugar Berry Jam

*Jams using agar agar powder (page 341) can be prepared with much less sugar than traditional jams which rely on the sugar and fruit juice forming a 'jell'. Try this delicious jam and you will be amazed at the flavour and sweetness that shines through.*

2 punnets (cartons) berries such as blackberries
   *or* loganberries *or* strawberries
4 tablespoons honey
1 tablespoon lemon juice
1 teaspoon pure agar agar powder (page 341)

Place the berries, honey, lemon juice and agar agar powder in a saucepan and bring the mixture to the boil. Reduce the heat and simmer for 1 minute. Pour the jam into heated jars and set aside to cool. At this stage the jam appears to be a little too runny, but rest assured that it will thicken up upon cooling to room temperature. Cover the jars and store them in the refrigerator.
*Makes about 2 cups*

## Shelf Life

Low-sugar jam only keeps for up to two weeks in the refrigerator so I suggest buying fresh berries as required and when they are not available, keeping a supply of frozen berries on hand for making this simple jam in batches as required.

# Zesty Apricot Spread

*Although this spread cannot be kept at room temperature, it can be frozen and then thawed before use. Try it on hot toast when you have the time to savour the flavour.*

500 g (1 lb) dried apricots
2 cups (500 mL/16 fl oz) fruit juice
4 slices lemon
2 tablespoons honey
1 tablespoon lemon juice

Place the apricots, fruit juice and lemon slices into a saucepan and bring the mixture to the boil. Reduce the heat and simmer until the apricots become quite tender, about 20–25 minutes. Remove the lemon slices. Using a blender, blend the mixture until smooth with the honey and lemon juice. Place in jars if storing in the refrigerator, or in freezer containers if you intend storing the spread in the freezer.
*Makes about 3 cups*

## A Quick Sauce

Low-sugar jam can be thinned down with pure fruit juice to make a quick tasty fruit sauce.

# Date and Orange Spread

1 kg (2 lb) pitted dates, chopped
2 cups (500 mL/16 fl oz) orange juice
4 slices orange
1 tablespoon lemon juice
2 teaspoons honey

Place the dates, orange juice and orange slices into a saucepan and bring the mixture to the boil. Reduce the heat and simmer for 10–15 minutes. Remove the orange slices and, using a blender, blend the mixture until smooth. Add the lemon juice and honey and blend for a further 20 seconds. Place the spread in an airtight container and refrigerate until required.
*Makes about 3 cups*

# Gum Flowers in Leatherwood Honey

*Scented honeys made from flowers or herbs are great with herb teas or spread on fresh bread and topped with fresh berries or soft fruits.*

**2 heads gum flowers**
**500 g (1 lb) leatherwood honey**

Wash and thoroughly dry the gum flowers and place them into clean, dry jars. Top with the honey and seal. Allow to stand for 1 week to allow the flavour to infuse.
*Makes about 2 x 250 g (8 oz) jars*

# Frangipani Honey

*The perfume of this exquisite blossom is captured beautifully in the lightly scented orange blossom honey. It only takes a few spoonfuls of this honey, combined with the freshly squeezed juice of an orange, to create a fragrant dressing for fresh pawpaw (papaya) or mangoes.*

**6–12 frangipani blossoms**
**500 g (1 lb) orange blossom honey**

Wash and thoroughly dry the blossoms and place them into clean, dry jars. Top with the honey and seal.
*Makes about 3 x 250 g (8 oz) jars*

**Edible Blossoms**
Capture the 'scent of each season' by steeping new season's edible blossoms in honey. Make sure the flowers have not been sprayed with pesticides and that they are indeed edible (page 341)! Wash and thoroughly dry the flowers. Place them into clean, dry jars. Top with the honey and seal.

# Honeysuckle Honey

*This lightly scented honey adds a lift to iced herb teas.*

**10 honeysuckle blossoms**
**500 g (1 lb) orange blossom honey**

Wash and thoroughly dry the honeysuckle blossoms and place them into clean dry jars. Top with the honey and seal.
*Makes about 2 x 250 g (8 oz) jars*

# Jasmine Honey

*Opening a jar of jasmine honey is like taking a deep breath in my garden in early spring when jasmine has just started to bloom. This honey is superb drizzled over hot waffles and topped with a scoop of Yoghurt Cheese (page 271).*

**4 good-sized sprigs jasmine**
**500 g (1 lb) clover honey**

Wash and thoroughly dry the jasmine and place into clean dry jars. Top with the honey and seal.
*Makes about 2 x 250 g (8 oz) jars*

# Orange Zest Honey

*This flavoursome honey is especially delicious added to hot or iced teas or fruit smoothies.*

**2 oranges, washed thoroughly**
**500 g (1 lb) orange blossom honey**

Pare the orange zest from the oranges, using a sharp serrated knife. Place the orange zest into clean, dry jars, top with the honey and seal.
*Makes about 2 x 250 g (8 oz) jars*

*Right: Fragrant honeys like Frangipani Honey and Cinnamon Honey (page 312) make beautiful gifts for special friends. Why not also try steeping herbs such as lemon thyme in honey as pictured, and enjoy adding herbed honey to dressings and marinades.*

# Cinnamon Honey

*Prepare this honey well ahead of time—it does take 6 to 8 weeks to take on the true spicy character of the cinnamon. I assure you it is well worth the wait. Enjoy it as a sweet spread on freshly baked bread or hot toast, or use it to lace the poaching liquid for fruits such as apples and pears.*

4 cinnamon sticks
500 g (1 lb) clover honey

Snap the cinnamon sticks into several pieces and place them in clean, dry jars. Pour the honey over and seal the jars.
*Makes about 2 x 250 g (8 oz) jars*

# Star Anise Honey

*As well as flavouring the honey, the star anise absorbs some of the honey causing them to expand after they have been steeping for a week or so.*

2 tablespoons star anise
500 g (1 lb) clover honey

Place the star anise into clean, dry jars. Top with the honey and seal.
*Makes about 2 x 250 g (8 oz) jars*

# Prunes in Red Wine

2 cups (500 mL/16 fl oz) dark grape juice
2 cups (500 mL/16 fl oz) red wine
½ cup (90 g/3 oz) soft brown sugar
1 cinnamon stick, broken into pieces
2 teaspoons whole cloves
1 kg (2 lb) pitted prunes

Place all the ingredients except for the prunes in a large saucepan and bring the mixture to the boil, stirring until the sugar has dissolved. Add the prunes and simmer until they are tender. Remove the spices and place the prunes into sterilised jars. Cover completely with the red wine mixture. Allow to cool, then seal.
*Makes about 4 x 500 g (1 lb) jars*

# Peaches in Red wine

*Wonderful to have in the pantry for unexpected guests, or expected guests for that matter, when you have no time to whip up a delicious dessert. Serve simply with whipping (double) cream or Greek Yoghurt (page 273).*

2 cups (500 mL/16 fl oz) dark grape juice
2 cups (500 mL/16 fl oz) red wine
½ cup (90 g/3 oz) soft brown sugar
1 cinnamon stick, broken into pieces
2 teaspoons whole cloves
2 kg (4 lb) peaches, blanched and peeled
   (page 306)

Place all the ingredients except for the peaches in a large saucepan and bring the mixture to the boil, stirring until the sugar has dissolved. Add the peaches and simmer until they are tender. Place the peaches into sterilised jars and cover completely with the red wine mixture. Allow to cool, then seal.
*Makes about 2 x 2 kg (4 lb) jars*

# Apples in White Wine

2 cups (500 mL/16 fl oz) apple juice
2 cups (500 mL/16 fl oz) sweet white wine
4–6 cloves
3 tablespoons soft brown sugar
1 cinnamon stick
4 lemon slices
2 kg (4 lb) apples, peeled and cut into quarters

Place the apple juice, wine, cloves, sugar, cinnamon stick and wine in a saucepan and bring the mixture to the boil, stirring until the sugar has dissolved. Add the apples and cook them gently until they are just tender. Remove the lemon slices and cinnamon stick and spoon the apples into sterilised jars. Pour the wine mixture over. Allow to cool before sealing.
*Makes about 2 x 1 kg (2 lb) jars*

# Prunes in Port

*An indulgent end to a special meal, served with freshly brewed coffee.*

750 g (1½ lb) pitted dessert prunes
125 g (4 oz) almonds
3 tablespoons soft brown sugar
2 cups (500 mL/16 fl oz) dark grape juice
1 cinnamon stick
2 cups (500 mL/16 fl oz) port

Open out the prunes slightly and place an almond inside each, then place the prunes in sterilised jars. Place the remaining ingredients in a saucepan and bring the mixture to the boil. Reduce the heat and simmer gently for 10 minutes. Remove the cinnamon stick and pour the liquid over the prunes so that they are completely submerged. Allow the mixture to cool before sealing.
*Makes 2 × 500 g (1 lb) jars*

# Apricots in Liqueur

*This is a delectable treat served at the end of a special meal.*

500 g (1 lb) whole dried apricots
90 g (3 oz) hazelnuts
2 cups (500 ml/16 fl oz) apricot nectar
1 teaspoon whole cloves
4 strips of lemon zest
1 cup (250 mL/8 fl oz) Apricot Liqueur (page 329)

Place one hazelnut in the centre of each apricot then place the apricots in sterilised jars. Combine the remaining ingredients in a saucepan and bring the mixture to the boil, then reduce the heat and simmer the mixture for 10 minutes. Strain the liquid and pour over the apricots so that they are completely submerged. Allow the mixture to cool before sealing.
*Makes 4 × 250 g (8 oz) jars*

# Brandied Kumquats

*Serve with Greek Yoghurt (page 273) or light sour cream.*

1 kg (2 lb) kumquats
2 cups (500 mL/16 fl oz) orange juice
1 cinnamon stick
2 teaspoons whole cloves *or* star anise
3 tablespoons soft brown sugar
3 tablespoons honey
2 cups (500 mL/16 fl oz) brandy

Pierce the kumquats with a sharp needle several times. This will allow the delicious spiced brandy to infuse and prevent the skins from bursting. Place the orange juice, cinnamon stick and cloves (or star anise) in a saucepan and bring the mixture to the boil. Reduce the heat and simmer the syrup for 10 minutes. Remove the cinnamon stick and cloves (or star anise). Add the kumquats and simmer gently for 5 minutes. Remove from the heat and allow the kumquats to stand in the syrup for a further 5 minutes. Using a slotted spoon, remove the kumquats from the syrup and spoon them into hot sterilised jars. Return the syrup to the stove, stir in the brandy and return the syrup to the boil. Cook uncovered for 5 minutes, then spoon the syrup over the kumquats so that they are completely submerged. Seal while still hot
*Makes 2 × 500 g (1 lb) jars*

# Basic Vanilla Ice Cream

*Making your own ice cream can be a lot of fun, and it is really very easy to do. It is a good way to capture the delights of fresh seasonal fruits such as mangoes and berries when they are economical. If you have an ice cream churn, you will be able to make smooth creamy ice cream with a soft texture. Using an agar agar 'custard' as the base, however, really does help to produce a smoother, less 'ice blocky' texture and is less bothersome than re-whipping the mixture once it has frozen. Most homemade ice creams need to be allowed to stand at room temperature for 20–30 minutes before serving, to allow the ice cream to soften.*

1 cup (250 mL/8 fl oz) water
½ cup (125 g/4 oz) sugar
2 teaspoons pure agar agar powder (page 341)
2 tablespoons honey
2 cups (500 mL/16 fl oz) milk
2 teaspoons vanilla extract (essence)
¾ cup (225 mL/7 fl oz) light (single) cream

Place the water, sugar and agar agar powder into a small saucepan and bring the mixture to the boil, stirring. Reduce the heat and simmer for 1 minute, stirring. Remove from the stove and set aside for a minute or two. Using a food processor or blender, blend the honey, milk and vanilla together until smooth. While the processor or blender is running, pour the agar agar mixture down the feeder tube. Blend for 20–30 seconds only. Set aside for 10 minutes or until the mixture sets to a custard consistency. Rewhip with the cream and pour the mixture immediately into a freezer container. Cover and freeze for several hours or overnight.
*Makes about 4 cups (1 litre/1¾ imp. pints)*

### A Gelatine Alternative

Agar agar is a useful ice cream ingredient as it helps prevent the ice cream from freezing in a solid block. Gelatine is often used in ice cream but vegetable alternatives like agar agar are preferred by vegetarians.

*Left: Terrine of Summer Fruits. Savour the flavour of each layer in this simply superb terrine and see if you can decide which layer is the best!*

# Ice Creams

*My imagination runs wild when I think of all the wonderful ingredients that can be incorporated into ice cream, a seemingly ever popular food for all age groups. Here you will discover a range of dishes from light and luscious ice creams and frozen yoghurts bursting with a fruity vitality to 'special occasions' ice creams, laced with real chocolate or a nip of liqueur.*

# Terrine of Summer Fruits

*An attractive dessert comprising pastel layers of delicious summer fruits. Spectacular enough to serve on its own with an edible blossom on the side, or surrounded with a fruit coulis. This terrine can be prepared over the course of a day, allowing 2–3 hours for each of the first two layers to freeze so the next layer can be added. Alternatively, prepare the terrine over several days.*

*Honeydew Layer*
½ ripe honeydew melon, peeled and pips removed
3 tablespoons caster (superfine) sugar
½ cup (155 mL/5 fl oz) light (single) cream
*Strawberry Layer*
1 punnet (carton) strawberries, hulls removed
2–3 tablespoons caster (superfine) sugar
½ cup (155 mL/5 fl oz) light (single) cream
*Mango Layer*
1–2 mangoes, peeled, pip removed and sliced
1–2 tablespoons caster (superfine) sugar
½ cup (155 mL/5 fl oz) light (single) cream

To prepare each layer, use a blender to blend the fruit with the sugar until smooth. Add the cream and blend until the cream is incorporated and the mixture is light and fluffy. Pour the first mixture into a terrine dish, cover and freeze for several hours or overnight before adding the next layer of mixture. Freeze for a further 4 hours before eating.
*Serves 8–10*

# Strawberry Ice Cream

*An all-round favourite, it can be served on its own or scattered with succulent fresh strawberries and drizzled with Fresh Berry Coulis (page 178).*

1 cup (250 mL/8 fl oz) apple juice
½ cup (125 g/4 oz) caster (superfine) sugar
2 teaspoons pure agar agar powder (page 341)
1 punnet (carton) strawberries, hulls removed
2–3 tablespoons honey
2 cups (500 mL/16 fl oz) milk
¾ cup (225 mL/7 fl oz) light (single) cream

Place the apple juice, sugar and agar agar powder into a small saucepan and bring the mixture to the boil, stirring. Reduce the heat and simmer for 1 minute, stirring. Remove from the stove and set aside for a minute or two. Using a food processor or blender, blend the strawberries, honey and milk together until smooth. While the processor or blender is running, pour the agar agar mixture down the feeder tube. Blend for 20–30 seconds only. Set the mixture aside until it sets then rewhip with the cream. Pour the mixture immediately into a freezer container, cover and freeze for several hours or overnight.
*Makes about 4 cups (1 litre/1¾ imp. pints)*

### Honey in Ice Cream

I like to use honey in ice cream and frozen yoghurt because, like agar agar, it helps prevent the ice cream developing an 'ice block' texture. Remember, too, that you do not need to use as much honey as sugar as honey contributes its own nectar-like flavour as well as sweetening. Use low-flavoured honeys for fresh fruit ice creams and frozen yoghurt, or scented honeys (pages 310–12). Strong flavoured honeys are best used for dried fruit, chocolate, coffee or mocha ice creams.

# Banana Ice Cream

*Quick fruit ice cream recipes like this are best suited to pulpy fruits which have a softer texture when frozen than juicy fruits. This ice cream is delicious served on its own, or topped with a scoop of Greek Yoghurt (page 273) or a dollop of whipping (double) cream and walnut halves.*

6 ripe bananas, sliced
3 tablespoons honey
juice of 2 lemons
¾ cup (225 mL/7 fl oz) light (single) cream
1½ cups (375 mL/12 fl oz) milk
1 teaspoon vanilla essence (extract)

Using a food processor or blender, blend all the ingredients until smooth. Pour the mixture immediately into a freezer container, cover and freeze for several hours or overnight.
*Makes about 4 cups (1 litre/1¾ imp. pints)*

# Passion Fruit Ice Cream

*There is something luscious about passion fruit and even when just a little is added to desserts, it leaves its distinctive mark. Passion fruit also harmonises well with vanilla. Add a touch of the exotic with slices of star fruit and mango, or serve with a scoop each of Strawberry Ice Cream (opposite) and Honeydew Sorbet (page 318) for a wonderful contrast in flavours and colours.*

1 quantity Basic Vanilla Ice Cream (page 315)
½ cup (125 mL/4 fl oz) passion fruit pulp
1 tablespoon honey

Prepare the vanilla ice cream and whisk the passion fruit pulp and the honey into the mixture. Pour the mixture immediately into a freezer container, cover and freeze for several hours or overnight.
*Makes about 4 cups (1 litre/1¾ imp. pints)*

# Quick Berry Ice Cream

2½ cups (625 mL/20 fl oz) milk
2 teaspoons pure agar agar powder (page 341)
1 cup Low-Sugar Berry Jam (page 309)
¾ cup (225 mL/7 fl oz) light (single) cream

Place 1 cup (250 mL/8 fl oz) of the milk and the agar agar powder into a small saucepan and bring the mixture to the boil, stirring. Reduce the heat and simmer for 1 minute, stirring. Remove from the stove and set aside for a minute or two. Using a food processor or blender, blend the remaining milk and jam together until smooth. While the processor or blender is running, pour the agar agar mixture down the feeder tube. Blend for 20–30 seconds only. Set aside for 10 minutes or until the mixture sets to a custard consistency. Rewhip with the cream and pour the mixture immediately into a freezer container. Cover and freeze for several hours or overnight.
*Makes about 4 cups (1 litre/1¾ imp. pints)*

# Pineapple and Banana Ice Cream

*A prize-winning duo, the pineapple and banana flavours add a touch of the tropics to the ice cream, but it's their 'pulpy' character that makes this ice cream special—the fruit prevents the ice cream from setting into a solid ice block.*

½ ripe pineapple, peeled and chopped
3–4 bananas, sliced
½ cup (90 g/3 oz) caster (superfine) sugar
1 teaspoon vanilla essence (extract)
¾ cup (225 mL/7 fl oz) light (single) cream

Using a food processor or blender, blend the pineapple, bananas and sugar together until smooth, then add the vanilla and cream and blend for 30 seconds. Pour the mixture immediately into a freezer container. Cover and freeze for several hours or overnight.
*Makes about 4 cups (1 litre/1¾ imp. pints)*

# Kiwi Fruit Ice Cream

*It's not advisable to blend kiwi fruit because this pulverises the tiny pips and releases a bitter flavour.*

1 quantity Basic Vanilla Ice Cream (page 315) at pouring stage
6 ripe kiwi fruit, peeled and mashed roughly

Prepare the vanilla ice cream to the stage of pouring the mixture into the freezer container, then whisk the kiwi fruit through. Pour the mixture immediately into a freezer container, cover and freeze for several hours or overnight.
*Makes about 1¾ quarts (1.25 litres/2 imp. pints)*

# Raspberry and Coconut Ice Cream

*The vibrant flavour of raspberries is complemented by pure cream at any time, but coconut cream and honey add a touch of the exotic to this special ice cream.*

1 punnet (carton) raspberries
3 tablespoons honey
3 tablespoons caster (superfine) sugar
¾ cup (225 mL/7 fl oz) coconut cream
¾ cup (225 mL/7 fl oz) light (single) cream

Using a food processor or blender, blend all the ingredients together until smooth. Pour the mixture into a freezer container, cover and freeze for several hours or overnight.
*Makes about 2 cups (500 mL/16 fl oz)*

**A Health Hint**
A good alternative to cream for lighter 'healthier' ice creams is plain yoghurt. Greek Yoghurt (page 273), which has a thick and creamy texture, is particularly suitable.

# Kiwi Fruit Sorbet

*For a pretty effect, place scoops of several types of sorbet on one plate, for example, kiwi fruit, honeydew and strawberry.*

¾ cup (180 mL/6 fl oz) apple juice
1 teaspoon pure agar agar powder (page 341)
10 kiwi fruit, peeled and sliced
¾ cup (185g/6 oz) caster (superfine) sugar
juice of 1 lemon

Place the apple juice and agar agar powder in a small saucepan and, stirring constantly, bring the mixture to the boil. Reduce the heat and simmer for 1 minute. Set aside to cool slightly. Using a food processor or blender, purée the kiwi fruit with the sugar and lemon juice and push the mixture through a coarse sieve. Whisk the agar agar mixture briskly and pour the mixture immediately into a freezer container. Cover and freeze for several hours or overnight, stirring occasionally if possible.
*Makes about 4 cups (1 litre/1¾ imp. pints)*

# Honeydew Sorbet

¾ cup (185 mL/6 fl oz) apple juice
1 teaspoon pure agar agar powder (page 341)
1.5 kg (3 lb) honeydew melon, peeled, pips removed and chopped
¾ cup (185 g/6 oz) caster (superfine) sugar
juice of 2 lemons

Place the apple juice and agar agar powder in a small saucepan and, stirring constantly, bring the mixture to the boil. Reduce the heat and simmer for 1 minute. Set aside to cool slightly. Using a food processor or blender, purée the melon with the sugar and lemon juice. While the processor is operating, pour the agar agar mixture through the feeder tube. Pour the mixture immediately into a freezer container, cover and freeze for several hours or overnight, stirring occasionally if possible.
*Makes about 4 cups (1 litre/1¾ imp. pints)*

*Right: The rich colour and intense fruity flavour of Strawberry Sorbet makes this a memorable dish.*

# Strawberry Sorbet

*Quite often, eggs are used in sorbets to soften the ice crystals, making it easier to serve. I have used agar agar to achieve the same effect.*

¾ cup (185 mL/6 fl oz) apple and blackcurrant juice
1 teaspoon pure agar agar powder (page 341)
2 punnets (cartons) ripe strawberries, hulls removed
¾ cup (185 g/6 oz) caster (superfine) sugar
juice of 1 lemon

Place the apple juice and agar agar powder in a small saucepan and, stirring constantly, bring the mixture to the boil. Reduce the heat and simmer for 1 minute. Set aside to cool slightly. Using a food processor or blender, purée the strawberries with the sugar and lemon juice. While the processor is operating, pour the agar agar mixture through the feeder tube. Pour the mixture immediately into a freezer container, cover and freeze for several hours, or overnight, stirring occasionally if possible.
*Makes about 4 cups (1 litre/1¾ imp. pints)*

# Watermelon Sorbet

*Hot summer days and watermelon seem to go hand in hand, and what better way to refresh the palate at the beginning of a meal or between courses than with a scoop of this colourful sorbet. To top it off and accentuate the cooling effect of the watermelon, decorate each serve with a mint sprig.*

1 kg (2 lb) watermelon, skin removed and chopped
3 tablespoons caster (superfine) sugar
juice of 1 lemon

Remove the pips from the chopped watermelon. Using a blender, purée the watermelon flesh with the sugar and the lemon juice. Pour the mixture into a freezer container, cover and freeze for several hours, or overnight, stirring occasionally if possible.
*Makes about 4 cups (1 litre/1¾ imp. pints)*

# Basic Vanilla Frozen Yoghurt

1 cup (250 mL/8 fl oz) apple juice
3 tablespoons caster (superfine) sugar
2 teaspoons pure agar agar powder (page 341)
3 cups (750 mL/24 fl oz) plain yoghurt
3 tablespoons honey
1 teaspoon vanilla essence (extract)

Place the apple juice, sugar and agar agar powder into a small saucepan and bring the mixture to the boil, stirring. Reduce the heat and simmer for 1 minute, stirring. Remove from the stove and set aside for a minute or two. Using a food processor or blender, blend the yoghurt, honey and vanilla together until smooth. While the processor or blender is running, pour the agar agar mixture down the feeder tube. Blend for 20–30 seconds only. Pour the mixture immediately into a freezer container, cover and freeze for several hours or overnight.
*Makes about 4 cups (1 litre/1¾ imp. pints)*

# Loganberry Frozen Yoghurt

1 cup (250 mL/8 fl oz) apple and blackcurrant juice
2 tablespoons sugar
2 teaspoons pure agar agar powder (page 341)
2 punnets (cartons) loganberries
3 tablespoons honey
2 cups (500 mL/16 fl oz) Greek Yoghurt (page 273)

Place the juice, sugar and agar agar powder in a small saucepan and bring the mixture to the boil, stirring. Simmer for 1 minute, stirring. Set aside to cool slightly. Using a food processor or blender, blend the loganberries and honey until smooth. Add the yoghurt and while the food processor is operating, pour the agar agar mixture down the feeder tube and blend well. Pour into a freezer container, cover and freeze for several hours or overnight.
*Makes about 4 cups (1 litre/1¾ imp. pints)*

# Vanilla Tofu Ice Cream

500 g (1 lb) silken tofu, blanched
3 tablespoons honey
3 tablespoons caster (superfine) sugar
3 tablespoons oil
1 teaspoon vanilla essence (extract)
2 cups (500 mL/16 fl oz) soy milk

Using a food processor or blender, blend the tofu, honey, sugar, oil and vanilla together until smooth. Add the milk and continue to blend until the mixture becomes light and foamy. Pour the mixture immediately into a freezer container, cover and freeze for several hours or overnight.
*Makes about 4 cups (1 litre/1¾ imp. pints)*

# Almond Choc Tofu Ice Cream

125 g (4 oz) almonds
2 cups (500 mL/16 fl oz) soy milk
3 tablespoons honey
3 tablespoons soft brown sugar
500 g (1 lb) blanched tofu
4 tablespoons cocoa powder
3 tablespoons oil
1 teaspoon vanilla extract (essence)

Using a food processor or blender, blend the almonds and 1 cup (250 mL/8 fl oz) of the soy milk until smooth. Add the remaining ingredients and blend for 20–30 seconds or until the mixture is light and creamy. Pour the mixture immediately into a freezer container, cover and freeze for several hours or overnight.
*Makes about 4 cups (1 litre/1¾ imp. pints)*

**Blanching tofu**
Place the tofu in a heatproof bowl and cover it with boiling water. Allow to stand for 1–2 minutes then drain carefully. Plunge the tofu into a bowl of icy water and allow to stand for 1 minute. Drain well before using.

# Banana and Cashew Nut Ice Cream

225 g (7 oz) cashew nuts
1 cup (250 mL/8 fl oz) apple juice
3 ripe bananas, mashed
1 cup (250 mL/8 fl oz) soy milk
3 tablespoons honey
1 teaspoon vanilla extract (essence)

Using a food processor or blender, grind the cashews to a fine meal, then add the apple juice and blend until the mixture is smooth and creamy. Add the bananas, soy milk, honey and vanilla and blend until smooth. Pour the mixture immediately into a freezer container, cover and freeze for several hours or overnight.
*Makes about 4 cups (1 litre/1¾ imp. pints)*

# Almond Nougat Ice Cream

*The texture of this delectable ice cream defies the fact it contains no cream. The nougat-like flavour from the almonds and honey makes this a wonderful accompaniment for fresh figs, dates or poached peaches.*

225 g (7 oz) almonds
3½ cups (875 mL/28 fl oz) soy milk
3 tablespoons caster (superfine) sugar
3 tablespoons honey
2 tablespoons oil
1 teaspoon vanilla essence (extract)

Using a food processor or blender, grind the almonds to a fine meal, then add half the soy milk and blend the mixture until it becomes creamy. Add the remaining milk, sugar, honey, oil and vanilla and blend until smooth. Pour the mixture immediately into a freezer container, cover and freeze for several hours or overnight.
*Makes about 4 cups (1 litre/1¾ imp. pints)*

# Date and Walnut Ice Cream

*With its caramel-like flavour and interesting texture, this ice cream is a perfect example of how a delicious 'no added sugar' ice cream can be made. Serve with a scoop of Vanilla Tofu Vanilla Ice Cream (page 320) or fruit sorbet as a wonderful contrast.*

250 g (8 oz) pitted dates, chopped
2 cups (500 mL/8 fl oz) freshly squeezed orange juice
2 bananas, mashed
1 cup (250 mL/8 fl oz) soy milk
2 tablespoons oil
1 teaspoon vanilla essence (extract)
90 g (3 oz) walnuts, chopped roughly

Using a food processor or blender, blend the dates with the orange juice until smooth, then add the remaining ingredients, except for the walnuts. Place the mixture in a bowl and fold the walnuts in. Pour the mixture immediately into a freezer container, cover and freeze for several hours or overnight.
*Makes about 4 cups (1 litre/1¾ imp. pints)*

### Nuts in Ice Cream
Nut cream ice creams are very rich, so small servings are recommended. This will probably suit your food budget as well, as nuts are relatively expensive ingredients. Use raw nuts or dry roasted nuts (page 17) and make sure they are fresh.

# Rum and Raisin Ice Cream

*Enjoy indulging in this simple version of an old-time favourite ice cream.*

185 g (6 oz) raisins
½ cup (90 g/3 oz) soft brown sugar
4 tablespoons white rum
2 cups (500 mL/16 fl oz) milk
1 cup (250 mL/8 fl oz) light (single) cream
1 teaspoon vanilla essence (extract)

Combine the raisins and sugar in a small bowl and sprinkle the rum over. Cover and set aside to marinate for several hours. Using a blender, blend the raisins, milk, cream and vanilla for 20–30 seconds only. Pour into a freezer container, cover and freeze for several hours or overnight.
*Makes about 4 cups (1 litre/1¾ imp. pints)*

# Ginger Ice Cream

1 cup (250 mL/8 fl oz) apple juice
½ cup caster (superfine) sugar
2 teaspoons pure agar agar powder (page 341)
3 tablespoons preserved ginger syrup *or*
　½ teaspoon ground ginger and 3 tablespoons honey
¾ cup (225 mL/7 fl oz) single (light) cream
1½ cups (405 mL/13 fl oz) milk
4 tablespoons chopped preserved ginger

Place the apple juice, sugar and agar agar powder into a small saucepan and bring the mixture to the boil, stirring. Reduce the heat and simmer for 1 minute, stirring. Remove from the stove and set aside for a minute or two. Using a blender, blend the ginger syrup (or ginger and honey), cream and milk together until smooth. While the machine is running, pour the agar agar mixture down the feeder tube. Blend for 20–30 seconds only. Place the mixture into a bowl and fold in the chopped ginger. Pour the mixture immediately into a freezer container, cover and freeze for several hours or overnight.
*Makes about 4 cups (1 litre/1¾ imp. pints)*

# Amaretto and Honey Ice Cream

*A superb ice cream. Top it with lightly roasted slivered almonds and fresh or poached fruit, or serve on its own in a beautiful glass.*

2½ cups (625 mL/1 imp. pint) milk
1 cup (250 mL/8 fl oz) single (light) cream
½ cup (125 mL/4 fl oz) honey
4 tablespoons Amaretto Liqueur

Place all the ingredients in a blender or food processor and blend for 1 minute. Place in a freezer container, cover and freeze for several hours. When the mixture becomes icy, place it in the food processor once more and process until the mixture resembles soft serve ice cream. Alternatively, churn the blended mixture in an electric ice cream maker until it becomes a thick creamy consistency (about 45 minutes). Place the mixture in a freezer container, cover and freeze for several hours before serving.
*Makes about 4 cups (1 litre/1¾ imp.)*

# Mango Liqueur Ice Cream

2 large ripe mangoes, peeled, pip removed, sliced
3 tablespoons Mango Liqueur (page 328)
2 cups (500 mL/16 fl oz) milk
¾ cup (225 mL/7 fl oz) single (light) cream
1 teaspoon vanilla essence (extract)

Using a blender, purée the mango with the liqueur, then add the remaining ingredients and continue to blend the mixture until it becomes light and foamy. Pour the mixture into a freezer container, cover and freeze for several hours or overnight.
*Makes about 4 cups (1 litre/1¾ imp. pints)*

*Right: Enjoy indulging in the luscious caramel taste and creamy texture of Rum and Raisin Ice Cream scattered with melt-in-the-mouth curls of white and dark chocolate.*

# Pina Colada Ice Cream

*A dairy-free delight with a touch of the exotic, this is a delectable ice cream to serve with fresh tropical fruits.*

1 pineapple, peeled and chopped
3 tablespoons honey
2–3 tablespoons white rum
1 cup (250 mL/8 fl oz) coconut milk
¾ cup (225 mL/7 fl oz) coconut cream

Blend all the ingredients together until smooth, pour into a freezer container, cover and freeze for several hours or overnight.
*Makes about 4 cups (1 litre/1¾ imp. pints)*

# Plum Ice Cream

500 g (1 lb) plums, sliced roughly, pips removed
½ cup (125 mL/4 fl oz) dark grape juice
2 teaspoons pure agar agar powder (page 341)
3 tablespoons soft brown sugar
¾ cup (225 mL/7 fl oz) single (light) cream
1 cup (250 mL/8 fl oz) milk

Place the plums and the grape juice in a saucepan, cover and bring the mixture to the boil. Reduce the heat and stew the plums until they are tender, about 10–15 minutes. Sprinkle the agar agar powder over the top of the plums and cook the plums for a further 1 minute, stirring constantly. Remove the plums from the heat and set them aside to cool almost to room temperature. Using a blender, blend the sugar, cream and milk together until foamy. While the machine is running, pour the plum mixture down the feeder tube. Blend for 20–30 seconds only. Pour the mixture immediately into a freezer container, cover and freeze for several hours or overnight.
*Makes about 4 cups (1 litre/1¾ imp. pints)*

# Plum Pudding Ice Cream

*Terrific for the festive season, and as far as I am concerned, the festive season is all year round! To prepare mini plum pudding ice creams, spoon the mixture into 6–8 small bowls before freezing.*

2 cups (310 g/10 oz) mixed dried fruit (fruit cake mix)
2 teaspoons mixed spice*
3 tablespoons brandy *or* white rum
1 quantity Plum Ice Cream (opposite), prepared without milk
¾ cup (90 g/3 oz) ground almonds (almond meal)

Place the dried fruit in a small bowl and sprinkle with the spice and the brandy (or rum). Cover and allow to marinate for several hours or overnight. Prepare the plum ice cream and fold in the dried fruit and almonds just before freezing. Pour the mixture into a pudding basin and freeze for several hours or overnight before turning the mixture out and slicing.
*Makes about 4 cups (1 litre/1¾ imp. pints)*

# Chocolate Ice Cream

3 cups (750 mL/24 fl oz) milk
½ cup (90 g/3 oz) caster (superfine) sugar
2 teaspoons pure agar agar powder (page 341)
2–3 tablespoons honey
125 g (4 oz) chocolate, melted (page 206)
¾ cup (225 mL/7 fl oz) single (light) cream
2 teaspoons vanilla essence (extract)

Place the milk, sugar and agar agar powder into a small saucepan and bring the mixture to the boil, stirring. Reduce the heat and simmer for 1 minute, stirring. Remove from the stove and set aside for a minute or two. Using a food processor or blender, blend the honey, chocolate, cream and vanilla together until smooth. While the processor or blender is running, pour the agar agar mixture down the feeder tube. Blend for 20–30 seconds only. Pour the mixture immediately into a freezer container, cover and freeze for several hours or overnight.
*Makes about 4 cups (1 litre/1¾ imp. pints)*

*Please refer to the recipe for mixed spice in our Cook's Notes, page 8.

# Fruit Salad Icy Poles

½ cup chopped pineapple
2 ripe apricots, halved, pip removed and diced
3 tablespoons raspberries
3 tablespoons passion fruit pulp
3 cups (750 mL/24 fl oz) orange juice
6 icy pole sticks

Combine the pineapple and apricots then carefully fold in the raspberries and passion fruit pulp. Spoon the fruit into small cups or icy pole containers and pour the orange juice over. Insert one icy pole stick in the centre of each cup. Freeze for 2–3 hours before turning out and enjoying.
*Makes about 6*

### Frozen Raspberries

Freezing the raspberries beforehand will prevent them from being broken up when they are combined. Simply spread the raspberries out on a tray and freeze them for 30–40 minutes. Frozen raspberries make a refreshing snack for children and are also great for scattering over desserts.

# Mango Icy Poles

*Perfect for a cooling snack, these icy poles are a delectable way to enjoy mangoes when they are at their cheapest.*

1 large ripe mangoes, peeled, pip removed and chopped
3 cups (750 mL/24 fl oz) pure orange juice
6 icy pole sticks

Place the mango into small cups or icy pole containers and pour the orange juice over. Insert one icy pole stick in the centre of each cup. Freeze for 2–3 hours before serving.
*Makes about 6*

# Banana Yoghurt Icy Poles

*These delicious icy poles make a wonderful snack or even a dessert for hungry children—and remember, we are all children at heart!*

3 ripe bananas, sliced
1 cup (250 mL/8 fl oz) plain yoghurt
2 teaspoons honey
6 icy pole sticks

Using a blender, blend all the ingredients together until smooth. Place the mixture into small cups or icy pole containers and insert an icy pole stick in the centre of each cup. Freeze for 2–3 hours before turning out.
*Makes about 6*

# Frozen Grape Yoghurt Delights

*The talking point of these icy poles is their wonderful texture—crisp and creamy all at once.*

1 cup (250 mL/8 fl oz) plain yoghurt
1½ cups (375 mL/12 fl oz) dark grape juice
2 teaspoons honey
340 g (12 oz) red seedless grapes

Using a food processor or blender, blend the yoghurt, grape juice and honey together until smooth. Place the grapes into small cups or icy pole containers and pour the yoghurt mixture over. Insert one icy pole stick in the centre of each cup. Freeze for 2–3 hours before serving.
*Makes about 6*

# Basic Liqueur

*The alcohol I generally use is a good-quality vodka or gin but brandy and rum suit some flavours better. My favourite non-alcoholic creations are based on fresh summer fruits, crushed and blended with pure fruit juices and light nectarful honeys. Either way, both the alcoholic and non-alcoholic varieties are recommended in small quantities due to the high sugar content. But let me assure you that a small nip of these beautiful liqueurs will go a surprisingly long way!*

¾ cup (185 g/6 oz) sugar
1 cup (250 mL/8 fl oz) water *or* fruit juice
500 g (1 lb) fruit
2½ cups (625 mL/1 imp. pint) white spirits such as vodka *or* gin

Place the sugar and water (or fruit juice) in a small saucepan and stir over a medium heat until the sugar dissolves. Remove the saucepan from the heat and allow the syrup to cool (place the saucepan in a sink half-filled with cold water if you are in a hurry). Place the fruit in a large sterilised jar and pour the cool syrup over. Mix well. Top with the spirits and put the top on the jar. Allow to stand at room temperature for 7–10 days, shaking the jar occasionally to ensure the juice is extracted from the fruit.

Line a sieve or colander with a large piece of muslin and place it over a large bowl. Pour the fruit mixture into the sieve and collect the ends of the cloth. Gently twist the cloth to extract as much juice as possible from the fruit. Pour the mixture into attractive bottles, seal and store for 4 weeks before using, if you can bear to wait that long!
*Makes about 4 cups (1 litre/1¾ imp. pints)*

### Fruit Pulp

The fruit pulp left over from making your own liqueurs can be whipped up into devilish desserts and sauces, so don't throw it away! If you don't have enough time to prepare a dessert when you have strained the liqueur from the fruit pulp, place it in a container and refrigerate or freeze it until you are able to use it.

---

# LIQUEURS

*The following delectable liqueurs are my favourite concoctions which I enjoy serving to guests on special occasions. I have endeavoured to suit all tastes (and ages) by creating both alcohol-based and non-alcoholic blends, and both are resplendent in the colour and nectar of the fruits they are based on. Liqueurs based on alcohol actually improve with age so when your favourite fruits are in season, why not whip up a batch or two of liqueur to enjoy throughout the year?*

# Quince Liqueur

*This beautiful soft liqueur has a heavenly flavour. Liqueurs based on firm raw fruits like this one require a longer time to take on the wonderful flavour of the fruit. I love to make this liqueur when quinces are at their best, in late autumn.*

1 cup (250 mL/8 fl oz) water
1¼ cups (375 g/12 oz) sugar
5 quinces, washed, sliced and cored
2 vanilla beans (pods), slit open
2 cups (500 mL/16 fl oz) gin

Place the water and sugar into a saucepan and bring the mixture to the boil, stirring. Simmer, without stirring, for 1 minute. Pack the quinces into a sterilised jar, add the vanilla beans and pour the syrup over. Set aside and allow to cool. Pour the gin over, then seal and set the liqueur aside in a cool dark place for 3 months, shaking the jar occasionally. Strain the liqueur as for Basic Liqueur (opposite) and decant into attractive bottles.
*Makes about 4 cups (1 litre/1¾ imp. pints)*

*Left: Strawberry, quince and pear liqueurs, wonderful to have on hand to offer to guests at the end of a special meal or to warm you right down to your toes on a cold winter's night.*

# Pear Liqueur

1 cup (250 mL/8 fl oz) apple juice
1½ cups (375 g/12 oz) sugar
5 pears, sliced and cored
2 cinnamon sticks
2 cups (500 mL/16 fl oz) vodka

Place the apple juice and sugar into a saucepan and bring the mixture to the boil, stirring. Simmer, without stirring, for 1 minute. Pack the pears into a sterilised jar, add the cinnamon sticks and pour the syrup over. Set aside and allow to cool. Pour the vodka over, then seal and set the liqueur aside in a cool dark place for 3 months, shaking the jar occasionally. Remove the cinnamon sticks, strain the liqueur as for Basic Liqueur (page 327) and decant into bottles.
*Makes about 4 cups (1 litre/1¾ imp. pints)*

# Strawberry Liqueur

*This delicate liqueur is great to have on hand to splash onto fresh berries or whip into cream for special occasions.*

1 cup (250 mL/8 fl oz) water
¾ cup (185 g/6 oz) sugar
500 g (1 lb) strawberries, hulls removed, halved
2½ cups (625 mL/1 imp. pint) gin *or* vodka

Follow the method for Basic Liqueur (page 327).
*Makes about 4 cups (1 litre/1¾ imp. pints)*

# Raspberry Ratafia

1 cup (250 g/8 oz) sugar
1 cup (250 mL/8 fl oz) water
500 g (1 lb) raspberries
2½ cups (625 mL/1 imp. pint) white spirits such as vodka *or* gin

Follow the method for Basic Liqueur (page 327).
*Makes about 4 cups (1 litre/1¾ imp. pints)*

# Peach Liqueur

*Sweet, subtle and velvety smooth, this liqueur is wonderful served with a platter of fresh and dried fruits and soft cheeses.*

1 cup (250 mL/8 fl oz) water
¾ cup (185 g/6 oz) sugar
750 g (1½ lb) peaches, washed, stones removed and sliced
2½ cups (625 mL/1 imp. pint) vodka

Follow the method for Basic Liqueur (page 327).
*Makes about 4 cups (1 litre/1¾ imp. pints)*

**Versatile Liqueurs**
Apart from drinking liqueurs as a wonderful finale for special occasions, liqueurs are great to have on hand to add to fresh fruit desserts, sauces and ice creams.

# Mango Liqueur

*A wonderful way to indulge in luscious summer mangoes all year round.*

3 large mangoes, peeled, pip removed and sliced
1 cup (250 mL/8 fl oz) apricot nectar
1 cup (250 mL/8 fl oz) water
2 cups (500 mL/16 fl oz) gin

Follow the method for Basic Liqueur (page 327).
*Makes about 4 cups (1 litre/1¾ imp. pints)*

**Ornamental Liqueurs**
Liqueur-making has many benefits, the most obvious one being that you get to have a supply on hand to offer to special guests. But don't overlook the side benefits. Large jars of fruit steeping in alcohol and ornamental bottles of fully prepared liqueurs look wonderful in the kitchen.

# Pineapple Brandy

*Try a splash of this superb liqueur in summer fruit salads and cocktails to add a real depth of flavour.*

1 cup (250 mL/8 fl oz) pineapple juice
1 cup (250 g/8 oz) sugar
1 medium pineapple, peeled and chopped
2 cups (500 mL/16 fl oz) brandy

Place the pineapple juice and sugar in a large saucepan and bring the mixture to the boil, stirring until the sugar has dissolved. Simmer, without stirring, for 1 minute. Add the pineapple and simmer for 5 minutes. Spoon it into a large sterilised jar and pour the syrup over. Set the jar aside until the mixture cools, then top up with the brandy. Seal the jar and set it aside in a cool dark place for 4–6 weeks. Strain and decant, following the method for Basic Liqueur (page 327).
*Makes about 4 cups (1 litre/1¾ imp. pints)*

# Passion Fruit Liqueur

*A luscious liqueur, wonderful for after dinner, but truly blissful added to summer fruit sorbets—not only does it add an unmistakable flavour, but the alcohol softens the ice crystals in the sorbet making it a treat to serve as well as to eat.*

pulp of 10–12 passionfruit
1½ cups (375 mL/12 fl oz) apple juice
1 cup (225 g/7 oz) caster (superfine) sugar
2 cups (500 mL/16 fl oz) vodka

Follow the method for Basic Liqueur (page 327), allowing the mixture to stand for 14 days before straining.
*Makes about 4 cups (1 litre/1¾ imp. pints)*

# Apricot Liqueur

*Smooth is the word for this lovely light liqueur. The white wine softens the 'kick' associated with spirits.*

1 cup (250 mL/8 fl oz) apricot nectar
¾ cup (185 g/6 oz) sugar
1 cup (250 mL/8 fl oz) sweet white wine
500 g (1 lb) ripe apricots, stones removed and sliced
1½ cups (375 mL/12 fl oz) vodka

Place the apricot nectar and sugar in a small saucepan and stir over a medium heat until the sugar dissolves. Add the white wine and the apricots and bring the mixture to the boil slowly. Reduce the heat immediately and poach the apricots for 5–10 minutes or until they are tender. Allow the mixture to cool. Place the mixture in a large sterilised jar and add the vodka. Follow the method for Basic Liqueur (page 327).
*Makes about 4 cups (1 litre/1¾ imp. pints)*

**Liqueurs as Gifts**
Make a point of collecting attractive bottles to decant your homemade liqueurs. These make beautiful gifts for birthdays or the festive season, or for taking along to a gathering of friends instead of a bottle of wine.

# Orange Liqueur

*Great to have a bottle of this on hand to add to winter fruit compotes and sauces. And try a nip of this in freshly brewed coffee for a delectable drink.*

1 cup (250 mL/8 fl oz) orange juice
½ cup (125 g/4 oz) soft brown sugar
4 navel oranges, sliced
2 cups (500 mL/16 fl oz) brandy

Follow the method for Basic Liqueur (page 327), combining the fruit juice with the sugar and water.
*Makes about 3 cups (750 mL/24 fl oz)*

# Mango Nectar

*Has anyone ever asked you what a mango tastes like? And have you ever attempted to explain the wonderful flavour and texture of this beautiful fruit? The best way to explain it is to let the person savour a mango's sweetness themselves! The same goes for this recipe. Serve it as soon as possible after preparing. Break tradition, and actually start the meal with this nectar.*

2 large juicy ripe mangoes
2 cups (500 mL/16 fl oz) pineapple juice
2 tablespoons honey
juice of 1 lemon
frangipani blossoms for garnishing

Blend all the ingredients except the frangipani until smooth in a food processor or blender. Pour the fruit mixture into a sieve (or colander) lined with muslin and collect the ends of the cloth. Gently twist the cloth to extract as much juice as possible. Garnish glasses of the nectar with frangipani.
*Serves 4–6*

# Strawberry Nip

*Balsamic vinegar is wonderful with fresh ripe strawberries, as you will discover when you try this delicious drink. Serve it over ice for a 'mocktail' or in small liqueur glasses as a grand finale to a special meal.*

1 punnet (carton) strawberries, hulls removed
2 cups (500 mL/16 fl oz) apple and blackcurrant juice
2 tablespoons grenadine syrup
2 tablespoons balsamic vinegar (page 341)

Blend all the ingredients until smooth in a food processor or blender. Proceed as for Mango Nectar (above). Serve as soon as possible.
*Serves 4–6*

# Loganberry Nip

*This liqueur may be alcohol free but it is definitely not free of flavour. Loganberries certainly have that special fragrance of their own which shines through in this exquisite concoction.*

1 punnet (carton) loganberries
2 cups (500 mL/16 fl oz) apple juice
1 tablespoon honey

Blend all the ingredients together and proceed as for Mango Nectar (above). Serve at once, or store in the refrigerator for up to 2 days.
*Serves 4–6*

# Quick Passion Fruit Nip

*The sweet taste of summer shines through in this superb drink. Serve in small nips with freshly brewed coffee or use to drizzle over yoghurt or ice cream for a quick dessert. Wonderful added to fruit punches as well.*

pulp of 8 passion fruit
2 cups (500 mL/16 fl oz) pure apple juice
1 tablespoon honey
juice of 1 lemon

Whisk all the ingredients together thoroughly. Proceed as for Mango Nectar (above). Serve as soon as possible.
*Serves 4–6*

**Extracting Pulp**
A 'non-spatter' way to remove the pips and juice from passion fruit is to use a lemon juicer.

*Right: Loganberry Nip, a tantalising alcohol-free concoction served on its own in liqueur glasses or over ice for an especially refreshing long drink.*

# Pineapple Nectar

*Fresh lemon and lime juice really bring out the tropical sweetness of pineapple. Serve as a long drink over ice or with mineral water, or in small nips after dinner.*

500 g (1 lb) peeled pineapple, chopped
2 cups (500 mL/16 fl oz) unsweetened pineapple juice
2 tablespoons honey
juice of 2 lemons

Blend all the ingredients until smooth in a food processor or blender. Proceed as for Mango Nectar (page 330). Serve as soon as possible.
*Serves 4–6*

# Raspberry Nectar

1 punnet (carton) raspberries
2 cups (500 mL/16 fl oz) pure apple and blackcurrant juice
1 tablespoon honey
juice of 1 lemon

Blend all the ingredients together and strain as for Mango Nectar (page 330). Serve at once, or store in the refrigerator for up to 2 days.
*Serves 4–6*

# Redcurrant Lift

*The tang of ripe redcurrants makes this a delightful thirst quenching drink, served over ice or in small glasses after dessert.*

1 punnet (carton) redcurrants
2 cups (500 mL/16 fl oz) apple and blackcurrant juice
3 tablespoons honey

Blend all the ingredients together and strain as for Mango Nectar (page 330). Serve at once, or store in the refrigerator for 1 day.
*Serves 4–6*

# Guava Nectar

6 guavas, cut in half
1 cup (250 mL/8 fl oz) apple juice
pips and juice of 2 pomegranates
2 tablespoons honey

Squeeze the juice from the guavas and combine with the apple juice, pomegranate pips and juice and honey. Allow to stand for 2–3 minutes, then strain as for Mango Nectar (page 330).
*Serves 4–6*

**Pomegranate Substitute**
If you cannot obtain pomegranates, use 3 tablespoons grenadine syrup instead and omit the honey.

# Kiwi Fruit Nectar

*At their best in the cooler months, kiwi fruit can be popped on top of or into winter desserts for a burst of vitamin C. They can also be put to good use for this wonderful drink with a difference.*

3 kiwi fruit, peeled and sliced
2cups (500 mL/16 fl oz) pure apple juice
2 tablespoons honey
juice of 1 lemon

Blend all the ingredients together in a food processor, using the plastic blades. (This prevents the kiwi fruit pips from pulverising and releasing a bitter flavour.) Strain as for Mango Nectar (page 330). Serve at once, or store in the refrigerator for 1 day.
*Serves 4–6*

# Spiced Blackberry Liqueur

1 cup (250 mL/8 fl oz) apple juice
2 cups (500 g/1 lb) sugar
1 cinammon stock, broken into 3 pieces
1 lemon, sliced
2 punnets (cartons) blackberries
1 cup (250 mL/8 fl oz) water
2 cups (500 mL/16 fl oz) vodka

Place the apple juice, sugar, cinnamon stick and lemon slices in a saucepan and bring the mixture to the boil, stirring until the sugar dissolves. Reduce the heat and simmer for 5 minutes. Remove the lemon and set the syrup aside to cool. Place the blackberries in a large sterilised jar and add the cinnamon stick. Pour the syrup over. Top up with the vodka, seal and set aside for 2 months. To strain and decant, follow the method for Basic Liqueur (page 327).
*Makes about 6 cups (1.5 litres/2½ imp. pints)*

# Plum Liqueur

*A robust flavoured liqueur, wonderful to drink or add to special sauces.*

1 cup (250 mL/8 fl oz) dark grape juice
1 cup (250 mL/8 fl oz) red wine
1 cup (250 g/8 oz) sugar
500 g (1 lb) plums sliced
1 cinnamon stick, broken into 3 pieces
2 cups (500 mL/16 fl oz) vodka

Place the grape juice, red wine, sugar and cinnamon stick into a saucepan and bring the mixture to the boil, stirring. Simmer, without stirring, for 1 minute. Add the plums cover and simmer for 15–20 minutes. Leave covered and set aside to cool. Place the plums and juice into a large sterilised jar and top with the vodka. Allow to stand for 3–4 weeks, shaking the jar occasionally. Strain as for Basic Liqueur (page 327).
*Makes about 6 cups (1.5 litres/2½ imp. pints)*

# Coffee Liqueur

*Quick and easy to prepare and even easier to drink. Serve with a swirl of cream or use to make spiked hot or iced coffee.*

1 cup (150 g/5 oz) soft brown sugar
½ cup (125 mL/4 fl oz) water
1½ cups (405 mL/13 fl oz) strong brewed coffee
2 cups (500 mL/16 fl oz) brandy
1 teaspoon vanilla essence (extract)

Put the sugar and water into a small saucepan and bring the mixture to the boil, stirring. Simmer, without stirring, for 1 minute. Place the coffee, brandy and vanilla into an airtight container and add the brown sugar syrup. Cover and allow to stand for 3–4 weeks, shaking the container occasionally.
*Makes about 5 cups (1.25 litres/2 imp. pints)*

# Spiced Apricot Liqueur

*Star anise has a wonderful sensual fragrance, fruity and spicy all at once with a hint of licorice. It is used to flavour stone fruits such as plums, apricots and peaches as they are poaching.*

2 cups (500 mL/16 fl oz) apricot nectar
½ cup (125 mL/4 fl oz) Star Anise Honey (page 312)
500 g (1 lb) ripe apricots, sliced
2½ cups (625 mL/1 imp. pint) white spirits such as vodka *or* gin

Place the honey in a bowl and gradually whisk in the apricot nectar. Place the apricots in a large sterilised jar and pour the honey syrup over. Top up with the spirits, seal and set aside for 2–3 months. Strain and decant as for Basic Liqueur (page 327).
*Makes about 6 cups (1.5 litres/2½ imp. pints)*

**Honey Liqueurs**
Make use of light flavoured honeys such as clover, wild flower and orange blossom. Some of my favourite liqueurs are those sweetened by fragrant honeys (pages 310–12).

# Part Three: The Vegetarian Diet

*The word 'diet' makes many of us shudder, especially any of us who have ever embarked on a weight loss diet! But all a diet really means is 'a plan of eating'. And a vegetarian diet has so much going for it. There's an amazing variety of exciting foods, from a colourful cavalcade of fruits and vegetables to all varieties of bread, cereals, grains, pasta, pulses, nuts and seeds.*

# Choosing a Balanced Diet

To me, a balanced diet is one that takes the enjoyment of eating into just as much consideration as the importance of eating for health. And to go a step further, I feel it ought to include foods which are quick and easy to prepare as well as tasty, colourful and appetising! All this is possible with a vegetarian diet.

Getting down to the basics, nutritionally speaking, there are several guidelines that we need to consider. These days, vegetarians and non-vegetarians alike are advised to consume more breads, cereals, fruit and vegetables, adding moderate amounts of dairy products and a minimum of fat in the form of butter, margarine and cream. It's a good idea to keep our weight in check as well, without going overboard! Remember the key is to enjoy eating for health.

While enjoying a diet based on the recommendations above, take time to give your body the exercise it needs so it can enjoy living all the more. Talking of exercise, it really is important to choose a form of exercise you love to do—it shouldn't be a slog! After all, if you are going to embrace a regular exercise regime in your life, it ought to be an enjoyable one; not only will you be more likely to stick to it, but it will make you happy at the same time. There is no need to join a gymnasium or aerobics club unless you love to do that. Regular walking,

*Overleaf: A balanced and enjoyable diet is a major factor contributing to good health, but don't overlook the importance of fresh air, exercise and relaxation. A delicious picnic meal and a walk in beautiful surroundings are a good start.*

swimming or bike-riding, or even a mix of several types of exercise, works wonders.

Once upon a time we believed that breads and cereals were 'fattening'. Hooray at last, we are now being encouraged to eat more of these nutritious foods, but it doesn't stop there—we are advised to actually base our diets on them. The types of bread and cereals to go for are the wholemeal (whole-wheat) varieties. That's because they contain more dietary fibre, vitamins and minerals than their processed counterparts. When however, it comes to the crunch (pun relevant and intended) white bread can be better than no bread—that is, if the choice is between a pie encased in flaky pastry or a white bread sandwich, the sandwich would generally score better nutritionally because it would not be laden with the fat the pastry contains.

It is worthwhile incorporating whole grains and wholemeal (whole-wheat) flour into cooking. If you are unused to 100% wholemeal flour, start off with 50% white flour and 50% wholemeal flour and try your hand at Basic Pancakes (page 266), Basic Wholemeal Scones (page 196) or, if you have a little more time, have a go at whipping up a loaf or two of freshly baked bread (page 243). The same goes for wholegrains; try adding a little toasted muesli (page 264) to your usual breakfast cereal and gradually increase the ratio of muesli to breakfast cereal. Pasta has always been a popular food, but in the light of nutrition research for athletes, it has been adopted as a wonderful 'carbohydrate loading' food which, when consumed the evening before exercise, provides plenty of energy for performing the next day. The energy provided by complex carbohydrates such as pasta and grains is usually sustained, compared to energy from a simple carbohydrate such as refined sugar, which provides energy in quick bursts following its consumption.

Joy upon joy—we are now also encouraged to eat more fruits and vegetables, my favourite foods! Not only do I enjoy eating them, but I have so much fun conjuring up colourful and unusual dishes based on them. Like breads and cereals, fruits and vegetables contain complex carbohydrate, but it is from these foods that we can obtain much of our vitamin C intake, not to mention other vitamins and minerals. There are plenty of fruit and vegetable recipes in this book to try and most of them are literally prepared in minutes. Gone are the days when vegetable cooking involved submerging vegetables in boiling salted water and spending long hours making rich sauces to conceal their true beauty. The trick is to serve vegetables simply and savour the remarkable qualities of each type.

A vegetarian diet based on breads, cereals, legumes, vegetables and fruit is high in water and dietary fibre. Due to their bulk, vegetarian dishes can be comparatively low in fat and contain more nutrients. This depends, however, on just how the food is prepared; deep or shallow frying, rich sauces and oily dressings transform potentially nutritious foods into energy dense dishes—that is, dishes laden with excess fat and kilojoules (calories).

Apparently most of us consume far too much fat. The quantity needs to be reduced and the quality needs to be improved. We are advised to consume polyunsaturated and mono-unsaturated fats in preference to saturated fats such as butter and cream, and saturated vegetable oils such as coconut and palm oils. Common foods such as meat, poultry, milk, yoghurt, cheese, butter, margarine, cream and oil contain considerable yet varying amounts of fat, and generally saturated fat at that. Vegetarians are off to a head start by omitting fatty meats and poultry from their diets as long as they don't over compensate (as often happens!) by replacing the meat and poultry with copious amounts of full cream milk and cheese. For all of us, a good step is to use mainly reduced fat dairy products such as low fat or nonfat milk, yoghurt and cheese. Full fat cheese and cream can be enjoyed in small amounts or as an occasional extra. Many of the recipes in this book make use of low fat and reduced fat dairy products such as Yoghurt Cheese (page 271), ricotta cheese and nonfat plain yoghurt so if you haven't experimented with these foods much, now's your chance!

Unfortunately there is another negative on the horizon, and that's the amount of sugar we all seem to be consuming. The main problem with excess sugar consumption is the development of dental caries. And really, if anyone needs a good set of choppers, it's a vegetarian! Those of us who do not suffer from dental problems probably think we never will, and so often go on indulging excessively in sugary sweetened foods. And I'm not talking about the occasional indulgences either—for which I have supplied a number of recipes in this book.

Actually, much of the sugar we are eating these days is in the form of processed foods. For example a 375 mL (12 fl oz) can of soft drink (soda) contains at least 8 teaspoons of added sugar, as does a standard chocolate bar. Some sweetened breakfast cereals contain as many as 4 teaspoons of sugar per serve, not to mention the additional sugar that is sprinkled on top before it is eaten! This is not to say we shouldn't enjoy an occasional soft drink or chocolate bar, but it's worthwhile seeking out alternative drinks and snacks if these foods are presently a regular part of the diet. Too many sugary foods can crowd essential nutrients out of the diet. Children (and adults) who have just consumed sweet biscuits or cakes do not feel at all like sitting down to a nutritious meal, no matter how colourful and inviting it may be.

With the ever-increasing amounts of processed and pre-prepared foods we seem to be eating these days, care needs to be taken to keep our salt intake to a minimum too. And those of us who don't do the obligatory run around the plate with the salt shaker, or add handfuls of salt to our cooking, still cannot escape the salt attack completely. As in the case of sugar, much of the salt we consume is contained in processed foods such as bread, crackers, sauces, condiments and canned vegetables (unless specified as low or reduced salt).

The main health problem associated with excess salt consumption is that it increases the risk of hypertension in susceptible people. There is also the hidden problem of our tastes becoming so used to salty foods that we are not able to appreciate the wonderful natural flavours of foods. So instead of seasoning with salt, reach for fresh herbs, spices, citrus juices and flavoured vinegars to add a flavour burst.

How can vegetarians be sure they are achieving a nutritious, balanced diet?

Broadly speaking, a vegetarian diet is based on plant foods and does not contain flesh foods such as meat, poultry or fish. Within this general framework, there are three types of vegetarians:

Ova-lacto vegetarians—As the name implies (ova—eggs, lacto—milk), these vegetarians include eggs and dairy products in their diet as well as all plant foods.

Lacto-vegetarians—As the name implies (lacto—milk), these vegetarians include dairy products in their diets as well as all plant foods.

Vegans—These vegetarians do not include any foods derived from animals in their diets, so they base their diets wholly on plant foods.

We have all heard the saying 'variety is the spice of life' and when it comes to achieving a balanced nutritious diet I couldn't agree more. We are urged to consume a variety of foods to ensure we obtain a variety of nutrients from all food groups. The more we restrict our diets, the more care and planning is needed to ensure that we obtain all the nutrients necessary for optimum health and well being. When animal foods are restricted or omitted from the diet the nutrients they contain can often be replaced by plant foods, as follows:

### Iron

The animal foods that usually provide iron in the diet are meat, poultry and eggs. Legumes, pulses, dried fruits and green leafy vegetables, however, are also good sources of iron. It is important to note that the iron in plant foods is in a form that is not as readily absorbed by the body. This problem can be overcome by consuming a vitamin C rich food or drink at the same time as these foods are eaten, as vitamin C assists in the absorption of iron by the body. Fresh fruit or vegetable juices can be served at the same meal as a bean or lentil dish, or a salad of young spinach leaves could be dressed in a fresh lemon or lime juice dressing, and perhaps topped up with some fresh ripe tomatoes.

### Calcium

Most commonly provided by dairy products, calcium can also be obtained from green leafy vegetables, broccoli, legumes, pulses and sesame seeds. Tahini, a paste made from sesame seeds, is often used as a spread instead of butter or margarine by vegetarians. Care needs to be taken, however, not to consume more than one tablespoonful of tahini per day because it is a high fat food, albeit a quality fat.

### Riboflavin

Green leafy vegetables score again here—no wonder we were told to 'eat up your greens' as children! And thank goodness that green leafy vegetables have never been more appealing than today—the mustard scented greens popular in Asian cooking provide variety in taste and texture as well as vitamins and minerals, and tender salad greens such as butter lettuce, curly endive (frisée) and young spinach leaves also do much to whet our appetites.

### Vitamin B12

Commonly supplied by meat and dairy products, vitamin B12 can also be provided by mushrooms and fermented foods such as miso (page 343), tempeh (page 346) and sauerkraut.

### Vitamin D

Full cream dairy products contain vitamin D, but those who do not include these foods in their diet should ensure sensible and ample exposure to sunshine, the key word being sensible. Over-exposure to ultra-violet rays should be avoided, so enjoying fresh air and sunshine in the early-mid morning and late afternoon is the way to go. Sunshine is important in helping the body to assimilate vitamin D.

### Zinc

Peas, whole grain cereals and wholemeal (whole-wheat) flour, corn and peanut butter are good sources of zinc, so whip these foods up into delicious dishes such as vegetable satays, whole grain breakfast mixes such as Toasted Muesli (page 264) for delicious summer breakfasts, and steaming hot whole grain porridge for chilly winter mornings.

### Protein

Protein is essential for the growth, maintenance and repair of our bodies. It is made up of 21 amino acids, 8 of which cannot be manufactured by the body, or are made too slowly to meet the body's demand for them. To obtain an adequate

*Right: I derive great pleasure and inspiration from having baskets of fresh produce around me, rather like still life arrangements. Their beauty can be appreciated both before and after their preparation.*